Smart Sensor Technologies for IoT

Smart Sensor Technologies for IoT

Editors

Peter Brida
Ondrej Krejcar
Ali Selamat
Attila Kertesz

MDPI • Basel • Beijing • Wuhan • Barcelona • Belgrade • Manchester • Tokyo • Cluj • Tianjin

Editors
Peter Brida
University of Zilin
Slovakia

Ondrej Krejcar
University of Hradec Kralove
Czech Republic

Ali Selamat
Universiti Teknologi Malaysia
Malaysia

Attila Kertesz
University of Szeged
Hungary

Editorial Office
MDPI
St. Alban-Anlage 66
4052 Basel, Switzerland

This is a reprint of articles from the Special Issue published online in the open access journal *Sensors* (ISSN 1424-8220) (available at: https://www.mdpi.com/journal/sensors/special_issues/smart_sensor_iot).

For citation purposes, cite each article independently as indicated on the article page online and as indicated below:

LastName, A.A.; LastName, B.B.; LastName, C.C. Article Title. *Journal Name* **Year**, *Volume Number*, Page Range.

ISBN 978-3-0365-2462-7 (Hbk)
ISBN 978-3-0365-2463-4 (PDF)

Contents

About the Editors

Peter Brida obtained his M.Sc. and the Ph.D. degrees in Telecommunications from the University of Žilina, Faculty of Electrical Engineering, Slovakia in 2002 and 2006, respectively. He has been full professor since 2017. Since November 2016, he has held the position of Vice-dean for Development and International Co-operation at the Faculty of Electrical Engineering and Information Technology, University of Zilina. His research interests include wireless positioning in mobile radio networks, satellite navigation systems, location-based services, Internet of Things, cellular networks and intelligent transport systems. He is the author or co-author of more than 60 scientific papers published in scientific journals and presented at international conferences. He has been a guest editor and member of Technical Program Committees for several journals and conferences such as IPIN (Indoor Positioning and Indoor Navigation), ACIIDS (Asian Conference on Intelligent Information and Database Systems), ICCCI (International Conference on Computational Collective Intelligence), etc. In the past, he was chairman of several invited and special sessions at various conferences. He was guest editor of several Special Issues in high-impact journals, e.g., Sensors (MDPI), Mobile Information Systems (Hindawi) etc.

Ondrej Krejcar is a full professor in systems engineering and informatics at the University of Hradec Kralove, Faculty of Informatics and Management, Center for Basic and Applied Research, Czech Republic, and Research Fellow at Malaysia-Japan International Institute of Technology, University Technology Malaysia, Kuala Lumpur, Malaysia. In 2008, he received his Ph.D. title in technical cybernetics at Technical University of Ostrava, Czech Republic. He is currently a vice-rector for science and creative activities of the University of Hradec Kralove from June 2020. At present, he is also a director of the Center for Basic and Applied Research at the University of Hradec Kralove. In the years 2016–2020, he was vice-dean for science and research at Faculty of Informatics and Management, UHK. His h-index is 21, with more than 1500 citations received in the Web of Science, where more than 100 IF journal articles is indexed in JCR index. In 2018, he was the 14th top peer reviewer in Multidisciplinary in the World according to Publons and a Top Reviewer in the Global Peer Review Awards 2019 by Publons. Currently, he is on the editorial board of the MDPI Sensors IF journal (Q1/Q2 at JCR), and several other ESCI indexed journals. He is a Vice-leader and Management Committee member at WG4 at project COST CA17136, since 2018. He has also been a Management Committee member substitute at project COST CA16226 since 2017. Since 2019, he has been Chairman of the Program Committee of the KAPPA Program, Technological Agency of the Czech Republic as a regulator of the EEA/Norwegian Financial Mechanism in the Czech Republic (2019-2024). Since 2020, he has been Chairman of the Panel 1 (Computer, Physical and Chemical Sciences) of the ZETA Program, Technological Agency of the Czech Republic. From 2014 until 2019, he was Deputy Chairman of the Panel 7 (Processing Industry, Robotics, and Electrical Engineering) of the Epsilon Program, Technological Agency of the Czech Republic. At the University of Hradec Kralove, he is a guarantee of the doctoral study program in Applied Informatics, where he is focusing on lecturing on Smart Approaches to the Development of Information Systems and Applications in Ubiquitous Computing Environments.

His research interests include control systems, smart sensors, ubiquitous computing, manufacturing, wireless technology, portable devices, biomedicine, image segmentation and recognition, biometrics, technical cybernetics, and ubiquitous computing.

His second area of interest is in biomedicine (image analysis), as well as biotelemetric system architecture (portable device architecture, wireless biosensors), development of applications for mobile devices with use of remote or embedded biomedical sensors.

Ali Selamat has received a B.Sc. (Hons.) in IT from Teesside University, U.K. and M.Sc. in Distributed Multimedia Interactive Systems from Lancaster University, U.K. in 1997 and 1998, respectively. He has received a Dr. Eng. degree from Osaka Prefecture University, Japan, in 2003.

Ali Selamat is currently a professor at the School of Computing, Faculty of Engineering, Universiti Teknologi Malaysia (UTM). He is presently serving as a Dean of Malaysia Japan International Institute of Technology (MJIIT), Universiti Teknologi Malaysia. Before that, he was a Chief Information Officer (CIO) and a Director of Communication and Information Technology Director, UTM. He is currently elected as a Chair of IEEE Computer Society, Malaysia Section under the Institute of Electrical and Electronics Engineers (IEEE), USA, and a Malaysia Engineering Deans Council member. He previously held the position of research Dean on Knowledge Economy Research Alliance, UTM. He is currently elected as a fellow under Academy Professor Malaysia and a research fellow at Magicx - Media and Games Center of Excellence, Universiti Teknologi Malaysia. He was a principal consultant of Big Data Analytics, Ministry of Higher Education, Malaysia 201, and, currently, a member of Malaysia Artificial Intelligence Roadmaps (2020–2021) and a keynote speaker in many international conferences. He was a visiting professor at Kuwait University and few other universities in Japan, Saudi Arabia, and Indonesia. Currently, he is a visiting professor at Hradec-Kralove University, Czech Republic, and Kagoshima Institute of Technology, Japan.

He was serving as the Editorial Boards of International Journal of Knowledge-Based Systems Elsevier, Netherlands, and currently an associate editor for International Journal of Artificial Intelligence and Machine Learning (IJAIML), IGI Global and Journal of Service Oriented Computing and Application (SOCA), Springer. He is also an editorial member of the International Journal of Information and Database Systems (IJIIDS) under Inderscience Publications, Switzerland, and Vietnam Journal of Computer Science under Springer Publications. He is the Program co-chair of IEA/AIE 2021: The 34th International Conference on Industrial, Engineering and Other Applications of Applied Intelligent Systems in Kuala Lumpur, Malaysia. His research interests include data analytics, digital transformations, knowledge management in higher educations, key performance indicators, cloud-based software engineering, software agents, information retrievals, pattern recognition, genetic algorithms, neural networks, and soft-computing.

Attila Kertesz Ph.D. is an associate professor at the Department of Software Engineering, University of Szeged, leading the IoT Cloud research group at the department. His research interests include the federative management of Blockchain, IoT, Fog and Cloud systems, and interoperability issues of distributed systems in general. Currently, he is the leader of the FogBlock4Trust sub-grant project of the TruBlo EU H2020 project and a national project OTKA FK 131793, and a work package leader in the national GINOP Internet of Living Things project. He is also a Management Committee member of the CERCIRAS and INDAIRPOLLNET Cost Actions. He has more than 100 publications with more than 1000 citations.

sensors

MDPI

Editorial

Smart Sensor Technologies for IoT

Peter Brida [1,*], Ondrej Krejcar [2], Ali Selamat [3] and Attila Kertesz [4]

1 Faculty of Electrical Engineering and Information, University of Zilina, Univerzitna 1, 01026 Zilina, Slovakia
2 Center for Basic and Applied Research, Faculty of Informatics and Management, University of Hradec Kralove, Rokitanskeho 62, 500 03 Hradec Kralove, Czech Republic; ondrej.krejcar@uhk.cz
3 Malaysia Japan International Institute of Technology (MJIIT), Universiti Teknologi Malaysia, Jalan Sultan Yahya Petra, Kuala Lumpur 54100, Malaysia; aselamat@utm.my
4 Department of Software Engineering, University of Szeged, H-6720 Szeged, Hungary; keratt@inf.u-szeged.hu
* Correspondence: peter.brida@feit.uniza.sk; Tel.: +421-41-5132066

check for updates

Citation: Brida, P.; Krejcar, O.; Selamat, A.; Kertesz, A. Smart Sensor Technologies for IoT. *Sensors* **2021**, *21*, 5890. https://doi.org/10.3390/s21175890

Received: 27 August 2021
Accepted: 31 August 2021
Published: 1 September 2021

Publisher's Note: MDPI stays neutral with regard to jurisdictional claims in published maps and institutional affiliations.

The recent development in wireless networks and devices leads to novel services that will utilize wireless communication on a new level. It is possible to see a lot of effort and resources invested to establish new communication networks that will support massive machine-to-machine communication and the Internet of Things (IoT). In these systems, various smart and sensory devices are assumed to be deployed and connected, enabling the streaming of large amounts of data.

Smart services represent new trends in mobile services, i.e., a completely new spectrum of context-aware, personalized, and intelligent services and applications. A variety of existing services already utilize information about the position of the user or mobile device. In a lot of applications, the position of mobile devices is achieved thanks to the use of Global Navigation Satellite System (GNSS) chips that are integrated into all modern mobile devices (smartphones). However, GNSS is not always a reliable source of position estimates due to multipath propagation and signal blockage. Moreover, in foreseen IoT applications, the use of GNSS chips integrated into all devices might have a negative impact on their battery life. Therefore, alternative solutions for position estimation should be investigated and implemented in IoT applications.

Additionally, smart mobile sensors and devices could be able to fulfill an astonishingly wide range of demands of users and providers. One of the reasons behind the wireless device development is the ever-growing computing power together with the reduction of energy consumption and improved communication capabilities of devices.

In order to process a large amount of data from sensors, further investigation of mobile and dynamic cloud computing solutions is also envisioned. Implementation of new services will be with high probability based on the application of cloud services. This, however, produces additional challenges in such areas as management, security, technical solutions, infrastructure modelling, mobile devices support, and many others.

This Special Issue of Sensors aims at reporting on some of the recent research efforts on this increasingly important topic. The twelve accepted papers in this issue cover various aspects in Smart Sensor Technologies for IoT.

Paper [1] presents the Enhanced Multicast Repair (EM-REP) Fast ReRoute mechanism, which solves several limitations of the legacy M-REP Fast ReRoute mechanism. This means mainly supports for fast reroute in the event of continuous link and node failures throughout the whole network and that the destination host does not have to be directly connected to a network with a router that performs decapsulation, which also reduces the flooding process of M-REP packets in a network with multiple routing areas. The EM-REP mechanism does not require any preparatory calculations, which is effective for IoT devices such as sensors. In the area of WSN and the IoT, it can be used to distribute, for example, urgent messages across the WSN network or to assure the time-critical delivery of important information from sensors to gateways or behind to analytic servers.

1

In [2], the bit-repair (B-REP) Fast ReRoute mechanism is presented. The proposed mechanism provides advanced fast reroute solutions for IoT and IP network infrastructures. B-REP uses a standardized BIER header with a special bit-string field. That allows to use a standardized header and its fields to define an alternative path as well as to transfer user data. The bit-string, in addition, allows to efficiently define an exact alternative FRR path, which can be calculated by the Dijkstra algorithm or even manually defined by the administrator.

In [3], the new Multilayered Network Model (MNM) for the 5G mobile network's disrupted infrastructure is introduced. The MNM concept is composed of three independent layers of networks, which are capable of collaboration if disruption of fixed infrastructure occurs. The whole model is able to perform data collection at WSN layer using sensors, which mimic the IoT behaviour by sending those data to the Cloud. If a disruption scenario occurs, only urgent data are allowed to pass into higher layers through the introduced system of WSN gateways. Along with MNM, recommendations for the use of possible wireless technologies with routing protocols are provided. In addition to these recommendations, the exception mechanism for urgent data delivery in routing algorithms is introduced to all layers.

The authors of [4] present a complex IoT-based solution for detecting the position of a lying person. They produced a smart topper based on our novel pressure sensor for measuring the pressure distribution of the lying person. The novel sensor is based on the electrically conductive yarn and the Velostat. The performed experiments indicate a stable resistive response. The functionality of the whole solution and application to the operational staff using the challenging dataset are presented. The modified Convolutional Neural Network classifies the collected data into one of the four lying postures. It achieved an overall accuracy of 82.22% and with the best F1 score of 84%.

The aim of the paper [5] is to compare available sensors from the viewpoint of their suitability for traffic measurements. A summary of the achieved results is given in the form of the score for each sensor. The introduced sensor chart should provide the audience with knowledge about the pros and cons of sensors, especially, if intended for the purposes of road traffic surveillance. The authors in this research focused on the specific situation of road traffic monitoring with magnetometers placed at the roadside. The analysis presented in the paper will serve to the future research when the special sensor node for traffic surveillance will be designed.

Paper [6] presents the concept and pilot implementation of an indoor tracking system. It is based on an overlapping-resistant Internet of Things (IoT) solution for a Bluetooth Low Energy (BLE)-based indoor tracking system (BLE-ITS). The BLE-ITS is a promising, inexpensive alternative to the well-known GPS. It can be used in human traffic analysis, such as indoor tourist facilities. Tourists or other customers are tagged by a unique MAC address assigned to a simple and energy-saving BLE beacon emitter. Their location is determined by a distributed and scalable network of popular Raspberry Pi microcomputers equipped with BLE and WiFi/Ethernet modules. The authors implemented the prototype and demonstrated its usefulness in a controlled environment.

The growing demand for extensive and reliable structural health monitoring resulted in the development of advanced optical sensing systems that, in conjunction with Wireless Optical Networks (WON), are capable of extending the reach of optical sensing to places where fibre provision is not feasible. To support this effort, the authors of [7] propose a novel MultiWeight Zero Cross-Correlation (MW-ZCC) coding scheme with a low cross-correlation function for Wireless Optical Networks Based Optical Code Division Multiple Access (WON-OCDMA) system. Codes are easy to convert into multiweight power of two codes, thus suitable for supporting a variety of QoS services in WON, including sensing, datacomms and video surveillance applications. The effect of a free space transmission with medium turbulence on the signal transmission and received optical power was analysed. The simulations results revealed that for a minimum allowable BER of $10-3$, $10-9$, when supporting triple-play services (sensing, datacomms and video surveillance), the proposed

WON-OCDMA employing MW-ZCC codes could carry up to 32 services simultaneously at a distance of 32 km in the presence of moderate turbulence in the atmosphere.

In the paper [8], the authors propose an Energy-Efficient Clustering Multi-hop Routing Protocol (EECMR) for routing data packets in Underwater Wireless Sensor Networks (UWSNs). EECMR is a depth-based clustering protocol that uses the depth level of the node to select cluster head nodes and forwarder nodes for multi-hop routing. EECMR considers the residual energy of the node, which elects cluster heads in turns. The nodes can change roles as cluster head, cluster member, and cluster relay. The cluster relay node forwards data from a deeper level to the sink. With the aid of a cluster relay, the energy consumption for transmission is decreased, leading to fewer dead nodes. The simulation results showed that EECMR achieves better performance in terms of higher residual energy, longer network lifetime, and higher received packets at the sink.

In [9], a new and highly precise system has been presented for electromagnetically scanning large structures. The system combines the range information provided as point clouds by an array of mm-wave radars with the highly accurate positioning data provided by Global Navigation Satellite System-Real-Time Kinematic (GNSS-RTK) modules, forming a sensor-fusion system that enables to merge the point clouds taken from different arbitrary positions. Moreover, communication and control components have been employed to send and receive data from the sensors and manage the system status. As a proof of concept, the system has been tested on a stockpile-like model and in a realistic environment at a seaport with a scaled coal stockpile, obtaining accurate results in both cases.

In [10], the solution for a dynamic radio map collection is introduced. The proposed solution is based on simultaneous measurements of Received Signal Strength (RSS) from Wi-Fi networks and the Inertial Measurement Unit (IMU) data collection. The dead reckoning algorithm processes the IMU data with particle filtering, which helps reduce the localization error of the recovered track. The proposed solution was tested in a real-world environment. The mean localization error of the recovered track was less than 0.6 m, with a maximum error of approximately 2.5 m.

Paper [11] presents a novel human activity recognition system, named WiLiMetaSensing. It realizes location-independent sensing with very few samples in the Wi-Fi environment. Inspired by the idea of meta-learning, the authors endow the system with the ability that can utilize the knowledge acquired from one location for others. The authors proposed a Convolutional Neural Network and Long Short-Term Memory (CNN-LSTM) feature representation and metric learning-based human activity recognition system. The model focuses on the common characteristics of different locations and extracts discriminative features for different activities. The performance evaluation is conducted on the comprehensive dataset built by authors. It demonstrates that the WiLiMetaSensing system can achieve an average accuracy of 91.11%, with four locations for training, given only one sample for other testing locations.

Paper [12] deals with the impact of content on the perceived video quality evaluated using the subjective Absolute Category Rating (ACR) method. The assessment was conducted on eight types of video sequences with diverse content obtained from the SJTU dataset. The sequences were encoded at five different constant bitrates in the two widely used video compression standards H.264/AVC and H.265/HEVC, at Full HD and Ultra HD resolutions, which means 160 annotated video sequences were created. The evaluation was performed in two laboratories: at the University of Zilina, and at the VSB—Technical University in Ostrava. The results acquired in both laboratories showed a high correlation. The evaluation results concluded that it is unnecessary to use the H.265/HEVC codec for compression of Full HD sequences and the compression efficiency of the H.265 codec by the Ultra HD resolution reaches the compression efficiency of both codecs by the Full HD resolution.

Funding: This research received no external funding.

Acknowledgments: The guest editors of this Special Issue would like to thank all authors who have submitted their manuscripts for considering the Sensors journal and the reviewers for their hard work during the review process. Furthermore, our sincere thanks go to the editors of Sensors for their kind help and support. We hope that the readers enjoy reading the articles within this Special Issue. Finally, the guest editors wish to acknowledge partial support from the Slovak VEGA grant agency, Project No. 1/0626/19 "Research of mobile objects localization in IoT environment".

Conflicts of Interest: The authors declare no conflict of interest.

References

1. Papan, J.; Segec, P.; Yeremenko, O.; Bridova, I.; Hodon, M. Enhanced Multicast Repair Fast Reroute Mechanism for Smart Sensors IoT and Network Infrastructure. *Sensors* **2020**, *20*, 3428. [CrossRef]
2. Papan, J.; Segec, P.; Yeremenko, O.; Bridova, I.; Hodon, M. A New Bit Repair Fast Reroute Mechanism for Smart Sensors IoT Network Infrastructure. *Sensors* **2020**, *20*, 5230. [CrossRef]
3. Hrabcak, D.; Dobos, L.; Papaj, J.; Ovsenik, L. Multilayered Network Model for Mobile Network Infrastructure Disruption. *Sensors* **2020**, *20*, 5491. [CrossRef] [PubMed]
4. Hudec, R.; Matúška, S.; Kamencay, P.; Benco, M. A Smart IoT System for Detecting the Position of a Lying Person Using a Novel Textile Pressure Sensor. *Sensors* **2021**, *21*, 206. [CrossRef] [PubMed]
5. Hodoň, M.; Karpiš, O.; Ševčík, P.; Kociánová, A. Which Digital-Output MEMS Magnetometer Meets the Requirements of Modern Road Traffic Survey? *Sensors* **2021**, *21*, 266. [CrossRef] [PubMed]
6. Belka, R.; Deniziak, R.; Łukawski, G.; Pięta, P. BLE-Based Indoor Tracking System with Overlapping-Resistant IoT Solution for Tourism Applications. *Sensors* **2021**, *21*, 329. [CrossRef] [PubMed]
7. Seyedzadeh, S.; Agapiou, A.; Moghaddasi, M.; Dado, M.; Glesk, I. WON-OCDMA System Based on MW-ZCC Codes for Applications in Optical Wireless Sensor Networks. *Sensors* **2021**, *21*, 539. [CrossRef] [PubMed]
8. Nguyen, N.; Le, T.; Nguyen, H.; Voznak, M. Energy-Efficient Clustering Multi-Hop Routing Protocol in a UWSN. *Sensors* **2021**, *21*, 627. [CrossRef]
9. Fernández Álvarez, H.; Álvarez-Narciandi, G.; García-Fernández, M.; Laviada, J.; Álvarez López, Y.; Las-Heras Andrés, F. A Portable Electromagnetic System Based on mm-Wave Radars and GNSS-RTK Solutions for 3D Scanning of Large Material Piles. *Sensors* **2021**, *21*, 757. [CrossRef]
10. Brida, P.; Machaj, J.; Racko, J.; Krejcar, O. Algorithm for Dynamic Fingerprinting Radio Map Creation Using IMU Measurements. *Sensors* **2021**, *21*, 2283. [CrossRef] [PubMed]
11. Ding, X.; Jiang, T.; Zhong, Y.; Huang, Y.; Li, Z. Wi-Fi-Based Location-Independent Human Activity Recognition via Meta Learning. *Sensors* **2021**, *21*, 2654. [CrossRef] [PubMed]
12. Uhrina, M.; Holesova, A.; Bienik, J.; Sevcik, L. Impact of Scene Content on High Resolution Video Quality. *Sensors* **2021**, *21*, 2872. [CrossRef] [PubMed]

Article

Enhanced Multicast Repair Fast Reroute Mechanism for Smart Sensors IoT and Network Infrastructure

Jozef Papan [1,*], Pavel Segec [1], Oleksandra Yeremenko [2], Ivana Bridova [1] and Michal Hodon [3]

[1] Department of InfoCom Networks, University of Žilina, 010 26 Žilina, Slovakia; pavel.segec@fri.uniza.sk (P.S.); ivana.bridova@fri.uniza.sk (I.B.)

[2] Department of Infocommunication Engineering, Kharkiv National University of Radio Electronics; 61000 Kharkiv, Ukraine; oleksandra.yeremenko.ua@ieee.org

[3] Department of Technical Cybernetics, University of Žilina, 010 26 Žilina, Slovakia; michal.hodon@fri.uniza.sk

[*] Correspondence: jozef.papan@fri.uniza.sk

Received: 22 May 2020; Accepted: 15 June 2020; Published: 17 June 2020

Abstract: The sprawling nature of Internet of Things (IoT) sensors require the comprehensive management and reliability of the entire network. Modern Internet Protocol (IP) networks demand specific qualitative and quantitative parameters that need to be met. One of these requirements is the minimal packet loss in the network. After a node or link failure within the network, the process of network convergence will begin. This process may take an unpredictable time, mostly depending on the size and the structure of the affected network segment and the routing protocol used within the network. The categories of proposed solutions for these problems are known as Fast ReRoute (FRR) mechanisms. The majority of current Fast ReRoute mechanisms use precomputation of alternative backup paths in advance. This paper presents an Enhanced Multicast Repair (EM-REP) FRR mechanism that uses multicast technology to create an alternate backup path and does not require pre-calculation. This principle creates a unique reactive behavior in the Fast ReRoute area. The enhanced M-REP FRR mechanism can find an alternative path in the event of multiple links or nodes failing at different times and places in the network. This unique behavior can be applied in the IoT sensors area, especially in network architecture that guarantees reliability of data transfer.

Keywords: Internet of Things (IoT); ReRoute; Multicast Repair (M-REP)

1. Introduction

The Internet of Things (IoT) model allows the connection and exchange of data between various types of smart devices. These smart devices, usually sensors, can be connected in the Wireless Sensor Network (WSN) [1–4] creating a unique sensor architecture [5,6]. With increasing numbers of sensors in the environment and the importance of measured data, the network platform must guarantee the reliability of connection.

Historically, Internet Protocol (IP) networks have been focused mainly on time-tolerant communication services, such as e-mail, file transfer and access to web content. However gradually, IP networks have evolved into converged platforms supporting several different types of services, including time-consuming and real-time applications such as voice transmission over IP, Internet of Things platform, sensors, streaming and multimedia services [7,8]. These services have higher network performance requirements, such as delay, availability, or packet loss, and are also negatively affected by unexpected link or node failures in the network. In case of network failures, network routing protocols (IGP), such as Open Shortest Path First (OSPF), respond to network failures by flooding topology updates and calculating new routes [7–11]. This process is also known as the network convergence process. Thus, in a period of network convergence, network routers have outdated information that can cause data loses and outages.

For this reason, IP networks must meet specific qualitative and quantitative parameters in order to ensure an acceptable quality of service, e.g., availability and short repair time after a specific network failure. To do this, network providers must deploy appropriate technologies to ensure uninterrupted customer service. One such significant technology is a group of mechanisms for rapid network recovery, also known as Fast ReRoute (FRR) [12–15]. A key principle of FRR mechanisms is that the backup path for possible failure scenarios is calculated in advance before the failure occurs. This principle presumes that the switching to a precomputed backup path is faster than waiting for the network convergence process to complete. FRR mechanisms that are designed to work on IP networks are known as Internet Protocol Fast ReRoute (IP FRR) mechanisms.

The paper presents an enhanced version of Multicast Repair (M-REP) FRR mechanism (hereinafter EM-REP) that does not require pre-calculation of alternative routes in advance. At the same time, EM-REP is capable of finding an alternative path even in the case of multiple network failures. These features make EM-REP a unique IPFRR mechanism which can be also used in IoT architecture providing reliable connection for various types of sensor networks.

The rest of this paper is organized as follows. Section 2 provides an insight into the issues of Fast ReRoute, the purpose, and terminology used. Section 3 provides state-of-the-art analysis, where existing FRR solutions and identified problems are discussed. Section 4 presents the specification of the original M-REP FRR mechanism and Section 5 proposes its enhanced version, the EM-REP FRR mechanism. Section 6 focuses on the evaluation of the EM-REP mechanism and compares its features with the predecessor, the M-REP algorithm, as well as with the other FRR solutions. Finally, Section 7 presents the conclusions and directions for future research work.

2. The Fast ReRoute

One of the main reasons why Fast ReRoute mechanisms have started to be used is that the process of network convergence after a network failure usually takes a longer time than that expected by the network provider.

In the context of routing, the convergence state of a network is the state in which each network router has up-to-date, complete and consistent routing information [16,17]. This means that each router is informed of the current network status (up-to-date), of each available network (complete), and each router has chosen the optimal successor/next-hop for each network according to a common criterion (consistent). The convergence process is the operation of each individual routing protocol process to achieve a state of convergence. The time required to complete the process of network convergence depends on various factors, such as the number of devices, especially network routers; topology complexity; the type of routing protocol used (link-state or distance vector); and its individual operational parameter values (like update or hello timers). The time required to finalize the network convergence process usually ranges from hundreds of milliseconds up to a few seconds. The network convergence process may consist of several subprocesses, such as failure detection, response, the distribution of updated routing information, recalculation and, finally, the installation of new routes [7,18–20]. The resulting time of network convergence is the sum of durations of each individual subprocess.

First, from the router point of view, there is a need for mechanisms that perform failure detection. Failure detection is the time that the router's operating system (OS) needs to detect a failure, i.e., a failed link (network interface) or unavailable neighbor router. Interface failure detection may take up to several milliseconds on the physical layer of a router. The detection of neighbor router unavailability depends on the type of routing protocol used. This failure detection may take from tens of milliseconds when a link state protocols are used (OSPF/IS-IS hello mechanisms), or it may take up to tens of seconds in the case of distance vector routing protocols (RIPv2). During this period, the packets affected by the failure are permanently lost due to outdated routing information and resulting incorrect routing decisions. Next, the local router response to a link failure; it generates and distributes topology/routing updates that reflect actual state. The duration depends on actual load conditions of each individual router. The distribution of information to other routers is required to inform other routers about the situation and starts within 10 ms to 100 ms for each affected next-hop router [18–20]. All routers that have received actual routing information must recalculate their routing tables. The recalculation of routing tables depends mainly on the size of the network and the amount of topological information. This may take a few milliseconds for link-state routing protocols that use the Dijkstra algorithm. After the recalculation is complete, routers install new routes and update their routing tables. Again, this mainly depends on the type of router and the number of prefixes that were affected by the network failure.

2.1. The Principle of Fast ReRoute

For the proper understanding of the FRR technology, there is a need for terminology that denotes routers with special meaning for FRR mechanisms [21–25]. Here, we introduce the terms using the following simplified network topology described in Figure 1. The source router (S) is a router that has detected a link or neighboring router failure and then activates a locally implemented FRR repair mechanism. In other words, router S is actively involved in FRR repair (Figure 1). This router is also called Point of Local Repair (PLR). The destination router (D) is the destination router of the original data flow. Routers N1, N2, N3 and others are specific routers that are used as an alternative next router (hereafter referred to as next-hop router) for a specific FRR alternative path. R (R1) is a router that is not actively involved in FRR repair.

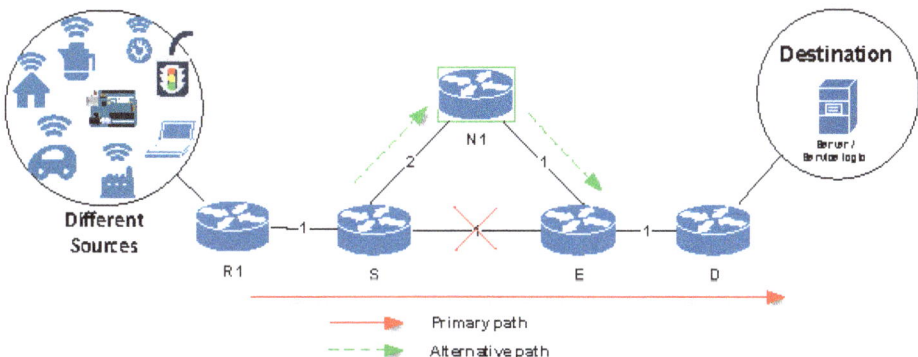

Figure 1. The principle of Fast ReRoute (FRR).

However, before starting the main FRR process, an administrator must set up protected links or prefixes that are managed by the router. Subsequently, the FRR mechanism pre-calculates an alternate next-hop router to be used in the event of a protected link or prefix failure. This is called Phase Zero (preparation). FRR can then proceed further through the following phases [26–28]:

- Phase One: Detection of a link failure by the specialized FRR technology. This phase activates the FRR mechanism. In the Figure 1, the Fast ReRoute process starts after a failure of the link between routers S and E has been detected. Here, following the terminology, the router S detects a link failure.
- Phase Two: Temporary modification of affected routing records by the FRR mechanism. During this phase, precalculated alternative routes are being installed (the FRR mechanism is active).
- Phase Three: Performing background routing protocol update. Routes installed using the FRR mechanism are used to route packets until the network convergence is completed (the FRR mechanism is active).

- Phase Four: The routing protocol completes the necessary routing information update. As the next step, the FRR mechanism is deactivated and the routing process is taken over by the routing protocol.

Once the update of routing information is completed, the deactivation of the FRR mechanism can be accomplished in several ways. One method used is to apply a hold-down timer. This timer should be set to a minimum time necessary to complete the network convergence process. After this timer expires, the temporary routing information installed by the FRR mechanism is removed and the FRR mechanism is subsequently deactivated [26].

The main advantage of the Fast ReRoute mechanism is that it offers several times faster network transmission recovery than a traditional routing protocol may achieve (OSPF). The average repair time of actual FRR mechanisms is up to 50 ms [26,29–31].

2.2. Precomputation Approach of Fast ReRoute

A key feature common to Fast ReRoute mechanisms is that they calculate the backup path in advance and therefore offer faster network recovery [32,33]. The precalculated backup path in the FRR terminology is also referred to as a precomputed backup path [34,35]. To ensure correct network recovery, the backup path cannot pass through the failure point. Depending on the FRR mechanism, a given router may also calculate several backup paths. When calculating and installing a pre-calculated alternative route, each router decides independent of other routers. The principle of precalculated alternative routes is currently used by all FRR mechanisms. This proactive approach is an important factor in minimizing the time required for fast network recovery after failures [32].

3. Related Works

In the IoT area, several existing solutions dealing with rerouting have been proposed. In paper [36], a new approach of jamming attack tolerant routing using multiple paths based on zones is presented. The proposed scheme in that paper separates the system network into specific number of zones and directs the candidate forward nodes of neighbor zones. After detecting a specific attack, detour nodes in the network determine zones for rerouting and detour packets destined for victim nodes through forward nodes in the decided zones.

In work [37], the authors present a detailed review of IoT sensing applications in WSN and the difficulties and challenges that need to be overcome. Some of these challenges are fault tolerance, the effectiveness of the energy harvesting, communication interference, cost feasibility, and an appropriate integration of these elements.

At present, there are many unicast IPFRR mechanisms that differ in the way that alternative routes are calculated. Three of the most common and widely used IPFRR mechanisms are the Equal-Cost Multi-Path (ECMP) [30,31], Loop Free Alternates (LFA) [24,31,38] and its extended version, Remote LFA (RLFA) [30,39].

The LFA mechanism calculates alternative routes based on conditions that consider metrics for each next-hop router. These conditions ensure that if a packet is redirected to this alternate next-hop router (that has met the conditions), the router delivers the packet to the destination over a longer path that is still loop-free and bypasses the network failure. The Remote LFA is an improved version of the original LFA. The idea of Remote LFA is to use a tunneling mechanism from the source router S to the remote LFA router. The tunnel is used to bypass the part of the network that, in the event of an error, would route packets (not tunneled) from the affected site back to the source router S or would forward them through a failed link or router. The RLFA router may be a few hops away from the source router S.

Other mechanisms, although less common, are Multiple Routing Configurations (MRC) [11,30,40–44] and Not-Via Addresses [35,45]. Furthermore, there are tunneling-based mechanisms, such as Maximally Redundant Trees (MRT) [46,47], and, finally, IPFRR mechanisms based on alternative trees [22,48–50]. IPFRR mechanisms such as Not-Via Addresses, Multiple Routing Configurations and

Maximally Redundant Trees can provide protection that is close to 100% of repair coverage [26,51]. The main challenge of these IPFRR mechanisms is the complexity of internal algorithms that calculate alternate paths.

There is also another FRR group of mechanisms that focus on the protection of multicast communication [52,53]. In general, these solutions utilize precomputed multicast disjoint trees. Examples of these mechanisms are Multicast Only Fast Re-Route (MoFRR) [54] and Bit Index Explicit Replication-Traffic Engineering (BIER-TE) [51,55].

We have been analyzing and researching FRR mechanisms for several years [21,56–61]. Based on the obtained results, we can summarize the most significant properties of the existing FRR mechanisms in Table 1.

Table 1. FRR mechanisms: features comparison.

FRR Mechanism	100% Repair Coverage	Precomputing	Packet Modification	Dependency on Link-State Routing Protocols
ECMP FRR	No	Yes	No	No
BIER-TE (M)	Yes	Yes	Yes	No
Directed LFA	Yes	Yes	Yes	Yes
LFA	No	Yes	No	No
MoFRR	No	Yes	No	No
MPLS-TE FRR	No	Yes	Yes	No
MRC	Yes	Yes	Yes	Yes
MRT	Yes	Yes	Yes	Yes
Not-Via Addresses	Yes	Yes	Yes	Yes
Remote LFA	No	Yes	Yes	Yes
TI-LFA	Yes	Yes	Yes	Yes

Notes: ECMP—Equal-Cost Multi-Path Routing; BIER-TE—Bit Index Explicit Replication—Traffic Engineering; LFA—Loop-Free Alternate; MoFRR—Multicast-Only Fast Reroute; MRC—Multiple Routing Configurations; MRT—Maximally Redundant Trees; TI-LFA—Topology Independent Loop-Free Alternate.

3.1. Problem Formulation

In analyzing the FRR mechanisms mentioned above, several issues have been identified. We can classify them into the three basic problem areas, which are briefly introduced in the following subsections.

3.1.1. Cost-Based Calculation of Alternative Route

The majority of existing FRR mechanisms, such as LFA [24,31,62], Remote LFA [14], Directed LFA [63], ECMP [23], MRC [11], and MRT [46,47], calculate an alternative backup route according to link metrics. Alternative routes are usually calculated using a Dijkstra SPF algorithm, which calculates the route path as the minimal total cost of each individual link. The main problem with this type of calculation is that a valid alternative route can only be calculated if the internal algorithm of the FRR mechanism is able to find the correct alternative route according to specific metric conditions. In other words, there are topologies or situations where one FRR mechanism can find an alternative path but another FRR mechanism is unable to do so. If link costs exceed mathematical conditions, the FRR mechanism cannot find an alternative route, even if the alternative route physically exists. The positive effect of the cost-based FRR mechanisms is that they guarantee the calculation of the most advantageous alternative route in the event of a failure. On the other hand, it should be noted that they depend on the correct cost of links in topology. Therefore, there is a need for an FRR algorithm that is able to find an alternative route without cost-based calculation of an alternative route.

3.1.2. Single Failure Recovery

Mechanisms such as Remote LFA [39], Directed LFA [63], and Not-Via Address [45] are designed to be able to protect networks only in the event of a single failure. In situations where more than one failure occurs, these FRR mechanisms cannot create an alternative path and to reroute affected traffic around the failed element in the network. Therefore, packets could be lost in this situation, as the mechanism was not designed to account for more than one point of failure. This is sometimes identified as a limitation of these mentioned FRR algorithms.

3.1.3. Dependency on Link-State Routing Protocols

Another important fact is that several analyzed FRR mechanisms require topological network information from a link-state routing protocol database to calculate an alternative path [26]. This feature limits the application of FRR mechanisms only to networks where a primary link-state routing protocol is deployed. Currently, most of the existing FRR mechanisms are dependent on information from link-state routing protocols.

3.1.4. Packet Modification

The key part of fast network recovery technology is the fast detection of the failure and the subsequent means of its notification to the other routers which were affected by the failure (disrupted routing). In some FRR mechanisms, specific link failure information is distributed by the following techniques:

- Modifying special bits in the IPv4 header (MRC [11]);
- Encapsulating the packet with another header (Remote LFA [30], Directed LFA [63]);
- Based on the interface through which the packet was received (LFA [46,64]).

It should be noted that packet modification causes various compatibility problems as well as problems with exceeding the Maximum Transmission Unit (MTU) on some network links [26].

3.1.5. Preparatory Calculations

The analyzed FRR mechanisms work on a principle which is based on the fast detection of link failure with a neighboring router and precalculated alternative routes (precomputing). The high complexity of these precalculations is a problem area [26].

The computational complexity of individual FRR mechanisms increases with the increasing number of routers in the network. These calculations must be repeated if there is a change in network topologies and they are typically performed on routers as specific low-priority processes when the router's Central Processing Unit (CPU) is idle [26]. Thus, the FRR mechanism calculations take up the valuable time and system resources of the router. Based on these facts, we conclude that one of the problem areas of FRR mechanisms are preparatory calculations. All existing FRR mechanisms work on this principle.

Based on the problems thus identified and their problem areas, this document proposes the EM-REP FRR mechanism, an improved version of the M-REP algorithm. The main improvements of the EM-REP proposal focus on the protection of important unicast flows in the event of subsequent and recurring failures occurring concurrently over time. This is a unique feature, as we identified that existing IPFRR mechanisms provide the single failure protection.

Our M-REP algorithms are not dependent on any of unicast routing protocols in general, but EM-REP is enhanced in a way that provides an advantage in specific deployment scenarios, where the area design is used (for example OSPF or IS-IS). Here, we propose the modification of the Area Border Router (ABR) router behavior. This modification adds flexibility to optimize packet delivery through an "on-the-go" decapsulation process, compared to the old M-REP approach where it must be performed on the last router in the delivery chain. This is the second M-REP algorithm enhancement introduced in the paper.

Sensors **2020**, *20*, 3428

4. M-REP FRR Mechanism

Based on the analysis and identified problem areas introduced in the previous section, a M-REP FRR mechanism has been proposed. The M-REP mechanism does not require precomputation of an alternative route, it is not dependent on any unicast routing protocol, it does not use a metric calculation of the alternative route, and, finally, it provides full repair coverage.

The M-REP FRR mechanism uses a multicast [65–67] routing protocol, Protocol Independent Multicast-Dense Mode (PIM-DM), as its basis. PIM-DM, at the beginning of multicast transmission, floods multicast packets to all PIM-enabled routers in a domain. We decided to use this flooding feature as the basic behavior of our M-REP algorithm. However, to fit PIM-DM to our purpose, we modified its Reverse Path Forwarding control mechanism.

In this section, the description of original M-REP mechanism is provided. In the next section, we will follow up with the presentation of its improved version, the Enhanced M-REP mechanism (EM-REP). EM-REP can create alternative route that allows recovery from the occurrence of multiple and even parallel failures.

4.1. Description of the Original M-REP Mechanism

To describe the M-REP mechanism, the role of routers in IPFRR is modified as follows:

- S router (source router) is a router that has detected a connection failure with its primary next-hop for a specific destination host. Router S begins to encapsulate the original unicast protected flow (or the protected flow, see Table 2) into packets of a specific multicast (S, G) flow. Here, the S address is the original address of the host, that sends packets. G is a specific, pre-configured multicast group address, that is used by the M-REP IPFRR to encapsulate packets of the protected flow. Router S becomes the root of the tree created by the M-REP mechanism.
- D router is a router that performs M-REP IPFRR multicast flow recovery back to the original unicast packets of the protected flow. Router D will further route and forward packets to the destination host as unicast. The destination host, i.e., the target for the original protected flow, must be directly connected or reachable through the D router.
- R router is a router with implemented IPFRR M-REP mechanism.

The M-REP mechanism is designed to protect only specific important customer data flows, delivered over an Internet Service Provider (ISP) network from the source S to the destination host D (Figure 2a, mark 1, red path). A router that detects a connection failure (link or node) becomes the source router S (Figure 2a, mark 2). At the same time as the failure was detected, routers start the process of network convergence. In this moment, the source router S begins to encapsulate the original unicast packets of the protected flow into a specific M-REP multicast flow identified by (S, G) pair. These multicast packets are sent directly out (utilizing the flooding process of Protocol Independent Multicast-Dense Mode protocol) on all active PIM-DM enabled interfaces of router S (Figure 2b, mark 3, dashed green arrows). This starts the process of creating a multicast distribution tree by the PIM-DM. The result of this flooding represents an alternative route around the detected failure (Figure 2b, mark 4, bold green arrows). Router S continues to perform this process of encapsulation and flooding of the protected unicast flow until the process of network convergence is completed.

However, before the network completes the convergence and the new shortest paths are calculated, R routers may receive a multicast packets of M-REP flow even through interfaces do not match their current selection of the correct Reverse Path Forwarding (RPF) interfaces. This statement is conditioned by the fact that the current routing tables have not yet been updated with the new information resulting from a link failure.

Table 2. Terminology used by the Multicast Repair (M-REP) mechanism.

Protected Flow	Unicast flow of packets with specified source and destination IP addresses (source, destination). The M-REP protects packets of a secured flow from losses during network failures. The unicast source address specifies a sending host, the unicast destination address specifies the receiving host.
M-REP Address	Special reserved multicast address used exclusively by the M-REP mechanism. The address represents a multicast G address of PIM-DM (S, G) pair, that is reserved and preconfigured for each protected flow. Each protected flow has unique G multicast address.
M-REP Flow	A multicast (S, G) flow that encapsulates packets of a protected flow in the event of a failure. The S address is the original source IP address of the protected flow. The G address is the multicast M-REP address. Together, they define a multicast distribution (Source, M-REP address) pair.
Received Packet	A packet of a protected flow received by a router. The router identifies the packet based on configured IP addresses of a protected flow.
Received Multicast Packet	A packet of the M-REP flow received by a router. The packet is identified by its M-REP address destination address.
Protected Interface	Router output interface selected according to the unicast routing table used. The interface is used for the routing of a protected flow (destination).
Failure of Protected Interface	Loss of connectivity on the protected interface.
Reverse-path forwarding (RPF) Interface	A router interface that first receives a multicast packet with the specified destination M-REP address (M-REP address). This interface has a similar role to the RPF interface in the "original" PIM-DM specification. Each router may have at most one RPF interface per M-REP address.
Connected Destination	The network that contains the host with a protected flow destination address. The D router is directly connected to this network by one of its interfaces.
M-REP Requirements	Point-to-point routers. The original destination of the original unicast communication must be directly connected to router D.

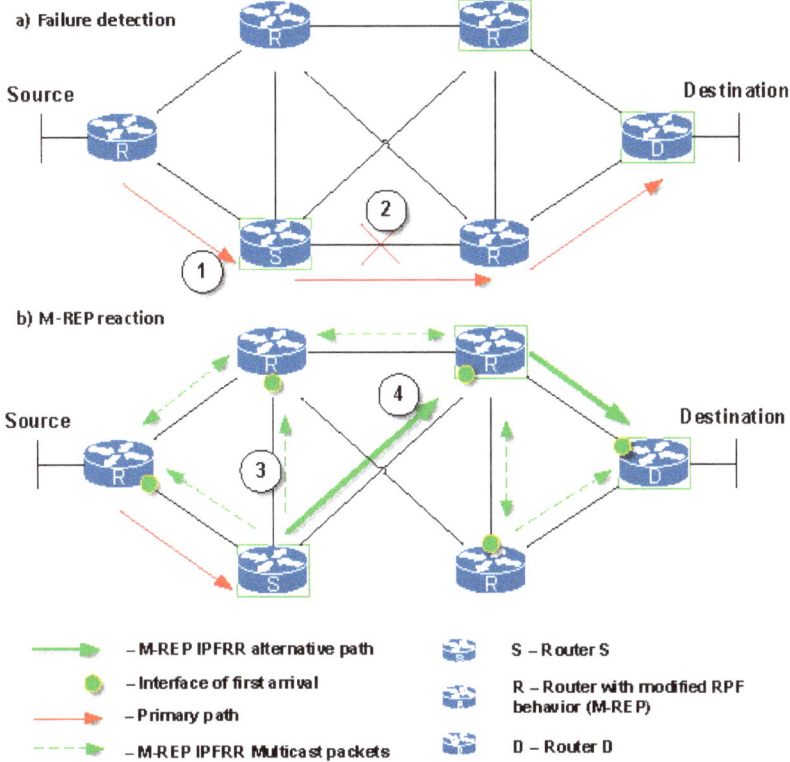

Figure 2. Principle of the M-REP mechanism

Incorrect selection of the RPF interface would prevent routers, with the M-REP mechanism implemented, to accept and forward the multicast M-REP flow. For this reason, we created the following modification to the RPF interface selection:

For a router that is not suitable for the M-REP multicast (S, G) flow, let an RPF interface be the one that allows the first multicast packet of a suitable multicast (S, G) flow.

The original PIM-DM communication processing and sending mechanism, as well as legacy PIM-DM RPF selection, are not modified. The revised RPF check will only apply to the specific range of multicast group addresses reserved for the M-REP mechanism.

The term "first packet" used in the modified RPF rule (the rule of first-arrival) refers to a multicast packet, the processing of which leads to the creation of a new multicast table entry for a specific (S, G) pair. This principle is in accordance with the standard rule of the PIM-DM protocol that the first multicast packet of a specific (S, G) pair requires the creation of a new entry in the multicast routing table. This record does not exist before the arrival of the first multicast packet of a specific multicast (S, G) pair.

After selecting a RPF interface, previous routers forward multicast packets from their other interfaces and active PIM-DMs. Each router has exactly one RPF interface for a specific multicast M-REP (S, G) pair.

An alternative path created by the M-REP IPFRR mechanism is random because its formation is conditional on the arrival of M-REP multicast packets to individual routers. Consequently, the alternative path created by the M-REP mechanism is not the shortest possible path (Figure 3). However, other IPFRR mechanisms do not generally provide the shortest alternative paths [30,62].

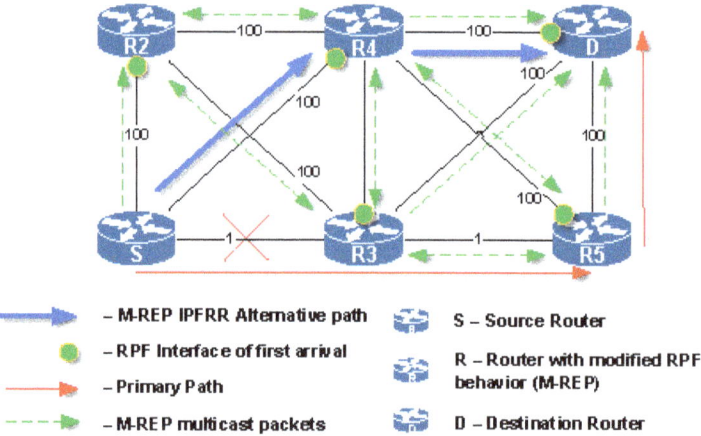

Figure 3. The first arrival rule.

The destination D router may be a provider edge (PE) router or a router that is directly connected to the destination network of the original protected unicast data flow. When multicast M-REP packets arrive at the destination D router, these encapsulated protected flow packets must be restored (decapsulated) to their original format and then routed according to the unicast routing table.

The decapsulation process of the M-REP multicast flow is performed by the destination router D. This router should be directly connected to the destination network of the original unicast packets. To restore the flow back to its original unicast form correctly, destination router D must have the original unicast flow information (source and destination addresses). The M-REP mechanism currently uses a tunneling technique, which means encapsulation of IPv4 unicast communication in new multicast packets (Figure 4). This technique is one of many possible solutions of how we can preserve the original source and destination address of the packet. Another option is to use extension headers (for example in IPv6).

IP header of the M-REP		Original packet			
Original Source Address	**Multicastic M-REP Address**	Source Address	Destination Address	Data	

Figure 4. The M-REP encapsulation of the unicast communication.

RPF in PIM-DM is a mechanism to ensure that packets are received on a correct interface and to prevent the creation of the micro-loops. For the needs of the M-REP mechanism, the original RPF was modified following the rule of First-Arrival. The research question we faced was whether this modification could cause micro-loops. The verification was performed using the mathematical proof by a contradiction [56], which confirmed that the modification does not cause routing loops. However, the M-REP mechanism operates in topologies which must meet two conditions, the network topology must use point-to-point links only and the target of original protected flow must be directly connected to router D.

The M-REP mechanism will result in exactly one path created between routers S and D. Switching from the alternate M-REP path back to the original unicast path after network convergence is controlled by a dedicated timer. This timer is set to a value greater than the unicast routing protocol convergence time.

It is important to point out that the legacy multicast tree creation procedure used in the PIM-DM protocol remains unmodified. A router with an empty list of output interfaces (OIL) for a specific flow (S, G) logs out of the multicast distribution tree by sending a Prune message from its RPF interface. The Prune message will also be sent out on non-RPF interfaces that received packets fom (S, G) pair.

4.2. M-REP State Machine

For a logical representation of the M-REP mechanism, state diagrams are created for S router (Figure 5), as well as D and R routers (Figure 6).

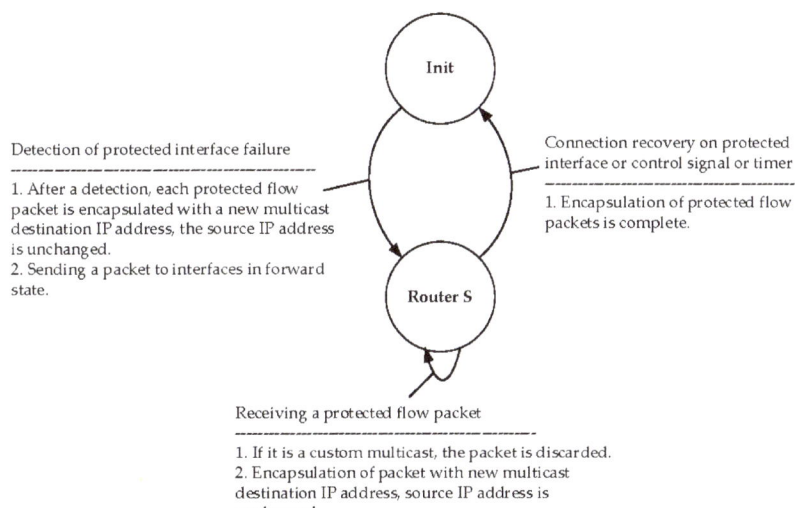

Figure 5. The M-REP mechanism state diagram of router S.

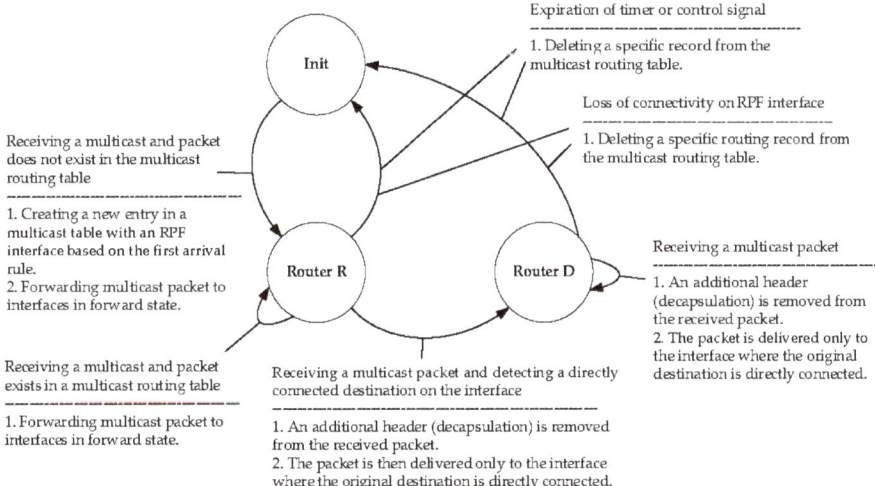

Figure 6. The M-REP state diagram for D and R routers.

The M-REP process of the mentioned routers can move between the states described in the Table 3:

Table 3. States of the M-REP mechanism.

State:	Any Condition
Event:	-
New state:	Init
Action:	Initializing the M-REP mechanism on the router. The mechanism is initialized only for the first time. After this action, it is in the monitoring mode.

State:	Init
Event:	Failure of a protected interface
New state:	Router S
Action:	If the router detects a connectivity failure on the output interface during the processing of protected packet flow (defined by source, destination addresses), it becomes router S. After the failure is detected, all packets within a protected flow are encapsulated with an additional packet header (source, M-REP add).
	Router S does not have an input RPF interface for the multicast flow, which means that it discards the packet (s) with the destination multicast address (M-REP add).
	Note: Deactivation of the M-REP mechanism can also be performed using a timer set to a time, which will ensure that the convergence process in the network has completed. In this case, the timer starts when the encapsulation starts.

State:	Router S
Event:	Recovery of connection on protected interface or control signal or timer.
New state:	Init
Action:	The router stops encapsulating the protected flow and enters the Init state.

State:	Init
Event:	Receiving a multicast packet and no entry in the multicast routing table.
New state:	Router R
Action:	The router has received a packet with the multicast address (M-REP add) and does not have a directly connected destination. If the router does not have an entry in its multicast routing table for (source, M-REP add) pair, it creates a new entry with the RPF interface that has first received the multicast packet. The RPF interface is just one. Interfaces other than RPF and with active PIM-DM, become output interfaces. Received multicast packet is then forwarded to all output interfaces. If the router has a multicast routing table entry for (source, M-REP add) pair and has received a multicast packet on the RPF interface, the packet is forwarded to all PIM-DM output interfaces.
	If the router has a multicast routing table entry for (source, M-REP add) pair and has received a multicast packet on the NON-RPF interface, the multicast packet is dropped.

State:	Router R
Event:	Receiving multicast packet and destination is directly connected on an interface.
New state:	Router D
Action:	The router has received a multicast packet (the multicast address M-REP add is used) and has directly connected destination. Router D is a router that has the original destination directly connected to one of its interfaces. Multicast header is then removed from the received multicast packet, which means that packet is decapsulated and returned to its original state. After decapsulation, the packet is sent out through the interface where the directly connected destination is located. Interfaces other than the RPF interface will send a Prune message.

State:	Router R, Router D
Event:	Timer expires or control signal
New state:	Init
Action:	Deletes the entry in the multicast routing table. After this action, mechanism moves to the Init state.

State:	Router R, Router D
Event:	Loss of connectivity on an RPF interface.
New state:	Init
Action:	Deletes the entry in the multicast routing table and move to the Init state.

5. Enhancements for M-REP

Although the M-REP mechanism represents a new approach to addressing the IPFRR, this mechanism contains some limitations, which we removed with the proposed extensions. In this section we present the results of further research on M-REP mechanism enhancements. We have primarily focused on the treatment of multiple failures and the enhancement of specific deployments, i.e., the Area Border Router extension.

5.1. Multiple Failures

So far, we have dealt with the failure of a single link or router at a time. In critical situations, multiple failures may occur at the same time (Figure 7). This situation is an issue for the M-REP mechanism because it is not able to find an alternative route, although an alternative path exists. Nevertheless, it should be noted, that most of FRR mechanisms analyzed are not able to solve this situation of multiple failures at the given time. Their principles simply do not allow for the correction of multiple failures.

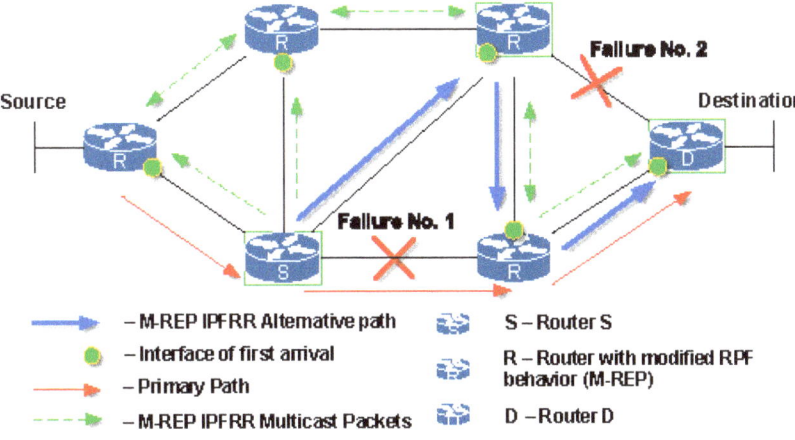

Figure 7. M-REP: reroute in the event of multiple failures.

To solve this problem, we propose an extension of the M-REP mechanism, which is called the Swap method. To explain its principle better, we can divide the method into three separate steps. We were inspired by the Multiprotocol Label Switching (MPLS) technology and its functions: Push, Swap and Pop. The step definitions are as follows:

- Push is defined as the encapsulation of an M-REP packet;
- Swap is defined as the replacement of a multicast M-REP address by another one;
- Pop is defined as the decapsulation of M-REP packets, i.e., the decapsulation of original unicast flow from the multicast M-REP packets.

The principle of the EM-REP mechanism in the event of a single failure is unchanged compared to the original design. If another failure occurs at a different time to the original failure, the method Swap shall be used.

This interpretation implies that the used M-REP multicast address (after the first failure at time t) will be in the event of a further failure (at time t + x, where x is the time difference between the first and second failure) replaced by another predefined multicast address. However, this behavior is not efficient and can be optimized further. This implies the following behavior.

A router that detects a new connection failure on already used M-REP backup path of a particular multicast flow will replace the multicast destination address of the existing M-REP header with another multicast address. That is, a router detecting a new failure on the original M-REP backup path becomes the next local repair point, the router S. This will force the router to start a new flooding process but using a different multicast address for the M-REP flow.

This behavior is shown in Figure 8. The primary path for delivering unicast packets from Source to Destination is through R1 → R2 → R5 → D (red arrows). Router R2, which has detected at time *t* the first link failure on the primary path, becomes the router S (Figure 8a, mark 1). Next, router S (R2) begins to encapsulate the protected unicast flow to a specific M-REP multicast flow identified by (S, G) pair, and initiates the flooding process in the topology (Figure 8a, mark 2). Routers that use PIM-DM with modified RPF control, receive multicast traffic (the first-arrival rule) and create an alternative M-REP pathway. The path goes through R2 (S) → R4 → D. Routers on interfaces that do not have receivers for the M-REP multicast flow or receive multicast traffic as the second ones are pruned using Prune messages.

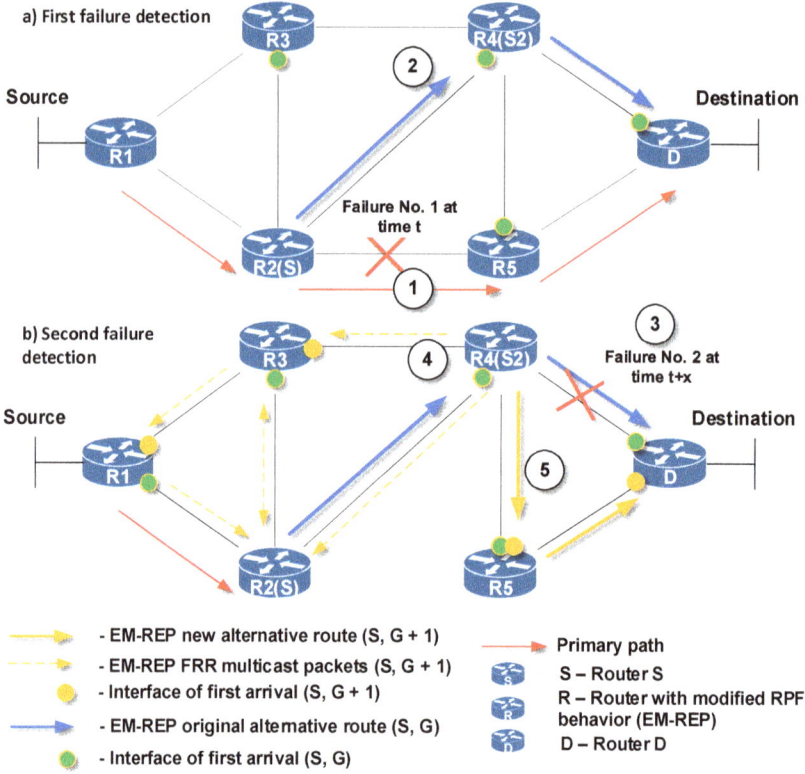

Figure 8. The EM-REP principle at multiple failures at different times.

At time t + x, router R4 has detected a second network failure (Figure 8b, mark 3), which occurred on the link through which the alternative M-REP route (S, G) leads. R4 becomes the next source router S2. R4 router replaces the destination multicast address of the original (S, G) multicast flow with the new destination multicast address (S, G + 1). Next, the flooding process in the network starts again (Figure 8b, mark 4). As a result, the new alternative M-REP path is created for the multicast flow (S, G + 1). The path goes through R4 (S2) → R5 → D (Figure 8b, mark 5). The whole resulting alternative M-REP path will go through R2 (S) → R4 (S2) → R5 → D. The part between R2 (S) → R4 (S2) was constructed as the multicast distribution tree for the (S, G) flow. The second part between R4 (S2) → R5 →D was constructed for the multicast flow (S, G + 1).

In the proposed solution, it is necessary to deal only with failures that have already occurred on the alternative route created by the EM-REP mechanism. Failures that occur outside of the alternative path do not affect or interfere with the path created and should not be addressed.

5.2. ABR Extension

The PIM-DM protocol, which is used by the M-REP mechanism, assumes that all connected end stations are interested in receiving the multicast traffic. Therefore, the PIM-DM router delivers multicast packets simply by flooding the packets to all active PIM-DM neighboring routers. PIM-DM routers that do not have receivers for a given multicast or have received multicast packets on interfaces, which do not pass RPF control, will be pruned from the distribution tree.

These processes take place in the beginning of multicast broadcasting and periodically later on, so they cause an unnecessary network load [68]. As the EM-REP mechanism uses these PIM-DM processes (flood and prune), they are only carried out until the network convergence process is complete. Subsequently, the routing protocol then takes control of the router's routing logic. From this point of view, networks consisting of several administrative areas appear to be problematic. In this case, the multicast (S, G) flow flooded by router S will be delivered to all routers in all administrative areas (Figure 9).

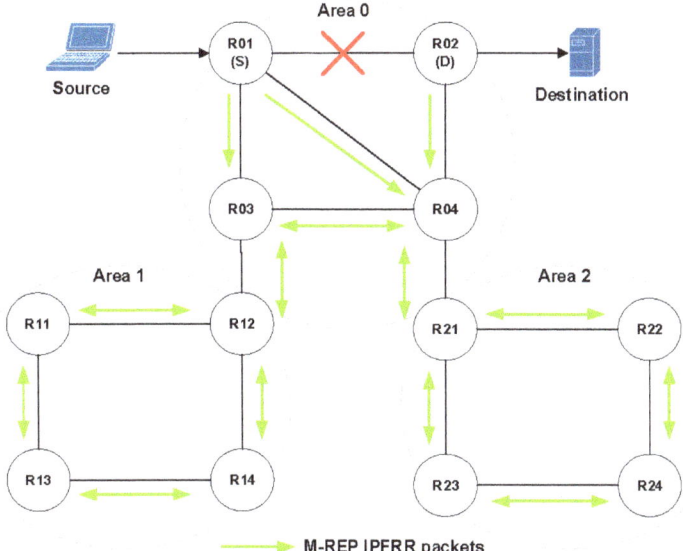

Figure 9. The process of PIM-DM flooding in multi-area Open Shortest Path First (OSPF).

Here, we propose the modification of the M-REP behavior applied on border routers of administrative areas (ABR). If we consider a network with applied OSPF routing, the area boundary routers are called the Area Border Router or the Autonomous System Boundary Router (ASBR). In this case, if a failure occurs in a given area, the ABR/ASBR router will act as a decapsulating router instead of the original D router. It means, that the ABR/ASBR router will decapsulate a specific M-REP multicast (S, G) flow back to the original unicast communication. The ABR behavioral design in OSPF is shown in the diagram (Figure 10).

Let us explain this process using the topology shown in Figure 11. The source sends its packets to the destination. R01 detects a link failure to the next-hop router and begins to encapsulate the unicast flow on the M-REP specific multicast flow (S, G). In this case, the boundary routers (ABR/ASBR) are

R02, R12 and R21. Using the modified behavior for the ABR/ASBR routers (Figure 10), the specific multicast M-REP flow will not pass to the other areas.

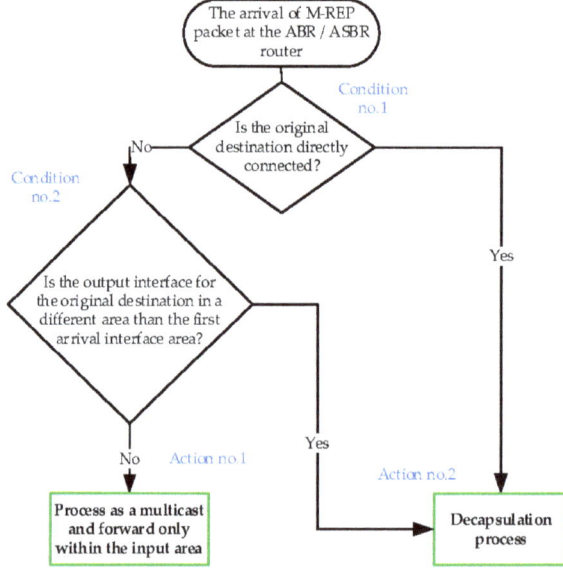

Figure 10. The Area Border Router (ABR) router behavior after the arrival of M-REP packet.

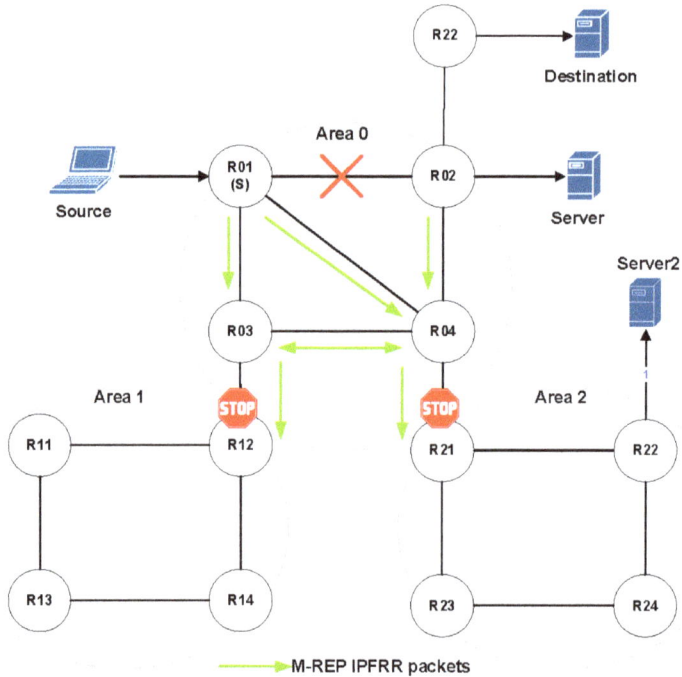

Figure 11. The flooding process with modified ABR.

This principle also removes the original M-REP mechanism design requirement, which assumes that the router D is directly connected to the destination. This solution requires that two different areas are connected over one link and only one failure has occurred there.

Routers R12 and R21 will behave according to Action no. 1 (Figure 10). This means that the M-REP multicast will not be forwarded to the next area. The R02 router, however, will behave according to the Action no. 2 (Figure 10), which causes the decapsulation of the multicast M-REP flow and its further delivery to the destination.

5.3. Manual Configuration of Router D

Another way to select a router that performs the decapsulation of the M-REP multicast flow back to unicast is to manually configure a router as the decapsulating router (router D). In practice, the network administrator would manually select and configure a router to perform the decapsulation process (Figure 12).

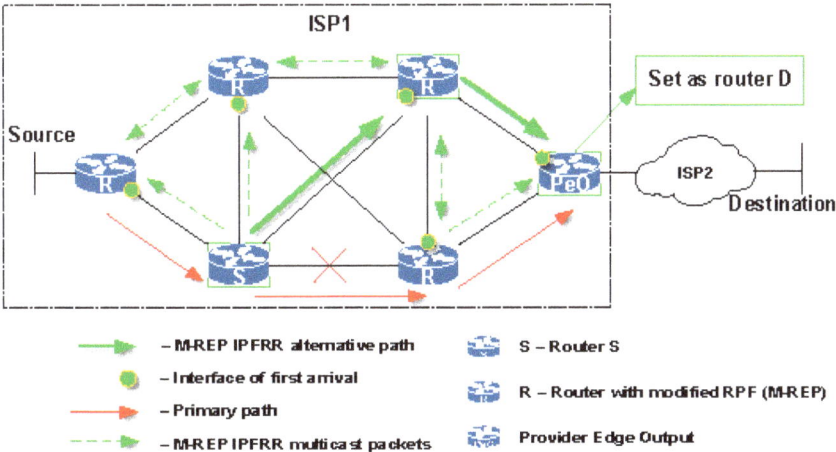

Figure 12. Manual configuration of Router D

An example of the situation, in which router D has to be manually configured when the destination of the protected unicast flow is not in the domain where a failure occurred is presented in Figure 12 (Manual configuration of Router D). In this case, the administrator must manually configure the Provider Edge Output (PeO) for router function D.

6. Evaluation of the EM-REP Proposal

The functionalities of the enhanced version of the M-REP algorithm (EM-REP) proposed in Sections 5.1 and 5.2 have been verified by simulations. The implementation of the algorithm itself together and its extensions, as well as the creation of testing scenarios, were performed in the OMNeT++ discrete event simulator. The implementation is based on modification of the Automated Network Simulation and Analysis (ANSA) [69] and INET Framework Objective Modular Network Testbed in C++ (OMNeT++) libraries [70]. The ANSA library implements the multicast technology and the INET provides OSPF routing functionalities.

The correct behavior of the enhanced M-REP algorithm functions proposed in the paper has been successfully tested using several scenarios. The scenarios simulate various types of failures for various topologies. In these scenarios, we focus on the correctness of the partial activities of the algorithm, as well as on the investigation of the correct delivery of packets belonging to the protected flow to its destination. In this section, we introduce one of the comprehensive testing scenarios. The topology used in the scenario is shown in Figure 13. As a unicast routing protocol, the OSPFv2 protocol in a multiarea deployment model has been used. The routing domain consists of five OSPF areas, 23 routers and three hosts. For testing purposes, we generate data flow originated from host H11 to the H42 receiver. This data represents a protected stream of user datagrams, the delivery of which is ensured by our algorithm. In the case of a stable and error-free network condition, the delivery of packets is following the shortest path selected by OSPF (in Figure 13 represented by red arrows). In this scenario, we simulate the occurrence of several (three) independent network failures (the improvement introduced in Section 5.1), that occurs inside of different OSPF areas. The purpose of the simulation is to observe how the algorithm will protect user data in the event of multiple network failures within three separated areas.

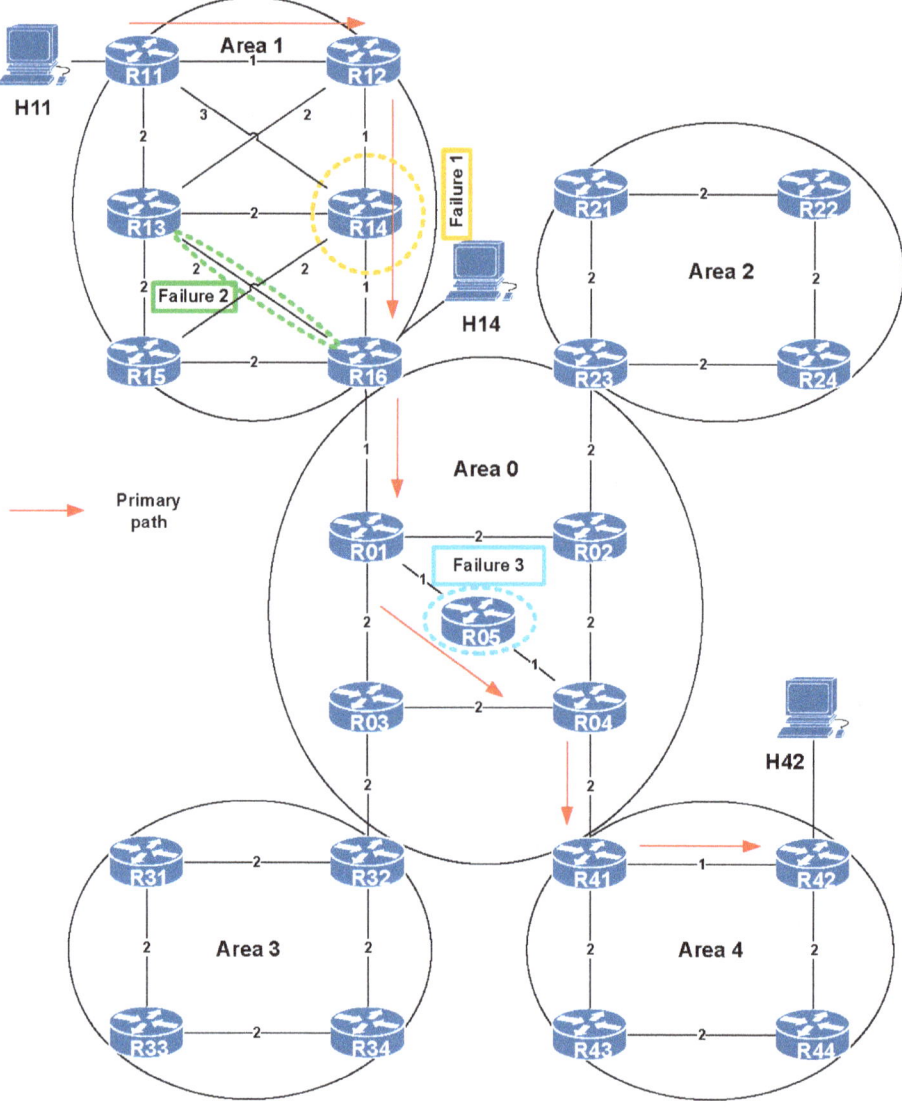

Figure 13. The OMNeT++ simulation topology.

The description of scenario is as follows. At the beginning of the simulation we wait 200 ms to complete the process of network convergence (i.e., the convergence of OSPF unicast routing), then at the time of 200 sims (simulation seconds) the H11 host starts generating data flow. The source is the H11 with IPv4 address 192.168.11.2, the destination is the host H42 with IPv4 address 192.168.66.2. At the time of 210 sims we simulate the first failure, and the R14 router is shut down. At 212 sims we simulate the second failure as a permanent connection failure between routers R13 and R16. Finally, at 215 sims we simulate another failure of router R05 (Table 4).

Table 4. Test description.

Time	Description of Action
<200	Time necessary for the OSPF convergence and stabilization of network processes.
200	H11 starts the flow
210	Router R14 failure
212	Drop of link R13 / R16
215	Router R05 failure

6.1. Simulation Process: Algorithm Behavior

After the simulation has been started, at 200 sims the H11 host starts to generate packets of protected flow with destination address of H42. This flow, as we have already mentioned, is called a protected flow because the routers in M-REP are configured to encapsulate and flood its packets around the point of failure on the way to the destination. Therefore, at the time of 210 sims, we simulate the first failure inside area 1, where we turn off the router R14. As the R14 router is on the best path to the destination, the OSPF will begin to flood its OSPF Link-State Advertisement (LSA) updates and will start to converge. However, until the convergence ends, the R12 router quickly detects that its neighbor has failed (they have either direct connection or use the BFD mechanism), and R12 becomes the source router (S router). That is, R12 begins encapsulating the unicast packets of the protected flow into new multicast packets of the (S, G1) pair, since it is configured to protect the flow from 192.168.11.2 to 192.168.66.2. When creating a multicast packet header, the router will use the original IP address as the source address S, i.e., the IP address of sender (H11). As the multicast destination address G1, the router will use the predefined M-REP multicast address (unique and configured for each protected flow); here it is 226.1.1.1. This behavior is shown in Figure 14. The original unicast destination address is stored for future decapsulation in a variable named MREPdestAddress. The multicast packet is then immediately flooded out using the PIM-DM mechanism. As a result, due to the M-REP algorithm modification (the rule of first arrival), the PIM-DM will construct an alternative path around the failure. The new path lead through R11 → R12 → R13 → R16 in this area.

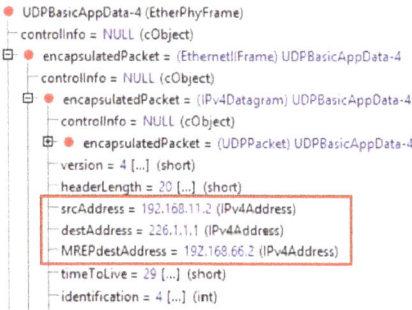

Figure 14. Encapsulated EM-REP packet.

At 212 sims, we have scheduled the second failure, in which the connection between R13/R16 will be interrupted. The link is already a part of the alternative route (distribution tree) constructed before. Here we have both, a second error and a protected flow, which is once encapsulated. The moment this failure occurs, R13 becomes the new source router S2. R13 as S2 detects that it is already on the previously constructed repair path of the first M-REP run (according to its record that includes interfaces list for (S, G1) tree). Therefore, for each multicast packets of (S, G1) pair, the router R13 replaces the previous M-REP G1 multicast address (226.1.1.1) by the new one, G2 (226.1.1.2, Figure 15). This event triggers a new flooding process, creating a new alternative path around the second failure. In this case, the path leads through the routers R11 → R13 → R15 of the area 1.

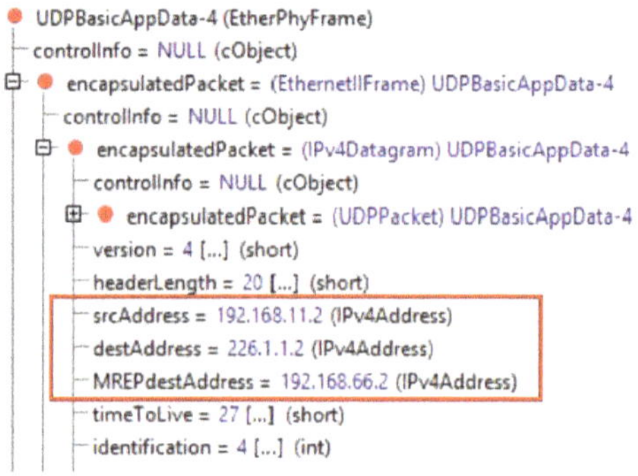

Figure 15. Second EM-REP run.

Our enhancement of the M-REP algorithm assumes, that the decapsulation of original unicast packets of a protected flow from the carrier multicast packets is performed on an ABR router. The ABR selection is performed according to the conditions specified in Section 5.2, which in our case is the R16 router. The modification proposed in Section 5.2 stops the flooding of M-REP packets from one area to other areas, except area 1. Router R16 replaces the destination address of the G2 M-REP packets back to the original unicast one (i.e., 192.168.66.2 taken from MREPdestAddress header, Figure 16). This converts the multicast communication back, and the flow from H11 to H42 is routed as unicast again.

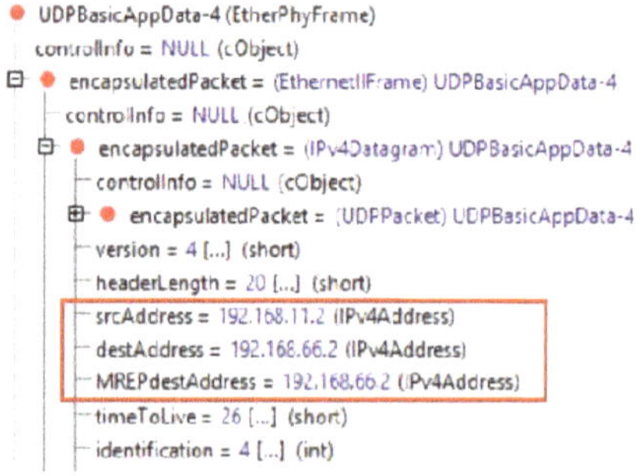

Figure 16. Restoration of EM-REP packet to original destination address.

The third and final simulated failure is scheduled at the time of 215 sims. The failure represents an error of the R05 router, that is located inside of the backbone area 0. Here, the process of encapsulating and PIM flooding is repeated. When this failure occurs, R01 becomes the next source router S and begins encapsulating packets of the protected flow using the predefined M-REP multicast address. The multicast address, as we mentioned, must be configured for the protected flow. The failure occurred in a different OSPF area than in the previous two cases. Our proposed solution reduces the flooding from one OSPF area to another, so that M-REP can use the same multicast destination address as in area 1, i.e., the multicast address 226.1.1.1.

Table 5 displays the output from OMNeT++ simulation, which shows how packets are handled in the moment of the R05 router failure, and which destination addresses are used to deliver packets of the protected flow. The M-REP constructs an alternative route that leads through routers R01 → R03 → R04.

Table 5. The result of the third failure simulation.

Time	Source/Destination	Name	Destination Address
215.00007242	→R01	UDPBasicAppData-185	192.168.66.2
215.00008484	R01 → R02	UDPBasicAppData-185	226.1.1.1
215.00008484	R01 → R03	UDPBasicAppData-185	226.1.1.1
215.00009726	R02 → R04	UDPBasicAppData-185	226.1.1.1
215.00009726	R02 → R23	UDPBasicAppData-185	226.1.1.1
215.00009726	R03 → R32	UDPBasicAppData-185	226.1.1.1
215.00010968	R04 → R41	UDPBasicAppData-185	226.1.1.1
215.0001221	R41 → R42	UDPBasicAppData-185	192.168.66.2
215.00013452	R42 → H42	UDPBasicAppData-185	192.168.66.2

6.2. Evaluation of the EM-REP Mechanism

The main advantage of the M-REP IPFRR mechanism is that the algorithm does not depend on precomputations and even on the unicast routing protocol used. Respecting these properties, we may argue that the M-REP IPFRR mechanism is unique compared to the analyzed ones, as well as other existing IPFRR solutions. The extensions of the M-REP proposed in this paper solve several limitations that have not been resolved in legacy M-REP proposal.

The enhancement described in Section 5.1 has introduced recovery mechanisms that support fast reroute in the event of multiple and persistent connection and node failures thorough the whole network. In situations when subsequent and recurring errors occur concurrently over time, the EM-REP mechanism encapsulates protected flow into several specific multicast distribution trees, or (S, G) traffic groups. For each multicast distribution group, its router S as the root of the distribution tree encapsulates and floods packets through any of its functional links to all PIM-DM neighbors. Therefore, even if a link or node failure occurs in several places, if there is still at least one possible path from the source S to the destination D, the EM-REP mechanism can find it and use it as an alternative path. This is a unique behavior of EM-REP that provides the 100% repair coverage. This behavior was among other ones simulated by the complex scenario just described. Here we have simulated three consecutive network failures. The simulation results confirmed expected core EM-REP behavior (detection, encapsulation, and flooding), as well as the extended protection against multiple failures, as we proposed in Section 5.1. The EM-REP mechanism has constructed several distribution trees and protects the data of the specified protected flow from multiple failures. The mechanism ensures that all packets of the protected flow were delivered to its destination D.

The second enhancement, which was described in Section 5.2, addresses the issue that in the original M- REP mechanism, the destination host has to be directly connected to a network with a router that performs decapsulation (router D). The extension also reduces a flooding process of M-REP packets in a network with multiple routing areas.

Compared to other existing IPFRR mechanisms, the concept of the M-REP mechanism (as well as its enhanced version EM-REP) brings several advantages in addition to the mentioned ones. Some of its drawbacks are also known. An overview of advantages and disadvantages of the EM-REP mechanism is given in the Table 6.

Table 6. Features of M-REP mechanism.

Advantages	Disadvantages
No pre-computation	
Suitable for networks of any size	
Independence of unicast routing protocols in general, but with optimized feature set when using OSPF	Does not support multiaccess network segments, i.e., only point-to-point links are supported
100% repair coverage	Random alternative route (hard to predetermine)
Support of multiple failure repairs at the same time	Packet modification (tunneling)
Fix multiple failures at different times (solution presented in Section 5.1)	Flooding/pruning process of PIM-DM distribution path
Relatively easy implementation through PIM-DM modification	

A more accurate comparison of the selected features with other existing IPFRR mechanisms is provided in Table 7 below. As we can see, the EM-REP mechanism is unique in several specific areas.

Table 7. Comparison of the innovative M-REP mechanism with existing solutions.

Title	100% Repair Coverage	Precalculations (Precomputing)	Packet Modification	Dependency on Link-State Routing Protocols
EM-REP	Yes	No	Yes	No
ECMP FRR	No	Yes	No	No
BIER-TE (M)	Yes	Yes	Yes	No
Directed LFA	Yes	Yes	Yes	Yes
LFA	No	Yes	No	No
MoFRR	No	Yes	No	No
MPLS-TE FRR	No	Yes	Yes	No
MRC	Yes	Yes	Yes	Yes
MRT	Yes	Yes	Yes	Yes
Not-Via Addresses	Yes	Yes	Yes	Yes
Remote LFA	No	Yes	Yes	Yes
TI-LFA	Yes	Yes	Yes	Yes

6.3. Time of Repair: Algorithm Speed

The network recovery time usually consists of two parts. The first part consists of the time in which a router is able to detect the failure of its link, or the unavailability of its connected neighbors. In practice, a specialized protocol is usually used for this purpose. The most used protocol is the Bidirectional Forwarding Detection (BFD), a protocol standardized by Internet Engineering Task Force (IETF) in Request for Comments (RFC) 5880. Using BFD, the router can detect a connection failure with a neighboring node in less than 30 ms, depending on the timer settings. Specifically, the mentioned time of 30 ms can be achieved by setting the hello interval to 10 ms. If no hello message is received from a neighboring node within three hello intervals, the BFD session with that neighbor is declared invalid, i.e., the neighbor is considered unavailable. It is the state of unavailability that subsequently triggers an IPFRR mechanism.

The second part, which defines the recovery time, is the amount of time required to create an alternative path and resume an interrupted communication. This time depends mainly on the speed of the specific IPFRR mechanism (or its algorithm). Current FRR mechanisms operate using a proactive approach. This means that all alternative paths for all possible destination are calculated in advance before the outage itself occurs. These preliminary calculations differ in their computational complexity and time depending on the IPFRR mechanism used. At the same time, different IPFRR mechanisms have different requirements regarding the required space needed to store their results. However, once a failure is detected, the installation and use of a pre-calculated alternative path is immediate. Compared to link failure detection, this time is minimal and negligible.

However, the EM-REP mechanism operates in principle in a reactive manner. An alternative path is created randomly as the result of flooding and pruning mechanisms used by our modified PIM-DM (i.e., EM-REP). The distribution path (single-branched tree), as has been already mentioned, is constructed using the principle of the first arrival of packets, i.e., packets that arrive first on individual router interfaces after the flooding process. This subsequently creates interfaces of the first arrival (PIM-DM RPF ports) and a chain of routers of an alternative path. Simulations show the speed of network recovery achieved by the EM-REP mechanism is comparable, respectively the same, as the network recovery speed achieved through the proactive FRR mechanisms. The main difference is that the EM-REP mechanism does not require preparatory calculations or additional router resources.

On the other hand, the network load is initially higher, as is the case with the proactive FRR mechanisms. This is the result of the initial EM-MREP flooding process. However, the EM-REP was not designed to protect all flows affected by a failure. EM-REP protects only specific but important customer data flows that require special treatment or lossless delivery through an ISP. These flows are only a subset of all flows affected by the error. In addition, we expect that the EM-REP mechanism, like other IPFRRs, will only work for a short time, not longer than a few tens of milliseconds or a few seconds. It ends when the network convergence process is complete, the multicast tree is no longer used, and packets of protected flows are routed again as unicast packets.

7. Conclusions

The paper presents the Enhanced Multicast Repair (EM-REP) FRR mechanism, which solves several limitations of the legacy M-REP FRR mechanism. This means mainly support for fast reroute in the event of continuous link and node failures throughout the whole network and that the destination host does not have to be directly connected to a network with a router that performs decapsulation, which also reduces a flooding process of M-REP packets in a network with multiple routing areas.

Both mechanisms belong to the family of Fast Reroute solutions. The EM-REP mechanism presented in this paper, makes it possible to create an alternate backup path that allows packets to bypass the failures of one or more links or nodes at a given time. To achieve this goal, the EM-REP has been built on two cornerstones, the PIM-DM protocol and tunneling. The PIM-DM delivers multicast data thorough a distribution tree constructed by the flooding and reverse pruning. The EM-REP is based on this behavior, where in the event of a failure (or even multiple failures), for specific traffic flow an alternate path is built by PIM-DM flooding and pruning. In this case, the router begins encapsulating unicast packets of the protected flow into multicast packets flooded out and around the failure. To ensure correct operation of routers, we have not modified the PIM-DM process as such, i.e., for a common multicast traffic the PIM-DM process works as usual. However, for the correct construction of alternative FRR paths (distribution trees), we have modified the PIM-DM RPF process, where we use the rule of the first arrival. Alternative paths are created only for protected flows, so the router must identify correct packets in some way. In short, we expect that flow identifiers are predefined and preconfigured by the network administrator in advance. However, in future, some dynamic distribution mechanism may be used, inspired, for example, by those used for a dynamic distribution of Rendezvous Point (RP) addresses (Auto-RP, BSR Bootstrap Router mechanism), but here used for the distribution of protected flow identifiers.

As has been already mentioned, most FRR mechanisms require the pre-calculation of alternative routes for different network failure scenarios. On the one hand, these preparatory calculations have undesirable effects on the router's limited resources, such as CPU load and memory. On the other hand, they may depend on a specific link-state routing protocol. The EM-REP mechanism does not require any preparatory calculations, which is effective for IoT devices such as sensors.

Moreover, the EM-REP does not depend on any unicast routing protocol. In addition, although EM-REP can bring benefits resulting from the use of a specific routing protocol supporting the organization of unicast routing to areas, as is presented here for OSPF, it could work for IS-IS as well. Furthermore, the EM-REP FRR mechanism provides 100% repair coverage for single as well as multiple failures occurring at different times and places in the network. Finally, EM-REP eliminates the condition of directly connected destination to router D of legacy M-REP.

The EM-REP mechanism uses the generic flooding process of the PIM-DM protocol to provide the protection for specific flows that expect special handling inside the network. The behavior and goal are generic enough with a wider application domain. In the area of WSN and the IoT, it can be used to distribute, for example, urgent messages across the WSN network or to assure the time-critical delivery of important information from sensors to gateways or behind to analytic servers.

The EM-REP was fully implemented, and its correctness was tested using the OMNeT++ simulator. We have performed extensive tests of the implementation in different networking scenarios, which validated the functional correctness of all the mechanism functions. The principle of the mechanism is unique, and it is possible to apply it in other networks such as WSN, IoT architecture, and other areas as well, which will be studied in future work.

Author Contributions: Conceptualization, J.P. and P.S.; software, J.P.; validation, J.P. and P.S.; formal analysis, J.P., P.S., O.Y., I.B., M.H.; investigation, J.P.; resources, J.P.; data curation, J.P.; writing—original draft preparation, J.P., P.S., O.Y.; writing—review and editing, J.P., P.S., O.Y., I.B., M.H.; investigation, J.P.; visualization, J.P.; supervision, J.P. and P.S.; project administration, J.P. and P.S.; funding acquisition, J.P. and I.B.. All authors have read and agreed to the published version of the manuscript.

Funding: This research was funded by UNIZA Grant System and Faculty Research Grant (FVG).

Acknowledgments: This work has been supported by the Slovak Scientific Grant Agency (VEGA) grant agency, Project No. 1/0626/19 "Research of mobile objects localization in IoT environment".

Conflicts of Interest: The authors declare no conflict of interest.

References

1. Kvist, F.; Urke, A.R.; Øvsthus, K. Energy efficient determinism in WSN through reverse packet elimination. *Sensors* **2020**, *20*, 2890. [CrossRef] [PubMed]

2. Moreno, J.; Matamoros, O.M.; Reyes, I.L.; Tejeida-Padilla, R.; Hernández, L.C.; Durán, J.P.F.P. Energy-efficient industrial internet of things software-defined network by means of the peano fractal. *Sensors* **2020**, *20*, 2855. [CrossRef] [PubMed]

3. Guerrero-Sanchez, A.E.; Rivas-Araiza, E.A.; Gonzalez-Cordoba, J.L.; Toledano-Ayala, M.; Takacs, A. Blockchain mechanism and symmetric encryption in a wireless sensor network. *Sensors* **2020**, *20*, 2798. [CrossRef] [PubMed]

4. Fathallah, K.; Abid, M.A.; Ben Hadj-Alouane, N. Enhancing energy saving in smart farming through aggregation and partition aware IOT routing protocol. *Sensors* **2020**, *20*, 2760. [CrossRef]

5. Haseeb, K.; Almogren, A.; Din, I.U.; Islam, N.; Altameem, A. SASC: Secure and authentication-based sensor cloud architecture for intelligent internet of things. *Sensors* **2020**, *20*, 2468. [CrossRef]

6. Lihakanga, R.; Ding, Y.; Medero, G.M.; Chapman, S.; Goussetis, G. A high-resolution open source platform for building envelope thermal performance assessment using a wireless sensor network. *Sensors* **2020**, *20*, 1755. [CrossRef]

7. Petija, R.; Michalko, M.; Jakab, F.; Fecil'ak, P. Convergence of routing protocols in real and simulated environments. In Proceedings of the 2018 16th International Conference on Emerging eLearning Technologies and Applications (ICETA), Stary Smokovec, Slovakia, 15–16 November 2018; pp. 425–430.

8. Harada, Y.; Hui, W.; Fukushima, Y.; Yokohira, T. A reroute method to recover fast from network failure. In Proceedings of the 2014 International Conference on Information and Communication Technology Convergence (ICTC), Busan, Korea, 22–24 October 2014; pp. 903–908.

9. Cheng, Z.; Zhang, X.; Li, Y.; Yu, S.; Lin, R.; He, L. Congestion-aware local reroute for fast failure recovery in software-defined networks. *J. Opt. Commun. Netw.* **2017**, *9*, 934. [CrossRef]

10. Antonakopoulos, S.; Bejerano, Y.; Koppol, P. A simple IP fast reroute scheme for full coverage. In Proceedings of the 2012 IEEE 13th International Conference on High Performance Switching and Routing, Belgrade, Serbia, 24 June 2012; pp. 15–22.

11. Csikor, L.; Rétvari, G. IP fast reroute with remote Loop-Free Alternates: The unit link cost case. In Proceedings of the 2012 IV International Congress on Ultra Modern Telecommunications and Control Systems, St. Petersburg, Russia, 3–5 October 2012; pp. 663–669. [CrossRef]

12. Yeremenko, O.; Yeremenko, O.; Hailan, A. Two-level method of fast ReRouting in software-defined networks. In Proceedings of the 2017 4th International Scientific-Practical Conference Problems of Infocommunications, Kharkiv, Ukraine, 10–13 October 2017; pp. 376–379.

13. Robertson, G.; Roy, N.; Penumarthi, P.K.; Nelakuditi, S.; O'Kane, J.M. Loop-free convergence with unordered updates. *IEEE Trans. Netw. Serv. Manag.* **2017**, *14*, 373–385. [CrossRef]

14. Malik, S.U.R.; Srinivasan, S.; Khan, S. Convergence time analysis of open shortest path first routing protocol in internet scale networks. *Electron. Lett.* **2012**, *48*, 1188. [CrossRef]

15. Pal, V.K.; Ramteke, S.M. A framework for fast IP rerouting. In Proceedings of the International Conference on Information Communication and Embedded Systems (ICICES2014), Chennai, India, 27–28 February 2014; pp. 1–6.

16. Muthumanikandan, V.; Valliyammai, C.; Harish, S. Link failure detection and alternate path tracing in openflow based Ethernet networks. In Proceedings of the 2017 Ninth International Conference on Advanced Computing (ICoAC), Chennai, India, 14–16 December 2017; pp. 352–356.

17. Gjoka, M.; Ram, V.; Yang, X. Evaluation of IP fast reroute proposals. In Proceedings of the 2007 2nd International Conference on Communication Systems Software and Middleware, Bangalore, India, 7–12 January 2007; pp. 1–8.

18. Krishnan, Y.N.; Shobha, G. Performance analysis of OSPF and EIGRP routing protocols for greener internetworking. In Proceedings of the 2013 International Conference on Green High Performance Computing (ICGHPC), Nagercoil, India, 14 March 2013; pp. 1–4.

19. Thorenoor, S.G. Dynamic routing protocol implementation decision between EIGRP, OSPF and RIP based on technical background using OPNET modeler. In Proceedings of the 2010 Second International Conference on Computer and Network Technology, ICCNT 2010, Bangkok, Thailand, 23–25 April 2010; pp. 191–195.

20. Masruroh, S.U.; Fiade, A.; Iman, M.F. Performance evaluation of routing protocol RIPv2, OSPF, EIGRP with BGP. In Proceedings of the 2017 International Conference on Innovative and Creative Information Technology: Computational Intelligence and IoT, ICITech, Salatiga, Indonesia, 2–4 November 2017; pp. 1–7.

21. Papán, J.; Segec, P.; Moravcik, M.; Kontsek, M.; Mikuš, L.; Uramova, J.; Konstek, M. Overview of IP fast reroute solutions. In Proceedings of the 2018 16th International Conference on Emerging eLearning Technologies and Applications (ICETA), Stary Smokovec, Slovakia, 15–16 November 2018; pp. 417–424.

22. Elhourani, T.; Gopalan, A.; Ramasubramanian, S. IP fast rerouting for multi-link failures. *IEEE/ACM Trans. Netw.* **2016**, *24*, 3014–3025. [CrossRef]

23. Gopalan, A.; Ramasubramanian, S. IP fast rerouting and disjoint multipath routing with three edge-independent spanning trees. *IEEE/ACM Trans. Netw.* **2016**, *24*, 1336–1349. [CrossRef]

24. Braun, W.; Menth, M. Loop-free alternates with loop detection for fast reroute in software-defined carrier and data center networks. *J. Netw. Syst. Manag.* **2016**, *24*, 470–490. [CrossRef]

25. Elhourani, T.; Gopalan, A.; Ramasubramanian, S. IP fast rerouting for multi-link failures. In Proceedings of the IEEE INFOCOM 2014—IEEE Conference on Computer Communications, Toronto, ON, Canada, 27 April–2 May 2014; pp. 2148–2156.

26. Shand, M.; Bryant, S. *IP Fast Reroute Framework*; Internet Engineering Task Force (IETF): Wilmington, DE, USA, 2010; ISSN 2070-1721, RFC5714.

27. Tavernier, W.; Papadimitriou, D.; Colle, D.; Pickavet, M.; Demeester, P. Packet loss reduction during rerouting using network traffic analysis. *Telecommun. Syst.* **2011**, *52*, 861–879. [CrossRef]

28. Fundo, A.; Bashllari, A.; Nace, D.; Shinko, I. A hybrid rerouting scheme. *Telecommun. Syst.* **2013**, *56*, 69–78. [CrossRef]

29. Rak, J.; Pickavet, M.; Trivedi, K.S.; Lopez, J.A.; Koster, A.M.; Sterbenz, J.P.; Cetinkaya, E.; Gomes, T.; Gunkel, M.; Walkowiak, K.; et al. Future research directions in design of reliable communication systems. *Telecommun. Syst.* **2015**, *60*, 423–450. [CrossRef]

30. Csikor, L.; Rétvári, G. On providing fast protection with remote loop-free alternates. *Telecommun. Syst.* **2015**, *60*, 485–502. [CrossRef]

31. Tavernier, W.; Papadimitriou, D.; Colle, D.; Pickavet, M.; Demeester, P. Self-configuring loop-free alternates with high link failure coverage. *Telecommun. Syst.* **2013**, *56*, 85–101. [CrossRef]

32. Tipper, D. Resilient network design: Challenges and future directions. *Telecommun. Syst.* **2013**, *56*, 5–16. [CrossRef]

33. Su, H.-K. A local fast-reroute mechanism for single node or link protection in hop-by-hop routed networks. *Comput. Commun.* **2012**, *35*, 970–979. [CrossRef]

34. Jarry, A. Fast reroute paths algorithms. *Telecommun. Syst.* **2011**, *52*, 881–888. [CrossRef]

35. Nagy, M.; Tapolcai, J.; Rétvári, G. Optimization methods for improving IP-level fast protection for local shared risk groups with loop-free alternates. *Telecommun. Syst.* **2013**, *56*, 103–119. [CrossRef]

36. Kim, M.; Chae, K. DMP: Detouring using multiple paths against jamming attack for ubiquitous networking system. *Sensors* **2010**, *10*, 3626–3640. [CrossRef] [PubMed]

37. Landaluce, H.; Arjona, L.; Perallos, A.; Falcone, F.; Angulo, I.; Muralter, F. A review of IoT sensing applications and challenges using RFID and wireless sensor networks. *Sensors* **2020**, *20*, 2495. [CrossRef] [PubMed]

38. Csikor, L.; Tapolcai, J.; Rétvári, G. Optimizing IGP link costs for improving IP-level resilience with Loop-Free Alternates. *Comput. Commun.* **2013**, *36*, 645–655. [CrossRef]

39. Hegde, S.; Bowers, C.; Gredler, H.; Litkowski, S. Remote-LFA node protection and manageability. *RFC Editor* **2017**. [CrossRef]

40. Cevher, S.; Ulutas, M.; Hökelek, I. Topology-aware multiple routing configurations for fault tolerant networking. *J. Netw. Syst. Manag.* **2015**, *24*, 944–973. [CrossRef]

41. Cevher, S.; Ulutaş, M.; Altun, S.; Hökelek, I. Multiple routing configurations for fast re-route in software defined networks. In Proceedings of the 2016 24th Signal Processing and Communication Application Conference (SIU), Zonguldak, Turkey, 16–19 May 2016; pp. 993–996.

42. Cevher, S.; Ulutaş, M.; Hökelek, I. Performance evaluation of multiple routing configurations. In Proceedings of the 2013 21st Signal Processing and Communications Applications Conference (SIU), Haspolat, Turkey, 24–26 April 2013; pp. 1–4.

43. El-Serafy, M.A.; Elsayed, A.M.; Aly, M.H.; El-Badawy, E.-S.A.; Ghaleb, I.A.; El-Badawy, E.-S. Multiple routing configurations for datacenter disaster recovery applicability and challenges. In Proceedings of the 2014 International Conference on Computer and Communication Engineering, Dwarahat, India, 22–23 February 2014; pp. 146–149.

44. Limin, Z.; Zheqing, L.; Hui, W.; Peiyu, L.; Xi, C. A new backup topology design method for IP fast recovery. In Proceedings of the 2016 2nd IEEE International Conference on Computer and Communications (ICCC), Chengdu, China, 14–17 October 2016; pp. 1992–1997.

45. Menth, M.; Hartmann, M.; Martin, R.; Čičić, T.; Kvalbein, A. Loop-free alternates and not-via addresses: A proper combination for IP fast reroute? *Comput. Netw.* **2010**, *54*, 1300–1315. [CrossRef]

46. Kuang, K.; Wang, S.; Wang, X. Discussion on the combination of loop-free alternates and maximally redundant trees for IP networks fast reroute. In Proceedings of the 2014 IEEE International Conference on Communications (ICC), Sydney, Australia, 10–14 June 2014; pp. 1131–1136.

47. Atlas, A.; Bowers, C.; Enyedi, G. *An Architecture for IP/LDP Fast Reroute Using Maximally Redundant Trees (MRT-FRR)*; Internet Engineering Task Force (IETF): Wilmington, DE, USA, 2016; ISSN 2070-1721, RFC7812.

48. Lemeshko, O.; Kinan, A.; Wahhab, M.A.J.A.; Yeremenko, O. Multicast fast re-route schemes for multiflow case. *Exp. Des. Appl. CAD Syst. Microelectron.* **2015**, 422–424. [CrossRef]

49. Aman, A.H.M.; Hashim, A.H.A.; Ramli, H.A.M. Mathematical evaluation of context transfer and multicast fast reroute in multicast enabled network mobility management. *Int. J. Control Autom.* **2017**, *10*, 207–216. [CrossRef]

50. Xu, M.; Li, Q.; Pan, L.; Li, Q.; Wang, D. Minimum protection cost tree: A tunnel-based IP fast reroute scheme. *Comput. Commun.* **2012**, *35*, 2082–2092. [CrossRef]

51. Braun, W.; Albert, M.; Eckert, T.; Menth, M. Performance comparison of resilience mechanisms for stateless multicast using BIER. In Proceedings of the 2017 IFIP/IEEE Symposium on Integrated Network and Service Management (IM), Lisbon, Portugal, 8–12 May 2017; pp. 230–238. [CrossRef]

52. Sundarrajan, A.; Ramasubramanian, S. Fast rerouting for IP multicast under single node failures. In Proceedings of the 2013 IEEE Global Communications Conference (GLOBECOM), Atlanta, GA, USA, 9–13 December 2013; pp. 2076–2081.

53. Chaitou, M. A new fast backup method for bidirectional multicast traffic in MPLS networks: Control plane procedures and evaluation by simulations. *J. Netw. Syst. Manag.* **2016**, *25*, 210–228. [CrossRef]

54. Karan, A.; Filsfils, C.; Decraene, B. *Multicast-Only Fast Reroute*; ISSN 2070-1721, RFC7431. Internet Engineering Task Force (IETF): Wilmington, DE, USA, 2015. [CrossRef]

55. Eckert, T.; Cauchie, G.; Menth, M. *Traffic Engineering for Bit Index Explicit Replication (BIER-TE)*; Internet-Draft; Internet Engineering Task Force (IETF): Wilmington, DE, USA, 2019.

56. Papán, J.; Segec, P.; Paluch, P.; Uramova, J.; Moravcik, M. The new Multicast Repair (M-REP) IP fast reroute mechanism. *Concurr. Comput. Pr. Exp.* **2018**. [CrossRef]

57. Papán, J.; Segec, P.; Drozdova, M.; Mikus, L.; Moravcik, M.; Hrabovsky, J. The IPFRR mechanism inspired by BIER algorithm. In Proceedings of the 2016 International Conference on Emerging eLearning Technologies and Applications (ICETA), High Tatras, Slovakia, 24–25 November 2016; pp. 257–262.

58. Papán, J.; Segec, P.; Moravcik, M.; Hrabovsky, J.; Mikus, L.; Uramova, J. Existing mechanisms of IP fast reroute. In Proceedings of the 2017 15th International Conference on Emerging eLearning Technologies and Applications (ICETA) 2017, High Tatras, Slovakia, 26–27 October 2017; pp. 1–7.

59. Papán, J.; Segec, P.; Palúch, P.; Mikuš, Ľ.; Moravcik, M. *The Survey of Current IPFRR Mechanisms*; Springer: Berlin/Heidelberg, Germany, 2016; Volume 511, pp. 229–240.

60. Papán, J.; Segec, P.; Palúch, P. Tunnels in IP fast reroute. In Proceedings of the 10th International Conference on Digital Technologies 2014, Zilina, Slovakia, 9–11 July 2014; pp. 270–274.

61. Papán, J.; Segec, P.; Palúch, P.; Jozef, P. Analysis of existing IP Fast Reroute mechanisms. In Proceedings of the 2015 International Conference on Information and Digital Technologies, Zilina, Slovakia, 7–9 July 2015; pp. 291–297.

62. Filsfils, C.; Francois, P.; Shand, M.; Decraene, B.; Uttaro, J.; Leymann, N.; Horneffer, M. *Loop-Free Alternate (LFA) Applicability in Service Provider (SP) Networks*; Internet Engineering Task Force (IETF): Wilmington, DE, USA, 2015; ISSN 2070-1721, RFC6571.

63. Litkowski, S.; Bashandy, A.; Filsfils, C.; Decraene, B.; Francois, P. *Topology Independent Fast Reroute using Segment Routing*; Internet-Draft; Internet Engineering Task Force (IETF): Wilmington, DE, USA, 2019.

64. Rožić, Ć.; Sasaki, G. Cost of loop-free alternates in IP-Over-WDM networks. *J. Opt. Commun. Netw.* **2015**, *7*, 368. [CrossRef]

65. Zhang, Y.; Wang, J.; Hao, G. An autonomous connectivity restoration algorithm based on finite state machine for wireless sensor-actor networks. *Sensors* **2018**, *18*, 153. [CrossRef]

66. Wang, L.; Li, Y.; Pan, B.; Wu, Q.; Yin, J.; Xu, L. Network coding for efficient video multicast in device-to-device communications. *Sensors* **2020**, *20*, 2254. [CrossRef]

67. Lin, Z.; Tao, D.; Wang, Z. Dynamic construction scheme for virtualization security service in software-defined networks. *Sensors* **2017**, *17*, 920. [CrossRef]

68. Minoli, D. Multicast routing-dense-mode protocols: PIM DM. In *IP Multicast with Applications to IPTV and Mobile DVB-H*; John Wiley & Sons, Inc.: Hoboken, NJ, USA, 2007; pp. 152–184.

69. ANSA by Brno University of Technology. Available online: https://ansa.omnetpp.org/ (accessed on 25 October 2019).

70. INET Framework—INET Framework. Available online: https://inet.omnetpp.org/ (accessed on 25 October 2019).

Article

A New Bit Repair Fast Reroute Mechanism for Smart Sensors IoT Network Infrastructure

Jozef Papan [1,*], Pavel Segec [1], Oleksandra Yeremenko [2], Ivana Bridova [1] and Michal Hodon [3]

[1] Department of InfoCom Networks, University of Žilina, 010 26 Žilina, Slovakia;
    pavel.segec@fri.uniza.sk (P.S.); ivana.bridova@fri.uniza.sk (I.B.)

[2] Department of Infocommunication Engineering, Kharkiv National University of Radio Electronics,
    61166 Kharkiv, Ukraine; oleksandra.yeremenko.ua@ieee.org

[3] Department of Technical Cybernetics, University of Žilina, 010 26 Žilina, Slovakia; michal.hodon@fri.uniza.sk

*   Correspondence: jozef.papan@fri.uniza.sk

Received: 21 August 2020; Accepted: 12 September 2020; Published: 14 September 2020

Abstract: Today's IP networks are experiencing a high increase in used and connected Internet of Things (IoT) devices and related deployed critical services. This puts increased demands on the reliability of underlayer transport networks. Therefore, modern networks must meet specific qualitative and quantitative parameters to satisfy customer service demands in line with the most common requirements of network fault tolerance and minimal packet loss. After a router or link failure within the transport network, the network convergence process begins. This process can take an unpredictable amount of time, usually depending on the size, the design of the network and the routing protocol used. Several solutions have been developed to address these issues, where one of which is the group of so-called Fast ReRoute (FRR) mechanisms. A general feature of these mechanisms is the fact that the resilience to network connectivity failures is addressed by calculating a pre-prepared alternative path. The path serves as a backup in the event of a network failure. This paper presents a new Bit Repair (B-REP) FRR mechanism that uses a special BIER header field (Bit-String) to explicitly indicate an alternative path used to route the packet. B-REP calculates an alternative path in advance as a majority of existing FRR solutions. The advantage of B-REP is the ability to define an alternative hop-by-hop path with full repair coverage throughout the network, where, unlike other solutions, we propose the use of a standardized solution for this purpose. The area of the B-REP application is communication networks working on the principle of packet switching, which use some link-state routing protocol. Therefore, B-REP can be successfully used in the IoT solutions especially in the field of ensuring communication from sensors in order to guarantee a minimum packet loss during data transmission.

Keywords: internet of things (IoT); Fast Reroute; bit repair (B-REP); failure repair

---

1. Introduction

IoT architectures operate many types of different smart devices. The most used smart devices in the IoT are sensors that can be connected to the network using several technologies. In most cases, they are connected via wireless sensor networks (WSNs) [1–4]. With the growing popularity of the Internet of Things solutions, the number of WSN deployments is growing, as is the number of sensors connected in them, which of course leads to an increase in the amount of data generated by these sensors. Such devices are no longer used only for simple tasks, but also in comprehensive scenarios and services. Consequently, from the communication point of view, new challenges arise here. The whole communication chain must meet new requirements not only for simple data delivery but also must guarantee some reliability parameters of different data transfers such as availability, reliability, and network fault tolerance [5–8].

For example, if there is a connectivity loss or a change of network topology within the delivery chain, routing protocols of external base stations (BS) networks [9,10], in analogy to the Open Shortest Path Free (OSPF), respond to this change by re-converging the network [7,8,11–13]. During this process, routing protocols must update their routing information. Therefore, routers affected by the failure begin to send update messages to other routers that include recorded changes in the network topology. Receiving routers can then respond to topological changes and adjust their routing decisions. The time of the network convergence process depends mainly on the size and complexity of the network (number, density of nodes and links), as well as the routing protocol used. In a period of network convergence, network routers do not have valid routing information needed to deliver data properly. The loss, duplication, or other negative effects on data flows may significantly increase, and applications, services, or hosts may be unreachable, interrupted, or may provide unsatisfactory quality. This may be unacceptable for the quality of some services, such as critical or real-time. To address this issue and limit the impact of different network convergence times on the correct delivery of transmitted data, the FRR mechanisms have been developed [14–17].

The primary feature of many existing FRR mechanisms is the proactive calculation of alternative routes for each expected failure scenario. Alternative paths are calculated in advance on each individual router locally and before an unexpected specific network failure occurs. Once a connectivity failure is detected, the FRR mechanism of a local router quickly uses the pre-calculated alternative path to bypass a faulty connection. A simplified example is illustrated in Figure 1. Here, in the event of a connection failure of the link between the routers S and E, the S router uses a pre-prepared alternative path through the router N1 to bypass the failure and successfully deliver critical data during the convergence period. The alternative path is active and used at least until the network convergence process will complete. Thus, the main idea of FRR is that their recovery time of the affected communication is much faster than the convergence time of a routing protocol. This reduces the negative impact of failure on data delivery (loss, delay).

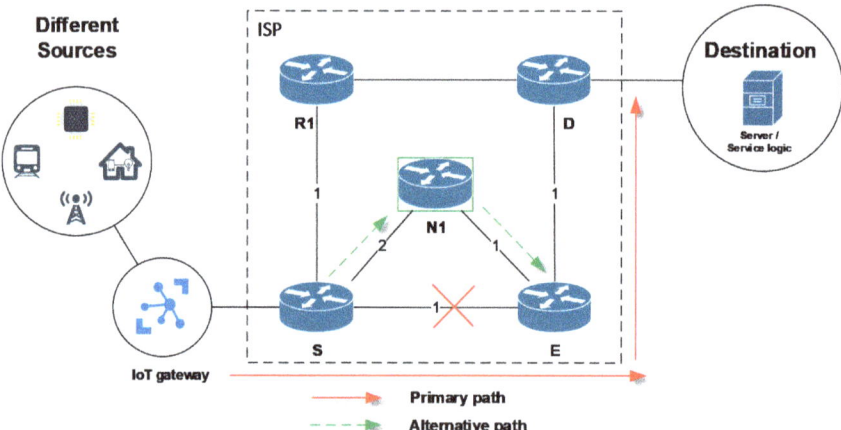

Figure 1. An example of the Fast ReRoute protection.

To further limit the effects of the error and to speed up the process of using the alternative route, FRR mechanisms may use other enhancement mechanisms, such as those for rapid detection of connection failure or neighbor unavailability (for example, bidirectional forwarding detection–BFD). These specialized mechanisms offer significantly faster detection of local failure than mechanisms built-in into current routing protocols (e.g., OSPF, IS-IS, EIGRP Hello mechanisms).

When using the FRR technology, the specific terms and definitions need to be introduced for denoting routers with unique FRR behavior [18–22]. The network topology shown in Figure 1 will be used for further explanation. The router that is detecting a link or neighboring router failure with the further activation of the FRR repair mechanism is defined as the source router (S). Consequently, router S becoming an active element of the FRR repair process (see Figure 1) referred to as the point of local repair (PLR). Router D denotes the destination router under discussion. Finally, the next-hop routers are specified by the routers N1, N2, N3, and others, which will compose the alternative path for FRR. The router not actively involved in the FRR repair process is designated the R router (here R1).

The paper presents a new bit repair (B-REP) FRR mechanism (hereinafter B-REP). The B-REP FRR mechanism is a type of proactive FRR mechanism. Unlike other FRR solutions, B-REP uses a standardized BIER header-based solution to circumvent failures. Mainly we focused on the ability to efficiently mark the entire alternative precalculated backup path thanks to its bit-string field. In addition, compared to other existing solutions (such as LFA or R-LFA), the B-REP mechanism can provide full repair coverage and repair all possible network failures within the topology. The B-REP can be deployed in an IP network that uses a link-state protocol, such as for example OSPF or intermediate system to intermediate system (IS-IS).

The B-REP is applicable to any network that operates the IP protocol stack and works with a link-state routing protocol. However, the deployment of the B-REP mechanism is more suitable for networks that are less dynamic, than usual WSN networks. B-REP works well for networks with static network nodes (some IoT deployments), or those networks behind the WSN BS towards the access/transport/ISP networks. In this environment, the B-REP mechanism provides the protection of important data flows generated from IoT/WSN devices–sensors and other devices. Our B-REP solution addresses the negative impacts of network failures and provides the solution that for the period of convergence guarantees correct packet delivery.

The remainder of this paper is structured as follows: Section 2 contains a summary of the latest knowledge in the FRR field and provides an analysis of existing solutions and their problem areas are discussed. Section 3 proposes the new B-REP FRR mechanism. Section 4 focuses on the evaluation of the B-REP mechanism and compares its features with other FRR solutions. Section 5 presents the conclusions of our work and plans for future research.

2. Related Works

Several existing solutions dealing with rerouting have been proposed in the IoT and IP network area. Reference [23] presents a new approach of jamming attack tolerant routing using multiple routes constructed on specific zones. This method separates the network into a number of zones and routes the candidate forward nodes of neighbor zones. When a system detects an attack, detour nodes in the network determine zones for proper rerouting and reroute packets intended for victim nodes through forwarding nodes in the obtained specific zones.

The authors of [24] present a comprehensive review of IoT sensing applications in WSNs, as well as the problems and tasks that need to be overcome. Some of the problem areas identified by authors are, for example, fault tolerance, the efficiency of the energy consumption, transmission interference, cost feasibility, and proper integration of these components.

Based on the identified issues and on our analysis of the IP FRR mechanisms properties, we can currently divide them into two generic groups/types. The first category of IP FRR mechanisms includes all proactive FRR mechanisms. The second category contains a family of reactive FRR mechanisms.

A characteristic of proactive FRR mechanisms is that these mechanisms calculate the alternative path in advance before a failure occurs. They act proactively when they already have alternative paths ready to respond to an error, depending on the location of the error. In the event of a failure, this backup path is then immediately installed into the routing table and used by a routing engine to redirect traffic around the failure. The interruption of operation caused by a network failure is therefore only for the time necessary to install a pre-prepared alternative route. This is considered as their undeniable advantage [25]. However, mechanisms in this category also have certain disadvantages identified. These include such properties as the pre-computation, the dependence on link-state routing protocols, complexity of internal algorithm [21,26–29].

One of the first mechanisms developed in the field of fast network recovery is the loop-free alternates (LFA for short) mechanism. LFA uses alternative next-hop neighbors that are able to deliver data without creating a routing loop. The selection of a suitable LFA candidate is ensured by several mathematical conditions. The basic version of the LFA mechanism [21,26,27] is suitable for certain topologies that are characterized by a high number of redundant links and suitable routing metrics. For topologies that do not meet these parameters, an extension of the classical LFA has been proposed, which is called the remote LFA (RLFA) [28,29]. RLFA has been proposed for situations where, for some reason, it is not possible to find suitable next-hop candidates according to the LFA conditions. RLFA uses tunneling mechanism to get around the failure towards remote tunnel end. Compared to the original LFA, the R-LFA provides higher repair coverage.

Other existing proactive FRR mechanisms are built on different approaches. The equal-cost multi-path (ECMP) [26,28] uses multiple routing paths that have the same metric in parallel. Multiple routing configurations (MRC) [28,30,31] uses different routing tables, while not-via addresses mechanisms [32,33] use specific addresses for explicit identification of failure. Furthermore, there are several FRR mechanisms exist based on alternative trees [19,34,35]. Amongst them, the maximally redundant trees (MRT) one is the most used [36,37].

The behavior of the reactive mechanism is different in that the alternative path is not calculated in advance. The backup path is constructed as an immediate reaction to the failure of the link itself and the protected flow transmitting through this link. Reactive FRR solutions do not calculate an alternative path in advance. However, the backup path is created after failure detection.

Reactive FRR mechanisms are not very numerous. They include the innovative multicast repair (M-REP) mechanism [36] and its enhanced version EM-REP [38]. The M-REP FRR mechanism uses the multicast [39–41] routing protocol—protocol independent multicast—dense mode (PIM DM) to flood traffic around failed element and create alternative FRR path. Enhanced version EM-REP adds support for the repair of multiple failures and link-state routing protocol such as OSPF or IS-IS.

The mechanisms mentioned so far have focused on addressing failure protection and convergence routing issues within the autonomous system (AS). Another FRR approach is represented by a mechanism called SWIFT. SWIFT is an FRR mechanism that is designed for the border gateway protocol (BGP), a protocol aimed at use for inter-AS routing. This mechanism is based on two approaches. First, a BGP router runs the SWIFT deduction algorithm that locates the failure and then tries to predict all prefixes that will be affected by the failure. The algorithm starts just after a router receives the routing update that contains first withdraw route information (prefix). Based on the calculations of this deduction algorithm, the router redirects the traffic to potentially affected prefixes to alternative routes that are not influenced by the failure (Figure 2).

In the case of BGP, the failure affects many prefixes at once. Therefore, as the second approach, the SWIFT introduces a new data plane coding scheme that allows the routing records concerned to be updated in a quick and flexible manner.

With the advent of relatively new approaches such as software defined networking (SDN), the FRR is emerging and being addressed in these application domains as well. The ability to calculate an alternate path in SDN depends on the option whether the SDN controller has access to a device imminently affected by a failure. As well as it depends on the round-trip time required for the communication between the SDN controller and devices influenced by the failure. The area of SDN is very diverse with a lot of proprietary approaches. The OpenFlow protocol is generally considered to be the most common standardized abstraction of the SDN internal communication. OpenFlow is used to install the data-match-action forwarding decisions applied through flow tables [42]. Therefore, as the link/node fault protection techniques there is the OpenFlow fast-failover [43]. This technique only operates in situations where the local node that detected the failure knows the alternative path.

Unfortunately, such an alternative route may not always be available. In that case, the intervention of an SDN controller is required. However, as the controller is deployed remotely it may not have access to the node that detected the failure. If the controller is aware of the failure and the local node does not have an alternative path, the controller will setup the redirection at another SDN node in the network.

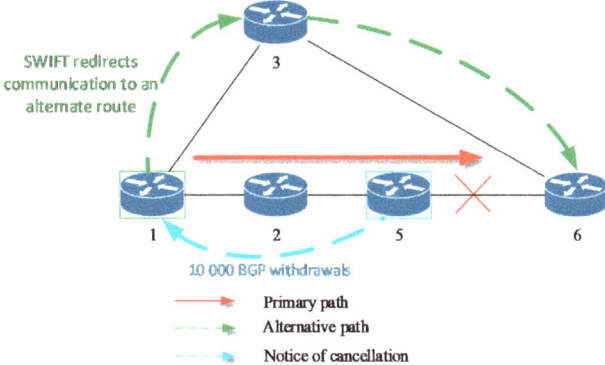

Figure 2. Principle of FRR mechanism SWIFT for BGP protocol.

One possible solution is to implement a stateful mechanism for determining the condition of links and other rules regarding alternative routes in each individual SDN node. There are several OpenFlow extensions exist that address this issue. The following solutions can be mentioned here: OpenState [44], FAST [44], and SPIDER [42]. For example, SPIDER is a neighbor detection mechanism inspired by known techniques such as bidirectional forwarding detection (BFD) and multiprotocol label switching (MPLS) FRR. Unlike other solutions that are based on OpenFlow, detection and redirection in SPIDER are implemented exclusively in the data plane without the need to rely on a slower control plane [42]. This mechanism contains four basic methods:

- Local failover, a specific node directly detects a failure and reroutes traffic to the alternative path.
- Remote failover (Figure 3), a specific node (Figure 3, node 2) receives information from another node about the failure (Figure 3, Tag = F) and reroutes traffic to the alternative path (Figure 3, node 5).
- Node testing (heartbeat request/reply), used to verify node availability.
- Path probing, nodes periodically generate packets to check the reachability of the node or the route.

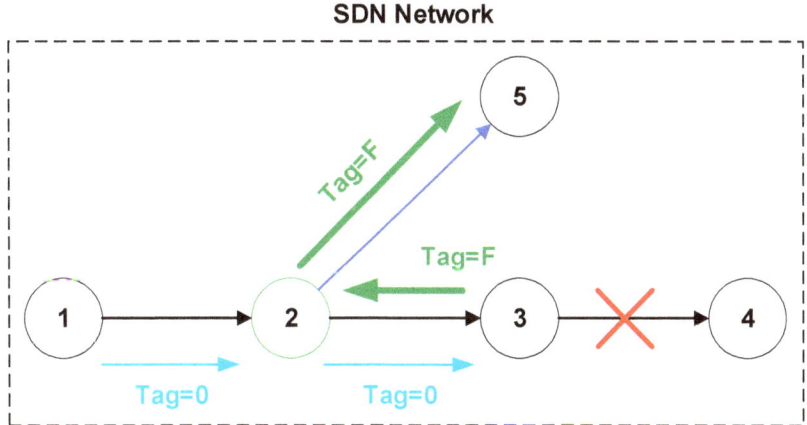

Figure 3. SPIDER—remote failover method.

An overview of the basic parameters of existing FRR solutions as the output of our research in this area [18,38,45–47] is summarized in Table 1. In this table, we compared the most important properties of existing FRR mechanisms such as repair coverage, proactive behavior, dependency on link-state routing protocols, and prediction.

Table 1. Comparison of FRR solutions.

Solution	Full Repair Coverage	Proactive Behavior	Dependency on Routing Protocols	Prediction
BIER-TE	Yes	Yes	No	No
Directed LFA	No	Yes	Yes	No
LFA	No	Yes	No	No
MPLS-TE	No	Yes	No	No
MRC	Yes	Yes	Yes	No
MRT	Yes	Yes	Yes	No
Not-Via	Yes	Yes	Yes	No
Remote LFA	No	Yes	Yes	No
TI-LFA	Yes	Yes	Yes	No
SWIFT (BGP)	Yes	Yes	Yes	Yes
M-REP	Yes	No	No	No
EM-REP	Yes	No	No	No

BIER-TE-Bit Index Explicit Replication-Traffic Engineering. LFA-Loop-Free Alternate. MRC-Multiple Routing Configurations. MRT-Maximally Redundant Trees. TI-LFA–Topology Independent Loop-Free Alternate.

2.1. Problem Areas

According to the analysis given in the previous section, we have identified several FRR problems that can be classified into three basic areas which are described in the following subsections.

2.1.1. Full Repair Coverage

According to the state-of-the-art analysis, we can state that some existing FRR mechanisms cannot provide full repair coverage. In other words, not all FRR mechanisms are able to repair and construct alternative backup paths for all possible failure scenarios. Furthermore, we can state that with the increasing repair coverage in most cases the complexity of the internal FRR algorithm also grows [48]. This may be an issue for complex and frequently changing network environment where routers with limited computation resources are installed, or low-priority FRR processes are used [48]. Therefore, one of the problem areas of current FRR solutions that provides full repair coverage is the complexity of an internal algorithm.

2.1.2. Custom Alternative Path and Cost-Based Calculations

In some situations, a network administrator should also have the possibility to manually specify an alternative path. The administrator can define a custom alternative path that can avoid a group of routers potentially affected by the failure.

Existing FRR solutions such as LFA [33], R-LFA [16], TI-LFA [49] calculate alternative FRR paths according to the link metrics of used routing protocols. The calculation and construction of alternative paths must usually meet specific algorithm conditions. Only paths that satisfy them can be then selected as valid alternative routes. In certain topological situations, problems may arise where an alternative path exists, although it is possible that based on its metrics it does not meet mathematical conditions of an algorithm and cannot be used as an alternative path. Therefore, some existing paths are unnecessarily excluded under the given conditions. The alternative path is defined in each of the existing FRR mechanisms differently (tunneling, adding specific bits in the IP header).

2.1.3. Research Goal (Research Aims and Objectives)

In previous subsections, we have identified some of the limitations of current FRR solutions that can be addressed and therefore offer new solutions that overcome them. Our work focused on the development of a new FRR mechanism concerned with the identified issues. Then the main contribution of this work is the proposal of the so-called Bit Repair (B-REP) algorithm. The B-REP algorithm is designed to repair of all possible failures within the specific network (100% repair coverage) with low calculation complexity.

The B-REP algorithm allows calculating an alternative path using standard link metrics or ignoring them, which means calculation without considering the metric's limitations. Accordingly, if a path exists, it will be found and used. At the same time with the B-REP mechanism, an administrator can define manually a custom alternative path.

Several FRR mechanisms use various proprietary solutions to define an alternative route and to transit mechanisms related data. We opted for a standardized solution, namely multicast protocol–bit index explicit replication (BIER) [50]. This protocol uses a standardized BIER header (Figure 4) that contains a special field called bit-string (B-S, Figure 5). That allows us to use a header and its fields to define an alternative path as well as to transfer user data.

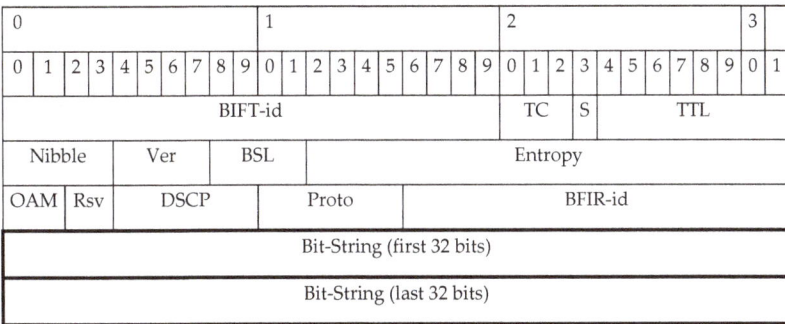

Figure 4. BIER header [51].

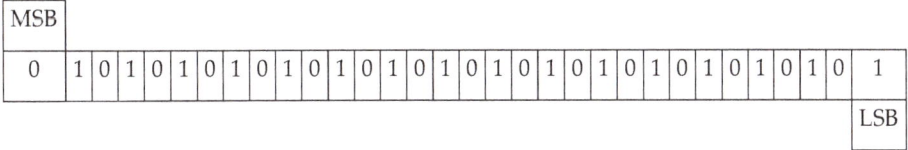

Figure 5. Bit-String.

Bit-string is an array of bits, in which each bit indicates exactly one specific router in the BIER domain [52,53]. In other words, bit-string is an array data structure that efficiently stores router related information. The bits are arranged from the least significant bit (LSB) to the most significant bit (MSB). The use of bit-string in the FRR area will allow defining effectively an alternative backup path in the event of a link or node failure. The B-S value with the specified bits represents the routers through which the packet will be routed in the event of an error. It was the idea of using bit-strings that inspired us to develop the B-REP mechanism. A similar idea was used by greedy algorithms designed for fault-tolerant multicast delivery in the hypercube [54–56]. The authors suggested using a bit address to select the optimal hop-by-ho routing.

3. The Proposal of the B-REP FRR Mechanism

In this section, we provide a more detailed description of the B-REP mechanism operation principles. As mentioned before, the B-REP belongs to FRR mechanisms. However, it is designed to protect specific unicast flows delivered from customer devices or IoT sensors over the transport network. This network comprising the devices responsible for data delivery (i.e., layer 3 routers) is typically organized into administrative or policy areas or domains. For the proper operation of the B-REP mechanism, two new parameters and one mandatory condition are introduced.

The first necessary parameter is the device or router identifier (ID). We require that each router in such a common network domain must have a unique identifier. This means that if a given router is assigned a certain ID, no other router can use it within the domain. Therefore, we propose a new router ID, which we will call the B-REP router-ID (B-REP R-ID). The R-ID is similar to, for example, the BFR-ID in BIER enabled networks [50] and is crucial for the proper operation of the B-REP. The assignment process is not precisely specified. B-REP R-ID can be set manually (preferred option) by the administrator for example, or it can be created and derived from another unique identifier that is already assigned to the router. The second parameter is the bit-string (B-S) that is the special variable length array where the B-REP IDs of B-REP enabled routers are defined. Thereby de facto the whole alternative transport path can be defined. Being able to do this, we finally assume, as a prerequisite for the proper functioning of B-REP, that some type of link-state (LS) routing protocol is enabled and is running in the transport network. Link-state routing protocols provide all area routers with accurate topological information about all other LS routers in the area and therefore allow B-REP to specify precise bit string parameter as a definition of alternative paths applicable to different failure scenarios. B-REP requires access to the LSDB database of the given LS protocol. The obtained data are then processed by B-REP and the Dijkstra algorithm is used to calculate the alternative route. Dijkstra can run as a specific low-priority process when the router's central processing unit (CPU) is idle. Therefore, the B-REP mechanism also calculates an alternative path during the CPU idle time. The alternative B-REP route is then stored in the B-REP backup path (B-REP BP) table (Table 2).

Table 2. B-REP BP table.

Protected Interface	Destination B-REP R-ID (OSPF Router ID)	Bit-String Value
Interface R1-R3	3 (3.3.3.3)	… 01110 (LSB)
Interface R1-R3	4 (4.4.4.4)	… 01010 (LSB)
…	…	…

Let us show the use of these parameters on the example of a network running the OSPF routing protocol (Figure 6). OSPF is a LS routing protocol. In OSPF all active routers must be assigned unique router-IDs (R-ID). OSPF R-ID can be set manually or automatically. In the case of automatic assignment, the OSPF R-ID is assigned based on one of the local IP addresses of the router. Therefore, as one of the alternatives, it allows setting the B-REP R-ID according to the OSPF R-ID, which perfectly meets the condition of uniqueness. The mapping process is not specified however there can be applied some kind of algorithmic mapping. An example of R-ID and corresponding B-REP ID mapping is illustrated in Table 3.

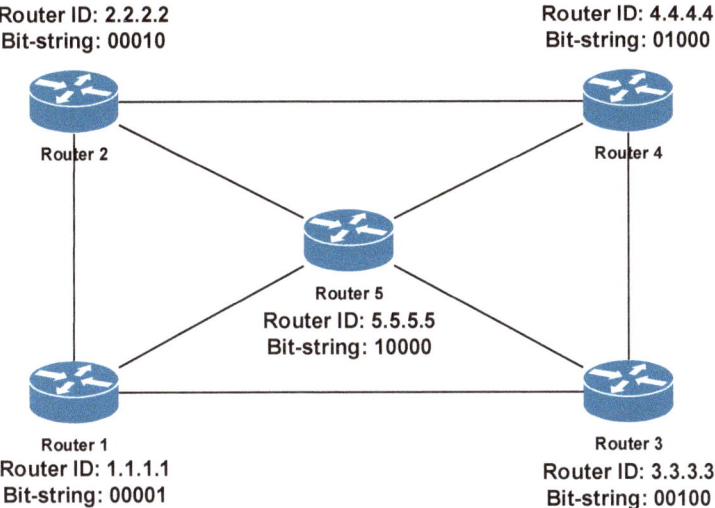

Figure 6. Allocation of Bit-Strings by the Router ID.

Table 3. B-REP Table—Bit allocation according to Bit-String.

Router	Router ID (OSPF)	B-REP R-ID	Bit-String Position (B-REP)
Router 1	1.1.1.1	1	... 00001 (LSB)
Router 2	2.2.2.2	2	... 00010
Router 3	3.3.3.3	3	... 00100
Router 4	4.4.4.4	4	... 01000
Router 5	5.5.5.5	5	... 10000

OSPF as an LS routing protocol that allows a router to obtain and maintain precise topological information about all other routers, their interconnections, and network links of the area. This information is identical on all routers, which store it locally in a database called the link-state database (LSDB) database. Because all routers have the same LSDB databases that contain all topological information, including all routers, each B-REP router will assign a unique B-REP R-ID to itself as well as to all other routers in the area. As the next step, the router specifies corresponding bit-string values for each area router. This information is stored, and operations are performed inside of the B-REP Table (Table 3). The table is created by each B-REP router when the B-REP is activated and finally it will be the same on each router. The table is constructed by sorting all routers of the given area according to their OSPF router IDs ascending. Then the B-REP algorithm assigns them unique B-REP IDs and positions in the bit-string (Table 3). Because the LSDB is the same on all routers, the final B-REP table will be the same too. In case of a network failure, the content of the B-REP table is frozen because it is used to construct an alternative reroute path. When the convergence of the OSPF protocol ends, the process of creating the B-REP table is performed again, i.e., each B-REP router refreshes its own B-REP table.

As we can see from the example, the router with the lowest OSPF Router ID is Router 1. Its OSPF router ID is 1.1.1.1, therefore, it gets B-REP R-ID of 1. That gives R1 the least significant bit (LSB) position in the bit-string (... 00001, Table 3, Figure 6). The Router 2, which is the second with the OSPF Router-ID 2.2.2.2 gets B-REP R-ID of 2 and the second position in bit-string (... 00010, Table 3, Figure 6).

The basic idea of FRR mechanisms is to calculate an alternative route to bypass the local router's failure in advance. The B-REP mechanism maintains this idea, as it also preliminary calculates an alternative route. Calculating an alternate route beforehand ensures that the routing engine of the router is able to quickly install and use the alternative route in the event of an error. Each B-REP-enabled router calculates alternative paths based on the protected link. In FRR terminology, the protected link is a link against whose failure (or by the failure of a directly connected neighbor) the network wants to be preserved. By default, the protected link in B-REP is set manually by an administrator. Next, based on the settings, B-REP calculates alternative paths to all destinations of protected flows routed over the protected link in order to decrease the impact of the link failure. For the simulation purposes, we expect one flow and one destination.

An alternative route is then used in the event of a protected link or its neighboring router failure. The B-REP mechanism uses Dijkstra's algorithm to calculate an alternative path for each given destination by setting the protected link to a metric with a value at infinity.

When the router detects a connection failure with the primary next-hop router for a specific destination, it becomes the S router. The destination of an alternate path in terms of reroute scheme is the D router. In the considered case, it is Router 3 (Figure 7). The path from the router S to the router D must bypass the local failure detected by router S.

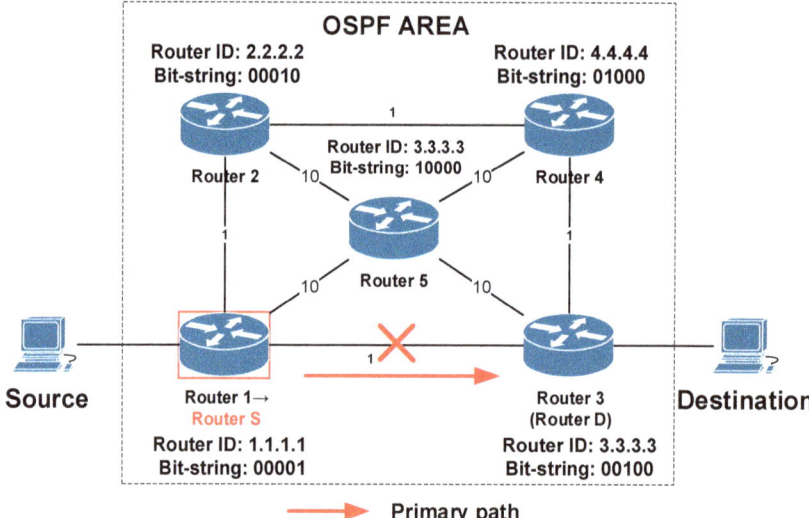

Figure 7. Detection of a failure and the reaction of the B-REP mechanism.

In the case of a link failure and specific protected flow of the customer, the router S already has a pre-calculated alternative path that contains all routers on the path including the destination router D. Following the failure protection procedures, the router S encapsulates packets of the original unicast protected flow with a new BIER header.

The BIER header includes the bit-string (Figure 8) field (BS field), which contains the exact definition of the pre-calculated path along which the packet will be routed (Figure 6). In case of several failures on the existing B-REP repair path, we assume the following behavior. The router that detects the failure adds a new/modified bit-string value that specifies the new alternative path. This means that packets are not again re-encapsulated, but only their LS field is modified. However, this property is still under further investigation.

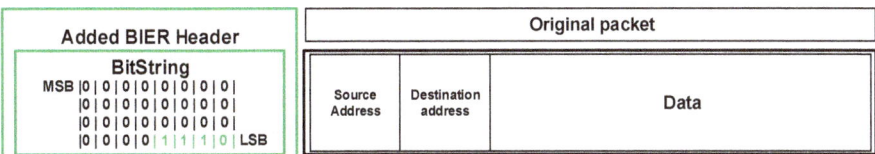

Figure 8. B-REP encapsulation of the IP packet.

Using the example of topology and link metrics from the Figure 7, the alternative path from the source to the destination is constructed via Router 2, Router 4 to Router 3 (Figure 9). The source router S (Router 1) will start encapsulating the original packets of a protected flow with a new BIER header immediately after the failure is detected. The router inserts the bit-string value " ... 01110" into the BS field (Figure 9, mark 1) that specifies the alternative route via Routers 2, 4, and 3. That BS value indicates the alternative path for other routers. An example of B-REP encapsulated packet is illustrated.

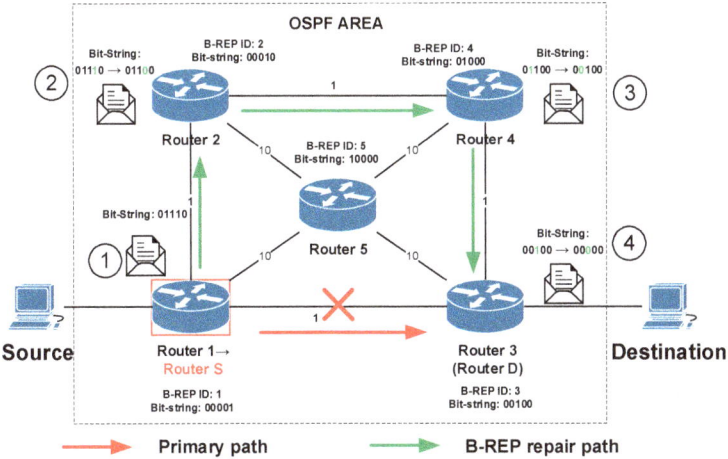

Figure 9. Example of a modified bit-string.

When a specific router, namely Router 2, receives a packet with a BIER header, it checks the bit-string value, finds the associated bit with its B-REP R-ID, and sets it to 0. The new BS value on R2 in our case is " ... 01100". This operation ensures that the router that received the B-REP FRR packet does not receive it again. Without this operation, the router could receive the same packet again resulting in a micro-loop. After this operation, the router will need to specify the next-hop router on the way to the destination. The router checks the bit-string, and if it finds that it has a directly connected neighbor according to the bit-string value, it then forwards the packet to the given router. For our example, Router 2 has directly connected Router 4 with the bit-string position 01000. Therefore, Router 2 sends the packet to Router 4 (Figure 9, mark 2). Router 4 repeats the process and sends the packet to Router 3 (Figure 9, mark 3).

The bit-string field with a value that contains only one bit set to 1 indicates to a router that it is the destination router D. Router D then sets the last bit to 0 and removes the BIER header, i.e., router decapsulated the original packet. During the decapsulation process, the modified packet is restored to its original state. Router D then routes the packet according to its unicast routing table.

In the presented example, such a packet is received by the router 3. Router 3 receives a packet with the last bit set in the bit-string field (mark 4, 00100, Figure 9). Router 3, therefore, knows that it becomes the destination router D (the last one). It removes the BIER header and routes the packet to its destination based on the content of its unicast routing table as usual.

For clarity, we can also describe the activities of the B-REP mechanism using the following descriptive diagrams of B-REP activities. Figure 10 shows the process of B-REP activation and error response. Figure 11 shows the packet processing used on each B-REP router.

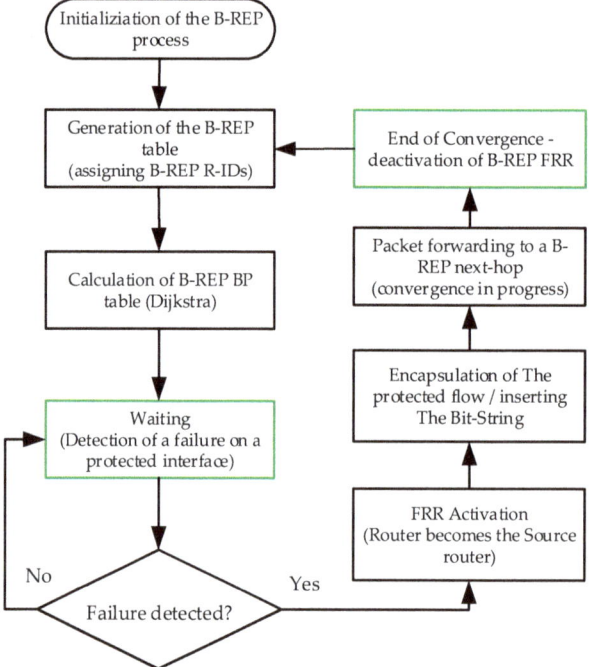

Figure 10. Diagram of B-REP activation and error response process.

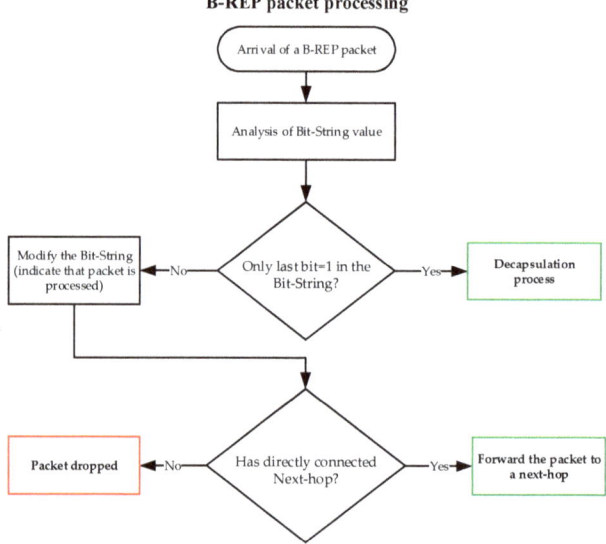

Figure 11. Processing of B-REP packet.

Sensors **2020**, *20*, 5230

4. Evaluation

In this section, we provide the evaluation of the proposed B-REP mechanism. In its verification, we used simulations performed in the OMNeT ++ simulator. The results obtained from simulations performed in the OMNeT++ simulator are presented. In addition, a comparison with other existing FRR mechanisms has been performed.

4.1. Simulation in Deterministic Simulator

The correctness of the proposed B-REP FRR algorithm has been verified through the means of simulations performed in the Objective Modular Network Testbed in C++ (OMNeT++) discrete event simulator [57]. For the implementation of the algorithm, we used the INET [58] Framework library. The INET library provides OSPF routing capabilities. We tested the accuracy of the algorithm in several scenarios that simulated numerous types of failures for different topologies consisting of different numbers of interconnected routers. In these scenarios, we focused mainly on examining the appropriate delivery of packets belonging to the protected flow. These packets have to be correctly delivered to its destination in the event of a single failure. In the following section, we present an example of one of the comprehensive testing scenarios.

The topology used in the scenario is shown in Figure 12. It consists of the matrix of seventeen routers and four hosts, which form the routing domain. As the unicast routing protocol, we used the OSPFv2 protocol deployed in a single area deployment model. For the purpose of the simulation, we generate a data flow originated from a host named the Source to the destination, the host H3. This flow of data represents a protected flow of user packets, a correct delivery of which in the event of a link failure is insured by the B-REP algorithm.

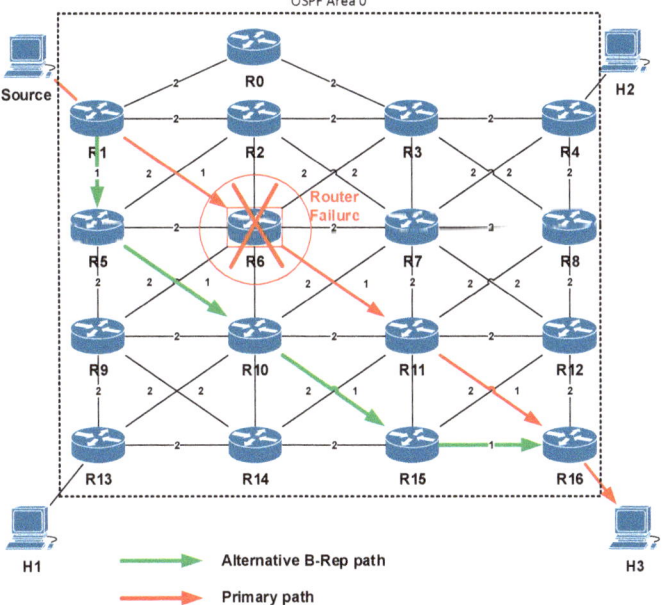

Figure 12. Simulation topology.

In a stable network situation, unicast packets are delivered from the source to H3 along the shortest path selected by the OSPF (represented in Figures 12 and 13 by the red line). Next in this scenario, we simulate a network failure, which is represented by shutting down the R6 router (all R6 interfaces go down). We then focus on verifying how the B-REP algorithm calculates the alternative path and how it uses it to protect user data in the event of the network failure.

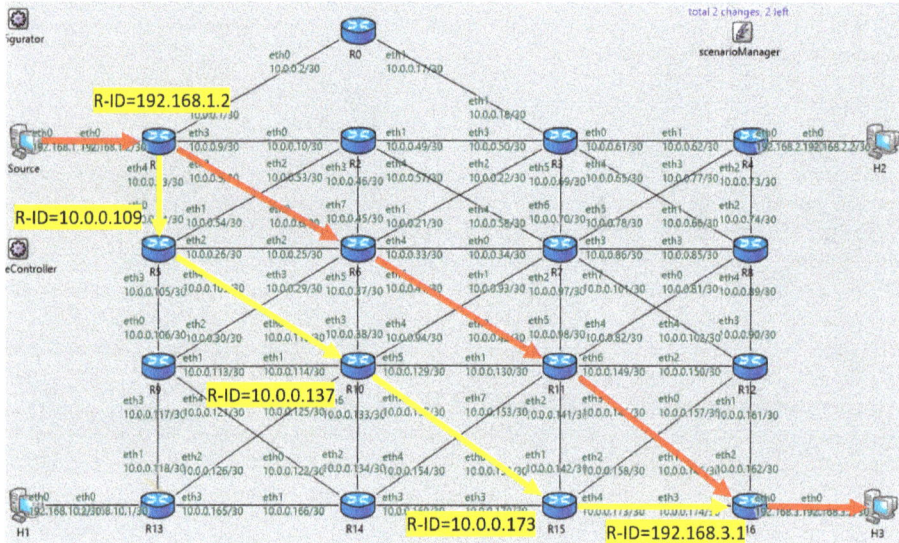

Figure 13. Visual output from the OMNeT++ simulation.

We expect that based on the link metrics the second shortest path is selected as an alternative (in Figures 12 and 13 represented by the green line), then the correct entries in the B-REP table of all routers are created. We also examined the correct addition of BIER header to packets of the protected flow affected by a failure, correct reroute to an alternative path, and routing based on the BIER header to the destination router. Finally, we checked if all packets of the protected flow are correctly delivered.

The description of the simulation scenario is as follows. In the beginning, we need to wait the 50 simulation seconds (sims) that are required to complete all of the OSPF unicast routing processes, i.e., the creation and synchronization of LSDBs and the calculation of unicast routing tables. Then, at the time of 56 sims, the Source host starts generating its data flow towards the host H3. We call this flow a protected flow. At the time of 60 sims, we simulate the failure on the primary routing path, where all interfaces of the router R6 are turned off. This is where the B-REP mechanism starts working and delivers packets of the protected flow using an alternative route. At the time 70 sims, we restore the router R6 to original state. Here the B-REP FRR stops working and routers use their converged unicast routing tables (Table 4).

Table 4. Description of the simulation scenario.

Time	Description of Action
<50	Time necessary for the OSPF convergence and stabilization of network processes.
56	Source host begins generating the flow
60	Router R6 failure
70	Restoration of R6

In the simulation, the B-REP mechanism deactivates when the source router detects that the protected interface is UP. In a real-life scenario, the B-REP will be deactivated by hold-down timer that is set to specific period. The duration of this period should be long enough so that the network can again successfully complete the convergence process.

Algorithm Behavior and Simulation Outputs

At the beginning of the simulation, once all OSPF processes have been finished (<50 ms), routers will compile their B-REP tables. Therefore, each router reads own OSPF LSDB, sorts the routers according to router's OSPF-ID, and assigns them unique B-REP R-ID.

Next, all B-REP enabled routers precalculate alternative paths for its protected interfaces and protected flow according to OSPF LSDB. These pre-calculated backup paths are stored in B-REP BP table.

At time 56 sims, the source host starts generating packets of the protected flow sent with the destination address of the host H3. The B-REP algorithm is designed to protect only specific customers' flows, i.e., flows that are identified by their source and destination addresses. Addresses as identifiers of protected flows must be preconfigured on the routers. Packets are delivered from the source to H3 along the shortest route as is selected by OSPF. At the time 60 sims, the described error occurs as is mentioned above. Disabling all interfaces of the R6 router will cause all its neighbors to detect its unavailability and thus, the network change. The speed of detection depends on the mechanism that routers use to check neighbors. Rapid failure detection can be guaranteed, for example, by a standardized BFD mechanism.

Next, all affected routers (R1, R2, R3, R5, R7, R9, R10, and R11) through OSPF update messages will begin flooding their new OSPF link-state advertisement (LSA) updates and begin the network convergence process. However, this process can take an unpredictable amount of time. Therefore, when the router R1 detects that the output interface with its primary next-hop router is no longer available, it begins to use B-REP. The R1 becomes the B-REP source router S. Subsequently, R1 start encapsulating unicast packets of the protected flows with a BIER header, into which it inserts the Bit-String routing value of the alternative path. The bit-string contains information about the pre-computed alternative path that will be used to route packets around the detected failure. This alternative path goes via R5 → R10 → R15 → R16 and is represented with the BS value of 000000010100010010 (Figure 14, Table 5).

```
Router: 192.168.1.2  |  00000000000001000
A route has found!
setting: 10.0.0.14
60.s - Sending datagram with bitstring: 00000010100010010
```

Figure 14. Inserting Bit-String (Source router).

Table 5. B-REP table.

Bit-String	Name	OSPF R-ID	B-REP ID
000000000000000010	R16 (Destination router)	192.168.3.1	2
000000000000001000	R1 (Source router)	192.168.1.2	4
000000000000010000	R15	10.0.0.173	5
000000000100000000	R10	10.0.0.137	9
000000010000000000	R5	10.0.0.109	11

Afterward, the packet with a new BIER header is subsequently routed to the next-hop router R5. Take note that, if the packet has a B-REP header, packet is not routed directly through the routing engine, but it is processed and routed through the B-REP process.

The explanation of Figure 14 is as follows: 192.168.1.2–OSPF router ID, 10.0.0.14–OSPF router ID of next next-hop router for the B-REP routing, 000000010100010010–bit-string that is inserted to the packet with BIER header.

The R5 receives the packet and starts to analyze its bit-string value. Accordingly, the R5 router detects its next-hop router, which is the R10 router with the B-REP ID = 9 (Table 5) and OSPF R-ID = 10.0.0.137. Subsequently, R5 modifies the BS value of the packet by setting its bit to zero.

Then R5 immediately selects an outgoing interface that leads to the R10 neighbor and forwards the packet towards R10 (Figure 15).

```
Router: 10.0.0.109 | 00000010000000000
Datagram with bitstring arrived: 00000010100010010
A route has found!
setting: 10.0.0.110
60.s - Sending datagram with bitstring: 00000000100010010
```

Figure 15. Processing of B-REP packet (R5).

Routers R10 and R15 repeat the same process as the R5 router forwards a packet to their next-hops (which is R15, respectively R16). The behavior is changed on the R16 router as it is the destination router D. R16 receives the packet, analyses the Bit-string value, and recognizes that only one bit in the bit-string is set to 1. This indicates that R16 is a decapsulation router. Therefore, R16 removes the BIER header and restores the packet of the protected flow to its original format (Figure 16). The decapsulation router is the end of the B-REP alternative path.

```
Router: 192.168.3.1 | 00000000000000010
Datagram with bitstring arrived: 00000000000000010
60.0001.s - Sending datagram with bitstring:
```

Figure 16. Output from the OMNeT++ console.

The behavior described above can be observed on the output obtained from the OMNeT ++ console listed in Table 6. We may see that at the time 56 sims, the source host starts sending packets of the protected data flow intended to the host H3. Packets follow the shortest route via routers: R1 → R6 → R11 → R16 → H3 (Table 6, green lines). At 60 sims, we simulate the failure of the R6 router. R1 detects its unavailability using the BFD connection failure detection mechanism. Therefore, the R1 becomes the Source router S and starts using the B-REP pre-calculated alternative path which goes through R1 → R5 → R10 → R15 → R16 → R10 (Table 6, blue lines). At the same time, all R6 neighbors are starting the OSPF update process. Until the OSPF R1 process completes and will provide actualized routing information, R1 will insert the pre-calculated path into the bit-string field of packet's header. According to obtained simulation results, packets were successfully delivered using the B-REP algorithm around the failure router (Table 6, blue lines). At 70 sims, the router R6 is restored (all interfaces go UP), which means the Source router detects reconnection with R6 and disables B-REP mechanism. Packets are routed via original route as before (Table 6, black lines).

4.2. Evaluation of the B-REP Mechanism

The B-REP algorithm implementation uses the SPF algorithm in conjunction with any type of LS routing protocol, although we used OSPF for the pilot implementation. The B-REP SPF algorithm is applied to calculate the alternative shortest path used in the event of a failure. The main advantage of the B-REP FRR mechanism is that the algorithm implements an efficient and standardized way to mark an alternative path using the B-S field.

In the B-REP we use the bit-string to exactly define hop-by-hop routing behavior, where due to B-S we can precisely define the whole alternative path of routers chain. This feature might be used for an administrator to manually configure the alternative route in the event of a need.

Table 6. Output from the OMNeT++ simulation.

Time	Source/Destination	Name	Destination Address	
0.079876921815	R12 –> R16	OSPF_HelloPacket	IPv4: 10.0.0.161 > 224.0.0.5	Network convergence
0.079977739817	R15 –> R16	OSPF_HelloPacket	IPv4: 10.0.0.173 > 224.0.0.5	
0.081024165641	R1 –> R6	OSPF_HelloPacket	IPv4: 10.0.0.5 > 224.0.0.5	
0.081275865377	R10 –> R13	OSPF_HelloPacket	IPv4: 10.0.0.125 > 224.0.0.5	
0.082012804148	R6 –> R9	OSPF_HelloPacket	IPv4: 10.0.0.29 > 224.0.0.5	
0.082307311152	R14 –> R10	OSPF_HelloPacket	IPv4: 10.0.0.134 > 224.0.0.5	
0.079876921815	R12 –> R16	OSPF_HelloPacket	IPv4: 10.0.0.161 > 224.0.0.5	
0.079977739817	R15 –> R16	OSPF_HelloPacket	IPv4: 10.0.0.173 > 224.0.0.5	
	... the output has been shortened ...			
56.00006842	→R1	UDPBasicAppData-185	192.168.3.2	Network without errors
56.00008084	R01 → R06	UDPBasicAppData-185	192.168.3.2	
56.00009326	R06 → R11	UDPBasicAppData-185	192.168.3.2	
56.00010568	R11 → R16	UDPBasicAppData-185	192.168.3.2	
56.0001181	R16 → H3	UDPBasicAppData-185	192.168.3.2	
58.00007242	→R1	UDPBasicAppData-185	192.168.3.2	
58.00008484	R1 → R06	UDPBasicAppData-185	192.168.3.2	
58.00009726	R06 → R11	UDPBasicAppData-185	192.168.3.2	
58.00010968	R11 → R16	UDPBasicAppData-185	192.168.3.2	
58.0001221	R16 → H3	UDPBasicAppData-185	192.168.3.2	
	... the output has been shortened ...			
60.00009726	→R1	UDPBasicAppData-B-REP	192.168.3.2	B-REP FAST REROUTE
60.00010968	R1 → R5	UDPBasicAppData-B-REP	192.168.3.2	
60.0001221	R5 → R10	UDPBasicAppData-B-REP	192.168.3.2	
60.00013452	R10 → R15	UDPBasicAppData-B-REP	192.168.3.2	
60.00014694	R15 → R16	UDPBasicAppData-B-REP	192.168.3.2	
60.00015936	R10→ H3	UDPBasicAppData-B-REP	192.168.3.2	
60.00017178	→R1	UDPBasicAppData-B-REP	192.168.3.2	
60.0001842	R1 → R5	UDPBasicAppData-B-REP	192.168.3.2	
60.00019662	R5 → R10	UDPBasicAppData-B-REP	192.168.3.2	
60.00020904	R10 → R15	UDPBasicAppData-B-REP	192.168.3.2	
60.00022146	R15 → R16	UDPBasicAppData-B-REP	192.168.3.2	
60.00023388	R16→ H3	UDPBasicAppData-B-REP	192.168.3.2	
	... the output has been shortened ...			
70.00007242	→R1	UDPBasicAppData-185	192.168.3.2	Restoration
70.00008484	R01 → R06	UDPBasicAppData-185	192.168.3.2	
70.00009726	R06 → R11	UDPBasicAppData-185	192.168.3.2	
70.00010968	R11 → R16	UDPBasicAppData-185	192.168.3.2	
70.0001221	R16 → H3	UDPBasicAppData-185	192.168.3.2	

Possibility of the explicitly defined alternative path can not only define the backup path close to a failed element in the network but also across the whole area which statistically can also be damaged.

Compared to other existing FRR mechanisms, the B-REP mechanism brings the new approach of defining alternative path (bit-string) into the FRR area and provides advantages in comparison with other mechanisms such as custom alternative path, easy implementation into existing architecture because of bit-string and 100% repair coverage. A summary of the advantages and disadvantages of the B-REP mechanism is given in Table 7.

Table 7. Properties of the B-REP algorithm.

Advantages	Disadvantages
Suitable for networks of any size	Pre-computation
Applicable for a link-state routing protocol	Encapsulation packet overhead
100% repair coverage	
Possibility to define a custom path	
Relatively easy implementation (Bit-String)	

A more exact comparison of the selected features with other existing FRR solutions is presented in Table 8 below. In this table we compare possibility of repairing all failures within the network, precomputing, modification of packets and support of custom alternative path.

Table 8. Comparison of the B-REP mechanism with existing solutions.

Title	100% Repair Coverage	Custom Alternative Path	Precomputing	Packet Modification
B-REP	Yes	Yes	Yes	Yes
EM-REP	Yes	No	No	Yes
ECMP FRR	No	No	Yes	No
BIER-TE (M)	Yes	No	Yes	Yes
Directed LFA	Yes	Yes	Yes	Yes
LFA	No	No	Yes	No
MPLS-TE FRR	No	Yes	Yes	Yes
MRC	Yes	Yes	Yes	Yes
MRT	Yes	No	Yes	Yes
Not-Via Addresses	Yes	No	Yes	Yes
Remote LFA	No	No	Yes	Yes
TI-LFA	Yes	No	Yes	Yes

The biggest time-consuming operation during the FRR process is the detection of link or node failure. For these purposes, the bidirectional forwarding detection (BFD) protocol is used. The BFD protocol is standardized by IETF in RFC 5880. Usually, the detection of the failure by BFD protocol is less than 30 ms depending on the timer settings. Another part of rerouting is switching to an alternate FRR path.

Existing proactive FRR solutions calculate alternative path in advance. Therefore, the rerouting time of the specific FRR mechanism is minimal because the alternative path is prepared and switchovers to that path immediately. B-REP algorithm calculates alternative path in advance, therefore its speed of recovery after link or node failure depends only on the time of failure detection, as is characteristic of proactive mechanisms.

5. Conclusions

The paper presents the bit-repair (B-REP) FRR mechanism, which provides advanced fast reroute solutions for IoT and IP network infrastructures. B-REP uses a standardized BIER header with a special bit-string field. That allows us to use a standardized header and its fields to define an alternative path as well as to transfer user data. The bit-string, in addition, allows us to efficiently define an exact alternative FRR path, which can be calculated by the Dijkstra algorithm or even manually defined by the administrator.

Some existing mechanisms, such as LFA or remote LFA calculate an alternative path according to specific metric conditions. However, in topologies with inappropriate metrics, these mechanisms are not able to choose an alternative path, but our algorithm is. We also add the ability to ignore metric-based calculations in our proposal, allowing us to select any possible physical alternative path. This mechanism can provide link or node protection and is suitable for any link-state protocols.

Sensors **2020**, *20*, 5230

These properties of the B-REP algorithm make it possible to achieve full repair coverage, which provides the protection against all possible failures in the network if a physically alternative path is presented.

The B-REP mechanism, as a proactive FRR mechanism, shares with other FRR mechanisms the properties of this family, which are identified as limitations. This includes CPU consumption during preliminary calculations and memory consumption for storing them. With FRR mechanisms that create a remote alternate path, B-REP uses the encapsulation of the original packets, which of course increases the overhead of the transmitted data. However, this limitation is partially addressed by using the Bit-String to define the entire transmission path. The speed of existing proactive FRR mechanisms including B-REP is similar, but the differences are in the way how they calculate alternative FRR path, how effective the results are and how the alternative path is constructed. According to our research, there is no FRR mechanism of all solutions. All of them have some advantages and disadvantages and B-REP brings his perspective on the solution to the issue.

The B-REP mechanism was fully implemented, and its correctness was tested using the OMNeT++ discrete event simulator. We have performed various extensive tests of the implementation in different network topologies, which validated the functional correctness of all B-REP sides. The use of Bit-String is unique, and it is possible to apply it in WSN networks, IoT design, and other areas as well, which will be studied in future work. Besides that, our future work will focus on the investigation of other related B-REP research issues, such as the addressing of multiple error occurrence, B-REP resource demands, and the B-REP bit-string-based source routing. We are also preparing the implementation of several existing FRR mechanisms into the OMNeT++ simulation tool, which will allow a better comparison of existing solutions and bring new knowledge in the field.

Author Contributions: Conceptualization, J.P. and P.S.; software, J.P.; validation, J.P. and P.S.; formal analysis, J.P., P.S., O.Y., I.B., M.H.; investigation, J.P.; resources, J.P.; data curation, J.P.; writing—original draft preparation, J.P., P.S., O.Y.; writing—review and editing, J.P., P.S., O.Y., I.B., M.H.; investigation, J.P.; visualization, J.P. and P.S.; supervision, J.P. and P.S.; project administration, J.P. and P.S.; funding acquisition, J.P., P.S. and I.B. All authors have read and agreed to the published version of the manuscript.

Funding: This research received no external funding.

Acknowledgments: This publication has been published with the support of the Operational Program Integrated Infrastructure within project: "Výskum v sieti SANET a možnosti jej ďalšieho využitia a rozvoja/ Research in the SANET network and possibilities of its further use and development", ITMS code 313011W988, co-financed by the ERDF.

Conflicts of Interest: The authors declare no conflict of interest.

References

1. Kvist, F.; Urke, A.R.; Øvsthus, K. Energy efficient determinism in wsn through reverse packet elimination. *Sensors* **2020**, *20*, 2890. [CrossRef]
2. Moreno Escobar, J.J.; Morales Matamoros, O.; Lina Reyes, I.; Tejeida-Padilla, R.; Chanona Hernández, L.; Posadas Durán, J.P.F. Energy-Efficient Industrial Internet of Things Software-Defined Network by Means of the Peano Fractal. *Sensors* **2020**, *20*, 2855. [CrossRef] [PubMed]
3. Guerrero-Sanchez, A.E.; Rivas-Araiza, E.A.; Gonzalez-Cordoba, J.L.; Toledano-Ayala, M.; Takacs, A. Blockchain Mechanism and Symmetric Encryption in A Wireless Sensor Network. *Sensors* **2020**, *20*, 2798. [CrossRef] [PubMed]
4. Fathallah, K.; Abid, M.A.; Hadj-Alouane, N. Ben Enhancing Energy Saving in Smart Farming Through Aggregation and Partition Aware IoT Routing Protocol. *Sensors* **2020**, *20*, 2760. [CrossRef] [PubMed]
5. Haseeb, K.; Almogren, A.; Ud Din, I.; Islam, N.; Altameem, A. SASC: Secure and Authentication-Based Sensor Cloud Architecture for Intelligent Internet of Things. *Sensors* **2020**, *20*, 2468. [CrossRef]
6. Lihakanga, R.; Ding, Y.; Medero, G.M.; Chapman, S.; Goussetis, G. A High-Resolution Open Source Platform for Building Envelope Thermal Performance Assessment Using a Wireless Sensor Network. *Sensors* **2020**, *20*, 1755. [CrossRef]

7. Petija, R.; Michalko, M.; Jakab, F.; Fecil'Ak, P. Convergence of Routing Protocols in Real and Simulated Environments. In Proceedings of the ICETA 2018-16th IEEE International Conference on Emerging eLearning Technologies and Applications, Stary Smokovec, Slovakia, 15–16 November 2018; pp. 425–430.

8. Harada, Y.; Hui, W.; Fukushima, Y.; Yokohira, T. A reroute method to recover fast from network failure. In Proceedings of the 2014 International Conference on Information and Communication Technology Convergence (ICTC), Busan, South Korea, 22–24 October 2014; pp. 903–908.

9. Shabbir, N.; Hassan, S.R. Routing Protocols for Wireless Sensor Networks (WSNs). In *Wireless Sensor Networks-Insights and Innovations*; IntechOpen: London, UK; GC University Lahore: Lahore, Pakistan, 2017. [CrossRef]

10. Burgos, U.; Amozarrain, U.; Gómez-Calzado, C.; Lafuente, A. Routing in mobile wireless sensor networks: A leader-based approach. *Sensors* **2017**, *17*, 1587. [CrossRef]

11. Robertson, G.; Roy, N.; Penumarthi, P.K.; Nelakuditi, S.; O'Kane, J.M. Loop-Free Convergence With Unordered Updates. *IEEE Trans. Netw. Serv. Manag.* **2017**, *14*, 373–385. [CrossRef]

12. Malik, S.U.; Srinivasan, S.K.; Khan, S.U. Convergence time analysis of open shortest path first routing protocol in internet scale networks. *Electron. Lett.* **2012**, *48*, 1188. [CrossRef]

13. Pal, V.K.; Ramteke, S.M. A framework for fast IP rerouting. In Proceedings of the International Conference on Information Communication and Embedded Systems (ICICES2014), Chennai, India, 27–28 February 2014; pp. 1–6.

14. Cheng, Z.; Zhang, X.; Li, Y.; Yu, S.; Lin, R.; He, L. Congestion-Aware Local Reroute for Fast Failure Recovery in Software-Defined Networks. *J. Opt. Commun. Netw.* **2017**, *9*, 934. [CrossRef]

15. Antonakopoulos, S.; Bejerano, Y.; Koppol, P. A simple IP fast reroute scheme for full coverage. In Proceedings of the 2012 IEEE 13th International Conference on High Performance Switching and Routing, Belgrade, Serbia, 24–27 June 2012; pp. 15–22.

16. Csikor, L.; Retvari, G. IP fast reroute with remote Loop-Free Alternates: The unit link cost case. In Proceedings of the 2012 IV International Congress on Ultra Modern Telecommunications and Control Systems, St. Petersburg, Russia, 3–5 October 2012; pp. 663–669.

17. Lemeshko, O.; Yeremenko, O.; Hailan, A.M. Two-level method of fast ReRouting in software-defined networks. In Proceedings of the 2017 4th International Scientific-Practical Conference Problems of Infocommunications Science and Technology, Kharkov, Ukraine, 10–13 October 2017; Volume 2018, pp. 376–379.

18. Papan, J.; Segec, P.; Moravcik, M.; Kontsek, M.; Mikus, L.; Uramova, J.; Segeč, P.; Moravčík, M.; Konštek, M.; Mikuš, L.; et al. Overview of IP Fast Reroute Solutions. In Proceedings of the ICETA 2018-16th IEEE International Conference on Emerging eLearning Technologies and Applications, Stary Smokovec, Slovakia, 15–16 November 2018; pp. 417–424.

19. Elhourani, T.; Gopalan, A.; Ramasubramanian, S.; Elhourani, T.; Gopalan, A.; Ramasubramanian, S. IP Fast Rerouting for Multi-Link Failures. *IEEE/ACM Trans. Netw.* **2016**, *24*, 3014–3025. [CrossRef]

20. Gopalan, A.; Ramasubramanian, S. IP Fast Rerouting and Disjoint Multipath Routing with Three Edge-Independent Spanning Trees. *IEEE/ACM Trans. Netw.* **2016**, *24*, 1336–1349. [CrossRef]

21. Braun, W.; Menth, M. Loop-Free Alternates with Loop Detection for Fast Reroute in Software-Defined Carrier and Data Center Networks. *J. Netw. Syst. Manag.* **2016**, *24*, 470–490. [CrossRef]

22. Elhourani, T.; Gopalan, A.; Ramasubramanian, S. IP fast rerouting for multi-link failures. In *IEEE INFOCOM 2014-IEEE Conference on Computer Communications*; IEEE: Piscataway, NJ, USA, 2014; pp. 2148–2156.

23. Kim, M.; Chae, K. DMP: Detouring Using Multiple Paths against Jamming Attack for Ubiquitous Networking System. *Sensors* **2010**, *10*, 3626–3640. [CrossRef]

24. Landaluce, H.; Arjona, L.; Perallos, A.; Falcone, F.; Angulo, I.; Muralter, F. A Review of IoT Sensing Applications and Challenges Using RFID and Wireless Sensor Networks. *Sensors* **2020**, *20*, 2495. [CrossRef]

25. Kamisinski, A. Evolution of IP fast-reroute strategies. In Proceedings of the 2018 10th International Workshop on Resilient Networks Design and Modeling, RNDM, Longyearbyen, Norway, 27–29 August 2018.

26. Tavernier, W.; Papadimitriou, D.; Colle, D.; Pickavet, M.; Demeester, P. Self-configuring loop-free alternates with high link failure coverage. *Telecommun. Syst.* **2014**, *56*, 85–101. [CrossRef]

27. Csikor, L.; Tapolcai, J.; Rétvári, G. Optimizing IGP link costs for improving IP-level resilience with Loop-Free Alternates. *Comput. Commun.* **2013**, *36*, 645–655. [CrossRef]

28. Csikor, L.; Rétvári, G. On providing fast protection with remote loop-free alternates. *Telecommun. Syst.* **2015**, *60*, 485–502. [CrossRef]

29. Sarkar, P.; Hegde, S.; Bowers, C.; Gredler, H.; Litkowski, S. *Remote-LFA Node Protection and Manageability*; Request for Comments: 8102; Internet Engineering Task Force (IETF): Fremont, CA, USA, 2017.

30. Cevher, S.; Ulutas, M.; Hokelek, I. Topology-Aware Multiple Routing Configurations for Fault Tolerant Networking. *J. Netw. Syst. Manag.* **2016**, *24*, 944–973. [CrossRef]

31. Cevher, S.; Ulutas, M.; Altun, S.; Hokelek, I. Multiple Routing Configurations for Fast Re-route in Software Defined Networks. In Proceedings of the 2016 24th Signal Processing and Communication Application Conference (SIU), Zonguldak, Turkey, 16–19 May 2016; pp. 993–996.

32. Nagy, M.; Tapolcai, J.; Rétvári, G. Optimization methods for improving IP-level fast protection for local shared risk groups with Loop-Free Alternates. *Telecommun. Syst.* **2014**, *56*, 103–119. [CrossRef]

33. Loop-free alternates and not-via addresses: A proper combination for IP fast reroute? *Comput. Netw.* **2010**, *54*, 1300–1315. [CrossRef]

34. Lemeshko, O.; Kinan, A.; Wahhab, M.A.A. Multicast fast re-route schemes for multiflow case. In Proceedings of the The Experience of Designing and Application of CAD Systems in Microelectronics, Lviv, Ukraine, 24–27 February 2015; pp. 422–424.

35. Aman, A.H.M.; Hashim, A.-H.A.; Ramli, H.A.M. Mathematical Evaluation of Context Transfer and Multicast Fast Reroute in Multicast Enabled Network Mobility Management. *Int. J. Control. Autom.* **2017**, *10*, 207–216. [CrossRef]

36. Kuang, K.; Wang, S.; Wang, X. Discussion on the combination of Loop-Free Alternates and Maximally Redundant Trees for IP networks Fast Reroute. In Proceedings of the 2014 IEEE International Conference on Communications (ICC), Sydney, NSW, Australia, 10–14 June 2014; pp. 1131–1136.

37. Atlas, A.; Bowers, C.; Enyedi, G. *An Architecture for IP/LDP Fast Reroute Using Maximally Redundant Trees (MRT-FRR)*; Request for Comments: 7812; Internet Engineering Task Force (IETF): Fremont, CA, USA, 2016.

38. Papan, J.; Segec, P.; Yeremenko, O.; Bridova, I.; Hodon, M. Enhanced Multicast Repair Fast Reroute Mechanism for Smart Sensors IoT and Network Infrastructure. *Sensors* **2020**, *20*, 3428. [CrossRef] [PubMed]

39. Zhang, Y.; Wang, J.; Hao, G. An Autonomous Connectivity Restoration Algorithm Based on Finite State Machine for Wireless Sensor-Actor Networks. *Sensors* **2018**, *18*, 153. [CrossRef]

40. Wang, L.; Li, Y.; Pan, B.; Wu, Q.; Yin, J.; Xu, L. Network Coding for Efficient Video Multicast in Device-to-Device Communications. *Sensors* **2020**, *20*, 2254. [CrossRef]

41. Lin, Z.; Tao, D.; Wang, Z. Dynamic Construction Scheme for Virtualization Security Service in Software-Defined Networks. *Sensors* **2017**, *17*, 920. [CrossRef]

42. Cascone, C.; Sanvito, D.; Pollini, L.; Capone, A.; Sansò, B. Fast failure detection and recovery in SDN with stateful data plane. *Int. J. Netw. Manag.* **2017**, *27*, 1–14. [CrossRef]

43. Ghannami, A.; Shao, C. Efficient fast recovery mechanism in Software-Defined Networks: Multipath routing approach. In Proceedings of the 2016 11th International Conference for Internet Technology and Secured Transactions (ICITST), Barcelona, Spain, 5–7 December 2016; pp. 432–435.

44. Bianchi, G.; Bonola, M.; Capone, A.; Cascone, C. OpenState. *ACM SIGCOMM Comput. Commun. Rev.* **2014**, *44*, 44–51. [CrossRef]

45. Papán, J.; Segeč, P.; Palúch, P.; Mikuš, Ľ.; Moravčík, M. The Survey of Current IPFRR Mechanisms. In *Federated Conference on Software Development and Object Technologies*; Springer: Cham, Switzerland, 2017; Volume 511, pp. 229–240. ISBN 9783319465340.

46. Papan, J.; Segec, P.; Paluch, P.; Uramova, J.; Moravcik, M. The new Multicast Repair (M-REP) IP fast reroute mechanism. *Concurr. Comput. Pract. Exp.* **2020**, *32*, e5105. [CrossRef]

47. Papan, J.; Segec, P.; Dobrota, J.; Koncz, L.; Kubala, F.; Kontsek, M.; Yeremenko, O. Fast ReRoute error detection-implementation of BFD mechanism. In Proceedings of the ICETA 2019-17th IEEE International Conference on Emerging eLearning Technologies and Applications, Smokovec, Slovakiam, 21–22 November 2019; pp. 593–599.

48. Shand, M.; Bryant, S. *IP Fast Reroute Framework*; Request for Comments: 5714; Internet Engineering Task Force (IETF): Fremont, CA, USA, 2010; ISSN: 2070-1721.

49. Xhonneux, M.; Bonaventure, O. Flexible failure detection and fast reroute using eBPF and SRv6. In Proceedings of the 2018 14th International Conference on Network and Service Management (CNSM), Rome, Italy, 5–9 November 2018; pp. 408–413.

50. Giorgetti, A.; Sgambelluri, A.; Paolucci, F.; Sambo, N.; Castoldi, P.; Cugini, F. Bit Index Explicit Replication (BIER) multicasting in transport networks. In Proceedings of the 2017 21st International Conference on Optical Network Design and Modeling, ONDM, Budapest, Hungary, 15–18 May 2017; pp. 1–5.

51. Wijnands, I.J.; Rosen, E.; Dolganow, A.; Przygienda, T.; Aldrin, S. *Multicast Using Bit Index Explicit Replication (BIER)*; Request for Comments: 8279; Internet Engineering Task Force (IETF): Fremont, CA, USA, 2017; ISSN: 2070-1721.

52. Eckert, T.; Cauchie, G.; Menth, M. Traffic Engineering for Bit Index Explicit Replication (BIER-TE). U.S. Patent 10,341,222, 2 July 2019.

53. Merling, D.; Lindner, S.; Menth, M. P4-based implementation of BIER and BIER-FRR for scalable and resilient multicast. *J. Netw. Comput. Appl.* **2020**, 102764. [CrossRef]

54. Lan, Y.; Esfahanian, A.-H.; Ni, L.M. Multicast in hypercube multiprocessors. *J. Parallel Distrib. Comput.* **1990**, *8*, 30–41. [CrossRef]

55. Chiu, G.M.; Chen, K.S. Efficient fault-tolerant multicast scheme for hypercube multicomputers. *IEEE Trans. Parallel Distrib. Syst.* **1998**, *9*, 952–962. [CrossRef]

56. Chiu, G.M.; Chen, K.S. Fault-tolerant routing strategy using routing capability in hypercube multicomputers. In Proceedings of the Proceedings of the Internatoinal Conference on Parallel and Distributed Systems, Tokyo, Japan, 3–6 June 1996; pp. 396–403.

57. OMNeT++ Discrete Event Simulator. Available online: https://omnetpp.org/ (accessed on 9 September 2019).

58. INET Framework-INET Framework. Available online: https://inet.omnetpp.org/ (accessed on 25 October 2019).

Article

Multilayered Network Model for Mobile Network Infrastructure Disruption

David Hrabcak, Lubomir Dobos, Jan Papaj * and Lubos Ovsenik

Department of Electronic and Multimedia Communication, Technical University of Kosice,
Bozeny Nemcovej 26/32, 040 01 Kosice, Slovakia; david.hrabcak@tuke.sk (D.H.); lubomir.dobos@tuke.sk (L.D.);
lubos.ovsenik@tuke.sk (L.O.)
* Correspondence: jan.papaj@tuke.sk

Received: 12 August 2020; Accepted: 22 September 2020; Published: 25 September 2020

Abstract: In this paper, the novel study of the multilayered network model for the disrupted infrastructure of the 5G mobile network is introduced. The aim of this study is to present the new way of incorporating different types of networks, such as Wireless Sensor Networks (WSN), Mobile Ad-Hoc Networks (MANET), and DRONET Networks into one fully functional multilayered network. The proposed multilayered network model also presents the resilient way to deal with infrastructure disruption due to different reasons, such as disaster scenarios or malicious actions. In the near future, new network technologies of 5G networks and the phenomenon known as the Internet of Things (IoT) will empower the functionality of different types of networks and interconnects them into one complex network. The proposed concept is oriented on resilient, smart city applications such as public safety and health and it is able to provide critical communication when fixed network infrastructure is destroyed by deploying smart sensors and unmanned aerial vehicles. The provided simulations shows that the proposed multilayered network concept is able to perform better than traditional WSN network in term of delivery time, average number of hops and data rate speed, when disruption scenario occurs.

Keywords: WSN; MANET; DRONET; multilayered network model; 5G; IoT; smart sensors

---

1. Introduction

New generation networks, also known as 5G networks, are slowly becoming the part of our lives. In the future, they will bring new opportunities and different views of the network of today. With the phenomenon known as the Internet of Things (IoT), the Internet will become increasingly complex, smart, and pervasive. Upcoming trends include smart homes, smart cities and Industry 4.0 with different applications, such as industrial automation, public health and information systems, city management, energy efficiency and public safety. Everything will be possible thanks to the new type of mobile networks, called heterogeneous network that will work as one functional complex network. New 5G networks are considered to be a promising technology that incorporates different types of networks to provide needed functionality and applications. Massive transport of the IoT data will require to use the alternative type of mobile network such as Wireless Sensor Networks (WSN), Mobile Ad-Hoc Networks (MANET), Drone Networks (DRONET) and use their benefits.

One of the urgent goals for the next generation networks are to provide uninterrupted public safety and health service in different scenarios, where fixed infrastructure will be disrupted. This scenario includes natural disasters (earthquakes, fires, floods, hurricanes), human errors (nuclear, chemical, biological, radiological exposures or railway and car accidents), and malicious criminal actions (terrorists or cyber-attacks) [1]. Other goals for designers of Public Protection and Disaster Relief (PPDR) agencies are not only to provide a reliable communication network for public safety agencies and departments such as police, emergency, etc., but to provide the data services to all people during emergency and disaster situations, where existing fixed communication infrastructure could be destroyed [2,3].

The one possible solution to these problems could be a resilient multilayered network model, which is able to provide necessary services even in unpredictable situations mentioned above. In this paper, the multilayered network model composed of Wireless Sensor Networks (WSN), Mobile Ad-Hoc Networks (MANET), and Drone Networks (DRONET) will be introduced. WSN networks are considered to be a type of IoT network composed of numerous low energy sensors, which are responsible for collecting measured data. WSN sensors could be situated in different types of environments, such as hospitals for collecting critical health data, on the beach to collect sea level data before the tsunami waves or to the amount of CO_2 and quality of the air during fires. Collected data are then distributed in a multihop ad-hoc manner to cloud data centers for processing.

Our proposal deals with destroyed fixed infrastructures, where fixed Access Points are not functional. Urgent data from the WSN network cannot be delivered and this could lead to system errors or misleading information on the server-side. The solution of this problem could be the MANET network, which is an autonomous self-organized network that could offer support for rescue operations and was used before by the military to surveying inaccessible areas. Thanks to the support of mobility, higher data rates, and lower energy constraints, urgent data could be delivered from the WSN network through the MANET network to another operational Access Point in a multihop manner with respect to device-to-device (D2D) communication principals. The reach can be extended by using unmanned aerial vehicles (UAVs) such as drones in DRONET network. UAVs can be used for data collection, or for delivery of urgent data from isolated MANET subnetworks, which were created by the movement of MANET nodes.

The aim of this study is to provide innovative and resilient way to deal with the failure or disruption of fixed infrastructure for upcoming 5G networks and its urgent applications. With a unique combination of WSN, MANET, and DRONET networks, it is possible to preserve the functionality of urgent applications, such as public health and safety, in different adverse situations. Based on this motivation, the multilayered model was build in order to use the advantages of mentioned networks and also empower the potential of new generation 5G networks and IoT solutions. The simulations of the proposed multilayered model show that it is able to provide a fully functional backup solution that preserves functionality and service demands required by 5G standards.

2. Related Work

In recent years, many studies investigated the possibilities of different networks convergence scenarios. Most of the works include MANET networks, WSN networks, Vehicular Ad-Hoc Networks (VANET) or networks composed of unmanned aerial vehicles (UAVs). Bellavista et al. [4] proposed a MANET and WSN convergence network model to support a cost-effective realization of wide-scale urban monitoring applications. The authors assumed a tree-based data collection for WSN with generic tree-based protocol to easily enable its deployment and immediate usage with all emerging collection solutions and standard specifications. The MANET network organized in small local clusters acts as a WSN backbone network that allows urgent data to pass.

Erdelj et al. [1] described the advances in wireless sensor network (WSN) technology and unmanned aerial vehicles (UAVs) to enhance the ability of network-assisted disaster prediction, assessment, and response. UAVs are responsible for the data collection from fixed WSN sensors deployed in different areas. The authors introduced recommendations for WSN and UAV use during different disaster stages, but there are missing technology and protocol background. In [5], the solution was extended about the measurement of major UAV communication technologies and authors discussed the possible communications technology with Quality of Service (QoS) point of view. A conceptual mobile UAV station for disaster management was proposed as well.

Mukherjee and Biswas [6] propose IoT network hierarchy comprising the Internet, WLAN and/or Internet gateway, MANET and WSN networks. Wireless sensor nodes were deployed in an IoT system that collecting data from the environment and sent them to the gateway node. Data can be directly sent to the Internet at the highest hierarchy level through WLAN Access Point or Internet gateway. MANET nodes are acting as intermediate nodes responsible for collecting data from WSN nodes if the direct Internet gateway is not available. Different communication technologies along with protocol stacks are also discussed [6]. In this work [6] to overcome interference between MANET (Wi-Fi IEEE802.11b) and WSN (ZigBee IEEE802.15.4) communication, the authors defined usable non-overlapping channels for WSN and MANET. Other related works considering convergence scenarios are [7–9].

Unlike the research presented above that interconnects different variations of networks, in our proposal, we introduce a convergence scenario that interconnects WSN, MANET, and DRONET networks into a layered model with the ability to collect data and send it to the cloud services for processing. The layers are independent, but in case of network disruption, urgent data can pass layers based on a system of gateways that enables the interconnection of multiple layers. For each network layer, we provide communication technology and routing protocols recommendation. Besides that, our contribution includes the description of necessary changing and exceptions for routing protocol deployed on each layer (i.e., network) that allows the transporting of urgent data through multiple layers in the multilayered network model. In particular, in DRONET layer, we provide a simplified mechanism for UAV management in order to cover MANET nodes by slicing MANET networks into clusters. The main aim of this proposal is to provide a conceptual way for critical data of urgent applications to be continuously delivered in disrupted network scenarios caused by unpredictable situations.

3. Proposal of Multilayered Network Model for Mobile Network Infrastructure Disruption

3.1. Overview

The proposed multilayered network model (MNM) is composed of three layers that accommodate three different types of wireless networks. The networks used in this multilayered concept are WSN, MANET, and DRONET. The main idea of this network model is to provide a backup network for destroying 5G and its infrastructure. In the case of MNM, WSN layer is supposed to provide IoT data collection functionality with the high number of static low energy wireless sensors. We assumed those data collected by the WSN network will be processed by cloud applications. Therefore, these data need to be transferred out of the WSN network to the Internet by gateways such as an Access Point (AP) of the Wi-Fi network. In the 5G network disruption scenario, we assumed that WSN gateways are unable to send data through AP since the fixed infrastructure is destroyed. In this case, data transfer to the part of the WSN network where Access Point is available could be very expensive in the term of energy consumption, data overload, delivery time, and so on. There is also a possibility that no functional Access Point exists in the WSN network.

Therefore, the ability to transfer critical data to the Internet could be handled by mobile inertial sensors in the MANET network [10]. Nodes of MANET network are not strictly energy-constrained and with mobility, higher radio ranges and data transfers are able to transfer data to the functional AP. There is also a possibility that the MANET network could fall apart into isolated sub-networks because of the mobility of nodes. This disadvantage is handled in MNM by UAVs of DRONET network. UAVs with appropriate communication technologies are able to communicate over long distances in the air without obstacles. DRONET network in MNM si playing the role of backbone network, which can transfer critical data from MANET sub-network without functional AP to the part of MANET network where the functional AP is presented. The structure of MNM is displayed in Figure 1.

Structure of MNM describes how this network model works. For example, WSN layer could be divided into three sub-WSN networks which all has its own connection to the Cloud on the Internet. The red area under WSN sub-network displayed at the left bottom expresses the part of fixed network that is disrupted. Since the AP connection to the Cloud is not functional, the special type of WSN sensor, called WSN gateway, passes critical data to the nearest mobile sensor of the MANET network. However, the isolated MANET sub-network could also suffer from not functional AP, so the node pass obtained data from the WSN network to the nearest MANET gateway - the MANET node chosen by network to be a gateway to the DRONET layer. This gateway is directly connected to the UAV of DRONET network. UAV than looks for the best opportunity to deliver critical data to the MANET sub-network with functional AP. Therefore, the data are transferred through another UAV to MANET sub-network, where AP connection to the Cloud is operational. The whole path from source WSN node to Cloud is displayed by orange colour.

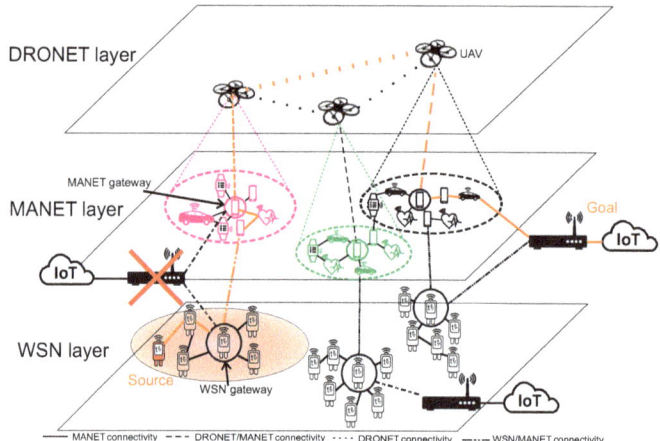

Figure 1. Structure of MNM.

Kazemzadeh et al. [11] presented a survey that addresses optimal multilayered network design identified by flow and design connectivity. Based on this survey, the MNM can be identified as a three-layer network model with one-to-one flow-connectivity design, where each layer is supporting or is supported by only one other layer. Urgent data from the WSN layer can be passed to the MANET layer and then to DRONET layer, while direct flow from WSN layer to DRONET layer does not exist. In MNM, the only urgent data in network disruption scenario can pass between layers, which is commodity of WSN layer. Therefore, MNM falls into multilayer single flow-type network, where only one layer has a commodity to route. When disruption scenario does not occur, the layers act independently and do not communicate.

In the following sections, the detailed functionality of all layers and interlayers interactivity will be described.

3.2. WSN Layer

The WSN layer in the MNM plays a role of the IoT network. It is composed of multiple low-energy wireless sensors that can be deployed in different environments. The biggest advantages of WSN networks are their localized and self-configuring capabilities, which can enable easier large-scale deployments even in inaccessible terrain. Market research suggests that WSN networks will be soon adopted by urban areas, mainly for public safety, localization, and environmental monitoring [4].

Sensors of WSN layer can communicate through different types of communication standards focused on low energy consumption and compatibility with a wireless interface of mobile devices. The most suitable standards for WSN layer are Bluetooth Low Energy (Bluetooth LE), Developers Alliance for Standards Harmonization of ISO 18000-7 (DASH7) and ZigBee IEEE 802.15.4 [12,13].

From the networking-layer point of view, the Bluetooth LE is designed for short ranges and higher data ranges. The main problem is energy consumption in the continuous data stream, where the energy consumption is almost similar with standard Bluetooth. Another problem is the supported star topology. Bluetooth LE operates primarily using ad hoc piconets, where the master device controls up to seven slaves per piconet. Slaves communicate only with the master and do not communicate with each other. However, a slave device may participate in one or more piconets [12]. This topology makes Bluetooth LE unsuitable for most of the WSN monitoring scenarios.

DASH7 is an open-source Wireless Sensor and Actuator Network protocol that provides multi-year battery life, long coverage range up to 2 km, and relatively low data rate down to 9.6 Kbps. The advantages are simple design and cheap chipset. However, its architecture is upload-centric, which means that it does not support mesh routing [13].

ZigBee [14] is one of the most suitable technologies for NMN. It able to communicate over distances from 10 to 50 m and with maximum transfer data rates of 250 Kbps. Newest embedded devices are able to communicate with lower transfer rates of 20 and 40 Kbit/s [15]. It is well analyzed and it is possible to adapt it to different deployment environments. With the combination with 6LoWPAN protocol [16], it provides powerful usability for WSN-Internet deployment. In the mesh network topology, 6LoWPAN protocol can enable connection of WSN sensors with the Internet by the edge router and it seamlessly combines IPv6 with standard IEEE 802.15.4 by performing header compression, fragmentation and reassembly. In addition, it supports the transition between IPv6 and IPv4. Another powerful specification for ZigBee is IPv6 Routing Protocol for Low-power and loss networks (RPL) [17]. RPL is basically an IPv6 multi-hop routing protocol that is suitable as a routing-layer protocol for ZigBee and is also enabled to connect WSN sensor nodes to the Internet. It adopts several techniques to tune routing for data collection optimization but requires a full-fledged IPv6 stack.

LoRa is a proprietary wireless data communication technology which specifies only a PHY layer. A popular MAC for use with LoRa is the open LoRaWAN specification. LoRa enables secure bi-directional, low cost and mobile communication for IoT, smart city, machine to machine (M2M) and industrial applications [18]. LoRa is a preferred technology for IoT embedded systems because of its long-range, high capacity of nodes in network, long battery life, bi-directional, secured and efficient network, interference immunity [18,19]. WSN makes use of Low-Power Wide-Area Networks (LPWANs), a wireless technology to transmit data over long distances with minimal power consumption. LoRaWAN is one of the most successful LPWAN technologies despite its low data rate and because of its low deployment and management costs. An experimental study on the range of LoRaWAN showed that it can achieve ranges up to 7.5 km using SF10 and packets with 10 bytes of payload [18]. The LoRaWAN technology transfer rates range between 0.3 kbps and 50 kbps. Since LoRa technology assures very large communication distances for an extremely low bandwidth, the standard is suitable for applications where a reduced amount of data is transferred and the information collected from the sensors does not change rapidly over time. In [19], the authors present multiple applications of LoRaWAN technology for WSN with IoT, such as water quality monitoring, agriculture, underground sensor networks or smart city. LoRaWAN is therefore another suitable technology for MNM.

Based on Zigbee, Bluetooth and WISA standards [20], several enhancements/related standards or products have been presented like the WirelessHART [21] and ISA 100.11a [22].

WirelessHART is an industrial control protocol that is extension of the Highway Addressable Remote Transducer (HART) communication protocol. It is designed to be reliable, easy to use, and interoperable protocol deployed in process control applications, alerting and monitoring systems. WirelessHART has low power consumption compared to ZigBee with higher security standards, and it can also establish large networks and can support different communication topologies [21]. However, while WirelessHART offers several features that complement its suitability in industry, it fails to offer appropriate solutions to facilitate interoperability. It is also not compatible with IP-based devices and the IoT [23].

ISA100.11a is a wireless network solution for IWSNs (Industrial WSN), developed by International Society of Automation (ISA). Like WirelessHART, it targets industrial applications in automation, process control and monitoring. It has the features of low power consumption, reliability, scalability, and security as well as high real-time data transfer [22]. It operates on 2.4 GHz frequency band, supports high data rates up to 250 kpbs [22]. The specification of an upper data link layer, network layer, UDP and TCP and application layer are defined. In addition, ISA100.11a is IP enabled and supports IPv6. Unlike WirelessHART, not all devices in ISA100.11a network must have routing capability. Without it, devices must be within one hop of a routing-capable device or the gateway. In larger networks, this disadvantage makes ISA100.11a unsuitable for MNM.

The best solution for MNM is ZigBee standard since it supports 6LoWPAN and RPL protocols to connect WSN nodes to the Internet. With appropriate routing protocols are also possible to establish the system of WSN gateways needed to provide interlayer communication. The role of WSN gateways will be further discussed in Section 3.5.

3.3. MANET Layer

The MANET network is usually composed of devices such as smartphones, tablets, laptops and so on. MANET layer in the MNM is composed of mobile smart sensors with communication based on IEEE 802.11 Wi-Fi using an Ad-Hoc mode. The advantages of the MANET network are the autonomous and self-organized network mobile nodes. Therefore, the establishment of the network is quick without needing fixed infrastructure, which enables MANET to be used in different scenarios and environments. The reason MANET is chosen as the second layer in MNM is due to the fact that MANET nodes are not strictly resource-constrained and offers longer radio ranges along with higher data rates. Standards like 802.11n offer data rate range from 54 Mbps to 600 Mbps with outdoor radio range up to 250 m [24]. With mobility, it is possible to send urgent data from the WSN layer through the MANET layer to the nearest functional AP.

The crucial part of MANET layer is communication without interference with other devices and with high spectrum efficiency in the highly congested 5G environment. One of the solutions to achieve higher spectral efficiency in 5G environment is D2D communication. Iqbal et al. [25] categorize D2D communication as Inband (licensed) and Outband (unlicenced) on the bases of spectrum in which D2D communication occurs. In Inband communication, D2D users share cellular resources, while in Outband communication is used to eliminate interference between D2D users and cellular users. It works in the unlicensed spectrum where Wi-Fi, Bluetooth and ZigBee operates. In terms of MANET networks, the solution to these problems is Cognitive Radio of Cognitive Radio Ad-Hoc Networks (CRAHN).

3.3.1. Cognitive Radio in MANET Layer

In [26] we introduce the Adaptive Routing for CR-MANET (AR-CRM) based on Fuzzy logic. This routing method is based on functional blocks that can provide the functionalities of MANET nodes to sense spectrum, provide intelligent management of Wi-Fi channels and routing communication. In the MNM it is possible to implement methods for spectrum sensing and intelligent method for channel management, which can result in lower interference between MANET nodes that uses Wi-Fi communication interfaces. Spectrum sensing provides input data for Fuzzy logic based on SIR (Signal-to Interference Ratio) calculated from RSSI (Received Signal Strength Indicator) and Traffic. The output of precisely adjusted membership functions of Fuzzy logic provides the set of the best optimal channels for each device.

With this method the manage Wi-Fi channels according to the WSN channels is also possible. If the WSN layer uses the standard IEEE 802.15.4 ZigBee, the interference among MANET nodes can occur. The authors in [6] describes standard IEEE 802.11b/g/n/ax (Wi-Fi) channels from 1 to 13 in the range of 2401 MHz to 2495 MHz. The Zigbee standard IEEE 802.15.4 uses 16 frequency channels (from '11' to '26') each of 2 MHz. Wi-Fi and ZigBee channels depiction can be seen in Figure 2.

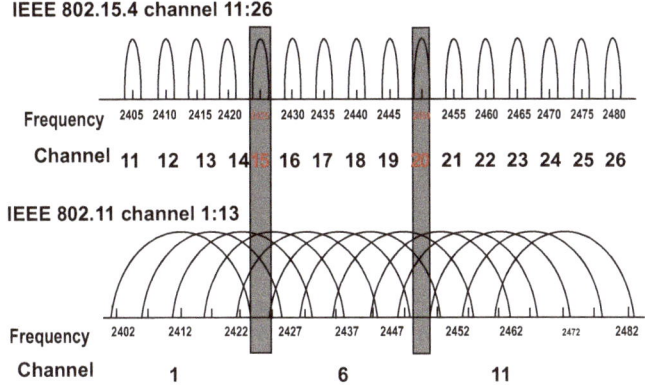

Figure 2. Frequency channels of Wi-Fi IEEE802.11 and ZigBee IEEE802.15.4 [6].

With the assumption of existing sensing methods for discovery of Zigbee channels, it is possible to arrange non-interfere MANET channels for each ZigBee channel based on the fuzzy logic model introduced with AR-CRM. Therefore, it would be possible to set MANET channels among MANET nodes according to nearby WSN channels to avoid interference. This paper does not describe the method of interference avoidance between the MANET and WSN nodes. The purpose of this section is to show the possible way to accomplish this problem. However, the AR-CRM is still possible to use as a protocol in the MNM MANET layer for interference avoidance among MANET nodes.

3.4. DRONET Layer

DRONET layer is composed of UAVs, also called drones. This layer in MNM is playing the role of back-up or backbone network. The reason is that MANET networks could split into subnetworks because of nodes mobility. Therefore, some MANET subnetworks could end-up without connectivity for functional AP. The main idea is to cover MANET subnetworks with UAVs of DRONET layer. With appropriate communication technologies of the DRONET layer it is possible to transfer urgent data over long distances from one MANET subnetwork to another with functional Access Point.

To perform such functionality, UAVs needs to support two protocol stacks. For DRONET communication, it is possible to use Wi-Fi standard IEEE 802.11 with appropriate MANET routing protocol to communicate with MANET nodes on the ground. For the communication between UAVs, it is possible to establish WiMAX IEEE 802.16 [27] communication with WiMAX routing protocol. This solution of two communication standards can overcome the interference of DRONET UAV's with MANET nodes. The WiMAX standard for the single-carrier modulation air interface, also known as WirelessMAN-SC [28], operates in the 10–66 GHz band with typical channel bandwidths of 25 MHz or 28 MHz. The raw data rates excesses 120 Mbps. In practice, the drone can carry the Raspberry Pi single-board computer with both Wi-Fi and WiMAX modules.

The assumption for the functionality of the DRONET network in MNM is the presence of a central point, which in this case will represent the so-called dock. Like MANET nodes, UAVs has also limited energy resources. Therefore, after some time it is necessary to replace used UAV by another UAV with a fully charged battery. The dock in MNM will serve as the headquarters for the DRONET network abilities to organize UAVs, replace fresh UAVs with drained UAVs and charge them or sends them to the required locations of the operation area.

Therefore, the dock will implement WiMAX communication technology. Beside UAVs organizing, the dock will also perform energy-intensive operations, such as clustering. Clustering will be required for the division of MANET nodes into clusters which will be covered by DRONES. This approach will be discussed in the followed section. An example of a such dock for UAVs was presented in [5].

Sanches-Garcia et al. [29] show that the most prefered communication technology for DRONET network is Wi-Fi standard IEEE 802.11. It could be used for UAV to UAV communication technology as well as UAV to MANET nodes on the ground. However, for the communication between UAVs, it is possible to establish WiMAX IEEE 802.16 communication with WiMAX routing protocol [27]. This solution of two communication standards can overcome the interference of DRONET UAV's with MANET nodes, which can be useful with the large number of MANET nodes in the network. To perform such functionality, UAVs needs to support two protocol stacks. Therefore, it is possible to use Wi-Fi standard IEEE 802.11 with appropriate MANET routing protocol to communicate with MANET nodes on the ground, and WiMAX with an appropriate routing protocol to communicate among UAVs.

The WiMAX standard for the single-carrier modulation air interface, also known as WirelessMAN-SC [28], operates in the 10–66 GHz band with typical channel bandwidths of 25 MHz or 28 MHz. The raw data rates excesses 120 Mbps. In practice, the drone can carry the Raspberry Pi single-board computer with both Wi-Fi and WiMAX modules.

3.5. Inter-Layer Communication

In this section, the inter-layer communication will be described. We assume that all layers operate independently. The WSN network requires the existence of communication based on IPv6, which enables WSN nodes to reach the Access Point. The best solution to this is ZigBee with 6LoWPAN or RPL protocol mentioned in Section 3.2. The MNM approach is using a system of gateways, called WSN gateways. The WSN sensors are therefore divided into two types: WSN sensor node and WSN gateway sensors. In the network disruption scenario, WSN gateway sensors will serve as a gateway for urgent data to the higher layers. The ordinary WSN sensor nodes will use IEEE 802.15.4 ZigBee communication technology to communicate with other sensors or WSN gateway sensors. On the other hand, beside ZigBee standard, WSN gateway sensors will also use IEEE 802.11 Wi-Fi. Therefore, WSN gateway sensors need to implement a dual protocol stack that is depicted in Figure 3.

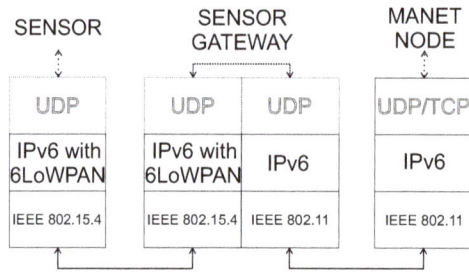

Figure 3. The example of dual protocol stack used in WSN gateway sensors.

Based on the dual protocol stack, WSN gateway senors will be able to communicate with WSN sensor nodes as well as MANET nodes. This scenario is depicted in Figure 4, where the source WSN sensor node is unable to send urgent data to AP_1 because of the disrupted link. However, urgent data can be delivered through the another WSN gateway sensor and MANET layer nodes to the functional AP_2.

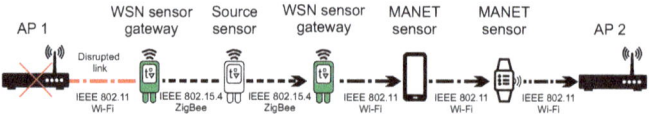

Figure 4. The example of communication between WSN sensor nodes, WSN gateway sensors and MANET layer nodes.

At the Data Link OSI layer, WSN sensor nodes use ZigBee, while WSN gateway sensors use both ZigBee and Wi-Fi. On the Network layer, WSN sensor nodes will use IPv6 routing protocol such as 6LoWPAN.In this paper, higher layers are not considered, which is highlighted by dotted parts in Figure 3. However, in terms of energy consumption, light protocols should be used, such as the UDP transport protocol on the Transport layer. UDP protocol is lighter than TCP and is useful for energy-constrained WSN sensors and WSN gateway sensors. Examples of protocols used in higher layers include Constrained Application Protocol (CoAP) for constrained RESTful Environment running over UDP with lightweight Efficient XML Interchange (EXI) protocol which is a counterpart of XML. Since MANET nodes are not strict energy-constrained and MANET network is an independent network, it is possible to use the TCP transport protocol. However, if critical data are transported in disruption scenario, used protocol in the transport layer has to be UDP. Therefore, the Transport layer of MANET nodes has to be flexible.

To use the WSN gateway system and optimize energy consumption, the routing protocol used in WSN should be cluster-based or use sink-mobility, where elected cluster-head or sink node will act as a gateway to higher MNM layers. The appropriate routing protocols will be described closely in Section 4.1.

The only used communication technology in MANET layer of MNM will be IEEE 802.11 Wi-Fi standard. From the WSN layer point of view, only the WSN gateway sensors are able to send urgent data to the MANET layer. On the other hand, all MANET nodes are able to receive those data. To maintain the integrity of these two layers, it is recommended for the MANET network to use the routing protocol based on IPv6 addressing. This will ensure that the MANET node will be able to deliver critical data to the access point within the 5G network and will also not require reverse conversion between IPv4 and IPv6.

The third layer of the DRONET network uses IEEE 802.11 Wi-Fi standard to connect to nodes of the MANET layer. Based on Wi-Fi standard is possible for UAV of DRONET layer to search for MANET nodes from the air and establish communication. However, the MANET network can be quite large in terms of several nodes and spread over a large area. In order to cover the MANET network with the UAV, it is necessary to perform an area exploration and identify the network topology. Based on the size of the MANET network, using clustering algorithms, it is possible to divide MANET nodes into individual logical subnets in which one Cluster Head (CH) will be selected. This CH will serve as MANET gateway for other MANET nodes in the cluster when urgent data needs to be sent to the DRONET layer. The information about clustering and MANET gateway selection will be discussed in Section 5.1.

Besides the Wi-Fi standard, UAV uses the WiMAX IEEE 802.16 standard for communications among other UAVs and the dock. All UAVs needs to use dual protocol stack in the same way as WSN gateway sensors, which is depicted in Figure 5.

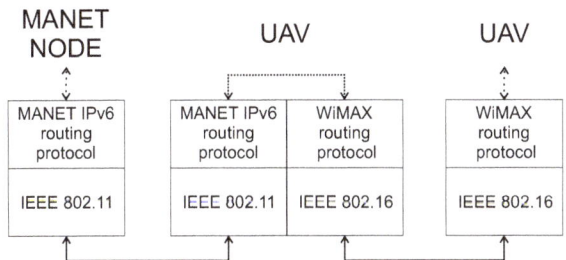

Figure 5. The example of dual protocol stack used in MANET node and UAV.

The first protocol stack implemented in UAV uses IEEE 802.11 Wi-Fi standard on the Data Link OSI layer and IPv6 MANET routing protocol on the Network layer. The second protocol stack used IEEE 802.16 WiMAX standard on the Data Link OSI layer and appropriate WiMAX routing protocol on the Network layer. Based on this approach, the UAV is able to communicate with MANET nodes and other UAV, which is depicted in Figure 6.

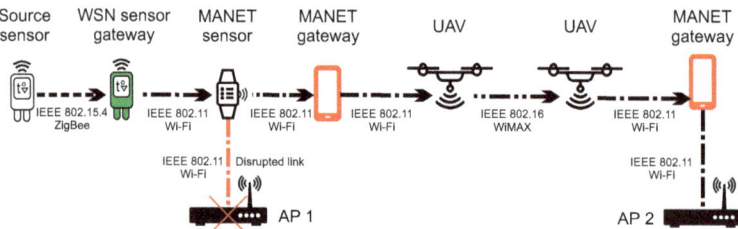

Figure 6. The example of communication between MANET nodes, MANET gateways and UAVs.

The scenario depicted in Figure 6 describes WSN source node that sends urgent data to AP_1. Since the link is disrupted, urgent data are transferred to the MANET layer through the WSN gateway sensor. MANET node is also unable to deliver urgent data to the same AP_1. Therefore, urgent data are transferred to DRONET layer through the MANET gateway in order to find another MANET subnet with functional AP_2.

4. Routing in MNM

As described in previous sections, the MNM is composed of three layers that work independently, so the routing protocols on each layer also works independently. The network disruption scenario is the exceptional situation, in which routing protocols used by each layer need to provide required actions to recognize urgent data and deliver it to the Cloud through AP. Therefore, the content of this section will focus on the recommendations of appropriate routing techniques and algorithms for individual layers and also on their necessary modifications for proper functioning in MNM.

4.1. Routing in WSN Layer

The routing of urgent data begins in the WSN layer. The sensors of the WSN layer periodically measure data and routes them into cloud services on the Internet if the AP is available on the network. In Section 3.2. we provide technology recommendations for WSN layer. The best way to make WSN data propagation to the Internet is the implementation of the routing protocols based on IPv6 protocols.

The most suitable technology for MNM is IEEE 802.15.4 ZigBee with 6LoWPAN or RPL protocol. In the MNM, we assume that sensors in the WSN layer will be fixed without mobility and also will be able to communicate in a multihop manner. The authors in [30] provide a protocols survey based on 6LoWPAN technology. Protocols are classified based on multihop support, Network or Host-based mobility or presence of local entity among other specifications. The classification of routing protocols with multihop support can be seen in Figure 7.

The same authors also point out that proactive protocols are most suitable for WSN with 6LoWPAN, since, it helps to reduce the handover delay by reducing the configuration time and also to avoid the disconnection of nodes, which reduces the data loss rate. Therefore, it is useful to use protocols in the Proactive branch chart. Another important division is based on mobility. The authors described Micro and Macro mobility, where the "Micro mobility" refers to the node mobility within the same sensor network domain and "Macro mobility"refers to the node mobility between different sensor networks. Since sensors in MNM are fixed, the maximum allowed mobility of sensor node is Micro mobility. Since WSN layer in MNM uses the gateway system, the best suitable routing protocols based on presented assumptions are Based-Cluster [31] and RPL-Weight [32].

In the case of the Based-Cluster protocol, the main advantage is network architecture based on a clustering tree topology, which leads from the lowest layers of sensors to one leading sensor (Cluster Head), which in the case of MNM can be considered to be a WSN gateway sensor. RPL-Weight is a hierarchical protocol based on Directed Acyclic Graph (DAG), which defines a network topology and uses Destination Oriented DAG (DODAG) algorithm for routing. It supports sink node mobility, which reduces power consumption and to increase the network lifetime. This is also very useful for MNM, where the sink node can act as a gateway to the MANET Layer or AP. The clustering tree topology of Based-Cluster protocol and sink node mobility of the RPL-Weight protocol are shown in Figure 8.

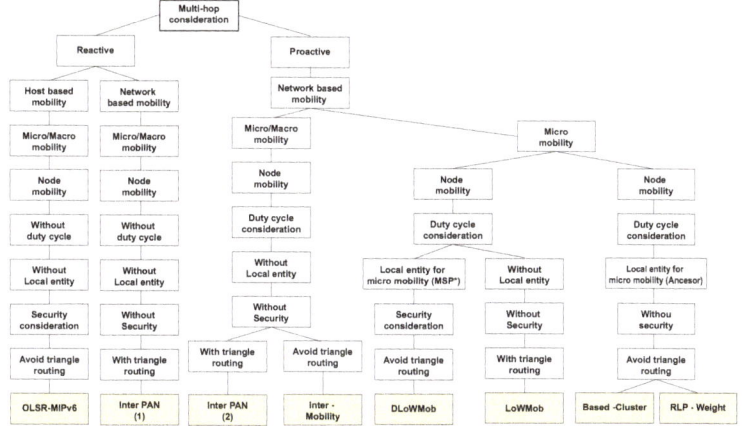

Figure 7. WSN protocols based on 6LoWPAN with multi-hop support [30].

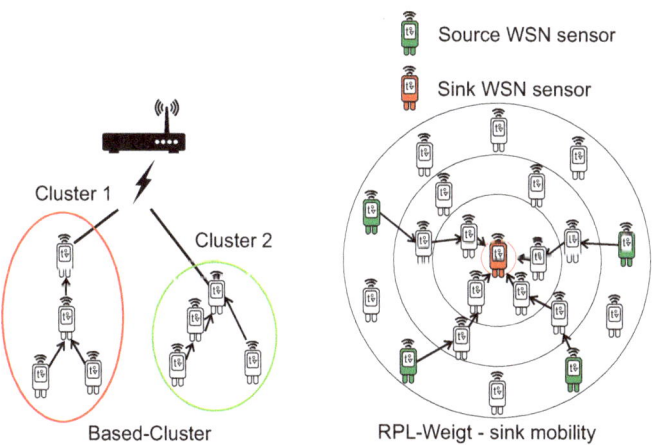

Figure 8. The example of Based-Cluster and RPL-Weight routing mechanisms.

However, both Based-Cluster and RPL-Weight protocols are not designed to support urgent data transmission through WSN gateway sensors to the MANET layer. Therefore, it is important to implement an exception mechanism for those or other deployed protocols. The algorithm responsible for the routing of urgent data in WSN layer of MNM is proposed in flowchart depicted in Figure 9.

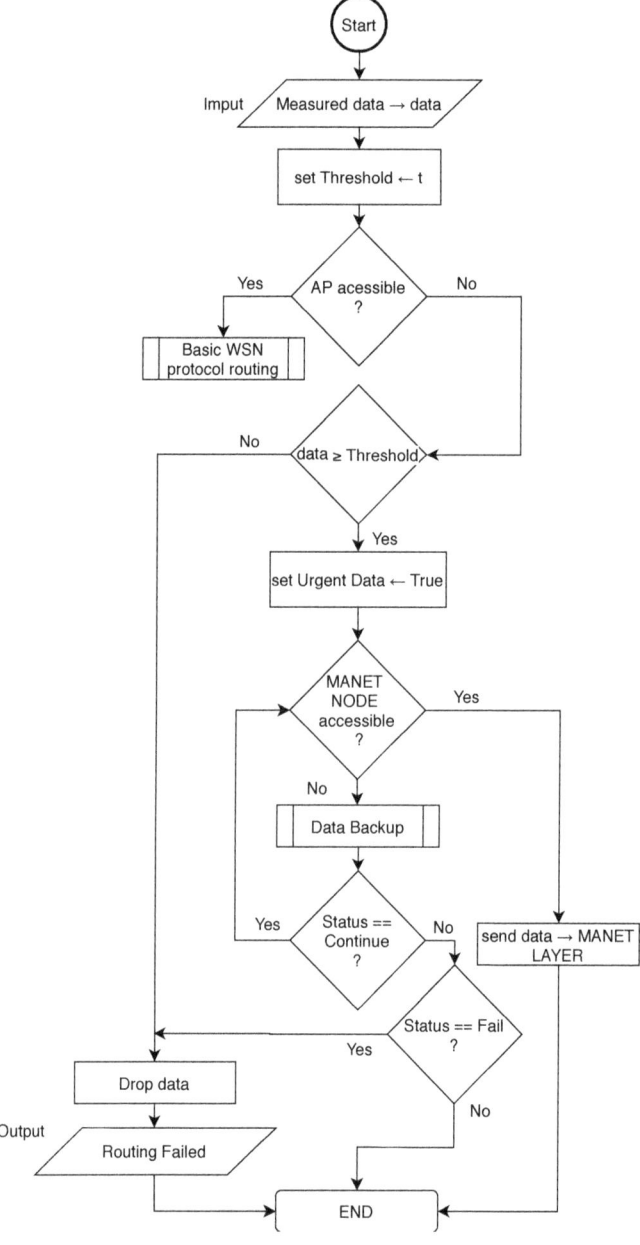

Figure 9. The WSN Layer routing flowchart.

This algorithm needs to be implemented as an exception to the main routing algorithm. In the beginning, if AP is available in the network, all measured data are processed as usual by the main routing algorithm. If AP is not available, measured data needs to be evaluated based on Threshold. This threshold is set based on type or nature of measured data that evaluates them as urgent. Since the sink routing model is considered, it is possible to assume, those nodes near the sink node connected to MANET layer will be asked to forward packets more frequently as nodes that are far. This could affect the energy consumption of those nodes and also cause traffic congestion. To address this problem and also lower the traffic load in the MANET layer, WSN sink node will forward only urgent data to MANET layer when AP is not accessible.

In order to lower processing on WSN gateway or sink node respectively, the process of urgent data evaluation is running on all nodes. When AP is not accessible and data are evaluated as non-urgent, nodes drop the data. Urgent data are transferred to the WSN gateway, which looks for an available MANET node. If the MANET node is accessible, data are transferred to the MANET layer, otherwise, data are processed by Data Backup algorithm described by Algorithm 1.

Algorithm 1: Data Backup algorithm for storing urgent data

---

    input :Data from NodeID$\rightarrow$ *DataID*

    if *DataID* is not *Repository* ? **then**

        if *Previous DataID from NodeID in Repository?* **then**

           | Detete previous DataID in Repository

        end

        if *AP* is *accessible* **then**

           | send *Data* $\rightarrow$ AP

           | Status $\leftarrow$ Succesfull

           | **Return**:Status

        else

           | DataID $\rightarrow$ Repository

           | set: *TimerID* $\leftarrow$ time

           | Status $\leftarrow$ Continue

           | **Return**:Status

        end

    else

        if *TimerID == 0* **then**

           | Delete *DataID* in Repository

           | Status $\leftarrow$ Fail

           | **Return**:Status

        else

           if *AP* is *accessible* **then**

               | send *Data* $\rightarrow$ AP

               | Status $\leftarrow$ Succesfull

               | **Return**:Status

           else

               | Upadte *TimerID*

               | Status $\leftarrow$ Continue

               | **Return**:Status

           end

        end

    end

A data backup algorithm is used to prevent dropping of urgent data if the MANET node is not available at the specific time for WSN gateway. The main idea is to store urgent data for a specific time. The node then waits for the MANET node or AP availability. If the time for giving data runs out, urgent data are dropped.

We assume that input data can be identified by its origin node with a unique ID. Then the input data are associated with the node's ID and marked as *DataID*.

In the beginning, *DataID* is checked, if the gateway node has an entry for the same data in the repository. If not, the algorithm then checks, if the gateway has an entry for input data from the same node according to its ID. If yes, it means that the gateway node obtained fresher data from the same node. Therefore, older data identified by the same node are deleted. Then the gateway node tries to access AP and if this attempt is successful, the algorithm returns the "Successful" status of the main algorithm. If AP is not accessible, then *DataID* is stored to the repository and associated with *TimerID*. This timer refers exactly to the stored *DataID*. Then the algorithm returns "Continue" status to the main algorithm.

If the gateway node has *DataID* stored in its repository, the algorithm checks if *TimerID* is equal to zero. If yes, *DataID* is deleted and algorithm returns "Fail" status to the main algorithm. Otherwise, the gateway node attempts to access AP and the main algorithm returns "Successful" status to the main algorithm if AP is available. If AP is not accessible, *TimerID* is decreased and "Continue" status is returned to the main algorithm.

4.2. Routing in MANET Layer

Routing in MANET layer of MNM is independent of routing in WSN layer when a local entity such as AP is available to all devices. When communication with AP is disrupted, sensors of WSN layer are unable to deliver its measured data to cloud services. Sensors, therefore, start to evaluate their data and produces only urgent data. Only those data are allowed to enter the MANET layer in order to enhance the delivery process. We assume that WSN gateway sensor is capable of using dual protocol stack with IEEE 802.11 WiFi connectivity. This allows the WSN gateway sensor to be seen by MANET nodes and vice versa. WSN gateway sensor is therefore allowed to send urgent data to any available MANET node.

Since WSN layer in MNM uses IPv6 protocol, it should be implemented in MANET layer as well. The routing protocol for MANET layer in MNM should be proactive, since topology maintained by proactive routing protocols is required for DRONET clustering algorithm. The example of MANET IPv6 protocols are IPv6 enabled DSR [33], AODV6 [34] or IPv6 OLSR [35]. Those routing protocols, however, do not support interference avoidance such as AR-CRM mentioned in Section 3.3.1. On the other hand, AR-CRM was not designed to support IPv6. This problem needs to be addressed by implementing interference avoidance mechanism of AR-CRM into mentioned routing protocols or implementing IPv6 into AR-CRM. It is also important to collect GPS positions since that information about topology could be used by DRONET layer to perform its clustering analyses. None of this is the scope of this paper and we assume that missing functionalities mentioned above are implemented.

Regardless of the selected routing protocol, the exception mechanism for urgent data delivery needs to be implemented to deployed routing protocol in order to work in MNM. The implemented exception helps main routing algorithm to recognize urgent data from WSN and provide necessary operations. This mechanism is described by flowchart depicted in Figure 10.

In the beginning, the MANET node that obtained urgent data needs to encapsulate IPv6 packet from WSN layer to recognize if obtained data are indeed urgent. If not, obtained data is recognized as not urgent and MANET node drops this data. If the obtained data are urgent, MANET node tries to access AP. If AP is available in the MANET network, data are sent to AP. If not, the MANET node is looking for MANET gateway.

If the MANET gateway is not recognized or is not available, the Data Backup algorithm described in Section 4.1 is called. If coming status from the Data Backup is Continue, algorithm check again for MANET gateway availability. If the status is Fail, the node drops the data. Otherwise, the status is Successful and it means the data was successfully delivered to AP and exception algorithm ends.

If MANET gateway node is available, urgent data is delivered to it. MANET gateway than check for UAV availability. If UAV is available, data are sent to DRONET layer and exception algorithm ends. If UAV is not available, gateway node calls Data Backup algorithm that stores data or tries to deliver it to AP. The urgent data are then dropped or the exception algorithm checks for UAV availability again according to the status obtained from Data Backup algorithm.

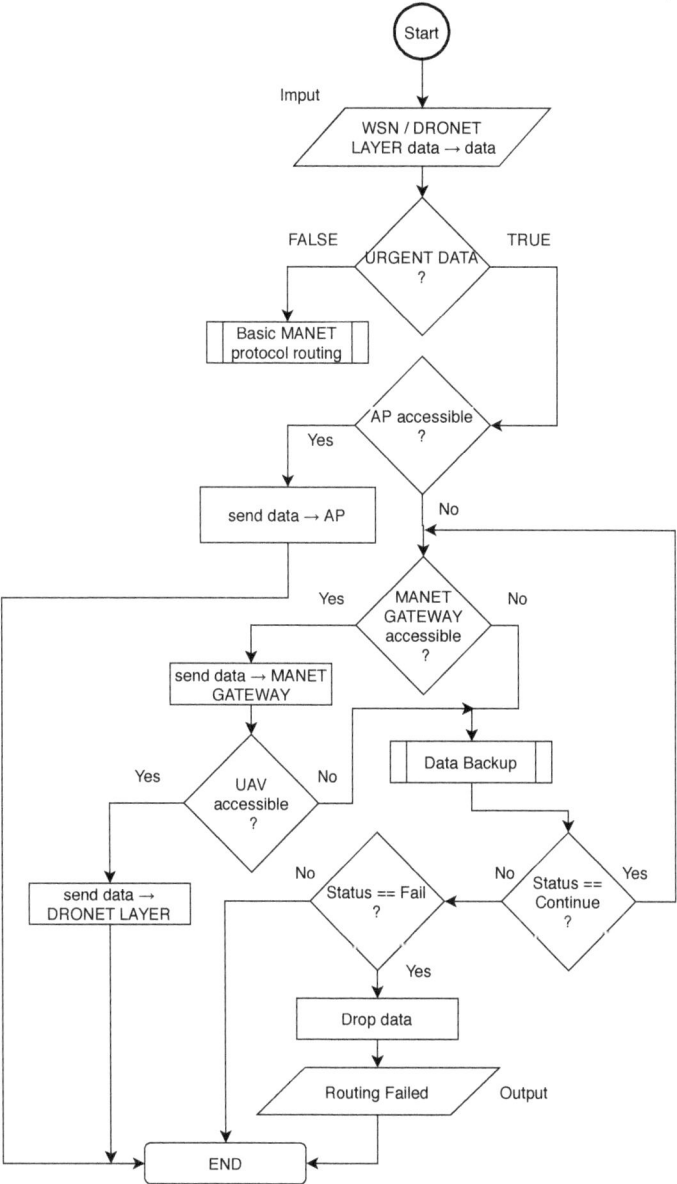

Figure 10. The MANET Layer routing flowchart.

5. Routing in DRONET Layer

The routing in DRONET layer is composed of two stages. The first stage is the Initial and search for MANET nodes to obtain positions of all nodes and possibly all MANET networks in the area. The second stage is routing itself, where the UAV communicates with MANET gateway nodes and within other Drones in order to provide a backup network for critical data transmission.

5.1. Initial and Search Stage of DRONET Layer

The main role of the Initial and search stage is to continuously search for MANET nodes in the desired area. Therefore, we assume that the operating area is known and it can be divided into multiple sub-areas. The size of sub-areas should be picked according to the UAVs antenna coverage perimeter. Another assumption is considering a local entity that is in fact the dock with operational PC and antenna. When the disruption of fixed infrastructure in the area occurs, the dock initiates the Initial and search stage until the disruption is over.

Dock continuously sends UAV's to all areas. The UAV is looking for MANET node. We assume that all UAVs are equipped with MANET IEEE 802.11 Wi-Fi communication technology and they are capable of discovering MANET nodes in the ground. When the UAV discovers the MANET node, it obtains the Topology info from each node along with GPS positions of all nodes in the network [36]. That information is sent back to the dock, where the clustering algorithm is provided. It is possible to use multiple clustering algorithms, such as simple lowest-ID or highest-connectivity (degree) algorithm [37], or more complex algorithms such as Particle Swarm Optimization (PSO) [38]. The dock returns the result of the clustering algorithm along with the cluster heads selections. The UAV then takes a position of the MANET gateway node and notifies it about cluster head election and nodes participated in its cluster. The MANET gateway node is then responsible for notification of other MANET nodes about its election.

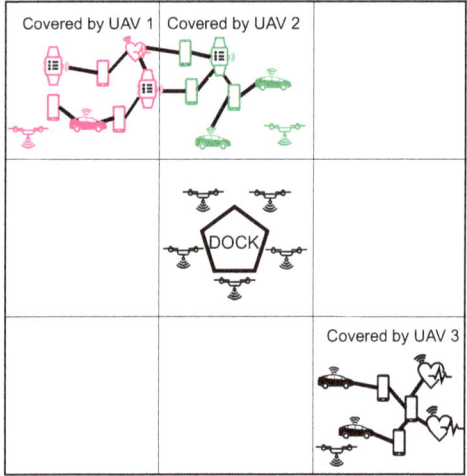

Figure 11. Example of multiple encountered cluster in the area.

When multiple clusters are discovered, UAV takes the position of free cluster and dock send another UAVs takes positions of remained clusters. The multiple clusters can occur if the MANET network contains a larger number of nodes. The situation is depicted in Figure 11, where the left upper part contains MANET network that was divided into two clusters, marked by magenta and green colour. The UAV that discovered the network covers one cluster and dock in the middle of the area sends another UAV to cover the second cluster. All steps of Initial and search stage are described by the flowchart in Figure 12.

The first step includes input in the form of information about the area. Then the area is divided into N subareas based on area size and coverage perimeter of UAV's antenna. Then, all subareas are marked by associated information $SUBAREAINFO(N)$ as "not searched". Algorithms proceed with an endless While loop, which termination is initiated by the ending of disruption scenario. One by one, UAVs are continuously sent to all subareas that are marked either as "searched" or "not searched" and at the same time as "uncovered". Only areas marked as "covered" are not searched again. This is because even previously searched subareas can exhibit new uncovered MANET nodes or MANET subnets.

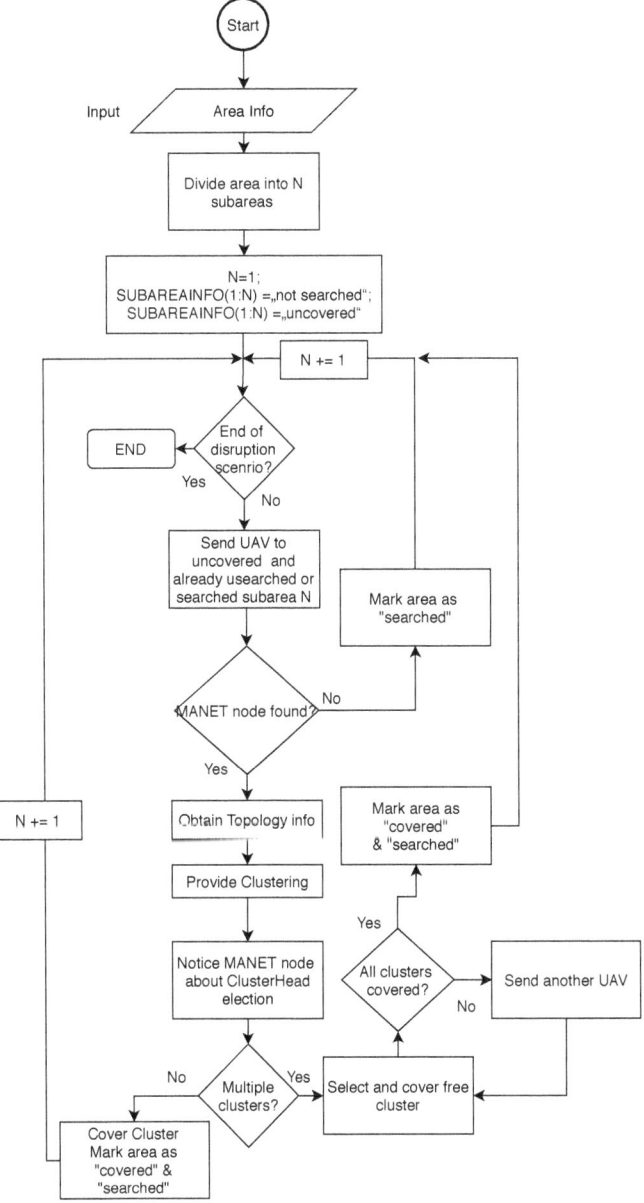

Figure 12. The DRONET initial and search stage flowchart.

If the MANET nodes are not discovered in the particular subarea, this area is marked as "searched" and UAV proceed to another subarea. If the MANET node is discovered, UAV request *TopologyINFO*, which includes the topology of the network and GPS positions of all nodes in the network, where discovered node participates. TopologyINFO is sent to the dock, where clustering is performed. The results of clustering are sent back to the UAV, which informs nodes about Cluster Head and participation in the cluster.

The algorithm then proceeds according to resulted clusters. If multiple clusters appear, UAV covers the randomly selected cluster and dock send another UAVs to cover remained clusters. Then, all subareas belonging to covered clusters are marked as "searched" and "covered".

5.2. Routing Stage of DRONET Layer

Routing stage in DRONET layer begins after the Initial and search stage, where at least two UAVs are connected to each other. As a communication technology, UAVs of DRONET layer in MNM should use at least IEEE 802.11 Wi-Fi. However, in terms of possible interference, it is better to use second technology such as IEEE 802.16 WiMAX. The same as in WSN layer, the UAVs, therefore, needs to implement dual protocol stack.

The earliest version of WiMAX is based on IEEE 802.16 and is optimized for fixed and roaming access. This solution was further extended to support portability and mobility based on IEEE 802.16e, also known as Mobile WiMAX. In recent years, multiple studies provide performance comparisons of routing protocols for WiMAX. Raseed et al. [39] perform a comparison of DSDV, DSR and AODV routing protocols, where table-driven protocol DSDV has the best performance in terms of the packet delivery fraction parameter. On the contrary, a AB Rahman [40] suggests, AODV outperforms DSR and DSDV routing protocols. The performance comparison in [41] shows that in a mobile environment, ZRP and AODV perform better than DSR and OLSR. Pathak et al. [42] also consider the performance of routing protocols for sending Health-care data over the WiMAX network. The results show that from studied protocols AODV, OLSR, ZRP and the LAR1, the last mentioned can offer better results in sending telemedicine data over the wireless channel with high throughput and better reproducibility.

In MNM, the reactive protocol is suggested, since periodic updates can be energy-demanding on limited UAVs resources. The deployed routing protocol also needs to implement necessary adjustments. We assume that the UAV is able to extract information about AP availability from topology obtained from a MANET gateway node. Therefore, this information should be taken into account in the routing metrics. The routing algorithm is described by the flowchart depicted in Figure 13.

The routing algorithm begins with urgent data obtained from the MANET layer. UAV than check for available UAV that has connectivity to MANET network with accessible AP. If UAV with MANET connectivity to accessible AP is not available, the Data Backup algorithm for DRONET layer is called. This algorithm store data and set timer. If the timer is zero, Data Backup returns Fail Status. If Continue status is returned, UAV check for UAV with MANET connectivity to accessible AP again. Otherwise, data are dropped. The timer is decremented and Continue status is returned. Since the DRONET layer is not connected to AP, Data Backup algorithm presented by Algorithm 1 needs to be edited. Data Backup algorithm for DRONET layer is, therefore, described by Algorithm 2.

If UAV with MANET connectivity to accessible AP is available, the urgent data are transported to particular UAV. This UAV then tries to send data to the MANET gateway node. If this node is not available, the main algorithm calls Data Backup. If the returned status is Continue, UAV check MANET gateway node again. Otherwise, data are dropped.

Algorithm 2: Data Backup algorithm for DRONET layer

---

input : *Data* from NodeID→ *DataID*

if *DataID* is not *Repository?* **then**

 if *New DataID from NodeID in Repository?* **then**

  do: delete previous DataID in Repository

  go to: line 6

 else

  DataID → Repository, set: *TimerID* ← *time*

  Status ← Begin

  Return:Status

 end

else

 if *TimerID == 0* **then**

  Delete *DataID* in Repository

  Status ← Fail

  Return:Status

 else

  Update *TimerID*

  Status ← Continue

  Return:Status

 end

end

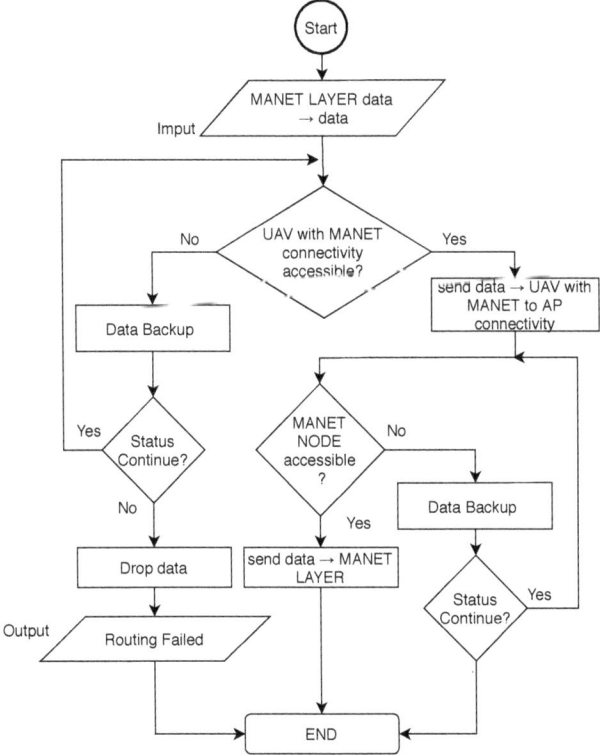

Figure 13. DRONET routing stage algorithm flowchart.

6. Simulations and Results

Based on the theoretical analysis of the MNM concept, simulations in the Matlab environment were designed to simulate the behavior and forwarding of urgent data within the model. The aim of these simulations is to point out the fact that in case of disruption scenario of the fixed infrastructure of 5G and IoT networks, the proposed concept of MNM can take over the role of critical applications and services. Simulations point out that the interconnection of several networks into a hierarchically composed multilayer model has advantages over the use of purely wireless sensor networks in the form of transmission of critical data to functional access points with higher transmission speed and lower delay. The exact description of the simulation scenarios will be provided in following subsections.

Simulations in Matlab do not account rerouting, network reconfiguration and do not use a lot of network parameters like other simulators such as Ns-3 or OPNET Modeler. However, Matlab enables us to simplify the concept of MNM network and provide proof of concept. With Matlab, it is also possible to use a variety of different mobility models for MANET networks such as Random-Way Point or social-based mobility model described in [43]. Matlab also provides possibilities to implement computationally intensive algorithms such as PSO for clustering. In future, we planed to merge Matlab implemented algorithms with OPNET Modeler to further extend simulations with all network parameters.

6.1. Simulation Scenarios

The simulations of the MNM concept were divided into three simulation scenarios, which are intended to illustrate the advantage of using multiple layers of the MNM model compared to the deployment of only WSN networks in the area affected by the disruption of fixed 5G and IoT infrastructure.

The simulation presupposes that there is an area where the fixed infrastructure has been disrupted and there is only one functional AP. Another prerequisite is the location of the WSN wireless sensors in the area intended for data collection, while the occurrence of mobile MANET devices is also considered in the same area. In the network disruption scenario, UAVs of DRONET networks are also present, arranged in the area to cover the MANET network.

6.1.1. Simulation Scenario 1

This simulation scenario is intended to highlight the benefits of adding a MANET layer to a WSN network. The scenario itself consists of a 100 m × 100 m simulation area, where 400 WSN sensors are randomly distributed. The simulation assumes the use of IEEE 802.15.4 ZigBee communication technology with the RPL-Weigth routing protocol using the 6LoWPAN in WSN layer.

Based on ZigBee technology, a radio range between WSN sensors is set to 10 m with a data rate of 30 Kbps. Data rate was randomly generated on each link between WSN sensors in the range of ±50%. This range should take into account the unforeseen effects of the environment on the data rate.

Besides the WSN layer sensors, 20 MANET nodes are also randomly placed in the area. MANET nodes uses IEEE 802.11 Wi-Fi technology with the 802.11n standard for communication and IPv6 OLSR protocol. This allows the nodes to set the radio range to 40 m at a data rate of 100 Mbps.

Data rates of MANET layer were randomly generated on each MANET link from the range of ±50%. There is also one AP in the network, which has the same radio range and data rate as MANET nodes. The individual variables of the simulation scenario can be seen in Table 1.

In this scenario, one WSN sensor is chosen as a source node that attempts to send urgent data for processing to the relevant application or service on the Internet. The role of routing protocols in all simulation scenarios mentioned in this paper used by each layer of MNM is to find the optimal routing path. All routing paths are selected according to the data rates generated on each link and number of hops in therm of Dijkstra shortest path algorithm.

To illustrate the benefits over traditional WSN network and two layers of WSN and MANET networks, a single access point in the network was strategically placed sequentially in three different positions:

- *Position 1*—left upper corner of the simulation area, relatively in close proximity to AP
- *Position 2*—in the middle of simulation area
- *Position 3*—right lower corner of the simulation area. The farthest point from WSN source sensor

The positions of AP mentioned above with devices placed in the simulation area are depicted in Figure 14a for WSN scenario and in Figure 15a for WSN-MANET scenario. Optimal routing paths for both scenarios are depicted on second part of mentioned figures marked as Figure 14b and Figure 15b respectivel.

Figure 14 illustrates the network layout with WSN nodes (blue markers), WSN sensor gateways (green markers) and AP depicted by the Wi-Fi router illustration. The WSN sensor gateways are selected by the RPL-Weight protocol in the sense of so-called "sink mobility" (Section 4.1). WSN source sensor is marked with the ID number of 393 and highlighted by a blue mark with a red edge.

Figure 15 illustrates the first layer of the WSN sensors (blue marks) with WSN sensor gateways (green marks). The MANET nodes (red marks) of second layer are distributed evenly throughout the area. There is an AP depicted by Wi-Fi router illustration and the WSN source sensor depicted by a blue mark with a red edge and ID number of 393.

These simulation scenarios were run 1000 times, always with the same position distribution of WSN and MANET nodes in an effort to illustrate the difference in performance and parameters of the two networks.

Table 1. Scenario 1 simulation variables

Variable	Value
Area size [m]	100×100
WSN sensors number	400
WSN sensors radio range [m]	10
WSN sensors data rate [Kbps]	30
MANET nodes number	20
MANET nodes radio range [m]	40
MANET nodes data rate [Mbps]	100
AP number	1
AP radio range [m]	40
AP data rate [Mbps]	100

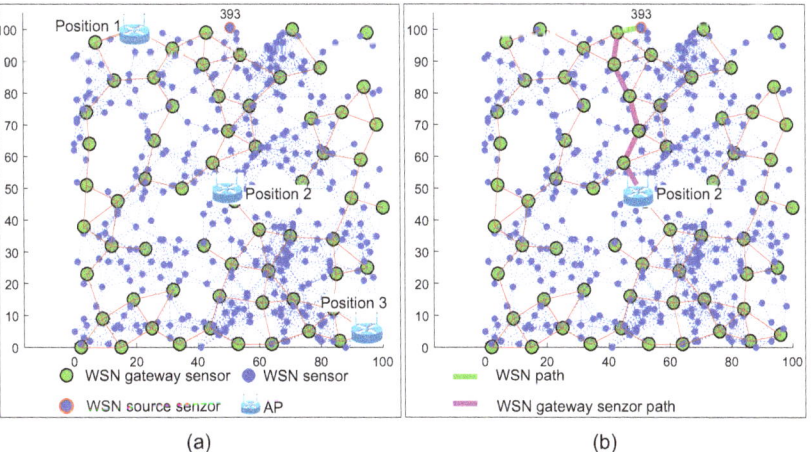

(a)　　　　　　　　　　　　　　　　(b)

Figure 14. (**a**) Example of simulation scenario 1 with all positions of AP for WSN network. (**b**) Example of optimal routing path from WSNT source sensor to AP deployed in Position 2 (in the middle of the simulation area).

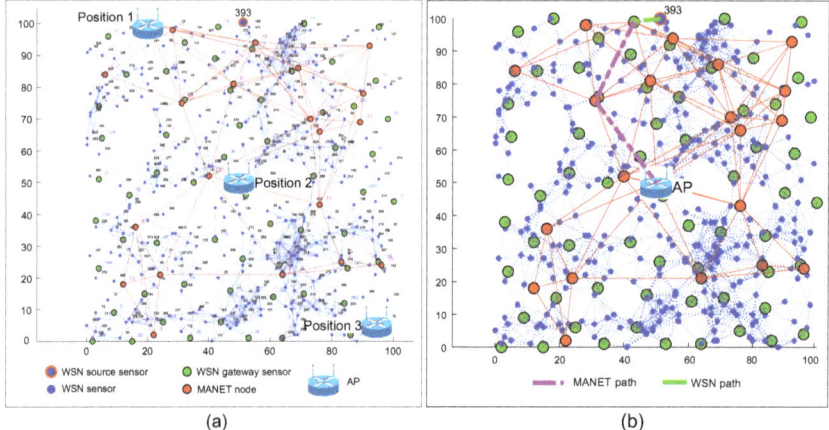

(a)   (b)

Figure 15. (**a**) Example of simulation scenario 1 with all positions of AP for WSN-MANET network. (**b**) Example of optimal routing path from WSN-MANET source sensor to AP deployed in Position 2 (in the middle of the simulation area).

6.1.2. Simulation Scenario 2

The second simulation scenario extends the first scenario by adding a DRONET layer to the multilayered model, which performance will be compared to the traditional WSN network depicted in Figure 14. The distribution of WSN nodes with their parameters and technologies is the same as in the case of the first simulation scenario.The number and parameters of MANET nodes remained unchanged, but some positions of MANET nodes were partially modified in order to divide the original MANET network into two subnets. This change was made to simulate the division of the MANET network into individual subnets in order to use UAVs of the DRONET network.

The UAVs uses IEEE 802.16 WiMAX technology with the AODV protocol to communicate with other UAVs and dock. Therefore, the radio range of UAVs was set to 200 m with a data rate of 250 Mbps. The number of UAVs and their distribution in the area is determined by the number of clusters and their location in the area. The PSO clustering algorithm was used in this task, which divided the individual MANET nodes into 4 clusters or logical subnets based on positions of the MANET nodes. The output of the clustering algorithm can be seen in Figure 16.

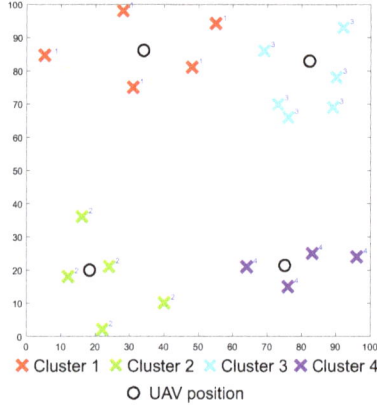

Figure 16. The example of the PSO clustering output.

Based on the assumptions mentioned above, the variables of the simulation scenario 2 were set according to Table 2.

Table 2. Scenario 2 simulation variables

Variable	Value
Area size [m]	100×100
WSN sensors number	400
WSN sensors radio range [m]	10
WSN sensors data rate [Kbps]	30
MANET nodes number	20
MANET nodes radio range [m]	40
MANET nodes data rate [Mbps]	100
AP number	1
AP radio range [m]	40
AP data rate [Mbps]	100
Number of UAV	4 (based on clustering algorithm)
DRONET radio range [m]	200
DRONET data rate [Mbps]	250

As in the first simulation scenario, three different access point positions were used in the second simulation scenario as well. The specific locations coincide with the first simulation scenario and together with the locations of the WSN, MANET and UAV nodes are depicted in Figure 17. As in the case of the first simulation scenario, the second simulation scenario was run 1.000 times for all AP positions with the same initial positions of WSN, MANET and UAV.

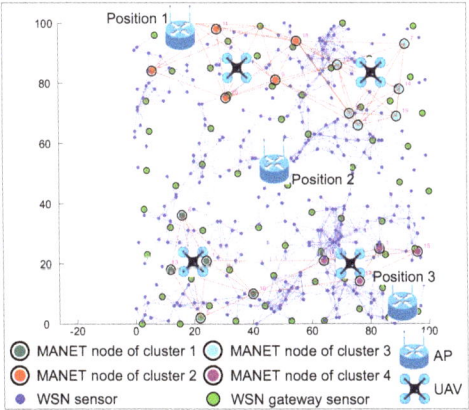

Figure 17. Example of simulation scenario 2 with the positions of AP, WSN, MANET and UAV nodes.

6.1.3. Simulation Scenario 3

The third simulation scenario is focused on the ability of the MNM concept to collect data by MANET nodes from the WSN network. The scenario consists of 2000 WSN sensors, which are static. Mobile MANET nodes were also placed in the simulation area, but the number of those nodes will be changed from 50 to 75 and 100. The movement of nodes was based on Random-Way Point mobility model with the speed of nodes set at 5 km/h, or 1.4 ms respectively, which is the speed of human walk. Radio ranges of MANET nodes were set to 50 m. This simulation scenario aims to observe the time that MANET nodes needs to cover all WSN nodes compared to WSN gateway sensors with its radio range. If the WSN sensor or WSN gateway sensor are within radio ranges of MANET nodes, we assume that contact is negotiated and data transfer can occur. The simulation begins with the initial position of MANET nodes that starts to move. The simulation ends when all WSN sensors or WSN gateway sensors are covered by MANET nodes at least one time. The simulations were run 1000 times with the same initial positions of WSN sensors, WSN gateway sensors and MANET nodes. This simulation with the position of WSN sensors, WSN gateway sensors and MANET nodes is depicted in Figure 18. The simulation variables are set according to Table 3.

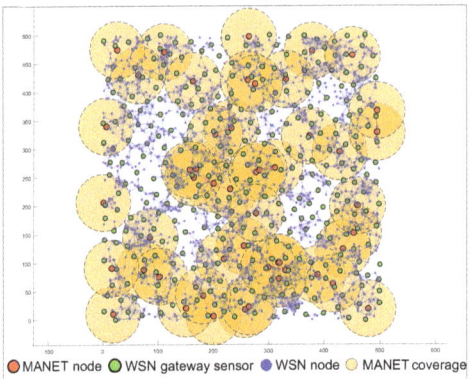

Figure 18. Example of simulation scenario 3. The brown circles are illustrations of MANET node's radio ranges.

Table 3. Scenario 3 simulation variables

Variable	Value
Area size [m]	500×500
WSN sensors number	2000
WSN sensors radio range [m]	10
MANET nodes number	50, 75, 100
MANET nodes radio range [m]	50
Speed of MANET nodes [m/s]	1.4
Mobility model	Random-Way Point

6.1.4. Results of Simulation Scenario 1

In the first simulation scenario, we consider a WSN network with wireless sensors and WSN gateways according to the "sink mobility" of the RPL-Weight protocol. In all simulations, only one AP was functional and its positions were changed according to the description in Section 6.1.1. In the case of WSN-MANET simulation, the routing protocol starts at WSN sensor 393, which is the source of urgent data. This sensor searches an optimal routing path to the WSN gateway sensor, which transfers data to the MANET node if AP is not in its radio range. The MANET network, then transfers urgent data to the functional AP by optimal routing path. Amount of urgent data was set to 100 KB. The results are examined data rates, the time required to transfer the data, and the number of hops from the source node to the access point.

The first result examines the total average delivery time of 100 Kb urgent data from the source sensor to the AP. This result is depicted by the graph in Figure 19. The graph shows the total average time required to deliver data via the traditional WSN network and via WSN-MANET network within the multilayer network model. The time required to redirect data on individual devices was not considered in these simulations.

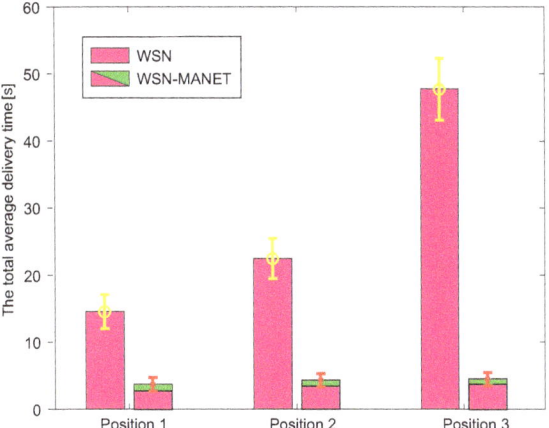

Figure 19. The total average delivery time of 100 Kb urgent data from the source sensor to the AP.

In the case of the WSN-MANET network, it is possible to observe a double component of time in bar graphs. Full time is composed of the time required for urgent data transmission via the WSN network and subsequently via the MANET network. With the help of this graphical representation, it can be seen that the majority of the total time required to transmit data is formed by the time required to transmit data over the WSN network. Therefore, it is possible to say that MANET network significantly speeds up data transmission.

The overall result for all AP positions shows a significant reduction of data transfer time in the case of WSN-MANET model, with the trend being more pronounced when the distance between the WSN source sensor and AP increases. Although the total data delivery time in the WSN network increases significantly with increased distance between the WSN source sensor and AP, in the WSN-MANET network this trend increases only very slowly. This is due to the fact that the delivery time of the WSN component is almost the same for each AP position since the WSN sensor gate was available for one jump in most cases and also due to MANET data rate, where transmission of 100 Kb urgent data is fast.

The second result depicted by the graph in Figure 20 expresses the average number of hops from the source WSN sensor to the AP. As with the first result, hops in the WSN-MANET network graph bar are represented as individual components of WSN and MANET networks.

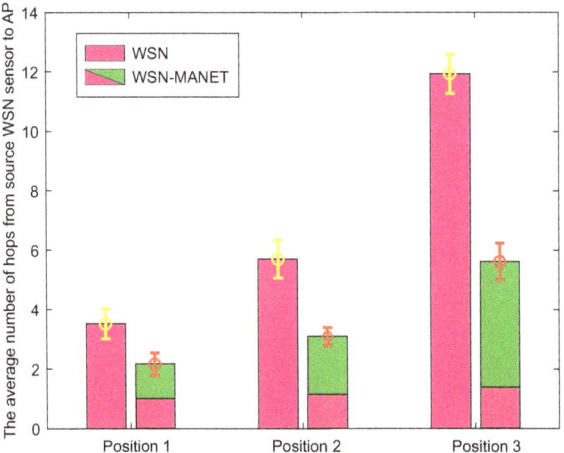

Figure 20. The average number of hops from source WSN sensor to AP.

In contrast to the first result, increasing transmission time of WSN-MANET network through all AP positions shows insignificant trend, while the increasing trend of hops in the case of the WSN-MANET network in the case of the second result is more pronounced. However, the number of hops in the WSN-MANET network is lower in each simulation. For position 1, the number of hops decreases approximately by 42%, while for the other positions the interconnection of WSN and MANET networks reduces the number of hops by more than 50%. This reduction increases with the highest distance between the source WSN sensor and AP. The reason is the fact that in addition the highest transmission speeds, the nodes of the MANET network provide also a higher radio range.

The third result (Table 4) shows the average values of the data rate that was achieved on the individual optimal paths in the case of 100 Kb urgent data delivery. Those values were achieved by averaging the data rates achieved on the individual parts of the optimal paths.

Table 4. The average data rates in 100 Kb urgent data delivery from source WSN sensor to AP.

| | The Average Data Rates in 100 Kb Urgent Data Delivery [Mbps] | | | |
| | WSN | | WSN-MANET | |
AP Position	Average	Standard Deviation	Average	Standard Deviation
Position 1	0.0264	0.0035	45.41	17.74
Position 2	0.0276	0.0035	68.97	14.17
Position 3	0.0275	0.0025	82.00	10.29

Table 4 shows that the data rates in the case of urgent data transmission via the WSN network are many times lower than in the case of urgent data transmission via the MANET network. In the WSN network, the average data rate ranges from 26 to 28 Kbps, while in the case of the WSN-MANET network data rate ranges from 45 to 82 Mbps. It is also possible to observe an increasing trend of the average data rate in the case of the WSN-MANET network. This phenomenon is caused by the fact that transmission of the data with increasing distance between the source WSN node and AP takes place in an increasing part of the MANET network. This fact is supported by the second result in Figure 20, where the number of hops in MANET networks is highest in the case of AP Position 3. A higher number of hops in the MANET part of WSN-MANET network resulted in a higher average data rate.

6.1.5. Results of Simulation Scenario 2

The second simulation scenario adds UAV devices of DRONET layer to the WSN-MANET network, which complement the concept of MNM. This concept will be compared with the WSN network the same way as in the case of the first simulation scenario. In the case of the WSN-MANET-DRONET network, routing protocols use the same algorithm to find optimal paths like in scenario 1. To save energy in the DRONET layer, routing protocols deliver urgent data primarily using the MANET layer. Despite UAV accessibility, urgent data are transferred to DRONET layer only if the AP is not presented in a particular MANET subnet. The example of this scenario with the optimal routing path is depicted in Figure 21.

The routing starts at the WSN layer, where the source WSN sensor finds the most optimal path in terms of the number of hops and data rate to the nearest WSN gateway sensor, which delivers the urgent data to the nearest MANET node. If functional AP is presented in the MANET subnet, the urgent data are transferred to this point. If the AP is not presented in the MANET subnet, the data are routed to the nearest available MANET gateway. Those MANET gateways are known because of the clustering algorithm performed by DRONET layer. After transferring the data to the DRONET network, the corresponding UAV selects the routing path according to OSLR routing protocol to the UAV, which is connected to the MANET subnet with functional AP. After the urgent data are transferred back to the new MANET subnet, the routing algorithm looks for the most optimal path to the AP.

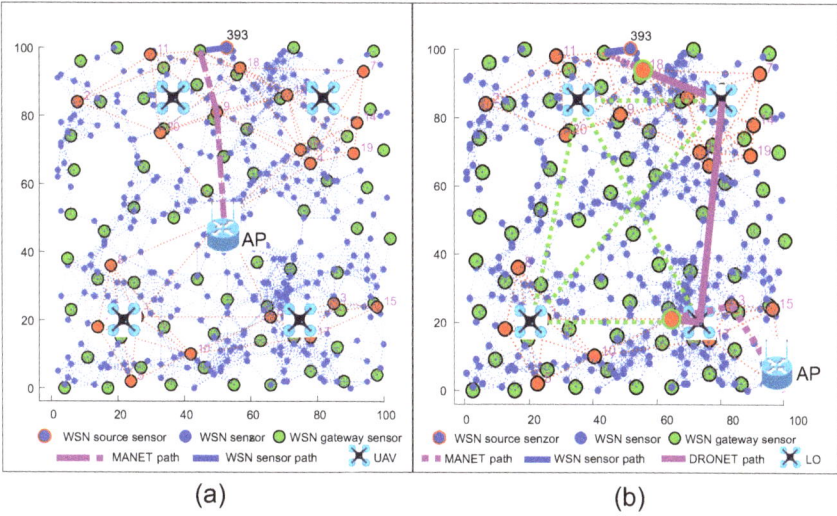

(a)   (b)

Figure 21. The example of optimal routing path in WSN-MANET-DRONET network. (**a**) Expample of optimal routing path through WSN and MANET layer. (**b**) Example of optimal routing path through WSN, MANET and DRONET layer.

The first result shows the total average delivery time of 100 Kb of urgent data from the source WSN sensor to the AP. However, in addition to WSN-MANET networks, these simulations also include DRONET networks. Therefore, it is possible to see a total of 3 delivery time components within AP Position 3 in the bar graph of WSN-MANET-DRONET network (Figure 22).

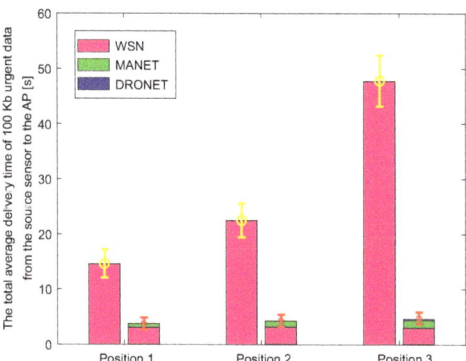

Figure 22. The total average delivery time of 100 Kb urgent data from the source sensor to the AP.

In the case of Position 1 and 2, the DRONET network was not used due to the direct connectivity of the MANET network with the AP. The DRONET layer was used in simulation with the AP on Position 3 since AP is in the separate MANET subnet. Even the farthest AP was reached quickly in terms of delivery time, despite the use of three layers. WSN-MANET-DRONET network reduces the delivery time of urgent data on Position 1 by almost 70% compared to WSN layer. In the case of Position 2, this difference has already increased to about 79% and in the third position by 90%. The time component of the DRONET network is responsible for the significant decreasing of the delivery time at Position 3 due to the highest data rate on the routing path. At this data rate, the time component of transferring 100 Kb of urgent data is very small. Despite the higher number of hops and distance between the source WSN sensor and AP, the DRONET layer was able to reduce the time of delivery that is comparable to the results on Position 1 and 2.

The second result depicted in Figure 23 shows the average number of hops between the source WSN node and AP. This result complements the informative value of the first result, as the achieved delivery times depend on the number of hops. Based on hops, it is possible to see why the time contribution of the MANET network in Position 3 was the highest.

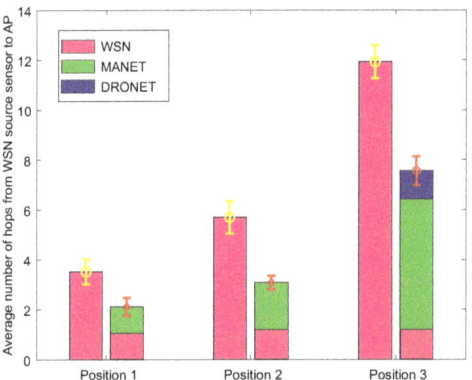

Figure 23. The average number of hops from source WSN sensor to AP.

The reason is the fact that most of the data transmission took place via the MANET network. On average, almost 6 hops within the MANET network in Position 3 compared to 1 to 3 hops within the MANET network in Position 1 and 2. In the overall comparison with the WSN network, the number of hops was reduced by 40 to 45% in the case of WSN-MANET-DRONET network. The third result presented in a tabular illustration (Table 5) shows the average data rates achieved on optimal routing paths when transmitting 100 Kb of urgent data. In the case of the WSN network, data rate ranges from approximately 27–28 Kbps, while interconnection of the WSN-MANET-DRONET network resulting in an average data rate ranges from 44 to 87 Mbps. An important factor of this increasing trend are the higher data rates of MANET and DRONET networks. This shows a great advantage over the deployment of the classic WSN network in the case of fixed infrastructure disruption.

Table 5. The average data rates in 100 Kb urgent data delivery from source WSN sensor to AP.

	The Average Data Rates in 100 Kb Urgent Data Delivery [Mbps]			
	WSN		WSN-MANET-DRONET	
AP Position	**Average**	**Standard Deviation**	**Average**	**Standard Deviation**
Position 1	0.0278	0.0034	44.51	16.26
Position 2	0.0274	0.0032	66.89	12.24
Position 3	0.0279	0.0024	87.29	11.64

6.1.6. Results of Simulation Scenario 3

The third simulation scenario deals with data collection of MNM concept. The MANET layer, which is hierarchically located above the WSN layer, is responsible for data collection in case of disruption of the fixed infrastructure. When disruption of the fixed infrastructure occurs, the WSN sensors transfer urgent data to the nearest WSN gateway sensor, which tries to locate MANET nodes if AP is unavailable. If the MANET node is not close to the WSN gateway sensor, the gateway stores the urgent data in its cache and waits for contact with MANET node. Therefore, it is crucial to compare the times needed to collect data by MANET nodes from WSN nodes and WSN gateway sensors. Those results are depicted in Figure 24.

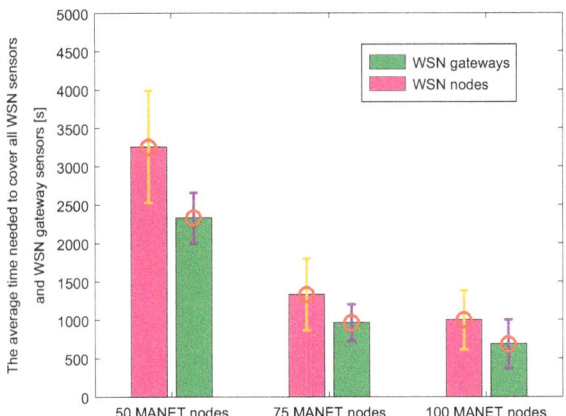

Figure 24. The average time needed to cover all WSN sensors and WSN gateway sensors.

Since the number of WSN gateway sensors is lower than the number of WSN sensors, results show that time needed to cover the last WSN sensor by MANET nodes is higher compared to the time needed to cover the last WSN gateway sensor. It can be also observed that with an increasing number of nodes, the time required to cover all nodes is lower. With twice the number of nodes, the time is even more than twice as low. This is due to the fact that the highest percentage of WSN nodes and gateways are covered with the same radio range of MANET nodes during the initial node distribution. More importantly, the time required to collect data from each WSN gateway sensor is approximately 30% lower than the time required to collect data from each WSN sensor.

A further reduction in the number of sensor gates would contribute to even less time, but a low number of gates would also increase energy costs and traffic at these nodes, as a "sink mobility" model is considered, where all communication converges to a single point. In the end, this result proves that the system of the gateway in the WSN network is useful for data collection in terms of time.

7. Brief Discussion about Future Steps of Proposed MNM Model

In these sections we will discuss the our future steps of the research.

7.1. Energy Consumption of Proposed MNM Model

A lot of the research activity today is focused on research into energy consumption in the routing process for either wireless networks or multilayered networks such as [44–46]. The energy is also considered in terms of UAV management [47,48]. In our paper, energy is also considered in different areas. For example, in a DRONET network, the presence of a central point (dock) is considered, which is responsible for UAV management, charging of drained UAVs, and performing energy-intensive operations, such as clustering. Energy is also considered in interlayer communication (Section 3.5), where using of light protocols such as UDP, CoAP or EXI is advised.

In the WSN network, the sink routing model is considered, so it is possible to assume, those nodes near the sink node connected to the MANET layer will be asked to forward packets more frequently. To address this problem and also lower the traffic load and energy consumption, the WSN sink node will forward only urgent data. In the DRONET layer the reactive protocol is suggested since periodic updates can be energy-demanding on limited UAVs resources. Also, urgent data are transferred to the DRONET layer only if the AP is not presented in a particular MANET subnet.

Although energy consumption in MNM is considered, it is nevertheless not evaluated in this paper. Energy consumption in MNM is a however important issue and its evaluation is part of future research, which needs to address multiple areas from network design to management of nodes and routing protocols.

7.2. Security Aspects of Proposed MNM Model

Security is very important and broadly discussed term in 5G networks. The goals of security solutions are to provide privacy, authentication, integrity, non-repudiation, and confidentiality [49–51]. Base on heterogeneity of the Internet of Thing-based systems, the proposed systems will need support different solutions and algorithms in the sense of security, privacy, secure transmission of information over the networks, interoperability and data management [52]. Based on the characteristics of networks, we have to take into account different items from the security solutions point of view. In MNM model, the term security gains importance, because this model integrates different types of wireless networks with specific technical challenges to attack vulnerabilities.

In MNM, public safety is a very important part of the security solution. Our solution enables to increase public safety by possibilities to transport emergency information between users without any infrastructure in a disaster and crisis. We must note that our solution does not record any sensitive information about users, we only deal with technology point of view.

A second look for security is a network and information security. Each network (MANET, DRONET, WSN, and Sensor) of the MNM model have varied security challenges. In the field of security, we will solve the problem of secure and robust transmission between different a source and destination nodes. Secure routing in sensor networks is a very hard problem due to inherent properties in comparison with MANET, DRONET and different types of wireless networks. In the field of security, our research activities in MNM model will be focused on:

- secure and robust communication between different wireless networks during disaster situations,
- secure and reliable transmission of the IoT information between a source and destination nodes over the wireless different networks,
- increase information and cybersecurity of the IoT by using the novel cryptographic techniques and blockchain algorithms to eliminate unauthorized access and malicious attacks.

Due to the nature of the proposed solution of the MNM, we will implement the game theory, namely cooperative, non-cooperative and evolution games to the process of finding reliable and secure communication paths between mobile terminals to transport IoT data. The game theory also gives us the possibilities to select reliable communication paths between terminals regarding the actual situation in the networks, and we will eliminate the different malicious nodes located in the networks.

Another solution is implementation trust-based routing algorithms to transport of the IoT data between isolated islands of the terminals with limited connectivity. We are working on the blockchain routing algorithm to provide a secure path selection between the source and destination nodes. The main idea of all security solutions is to provide secure communication between mobile terminals to provide robust, reliable and secure communication between mobile terminals to transmission IoT data. Another idea of the MNM is to provide a secure public safety network to communication between different terminals without any infrastructure.

8. Conclusions

In this paper, the new multilayered network model (MNM) for the disrupted infrastructure of the 5G mobile network was introduced. The main goal of this paper is to present possibilities and ideas, which describes how multilayered network models can be built and which technologies and routing protocols is possible to implement.

Therefore, the MNM concept is composed of three independent layers of networks, which are capable of collaboration if disruption of fixed infrastructure occurs. The whole model is able to perform data collection at WSN layer using sensors, which mimic the IoT behaviour by sending those data to the Cloud. If disruption scenario occurs, only urgent data are allowed to pass into higher layers through the introduced system of WSN gateways. The disrupted part of the network can be bypassed with MANET nodes of MANET layer, which offers longer radio ranges and higher data rates and thus faster delivery. If MANET subnetworks are unable to deliver urgent data, it is possible to use backbone DRONET network, which offers even longer radio ranges and higher data rates. The UAVs of DRONET are able to discover MANET nodes and perform clustering mechanism to effectively cover MANET subnetworks with UAVs. Along with MNM, recommendations for use of possible wireless technologies with routing protocols were provided. In addition to these recommendations, the exception mechanism for urgent data delivery in routing algorithms was introduced to all layers.

In order to show that the concept is capable of providing the intended functionalities and also highlighting the differences between typical WSN network and MNM, simplified Matlab simulations were provided. More complex simulations in simulators, such as OPNET Modeler or Ns-3, are in the process of preparation and will be included in future papers.

The MNM model provides new possibilities to use wireless networks without any infrastructure as a public safety network. This model should be used not only during an emergency and crises to transport IoT data between different terminals and sensors. MNM model enables to increase the mobility of the mobile terminals, design new services and applications as well.

Future research also includes implementation of IPv6 routing to Adaptive Routing protocol for CR-MANET (AR-CRM) in order to provide methods for spectrum sensing and intelligent method for channel management, which can result in lower interference between MANET nodes. Another step is to provide research of Fuzzy logic inside AR-CRM and spectrum sensing methods in order to manage MANET channels according ZigBee channels in WSN network. A detailed study of critical areas such as access control, both network and information security as well as evaluation of energy consumption in each layer by presenting a multilayered network model will be the subject of future studies and publications. The proposed MNM concept needs improvements, especially in the security area, which is mandatory for future networks. Improvements are also needed in terms of UAV management in DRONET network, where the complex algorithm needs to be established based on energy consumption constrains, security and privacy.

Author Contributions: Conceptualization, D.H. and J.P.; methodology, L.D.; data analysis, L.O.; validation, D.H, J.P. and L.D.; formal analysis, L.O.; investigation, D.H.; resources, J.P.; data curation, L.O.; writing—original draft preparation, D.H and J.P.; writing—review and editing, L.D.; visualization, J.P.; project administration, J.P.; funding acquisition, J.P. All authors have read and agreed to the published version of the manuscript.

Funding: This research received no external funding.

Acknowledgments: This work has been performed in the framework of the ministry of education of Slovak republic under research VEGA 1/0492/18 and APVV-17-0208.

Conflicts of Interest: The authors declare no conflict of interest.

References

1. Erdelj, M.; Natalizio, E.; Chowdhury, K.R.; Akyildiz, I.F. Help from the sky: Leveraging UAVs for disaster management. *IEEE Pervasive Comput.* **2017**, *16*, 24–32. [CrossRef]
2. Li, X.; Dongning, G.; Huarui, Y.; Guo, W. The public safety wireless broadband network with airdropped sensors. In Proceedings of the IEEE China Summit and International Conference on Signal and Information Processing (ChinaSIP), Chengdu, China , 12–15 July 2015; pp. 443–447.
3. Baldini, S.; Stan, K.; David, A.; Fabrizio, V. Survey of wireless communication technologies for public safety. *IEEE Commun. Tutor.* **2014**, *16*, 619–641. [CrossRef]
4. Bellavista, P.; Giuseppe, C.; Antonio, C.; Luca, F. Convergence of MANET and WSN in IoT urban scenarios. *IEEE Sens. J.* **2013**, *13*, 3558–3567. [CrossRef]
5. Erdelj, M.; Król, M.; Natalizio, E. Wireless sensor networks and multi-UAV systems for natural disaster management. *Comput. Netw.* **2017**, *124*, 72–86. [CrossRef]
6. Mukherjee, S.; Biswas, G.P. Networking for IoT and applications using existing communication technology. *Egypt. Inform. J.* **2018**, *19.2*, 107–127. [CrossRef]

7. Jain, B.; Gursewak, B.; Jyoteesh, M.; Shalli, R.; Hassan, A.S. A cross layer protocol for traffic management in Social Internet of Vehicles. *Future Gener. Comput. Syst.* **2018**, *82*, 707–714. [CrossRef]

8. Król, M.; Natalizio, E.; Zema, N.R. Tag-based data exchange in disaster relief scenarios. In Proceedings of the 2017 International Conference on Computing, Networking and Communications (ICNC), Valley, CA, USA, 26–29 January 2017; IEEE: New York, NY, USA, 2017; pp. 1068–1072.

9. Sharif, A.; Li, J.P.; Saleem, M.A. Internet of things enabled vehicular and ad hoc networks for smart city traffic monitoring and controlling: A review. *Int. J. Adv. Netw. Appl.* **2018**, *10*, 3833–3842. [CrossRef]

10. Racko, J.; Peter, B.; Arto, P.; Jussi, P.; Jussi, C. Pedestrian dead reckoning with particle filter for handheld smartphone. In Proceedings of the 2016 International Conference on Indoor Positioning and Indoor Navigation (IPIN), Alcala de Henares, Spain, 4–7 October 2016; IEEE: New York, NY, USA, 2016; pp. 1–7.

11. Kazemzadeh, M.R.A.; Crainic, T.G.; Gendron, B. *A Survey and Taxonomy of Multilayer Network Design*; CIRRELT, Centre interuniversitaire de recherche sur les réseaux d'entreprise, la logistique et le transport= Interuniversity Research Centre on Enterprise Networks, Logistics and Transportation: Montreal, QC, Canada, 2019.

12. Gomez, C.; Oller, J.; Paradells, J. Overview and evaluation of bluetooth low energy: An emerging low-power wireless technology. *Sensors* **2012**, *12*, 11734–11753. [CrossRef]

13. Ayoub, W.; Ellatif, S.A.; Fabienne, N.; Mohamad, M.; Christophe, P.J. Internet of mobile things: Overview of lorawan, dash7, and nb-iot in lpwans standards and supported mobility. *IEEE Commun. Surv. Tutor.* **2018**, *21*, 1561–1581. [CrossRef]

14. Alliance ZigBee. *ZigBee Specification*; ZigBee Standard Organization: Davis, CA, USA. 2005.

15. Lan/man Standards Committee. IEEE standard for local and metropolitan area networks-part 15.4: Low-rate wireless personal area networks (LR-WPANs). *IEEE Comput. Soc.* **2011**, doi: 10.1109/IEEESTD.2011.6012487. [CrossRef]

16. Kushalnagar, N.; Montenegro, G.; Schumacher, C. IPv6 over Low-Power Wireless Personal Area Networks (6LoWPANs): Overview, Assumptions, Problem Statement, and Goals, IETF RFC 4919, 2007. Available online: https://tools.ietf.org/html/rfc4919 (accessed on 25 May 2020).

17. Winter, T.; Tommaso, P.; Romano, F. RPL: IPv6 Routing Protocol for Low-Power and Lossy Networks. *rfc* **2012**, *6550*, 1–157.

18. PEÑA, Q.A.; Gia T.N.; Zou Z.; Tenhunen H.; Westerlund T. Comparative study of LPWAN technologies on unlicensed bands for M2M communication in the IoT: Beyond LoRa and LoRaWAN. *Procedia Comput. Sci.* **2019**, *155*, 43–350.

19. Subashini, S.; Venkateswari, R.; Mathiyalagan, P. A study on LoRaWAN for wireless sensor networks. In *Advances in Intelligent Systems and Computing*; Springer: Berlin, Germany, 2018.

20. Scheible, G.; Dzung, D.; Endresen, J.; Frey, J. E. Unplugged but connected - Design and implementation of a truly wireless real-time sensor/actuator interface. *IEEE Ind. Electron. Mag.* **2007**, *1*, 25–34. [CrossRef]

21. Chen. D.; Nixon, M.; Han, S.; Mok, A. K.; Zhu, X. WirelessHART and IEEE 802.15.4e. In Proceedings of the IEEE International Conference on Industrial Technology (ICIT), Busan, Korea, 26 February–1 March 2014; pp. 760–765.

22. Rezha, F.P.; Shin, S.Y. Performance analysis of ISA100.11a under interference from an IEEE 802.11b wireless network. *IEEE Trans. Ind. Inform.* **2014**, *10*, 919–927. [CrossRef]

23. Imran, M.A. *Wireless Automation as an Enabler for the Next Industrial Revolution*; Wiley-IEEE Press: Hoboken, NJ, USA, 2020.

24. Gast, M. *802.11 n: A Survival Guide*; O'Reilly Media, Inc.: Sebastopol, CA, USA, 2012.

25. Javed, I.; Iqbal, A, M.; AAwais, H.; Murad, K.; Affaq, Q.; Kijun, H. Comparison of spectral efficiency techniques in device-to-device communication for 5G. *IEEE Access* **2019**, *7* , 57440–57449.

26. Hrabcak, D.; Matis, M.; Dobos, L. The concept of adaptive routing in cognitive radio mobile ad-hoc network. In Proceedings of the 2018 28th International Conference Radioelektronika (RADIOELEKTRONIKA), Prague, Czech Republic, 19–20 April 2018; IEEE: New York, NY, USA, 2018; pp. 1–6.

27. IEEE 802.16 WORKING GROUP. IEEE standard for local and metropolitan area networks-part 16: Air interface for fixed broad-band wireless access systems. *IEEE Std 802.16-2004 (Revision of IEEE Std 802.16-2001)* **2004**, 1–857, doi: 10.1109/IEEESTD.2004.226664.

28. Marks, R.; Eklund, C.; Ponnuswamy, S.; Stanwood, K.L.; van Waes, N.J. *WirelessMAN: Inside the IEEE 802.16 Standard for Wireless Metropolitan Area Networks*; IEEE Press: Piscataway, NJ, USA, 2006.

29. SáNchez-GarcíA, J.; García-Campos, J. M.; Arzamendia, M.; Reina, D. G.; Toral, S. L.; Gregor, D. A survey on unmanned aerial and aquatic vehicle multi-hop networks: Wireless communications, evaluation tools and applications. *Comput. Commun.* **2018**, 43–65, doi:10.1016/j.comcom.2018.02.002. [CrossRef]

30. Bouaziz, M.; Rachedi, A. A survey on mobility management protocols in Wireless Sensor Networks based on 6LoWPAN technology. *Comput. Commun.* **2016**, *74*, 3–15. [CrossRef]

31. Wang, X.; Zhong, S.; Zhou, R. A mobility support scheme for 6LoWPAN. *Comput. Commun.* **2012**, *35*, 392–404. [CrossRef]

32. Saad, L.B.; Tourancheau, B. Sinks mobility strategy in IPv6-based WSNs for network lifetime improvement. In Proceedings of the 2011 4th IFIP International Conference on New Technologies, Mobility and Security, Paris, France, 7–10 February 2011; IEEE: New York, NY, USA, 2011; pp. 1–5.

33. Liu, Q.; Qin, H. Implementation and Improvement of DSR in Ipv6. *Procedia Eng.* **2012**, *29*, 716–720. [CrossRef]

34. Chadda, S.; Rai, M.K. A Novel Approach of Aodv for Stability and Energy Efficient Routing for Manet Using IPV6. *Int. J. Comput. Technol. Appl.* **2012**, *3*, 1071–1076.

35. Lamont, L.; Wang, M.; Villasenor, L.; Randhawa, T.; Hardy, R.; McConnel, P. An IPv6 and OLSR based architecture for integrating WLANs and MANETs to the Internet. In Proceedings of the 5th International Symposium on Wireless Personal Multimedia Communications, Honolulu, HI, USA, 27–30 October 2002; IEEE: New York, NY, USA, 2002; pp. 816–820.

36. Brida, P.; Cepel, P.; DúHa, J. Geometric algorithm for received signal strength based mobile positioning. *Radioengineering* **2005**, *14*, 1–7.

37. Gerla, M.; Tsai, J.T. Multicluster, mobile, multimedia radio network. *Wirel. Netw.* **1995**, *1*, 255–265. [CrossRef]

38. Loscri, V.; Natalizio, E.; Mitton, N. Performance evaluation of novel distributed coverage techniques for swarms of flying robots. In Proceedings of the 2014 IEEE Wireless Communications and Networking Conference (WCNC), Istanbul, Turkey, 6–9 April 2014; IEEE: New York, NY, USA, 2014; pp. 3278–3283.

39. Rasheed, M.R.; Khan, M. K.; Naseem, M.; Ajmal, A.; Hussain, I. M. Performance of routing protocols in WiMAX networks. *Int. J. Eng. Technol.* **2010**, *2*, 412. [CrossRef]

40. Ab Rahman, R.; Kassim, M.; Yahaya, C. K. H. C. K.; Ismail, M. Performance analysis of routing protocol in WiMAX network. In Proceedings of the 2011 IEEE International Conference on System Engineering and Technology, Shah Alam, Malaysia, 27–28 June 2011; IEEE: New York, NY, USA, 2011; pp. 153–157.

41. Azad, M.S.; Uddin, M. M.; Anwar, F.; Rahman, M. A. Performance evaluation of wireless routing protocols in mobile wimax environment. In Proceedings of the IAENG International Conference on Communication Systems and Applications, Hong Kong, China, 19–21 March 2008.

42. Pathak, S.; Kumar, B. Performance evaluation of routing protocols for sending healthcare data over WiMAX network. In Proceedings of the 2014 International Conference on Signal Processing and Integrated Networks (SPIN), Noida, India, 20–21 February 2014; IEEE: New York, NY, USA, 2014; pp. 269–274.

43. Hrabcak, D.; Matis, M.; Papaj, J. Students social based mobility model for MANET-DTN networks. *Mob. Inf. Syst.* **2017**, doi:10.1155/2017/2714595.

44. Chilamkurti, N.; Jabbar, S.; Minhas, A.A. Novel energy aware algorithm to design multilayer architecture for dense wireless sensor networks. In *Sensor Technology: Concepts, Methodologies, Tools, and Applications*; IGI Global: Hershey, PA, USA, 2020; pp. 372–399

45. Lipare, A.; Edla, D.R.; Dharavath, R. Energy Efficient Routing Structure to Avoid Energy Hole Problem in Multi-Layer Network Model. *Wirel. Pers. Commun.* **2020**, 1–22, doi:10.1007/s11277-020-07165-w. [CrossRef]

46. Kalaivanan, S. Quality of service (QoS) and priority aware models for energy efficient and demand routing procedure in mobile ad hoc networks. *J. Ambient. Intell. Humaniz. Comput.* **2020**, 1–8, doi:10.1007/s12652-020-01769-7. [CrossRef]

47. Chiaraviglio, L.; d'Andreagiovanni, F.; Liu, W.; Gutierrez, J.; Blefari-Melazzi, N.; Choo, K. K. R.; Alouini, M. S. Multi-Area Throughput and Energy Optimization of UAV-aided Cellular Networks Powered by Solar Panels and Grid. *IEEE Trans. Mob. Comput.* **2020**, doi:10.1109/TMC.2020.2980834. [CrossRef]

48. Trotta, A.; Andreagiovanni, F. D.; Di Felice, M.; Natalizio, E.; Chowdhury, K. R. When UAVs ride a bus: Towards energy-efficient city-scale video surveillance. In Proceedings of the IEEE Infocom 2018-IEEE Conference on Computer Communications, Honolulu, HI, USA, 16–19 April 2018; IEEE: New York, NY, USA, 2018; pp. 1043–1051.

49. Kizza, J.M. Security in Sensor Networks. In *Guide to Computer Network Security. Computer Communications and Networks*; Springer: Berlin/Heidelberg, Germany, 2017.

50. Sarika, S.; Pravin, A.; Vijayakumar, A.; Selvamani, K. Security issues in mobile ad hoc networks. *Procedia Comput. Sci.* **2016**, *92*, 329–335. [CrossRef]

51. Ahn, T.; Seok, J.; Lee, I.; Han, J. Reliable Flying IoT Networks for UAV Disaster Rescue Operations. *Mob. Inf. Syst.* **2018**, 1–12, doi:10.1155/2018/2572460. [CrossRef]

52. Tawalbeh, L.; Muheidat, F.; Tawalbeh, M.; Quwaider, M. IoT Privacy and Security: Challenges and Solutions. *Appl. Sci.* **2020**, *10*, 4102. [CrossRef]

Article

A Smart IoT System for Detecting the Position of a Lying Person Using a Novel Textile Pressure Sensor

Robert Hudec, Slavomír Matúška, Patrik Kamencay * and Miroslav Benco

Faculty of Electrical Engineering and Information Technology, University of Zilina, 01026 Zilina, Slovakia; robert.hudec@uniza.sk (R.H.); slavomir.matuska@uniza.sk (S.M.); miroslav.benco@uniza.sk (M.B.)
* Correspondence: patrik.kamencay@uniza.sk; Tel.: +421-41-513-2225

Abstract: Bedsores are one of the severe problems which could affect a long-term lying subject in the hospitals or the hospice. To prevent lying bedsores, we present a smart Internet of Things (IoT) system for detecting the position of a lying person using novel textile pressure sensors. To build such a system, it is necessary to use different technologies and techniques. We used sixty-four of our novel textile pressure sensors based on electrically conductive yarn and the Velostat to collect the information about the pressure distribution of the lying person. Using Message Queuing Telemetry Transport (MQTT) protocol and Arduino-based hardware, we send measured data to the server. On the server side, there is a Node-RED application responsible for data collection, evaluation, and provisioning. We are using a neural network to classify the subject lying posture on the separate device because of the computation complexity. We created the challenging dataset from the observation of twenty-one people in four lying positions. We achieved a best classification precision of 92% for fourth class (right side posture type). On the other hand, the best recall (91%) for first class (supine posture type) was obtained. The best F1 score (84%) was achieved for first class (supine posture type). After the classification, we send the information to the staff desktop application. The application reminds employees when it is necessary to change the lying position of individual subjects and thus prevent bedsores.

Keywords: smart sensor; IoT system; Velostat; pressure sensor; convolutional neural network; data classification; position detection

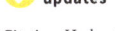

check for updates

Citation: Hudec, R.; Matúška, S.; Kamencay, P.; Benco, M. A Smart IoT System for Detecting the Position of a Lying Person Using a Novel Textile Pressure Sensor. *Sensors* **2021**, *21*, 206 . https://doi.org/10.3390/s21010206

Received: 4 December 2020
Accepted: 27 December 2020
Published: 31 December 2020

Publisher's Note: MDPI stays neutral with regard to jurisdictional claims in published maps and institutional affiliations.

1. Introduction

The expected population development shows that the process of population aging will intensify in the coming years and will deepen long into the future. Therefore, one of the state authorities' priorities is the aging of the population and the quality of their life. This priority is focusing on the health insurance of older fellow citizens, including assistance in the field of social security. A lot of elderly people rely on the help of either their family members or the hospice employees. Many of them are long-term lying subjects for health reasons. There is a significant risk of bedsores in long-term lying subjects. This risk is also present in patients hospitalized for a long time. The problems described above are the primary motivation for this article. To prevent lying bedsores, we have designed a smart IoT system for detecting the position of a lying person using novel textile pressure sensors. The proposed system is intended to help hospital and hospice staff, but also family members who take care of a person in the prevention of lying bedsores. Sixty-four novel textile pressure sensors placed on the mattress toppers provide us with information about the position of the lying subject. We transfer this information to the cloud, evaluate it, and then display it on a desktop application. The application reminds employees when it is necessary to change the lying position of individual subjects and thus prevent bedsores.

There are several papers published with a similar topic to our proposed complex solution. Authors in [1] presented a complex system based on an artificial neural network for in-bed posture classification. Unlike our solution, they used the commercially available pressure sensor mattress. The mattress consists of a 2.5 mm-thick bedsheet containing a matrix of 64 × 27 textile made piezo-resistive pressure sensors. They carried out the experiments on 12 healthy adults using histogram of gradients and local binary patterns feature extraction and feed-forward artificial neural network as a classification method. The method classifies the lying posture into one of the four postures (supine, prone, left, and right lateral side). They achieved accuracy at 97.9%. As the authors stated in the conclusion, their presented work did not offer a comprehensive solution to the problem. It presents a potential technique to make a fundamental step towards prevention.

Authors in [2–4] proposed the solution based on their own version of the bedsheet-sensing element. Hong [2], in his research article, presents a smart care bed for elderly patients. The smart bed features several pressure sensors FSR 408 and FSR 406. Their primary motivation was to prevent falls and bedsores. As the final implementation, he presented a real-time pressure-sensing algorithm capable of deciding on the possibilities of bedsores and falling accidents by considering both the intensity and the duration of the pressure of specific body parts. Abdelmoghith et al. [3] provide a solution that reduces the possibility of developing bedsores for long-term patients. They created an IoT-based healthcare monitoring system based on their prototype of a mattress. They used FSR 406 pressure sensors for body pressure distribution and DHT11 for temperature measurement. The proposed system did not classify the lying person's posture but only monitored the subject's mobility. The system provides crucial information using a mobile application based on the collected data. Authors in [4] also use the sensors from the FSR family to determine the pressure distribution of the lying person. They demonstrated the concept of a pressure sensing/monitoring system for pressure ulcer prevention. They equipped the bedsheet with 16 sensors and measured their resistance using an Arduino-based board. However, they did not solve the problem of laying person posture classification and provide only the concept of smart bedsheet.

The findings presented in [5] offer another approach to preventing bedsores. They used wearable computing and a deep learning approach to pressure ulcer prevention. To get the information about the lying person, they used a non-invasive system of wearable sensors based on inertial sensor. They can estimate the positions of the patients, and send an alert signal when the subject remains in the same position for too long a period. The disadvantage of this solution is that the lying person has to wear the same piece of electronic equipment. Authors in [6] propose a similar solution. They used a comprehensive approach for designing a sensor system that uses a single accelerometer along with machine learning algorithms for in-bed lying posture classification. They evaluated nine different accelerometer positions on the human body and they achieved the best F1 scores at 97.8% in lying postures detection.

In the papers mentioned above, authors use commercially available pressure sensors in their prototypes or accelerometer to get information about the lying person. On the other hand, the works presented in [7–9] propose the solution for pressure distribution measurement based on their own sensors. For instance, Saenz-Cogollo et al. [7] present a pressure mapping mat for tele-home care applications. They developed a mat-like pressure mapping system based on a single layer textile sensor. The sensor is fabricated by embroidering silver-coated yarns on a piece of light cotton fabric and creating pressure-sensitive resistive elements by stamping the conductive polymer at the crossing points of conductive stitches. The mat consists of an array of 32 × 32 sensing elements. They demonstrated the functionality and performance by comparing the proposed mat with the commercial pressure platform. Li et al. [8] present a low-cost textile smart map for step pressure sensing based on multiple layer structure with polyester textile, conductive copper taffeta, and Velostat. The matrix of sensors consists of 8 × 10 sensing points. They used an Arduino-based board for transferring the measured data into the personal computer for evaluation and visualization. The study presented in [9] describes a low-cost smart portable sitting mat that can measure the sitting plantar pressure distribution in real-time. The smart mat consists of 576 pressure-sensing elements made by a low-cost E-Textile. The presented solution uses voltage feedback non-scanning electrode to eliminate the cross-talk effect between the sensing elements. The primary goal of the presented work is the creation of a low-cost and effective sensing pressure mat.

Our system relies on novel textile pressure sensors based on electrically conductive yarn and the Velostat. Suprapto et al., in their study [10], also rely on the Velostat-based pressure sensors. They presented a characteristic of a 32 × 32 sensor matrix for foot pressure distribution measurements. The single proposed sensor is constructed from dual electrodes placed on the top and underneath Velostat as the sensing material with a size of 7 × 7 mm. Based on their findings, the proposed sensor shows a relatively linear force–conductance response. A similar sensor design is presented by the authors in [11]. Their sensor is an easy-to-build textile pressure sensor created from low-cost conventional anti-static sheets and conductive woven fabrics. The sensor consists of three layers, the top conductive layer, the middle low-density polyethylene with a carbon sheet, and the bottom conductive layer. The size of the sensor is approximately 23 × 23 mm. From the evaluated characteristics, they concluded that the proposed design is suitable for didactic, healthcare, and lifestyle applications. Authors in [12,13] also described Velostat-based pressure sensors; moreover, the sensor design pattern is the same. The sensor consists of three layers, where the Velostat is in the middle. Tihak and Boskovic [14] carried out the experiments demonstrating the development of pressure sensor using Velostat. They presented typical problems and also discussed the causes and possible remedies. Lin and Seet [15] present an improved design of a textile pressure sensor. The sensor is constructed of conductive yarns and a dual-layer piezoresistive polymer (Velostat) as the sensing material. The sensor size is 10 × 10 mm. The proposed sensor can detect the load up to 1000 kPa with a relatively linear response.

The structure of our paper is as follows. The next chapter describes the IoT system proposal in detail, the novel textile pressure sensors development, hardware development, and whole topper production. Software descriptions follow next. We will give a view of how communications work between the system parts and will describe the Node-RED and desktop applications. Then, we will present the neural network used for lying posture classification and achieved results from our experiments. The discussion and conclusion section are at the end of our paper.

2. IoT System Proposal

Our primary goal was to create a smart IoT-based system for the detection of the position of a laying person in bed. The system should help staff who take care of long-term lying persons. The main task is to warn the staff that the person is lying in one position for a long time and it is necessary to change the lying person's position. In this way, it is possible to prevent unwanted bedsores. Figure 1 shows the proposal for the system concept.

The system consists of one or more Arduino-based hardware solutions with attached pressure sensors on the mattress topper, the server, computation development board, and software application on the personal computer (PC). For every bed, 64 novel sensors detect the pressure distribution. Because the bed is usually placed in the same place, the hardware solution runs from the electrical network and does not need a battery power source. The network-attached storage from QNAP holds the server solution. It features the Message Queuing Telemetry Transport (MQTT) broker for communication, Node-RED for the logic, and Mongo database for data storage. For the position classification, we use the neural network. The neural network needs a lot of computation power. Because of this requirement, computation runs on a separate device.

In our case, it is the Nvidia Jetson TX2 development board. On the PC runs a Qt-based desktop application where the user interacts with the system. The communication flow is as follows:

- Arduino collects and sends pressure distribution to the server.
- Server receives and stores the data. Then the server requests the development board for data evaluation.
- The user gets all information from the server in the desktop application on the PC.

We will provide detailed information about the individual parts of our solution in the next sections.

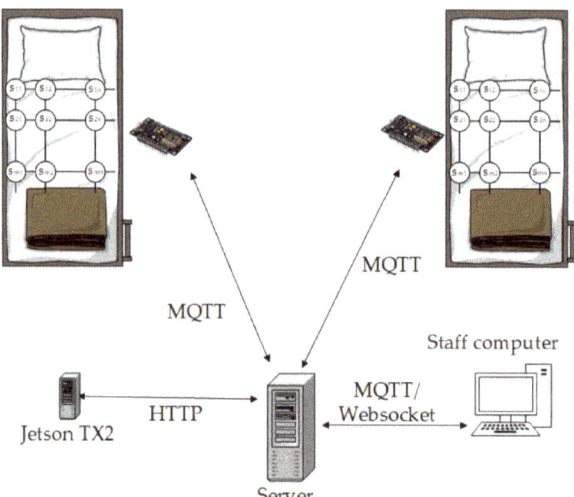

Figure 1. A smart IoT-based system concept proposal.

2.1. Sensor Design

The overall design of an intelligent topper should meet several requirements that are critical to its conventional use. One of the main requirements for long-term use is the application of an electrically conductive thread, which is not significantly damaged by abrasion and common detergents. Other relevant parameters are simple industrial production, low consumption of electrically conductive textile materials, the comfort of a person lying on a bed, or resistance of the conductive paths of the mattress to mechanical damage or tearing. In our designs and experiments, we tested three electroconductive yarns. Figure 2a shows two 50 mm copper wires with a silver coating blended with polyester yarns. Figure 2b illustrates the Elitex yarn based on polyamide yarns by a chemical silver coating. Figure 2c shows the third yarn, 3 ltex yarn based on two blended multifilaments of polyamide yarns by chemical silver coating with antioxidant treatment.

Based on our experiences with sewing electroconductive patterns, we chose the 3 eltex yarn with antioxidant treatment. Its core consists of polyamide coated by pure silver with a fineness of 278 dtex and surface electrical resistance of 260 Ω/m. The yarns based on the two blended 50 μm Cu/Ag wire with polyester yarns are uncomfortable for humans. Similarly, the Elitex yarn is not suitable for long-time use. The reason is the peeling of the silver layer from the surface of the fiber during washing and subsequent mechanical stress. The selected yarn is gentle on the human skin, it is more resistant to the oxidation process, and it has better embroidery properties. Our motivation was to choose a yarn that will be suitable for sewing with embroidery machines, and the design pattern will be strong enough and reliable even in cases of an extreme load, and also resistant to ordinary.

The primary sensor design was based on the change of resistance or capacitance principle. Moreover, electrodes will be embroidered in one step, fully textile, and fabricated on one or two textile layers. Following these conditions, we have developed and fabricated more than 30 designs. We focused on determining the influence of various factors that affect the production process or the overall parameters of the sensor. These include, for example, the stitch type and the number of yarn cross-connections, the type, and construction of electroconductive yarn, embroidering speed, and continuity of seeding with minimizing the number of yarn cuts, time and temperature of ironing. Figure 3 shows relevant milestone designs. The sensor abbreviation is explained in the following Table 1.

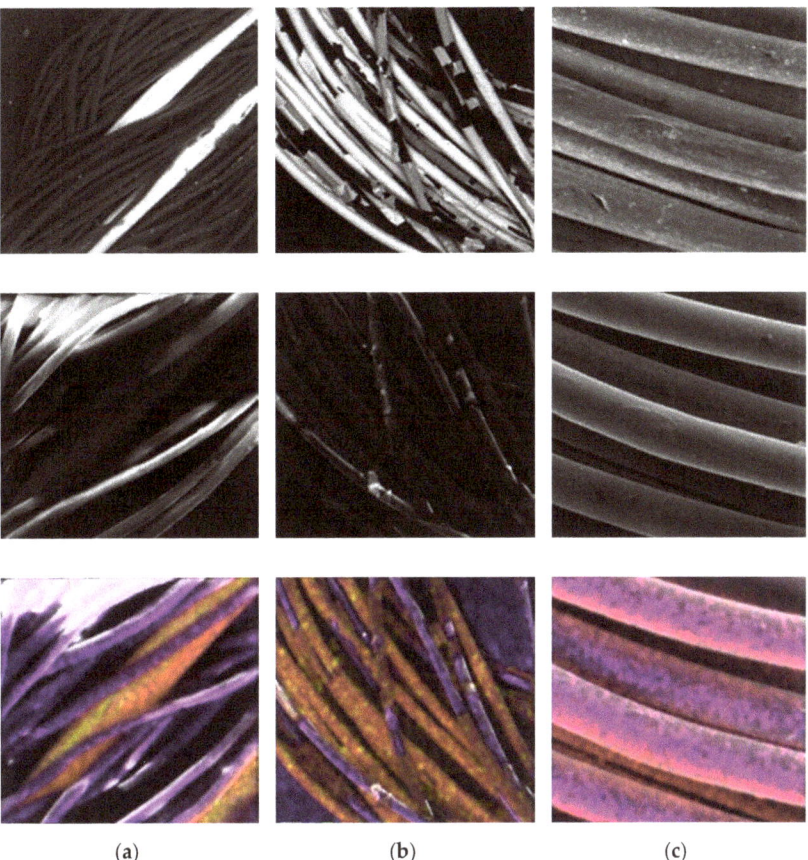

(a)   (b)   (c)

Figure 2. Electroconductive yarns with chemical analysis. (**a**) Two 50 mm Cu/Ag wires blended with polyester yarns; (**b**) Elitex yarn; (**c**) 3 ltex yarn with antioxidant treatment.

The sensing place at the topper covers approximately 0.7 m^2. This is an area where a person lies with an average figure and a weight of 90 kg. The sensing surface on which a person lies is defined by his/her shoulders and buttocks. Moreover, this part of a person's body accounts for about 60 percent of a person's total weight with an average load of approximately 7 g/cm^2. In experiments, we used a load weight of 11.5 kg to simulate the pressure of the human body. The load is placed on the sensor through a dielectric plate with a size of 40 × 40 mm which reaches a pressure equivalent to 100 times the human load (718 g/cm^2). It simulates extreme human strain and sensor resistance when a person is moving on a mattress. The goal is to achieve a change in measured values by at least two orders of magnitude with the lowest possible consumption of electrically conductive yarn. Table 2 presents the sensor's details and measured values. We used Velostat as the middle layer between the top and bottom electrodes in the sensor design. Velostat is a piezo-resistive material with high volume resistivity (<500/cm) and a thickness of only 200 microns. The Velostat is pressure sensitive, so squeezing it will reduce the resistance.

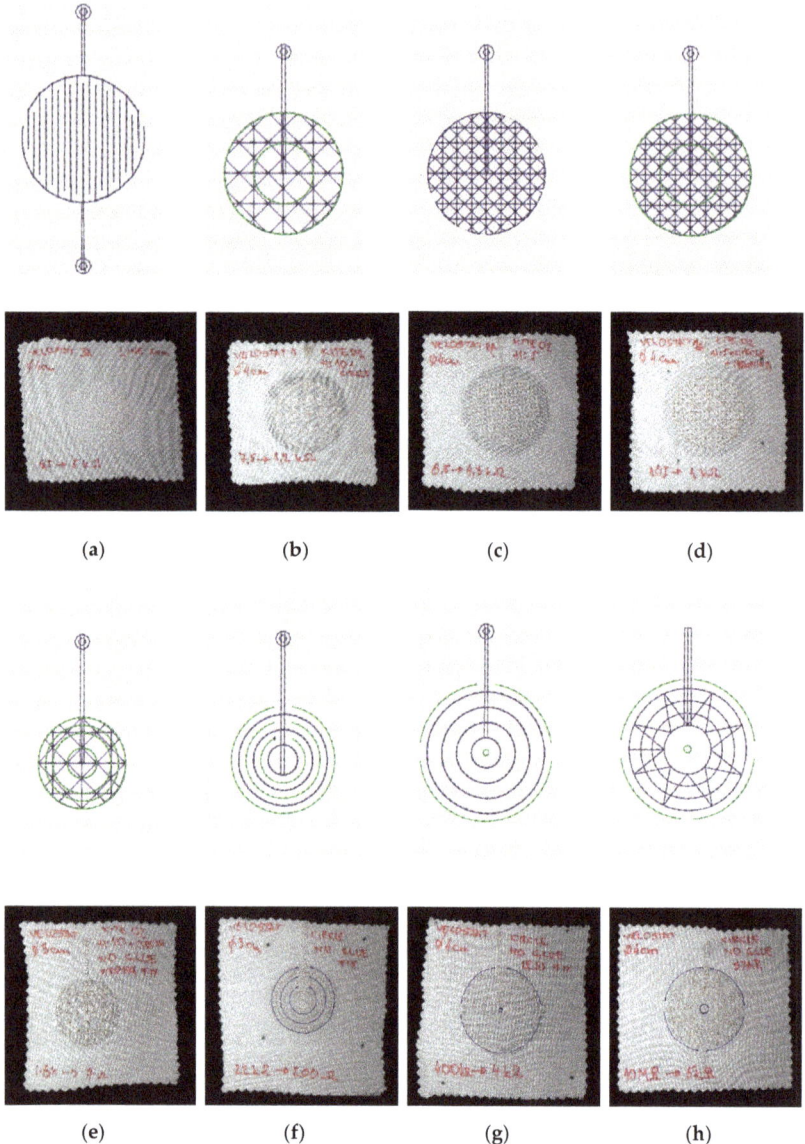

Figure 3. Sensing node designs in Wilcom DecoStudio and their fabrications. (**a**) PC2D; (**b**) PC3H; (**c**) PC3I; (**d**) PC3J; (**e**) PC3K; (**f**) PR4A; (**g**) PR4B; (**h**) PR4C.

Table 1. The definition of the sensor's abbreviations.

Abbreviation	Definition
P	Physical quantity, P—pressure
R	Measuring principle, R—resistance, C—capacitance
4	Generation, 1,2,3,4
B	Version, A,B … L

Table 2. Description of sensing node design based on the resistivity.

Mark	Description	Layers	Physical Quantity	Fixation	Uncompressed	Compressed
PC2D	ϕ 40 mm, stitch pattern: line	2	Capacity mode Resistivity mode with Velostat	Glue	5.5 pF 6.5 kΩ	10.0 pF 5.0 kΩ
PC3H	ϕ 40 mm, stitch pattern: kite	3	Resistivity mode with Velostat	Glue	7.5 kΩ	1.2 kΩ
PC3I	ϕ 40 mm, stitch pattern: kite soft ironing	3	Resistivity mode with Velostat	Glue	8.5 kΩ	4.3 kΩ
PC3J	ϕ 40 mm, stitch pattern: kite hard ironing	3	Resistivity mode with Velostat	Glue	105 kΩ	1.0 kΩ
PC3K	ϕ 30 mm, stitch pattern: kite strong fixation	3	Resistivity mode with Velostat	Glue	1.6 kΩ	7.0 Ω
PR4A	ϕ 30 mm, stitch pattern: line soft fixation	3	Resistivity mode with Velostat	Stitch	22.0 kΩ	200.0 Ω
PR4B	ϕ 40 mm, stitch pattern: line less fixation	3	Resistivity mode with Velostat	Stitch	400.0 kΩ	4.0 kΩ
PR4C	ϕ 40 mm, stitch pattern: line less fixation	3	Resistivity mode with Velostat	Stitch	10.0 MΩ	5.0 kΩ

As it can be seen in Figure 4a, the design marked as PR4C achieved the highest change in resistance. Figure 4b illustrates the top and transversal view of the best design.

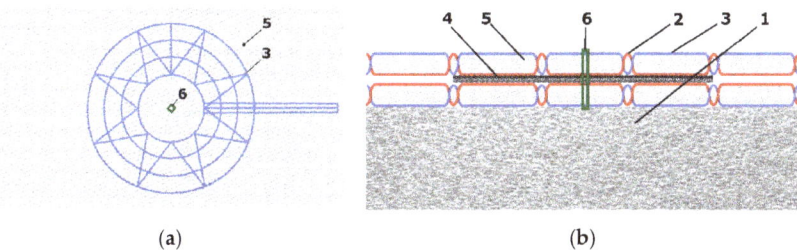

Figure 4. Measuring node realized by PR4C design. (**a**) Top view; (**b**) transversal view: (1) polyurethane foam, (2) electrically conductive yarn, (3) nonconductive yarn, (4) Velostat foil, (5) base fabric, (6) fixation with nonconductive yarn.

The developed primary sensor or sensing node of the intelligent topper should have the simplest design possible because it is a challenge to embroider a big sensor area. It will be used as a part of a sensing matrix of eight-by-eight sensing nodes, which should be sufficient to classify the person's sleep posture and to detect his/her activity during the night.

2.2. Hardware Design

We described the pressure sensor in previous part. Now it is necessary to design hardware solutions to measure, collect, and send the data to the server. In our design, we used a NodeMcu microcontroller. The NodeMcu is an Arduino-based board where the central processor is ESP8266. The communication via Wi-Fi with the server is also provided by this processor. The main advantage of this board is that it can be directly connected to the Wi-Fi and processing the data from sensors at the same time from one source code. The board features 16 general-purpose input–output pins and one analog input. In the hardware design, we followed the findings presented in [10–12]. We developed an electronic setup, which can measure each sensor pressure in the matrix of sensors using multiplexers. Figure 5 shows the proposed schematic.

Each sensor in the matrix of sensors is represented by its resistance R_s in parallel with a parasitic capacitance C_p. R_{top} and R_{bottom} represent the yarn resistance. While our proposed novel sensor decreases the resistance with the applied pressure, we adjust the sensor sensing ability by adding R_2 resistance in the front of trans-impedance amplifiers. NodeMCU manages the Mux1 and Mux2 to select a particular sensor sequentially, where Mux1 is responsible for selecting the column in the matrix and Mux2 for the row. We use the resistance R_{drain} to reduce the effect of C_p by referring the non-active columns to the ground. To minimize the cross-talk between rows of the matrix, we added the trans-impedance amplifiers for each row. Usage of the trans-impedance amplifiers allows us to measure voltage Vsignal that is inversely proportional to the measuring sensor resistance.

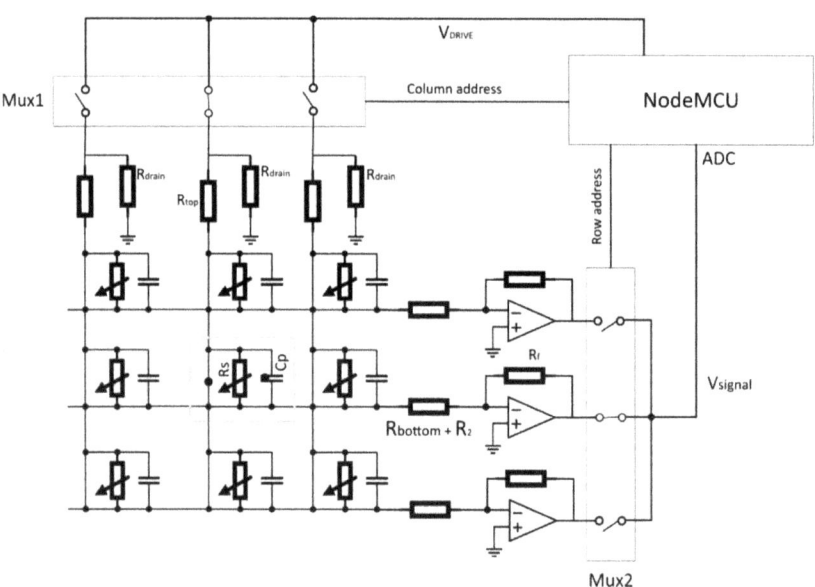

Figure 5. Schematic of the hardware solution based on multiplexers, the trans-impedance amplifiers, and NodeMCU board.

The Figure 6 illustrates the source code flowchart diagram. The diagram starts with the initialization of all the necessary components. Then, the general input/output pins and communication peripheries enter the default state. Using provided Wi-Fi credentials, the NodeMcu connects to the Wi-Fi network. If the connection to the network fails, the system waits for 5 s and then repeats this operation until the successful login. The next step is a connection to the MQTT broker using pre-defined credentials. The MQTT protocol communication is provided by an external library—Adafruit MQTT Library ESP8266. To establish the MQTT connection, we need the client instance of the class Adafruit_MQTT_Client. The client connects to the MQTT broker. We have to create an additional object for receiving the responses from the broker. The instance of the class Adafruit_MQTT_Subscribe provides such an interface. An Adafruit_MQTT_Publish class provides the application programming interface (API) for sending data. After a successful connection, the object from Adafruit_MQTT_Subscribe class fetches the data from the MQTT broker using the channel identifier for reading commands. On the server side, the MQTT broker resends the commands from the desktop application on the PC. The valid commands are to start and stop the measurements. The measurement is performed in cycles every 1 s. We are using two analog multiplexers to select the particular sensor in the matrix of sensors on the output and input side.

The first multiplexer sets the output voltage on a specific output and similarly, the second multiplexer sets the specific input, which transfers the signal to the NodeMcu. On the NodeMcu, we are measuring the signal amplitude using an analog input pin. The signal amplitude increases with the dropping resistance. After finishing the measurement of the signals, NodeMcu initiates sequential data sending to the server. It is necessary to send data sequentially because of the processor ram limitation. The data are sent in JavaScript Object Notation (JSON) format using Adafruit_MQTT_Publish object.

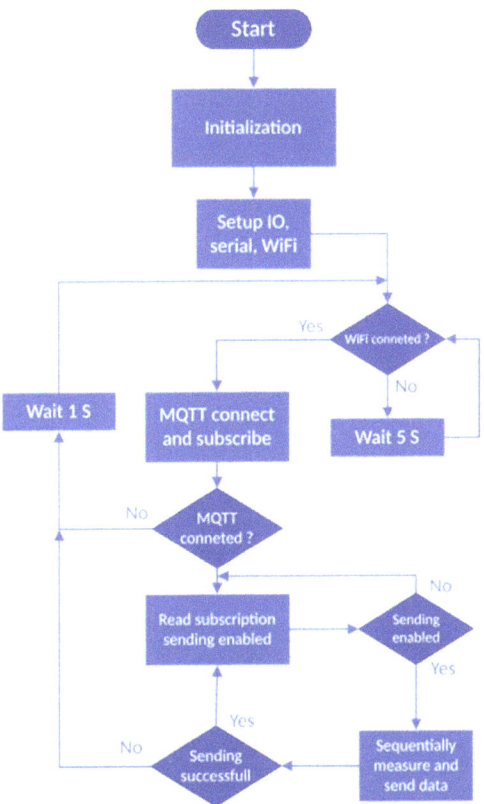

Figure 6. NodeMcu source code flowchart for pressure data acquisition and sending to the server.

2.3. Topper Design and Production

Based on realized experiments mentioned in Section 2.1, we decided to use the pressure sensor with Velostat foil. The overall topper's design consists of a partial pressure sensor creating a structure of eight by eight sensing nodes. We set the sensor diameter to 40 mm with 100 mm distances in horizontal and vertical axes. Figure 7 shows the sensor design for both layers.

The fabrication of the sensor starts by drawing a mesh of eight by eight dots on the base fabric. They mark the center of each sensing point. It is necessary because the overall sensor is too big to fabricate at one step and the material of the base fabric is a little bit elastic. Moreover, the precise final composition of both layers relative to one sensor at all 64 nodes is difficult to manufacture. We embroidered the partial sensors in the marked positions. In our prototype, we used the nonconductive viscose-based yarn for upper embroidery and silver-coated polyamide yarn as bottom embroidering filaments. After that, the rest of the connecting lines and connectors were embroidered too. It is a fact, that topper will be placed on the standard PolyURethane (PUR) foam mattress. From this point of view, the sensor prototype should be massive with a robust design able to resist a crackdown of the electroconductive yarns when a human is moving over the bed. For this reason, we secured the connections between sensor nodes by triple stitching. Figure 8 illustrates the fabrication of the sensor's layers.

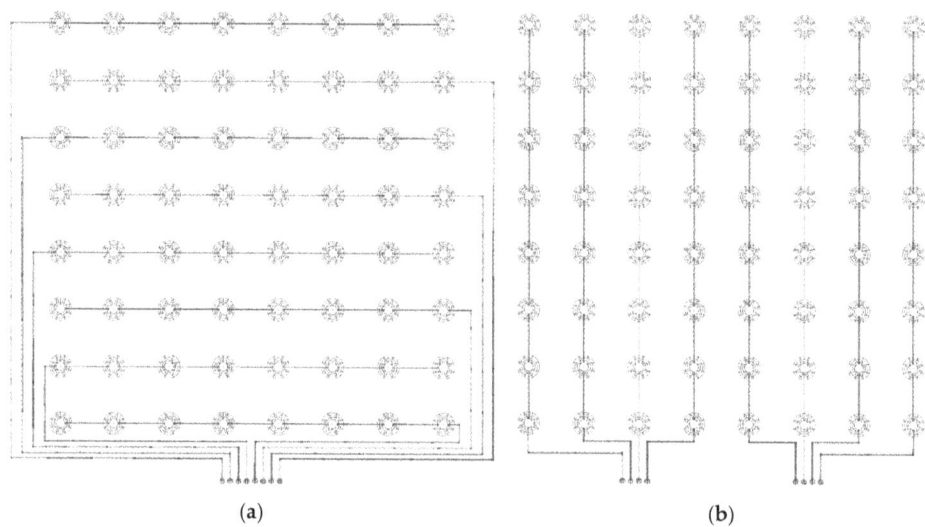

(a)   (b)

Figure 7. Final topper's pressure matrix design with eight by eight sensing nodes. (**a**) Top layer; (**b**) bottom layer.

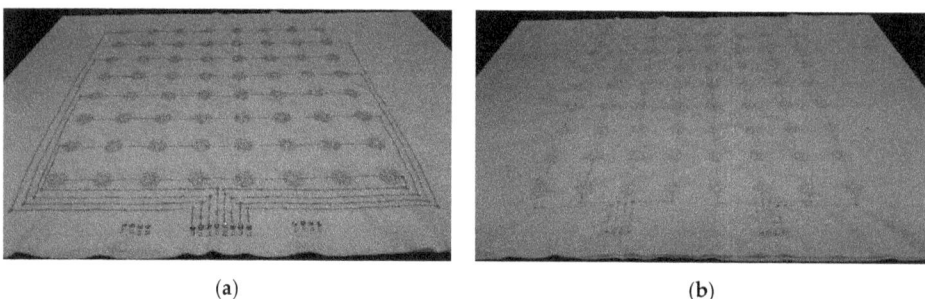

(a)   (b)

Figure 8. Embroidered patterns. (**a**) Top layer; (**b**) bottom layer.

As the next step, we inserted circle Velostat foils between the fabricated layers in the positions of the sensors. Using the embroidery machine, we fixed both layers of the sensors. Finally, we stabilized the sensor matrix and applied it to the polyurethane foam. Figure 9 illustrates the final smart topper with our novel sensors.

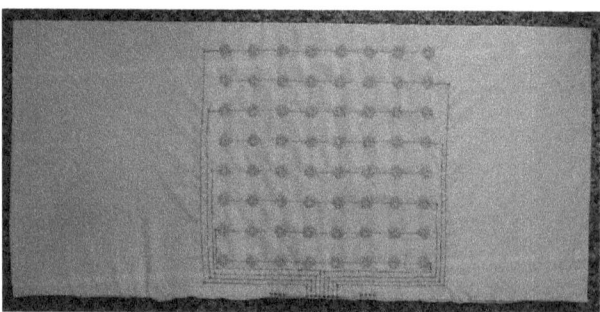

Figure 9. Final topper production applied on 40 mm polyurethane foam.

The topper was created as a liner of polyurethane foam for a standard mattress of 2000 mm by 900 mm dimension. We chose to experimentally position it on the topper's base fabric. The upper limit of the sensor location was determined by the shoulder position and its value was 550 mm from the edge of the topper. Likewise, the lower limit is determined by the buttocks at a distance of 1250 mm. The place between the shoulders and buttocks represents the dominant body footprint of a person.

Overall topper design was composed by Wilcom DecoStudio software, that produces a digital embroidery pattern of stitches. Both patterns have been stored on a PC hard drive as a file with EMB (Embroidery format) extension and DST (Data Stitch Tajima) for a programmable embroidery machine. Further, they were embroidered by Barudan BEXT-S1501CII separately.

2.4. IoT System Design

The central unit of our IoT system is the NAS from QNAP [16,17]. This unit runs programs and server services that provide connectivity, management, data storage, and communication between the system peripheries. Two primary services are running on the server:

- QIoT suite.
- Mongo DB [18,19].

The QIoT suite is an application, which could be installed directly from the application center on NAS. QIoT suite is a complete and practical IoT private cloud platform for building and managing IoT applications. It integrates different services, which are necessary to provide a complex solution in the IoT world, into one application. The QIoT suite leverages popular tools like the MQTT broker [17,20], Node-RED, Freeboard, and supports multiple protocols and dashboards. MongoDB is a popular, general-purpose, document-based, distributed database, which is common in a cloud solution and IoT world. We use MongoDB for data storage and provision. Figure 10 shows the flowchart of the system data flow.

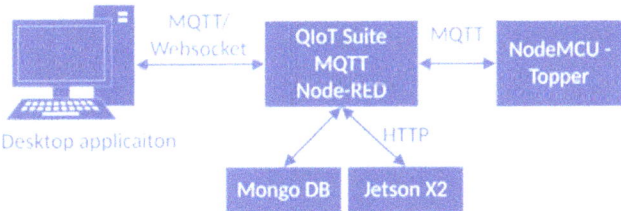

Figure 10. The system communication data flow between system components.

The primary data flow is as follows:

1. NodeMCU sends the measured data from the sensors to the QIoT using the MQTT protocol. On the QIot side, we are using Node-RED for data processing.
2. QIot receives the data, stores them to MongoDB, and issues the HTTP query to the Jetson X2 for data classification.
3. After the classification, QIot updates the record in the database with classified posture and sends the data to the desktop application.
4. The staff gets the current lying posture and other information.

2.4.1. Node-RED Application

The Node-RED application implements the logic part of the IoT system for detecting the position of a lying person using the private cloud platform. In our solution, we used two primary flows with the deployed application:

- A data processing flow.

- A command processing flow.

Figure 11 shows the command processing flow. HTTP request–response communication model implements the command processing in our solution. The flow starts with the input HTTP node. There is one compulsory argument in the HTTP request—command type.

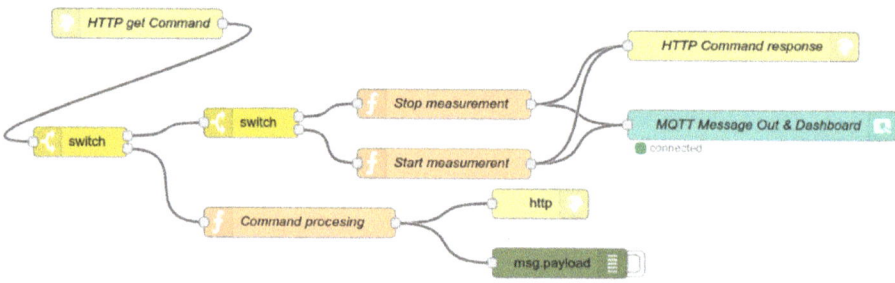

Figure 11. The Node-RED command processing flow for things based on HTTP request–response communication model.

There are two valid values for command type, controlSending, and manageStorage. Use controlSending type to start or stop sending data from the topper. In this scenario, function Start measurement and Stop measurement prepares the command message and Qbroker out node sends the message to the topper. The arguments from the HTTP request appear in Node-RED as a JSON object. An example of such a JSON command is:

{
"type":"controlSending",
"cmd":"1"
}

The manageStorage type serves as an API point during the experimental measurements and data acquisition for training and testing neural networks. We will describe this command type later in the section Data Acquisition. The Figure 12 illustrates the data processing flow.

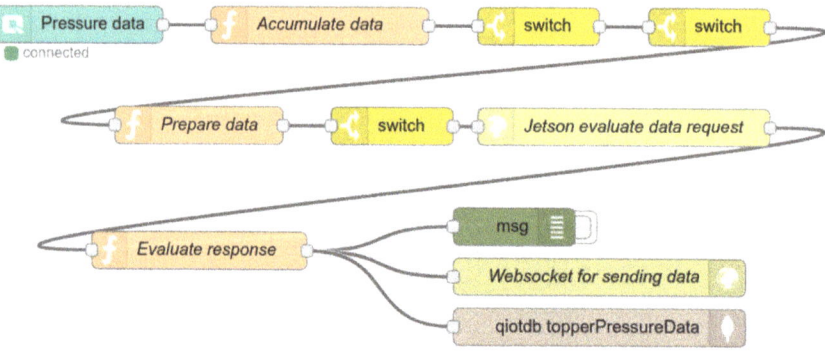

Figure 12. The Node-RED data processing flow for data collection, evaluation, propagation, and storage.

The flow starts with Qbroker in node. This input node listens on the topic "pressure-Data." The purpose of this flow is to collect, evaluate, and propagate the topper pressure data. The example of receiving data on the node is:

```
"payload": {
"row":4,
"data": ["52.00","52.00","86.00","122.00","132.00","113.00","32.00","38.00"]
}
```

Because of the NodeMCU ram limitation, we have to send the measured data in sequences. Therefore we need eight messages to send data from one measurement. One message contains the pressure data from one row in the matrix of sensors. The row tag indicates the row position. The function Accumulate data serves as a buffer function for one measurement. The IP network could cause different delays and therefore function task is to check the row order, sort the data if necessary, and prepare data from one measurement for later evaluation. The next two switch blocks inspect the data format and integrity. The next block is the Prepare data function. The function checks the topper state and prepares the data for the evaluation in the neural network. Afterward, the switch block validates the topper state. HTTP request–response block sends the data for evaluation in JSON format as a parameter in the HTTP request to the Jetson module. Data looks like:

```
payload: {
timestamp: 1605683032,
subjectID: "subjet12",
notes: "",
data: [
[7, 8, 12, 12, 20, 123, 0, 0],
[8, 10, 27, 21, 28, 26, 0, 0],
[2, 9, 6, 8, 12, 8, 0, 0],
[6, 11, 11, 16, 22, 13, 3, 0],
[19, 32, 39, 95, 103, 66, 8, 0],
[13, 16, 16, 28, 51, 24, 1, 0],
[18, 20, 24, 47, 82, 40, 6, 0],
[0, 0, 4, 10, 12, 6, 0, 0],
],
request: "evaluate"
}
```

After the evaluation in the Jetson module, the next function processes the HTTP response and sends information to the desktop application using web-socket and store all data to the database.

2.4.2. Data Provisioning in Neural Network Training

There is one more flow in our application. This flow serves as an API point for neural network training purposes. The Figure 13 shows this flow.

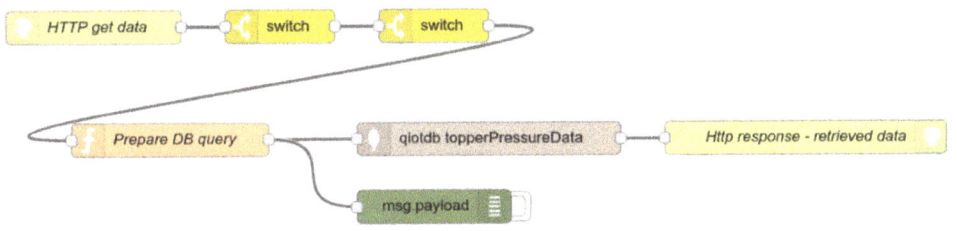

Figure 13. The Node-RED flow providing the application programming interface (API) for neural network based on HTTP request–response communication model.

The flow starts with HTTP in node, where there are two compulsory parameters in the HTTP request, the pose identification, and request type. Based on the request tag, the function block Prepare DB query prepares the query for getting the data from the database. There are two valid request types, training, and testing. For training purposes, 70% of the data are used for one pose. The rest (30%) use the neural network for testing. The HTTP out node response contains all valid data from databases in JSON format.

2.4.3. Desktop Application

We created a desktop application for the operating staff using the Qt framework. Figure 14 illustrates a primary application screen.

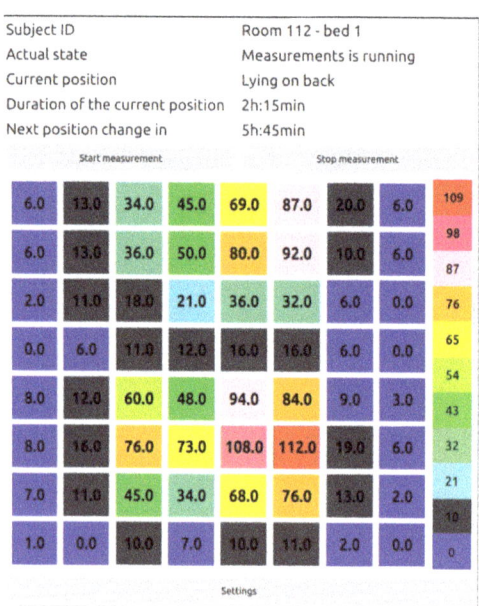

Figure 14. Desktop application for informing the staff about the subject identification, current state, current position, duration of the current position, and time to the next position change.

The application is using HTTP request–response model to send commands to start or stop measurements. Actual data like subject identification, current state, current position, duration of the current position, and time to the next position change give the staff the information about the subject lying on the smart topper. There is also a graphical representation of the current state of the lying subject. The red color represents the maximal pressure, while the blue color represents minimal or non-pressure on a particular sensor in the matrix of sensors. The displayed value represents the pressure in numerical form. This number goes from 0 to 140. The 0 value describes the state when there is no pressure applied to the sensor. The value of 140 represents the maximum load, which the sensor is capable of measuring.

3. Experimental Results

We will present the obtained experimental results in this section. First, we will provide the results from the single sensor resistive response measurements. Then, we will describe the data acquisition for training purposes. In the end, we will provide the results for lying posture detection using a Convolutional Neural Network (CNN) [21,22].

3.1. Single Sensor Resistive Response Measurements

We performed the resistive response of a single-sensor element to a load of 10 N over 200 cycles. We measured the sensor resistance every 100 ms. Figure 15a illustrates the obtained response. There is a little variability in zero load resistance and also with the applied load. The minimum measured resistance during the response measurements was 1.5 kΩ, but with more applied force, the resistance goes down to 300 Ω, and this value is stable. The zero-load variability makes no difference in our system. The proposed hardware solution is most sensitive in the range of 10 kΩ, more precisely from 22 to 32 kΩ. Therefore, small variation in a range more than 32 kΩ does not affect the system. This was the reason why we added a 22 kΩ resistor in the front of trans-impedance amplifiers.

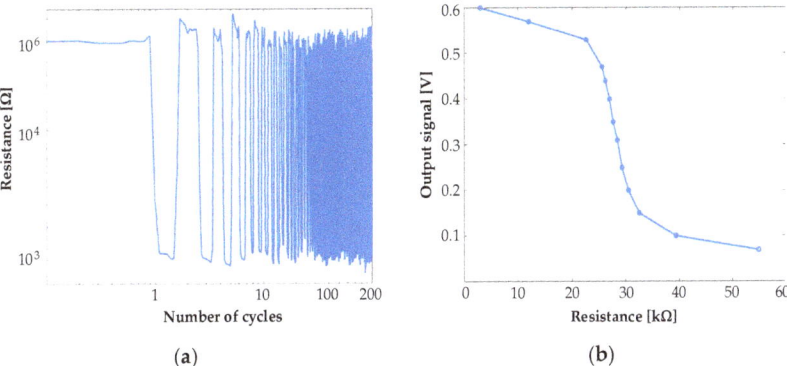

(a) (b)

Figure 15. (a) The resistive response of a single-sensor element to a load of 10 N over 200 cycles. (b) The value of output signal as a function of the changing resistance.

We determined the value of the resistor based on the performed analysis of the output value change in the response of changing the resistance with a potentiometer. Figure 15b describes this observation.

3.2. Data Acquisition

We had to create a dataset based on our proposed smart topper for neural network learning. Together, we collected data from 21 subjects, of which 3 were women and 18 men. The subjects' weights varied from 45 to 125 Kg. The database was divided into training and a test set randomly. In our case, we used data collected from 15 subjects for training. The data collected from the remaining six subjects serve to test the performance of the trained model. In our work, we determined four different postures for laying person classification, namely supine, the left side, prone, and the right side. Figure 16 shows samples of pressure images acquired from different subjects lying in one of the four postures. As mentioned above, the subject's weight varies a lot. Based on the wide weight variance, posture classification is a very challenging task. For example, when we compared the pressure distribution of one posture for the subject with the lowest weight and the heaviest subject, the difference was enormous.

We created an automated graphical tool for data collection and annotated storage in the MongoDB on the server and used the hardware described in the previous section on hardware design. The measurements repeat every second. The measuring range is from zero to 140. Zero means minimal or no pressure applied on the sensor, while 140 represents the maximal pressure on the sensors. Each subject spent 30 s in each posture. After ten seconds of measurement, we asked the subject to stand up and lay down in the same posture but in a different position. The subject could lay in any desired position for the given posture that feels comfortable. In the end, we had 120 samples for each subject, 30 samples per posture. For training purposes, 450 samples were used for one pose. The remaining 180 samples use neural network for testing (see Table 3).

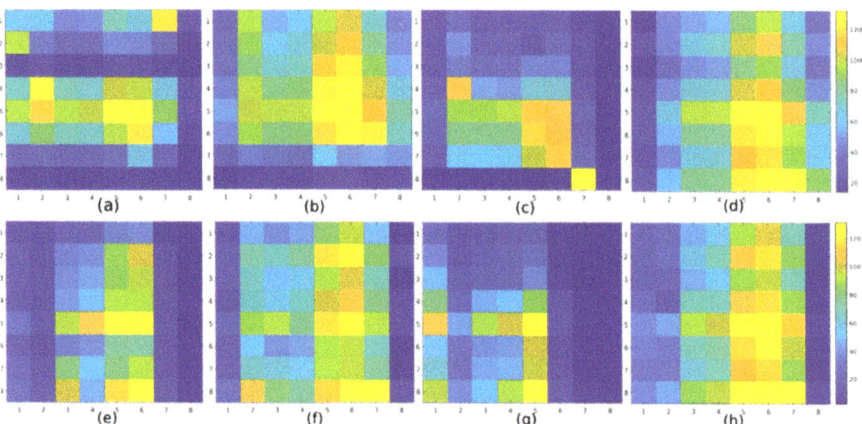

Figure 16. Pressure distribution example for lying postures, **Supine:** (**a**) subject 1, (**b**) subject 2, **Left side:** (**c**) subject 1, (**d**) subject 2, **Prone:** (**e**) subject 1, (**f**) subject 2, **Right side:** (**g**) subject 1, (**h**) subject 2.

Table 3. Dataset (four different postures).

Posture Type	Class	Train	Test
Supine	1	450	180
Left side	2	450	180
Prone	3	450	180
Right side	4	450	180

3.3. Proposed Methodology Using Modified CNN

This section describes the structure of the proposed CNN (Figure 17). The convolutional neural network classifies an input image into categories: supine, the left side, prone, and the right side. We performed the experiments using modified CNN and the precision, recall, and F1 parameter represents the achieved results. The model of the modified CNN consists of these primary layers:

keras.Input(shape=input_shape),
layers.Conv2D(16, kernel_size=(3, 3), activation="relu"),
layers.Conv2D(32, kernel_size=(3, 3), activation="relu"),
layers.Conv2D(32, kernel_size=(3, 3), activation="relu"),
layers.Flatten(),
layers.Dropout(0.25),
layers.Dense(num_classes, activation="softmax"),

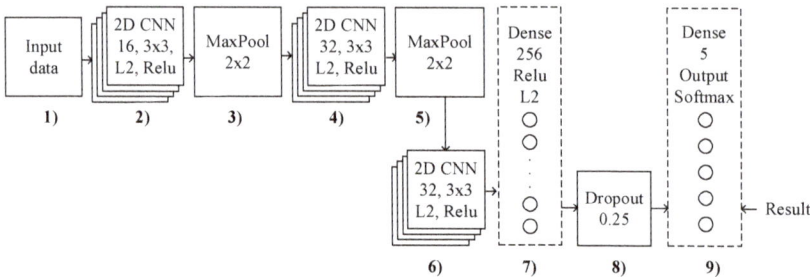

Figure 17. The block diagram of the modified convolutional neural network (CNN).

These basic operations (layers) form the core of almost every convolutional neural network. The task of the first layers is to extract the necessary samples from the input data. These first three layers are usually repeated several times. As you can see in Table 4, the layer consists of several functional maps. The main task of the functional map is the extraction of selected features using a convolution filter. The samples are then combined into feature map within the fully interconnected layers and perform a final operation called classification [23–25]. This modified CNN divides into nine main blocks (see Figure 17):

1. Reshaping the input data as vectors.
2. This block describes the 2D CNN layer which has 16 feature maps with a 3 × 3 kernel dimension. This layer creates a feature map to predict the class probabilities for each feature by applying a filter (kernel). The activation function uses the Rectified Linear Unit.
3. The MaxPooling layer with a size of 2 × 2 was used. These layers are inserted between the individual convolution layers to reduce the computation time.
4. This block uses the 2D CNN with the same parameters as in step 2, but the number of feature maps into value 32 was doubled.
5. The MaxPooling layer with a size of 2 × 2 was used. These layers are inserted between the individual convolution layers to reduce the computation time. The output from the feature map of the last convolution layer or subsampling layer (MaxPooling layer) is transformed into a one-dimensional vector.
6. In the block 6, the 2D CNN with same parameters as in step 4 was used.
7. In this step, dense layer with non-linearity activation function (ReLU) was used.
8. In this step, the dropout layer with a probability of 0.25 was added to prevent overtraining.
9. The last layer is the SoftMax function. The goal of this layer is to normalize the output of individual neurons to match the obtained probabilities (validation of the training progress).

Table 4. The structure of the modified CNN (layers description).

Layer Type	Output Shape	Parameters
conv2d_21 (Conv2D)	(None, 6, 6, 16)	160
conv2d_22 (Conv2D)	(None, 4, 4, 32)	4640
conv2d_23 (Conv2D)	(None, 2, 2, 32)	9248
flatten_7 (Flatten)	(None, 128)	0
dropout_7 (Dropout)	(None, 128)	0
dense_7 (Dense)	(None, 4)	516

In the other words, our modified CNN is trying to learn more and more abstract features. In the initial layers this network encodes low-level features such as edge detectors. In the following layers, the features for shapes such as multicolor gradients are described. In the last layers, there are features for individual objects or very complex shapes. Firstly, the input for CNN is data (8 × 8) which passes through the convolutional layer. These convolutional layers consist of a set of filters that are used to extract local image features. The activation function in the neural network determines the values of the outputs of the individual neurons based on their internal potential (the internal potential is calculated by multiplying the weights with the input). In our case, the Rectified Linear Unit (ReLu) as an activation function was used (this is a nonlinear function). Next, CNN applies the Max Pooling layer (sub-sampling) layer. In the Pooling operation, the feature map is divided into several sub-windows. Only the maximum value of each window is then left. The outputs from the individual windows are combined to create a new scaled-down feature map. When we apply this to all maps, a new set of feature maps is created, which then forms as an input to the next convolution layer, where the whole process is repeated. After the Max Pooling operation, the convolutional layer output is flattened through a fully connected layer. Finally, there is a SoftMax output layer for image classification. The SoftMax function assigns to each class the probability that the input image belongs to the appropriate class. The sum of all probabilities is equal to 1. The output from last layer (fully connected layer) can be used as a descriptor for other machine learning algorithms [24–26].

The confusion matrix (Table 5) holds the results from each tested method. This matrix summarizes the result of the classification and has rows indexed by output variable classes (reality) and columns by classes that the model predicted (estimation/prediction). The rows of the confusion matrix represent the actual class (supine, the left side, prone, and the right side). In our case, 180 samples in each row for testing were used. On the other hand, the column of confusion matrix represents the predicted class (supine, the left side, prone, and the right side).

Table 5. The achieved results using modified CNN for data classification (confusion matrix).

Class (Actual/Predicted)	Supine	Left Side	PRONE	Right Side
Supine	**164**	14	2	0
Left side	12	**161**	7	0
Prone	10	27	**131**	12
Right side	23	10	11	**136**

Based on the experiments carried out, the supine posture classification achieved the best results at 0.84 in the term of the F1 parameter (see Table 6). On the other hand, the prone posture classification gets the lowest value at 0.79 from all postures (see Table 5). The resulting accuracy is obtained as the sum of correctly predicted samples to the sums of all samples (0.82).

Table 6. The evaluation criterion of the modified CNN.

Class	Precision	Recall	F1 score
Supine	0.78	0.91	0.84
Left side	0.76	0.89	0.82
Prone	0.87	0.73	0.79
Right side	0.92	0.76	0.83

The parameters (P, R, F1) were calculated from the obtained values (see Table 6). The precision is the ratio between True Positive (TP) and the sum of positive data (True Positive (TP) + False Positive (FP)). The recall is the ratio between True Positive (TP) and the sum of data from the actual class (True Positive (TP) + False Negative (FN)) as shown in Figure 18. The F1 score is a combination of precision and recall (weighted average value of precision and recall). The TP value indicates the number of correctly classified patterns of the class true, the value FP indicates the number of incorrectly classified patterns of the class true. The value TN indicates the number of incorrectly classified patterns of class false, and the value FN represents the number of incorrectly classified patterns of class false.

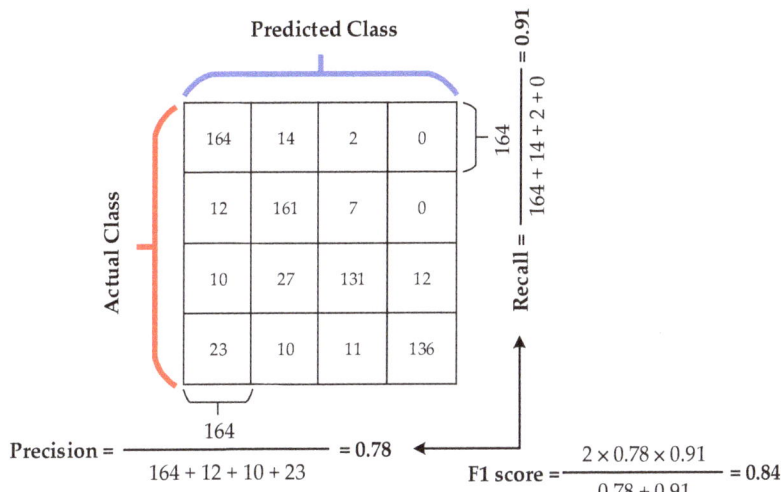

Figure 18. The evaluation metrices (precision, recall, F1 score).

4. Discussion

We have presented a smart IoT system for detecting the position of a lying person using novel textile pressure sensors. We introduced our novel textile pressure sensor based on the electrically conductive yarn and the Velostat. Our sensors showed a relatively stable resistive response. When we compare it with the pressure sensor presented in [7], which is also fabricated by sewing, their sensor provides a more stable resistive response to ours and is easier to manufacture. On the other hand, our sensor design is more robust and tear-resistant. Other works [10–12,15] use Velostat as the sensing element in their pressure sensors, but they do not use the sewing machine. In the comparison with other presented sensors, our sensor showed the biggest difference in measuring the resistance with the no-load and maximal load. For example, the resistance changes from 6 kΩ to approximately 700 Ω for the sensor presented in [10], respectively, from 2.5 kΩ to 400 Ω for the sensor proposed in [11]. The advantage of our sensor is also that it is based on materials which are gentle on the human skin and can be in direct contact with it.

To obtain the pressure distribution of the lying subject, we used sixty-four sensors. We created a matrix of sensors with eight rows and fabricated it on the base fabric. The final topper consisted of 40 mm thin polyurethane foam for a standard mattress of 2000 by 900 mm where the matrix of sensors is on the top side. Authors in [1] rely on the commercially available mattress for getting the laying person pressure distribution. The mattress has significantly more sensing points over our solution (1728). On the other hand, the works presented in [2–4] uses their version of the bedsheet sensing element and the number of the sensing elements used is 45 [2], 12 [3], 16 [4], respectively. They used commercially available sensors from the FSR family and only attach these sensors to the bed or sheet. The work presented in [1–4], and also our solution, use a non-invasive method and without electronics attached to the subject for the prevention of bedsores. In comparison, the works presented in [5,6] are also non-invasive, but they use an electronic component that needs to be attached to the subject. This can cause some level of discomfort for long-term patients.

In the end, we presented a complex solution for bedsores prevention based on our novel pressure sensor and deep learning. We determined four different postures for laying subject classification, namely supine, the left side, prone, and the right side. We created a challenging dataset and collect the data from 21 subjects. Three of them were women, and 18 were men. The dataset is challenging because the subject weight varies from 45 to 125 kg and the subject could choose the comfortable lying position in each posture. In terms of classification accuracy comparison, the work presented in [1], is the closest to our solution. These authors also used four different postures for classification, and their dataset consists of data from the observation of 12 healthy adults. The big disadvantage shown by classification accuracy comparison is that they have a more precise pressure distribution over our solution. They achieved a high testing prediction accuracy of 97.9% while our solution's accuracy is 82.22% with the best F1 score of 84%. On the other hand, the solution presented in [2] achieved the lying posture recognition 87.3% and they have only three different postures, left lateral, supine, and right lateral. The solution based on a deep learning approach and an electronic component attached to the subject [5] achieved a high accuracy of 99.56% with F1 1.00%. They used six different postures for classification, where they added sitting and movement posture over our solution. The accelerometer-based solution presented in [6] also achieved a high F1 score that ranges from 95.2% to 97.8%. Overall, the accelerometer-based solution gets better classification results over the sheet-based solution, but there is a disadvantage that the subject has to wear a piece of electronic equipment.

5. Conclusions

In this paper, we presented a complex IoT-based solution for detecting the position of a lying person. We produced a smart topper based on our novel pressure sensor for measuring the pressure distribution of the lying person. The novel sensor is based on the electrically conductive yarn and the Velostat. The performed experiments indicate a stable resistive response. We demonstrated the functionality of the whole solution and presented the application to the operating staff using the challenging dataset, which consists of data from 21 subjects. The modified CNN network classifies the collected data into one of the four lying postures. Our modified CNN achieved an overall accuracy of 82.22% and with the best F1 score of 84%.

Author Contributions: Conceptualization, S.M., R.H. and P.K.; methodology, R.H., P.K. and S.M.; software, M.B. and S.M.; validation, S.M., P.K. and R.H.; formal analysis, S.M. and R.H.; visualization, P.K.; supervision, R.H. All authors have read and agreed to the published version of the manuscript.

Funding: This work was funded by the Slovak Research and Development Agency under the project APVV-16-0190—Research of integration of textile functional system for biodata monitoring aimed at achievement synergy of human health, comfort and safety (BIO-IN-TEX) and APVV-18-0167—Smart clothing for E-health applications (E-clothing).

Data Availability Statement: The data presented in this study are available on request from the corresponding author.

Acknowledgments: We would like to thanks to Peter Palček for REM analyses and VÚTCH—CHEMITEX for providing the electrically conductive yarns. This work has been supported by the Slovak Research and Development Agency under the project No. PP-COVID-20-0100: DOLORES.AI: The pandemic guard system.

Conflicts of Interest: The authors declare no conflict of interest.

References

1. Matar, G.; Lina, J.-M.; Kaddoum, G. Artificial Neural Network for in-Bed Posture Classification Using Bed-Sheet Pressure Sensors. *IEEE J. Biomed. Health Inform.* **2020**, *24*, 101–110. [CrossRef] [PubMed]
2. Hong, Y.-S. Smart Care Beds for Elderly Patients with Impaired Mobility. *Wirel. Commun. Mobile Comput.* **2018**, *2018*, 1–12. [CrossRef]
3. Abdelmoghith, A.; Shaaban, R.; Alsheghri, Z.; Ismail, L. IoT-Based Healthcare Monitoring System: Bedsores Prevention. In Proceedings of the 2020 Fourth World Conference on Smart Trends in Systems, Security and Sustainability (WorldS4), London, UK, 27–28 July 2020; pp. 64–69.
4. Pereira, S.; Simoes, R.; Fonseca, J.; Carvalho, R.; Almeida, J. Textile Embedded Sensors Matrix for Pressure Sensing and Monitoring Applications for the Pressure Ulcer Prevention. In Proceedings of the 2018 International Conference on Biomedical Engineering and Applications (ICBEA, Funchal, Portugal, 9–12 July 2018; pp. 1–6.
5. Cicceri, G.; De Vita, F.; Bruneo, D.; Merlino, G.; Puliafito, A. A deep learning approach for pressure ulcer prevention using wearable computing. *Hum. Cent. Comput. Inf. Sci.* **2020**, *10*, 5. [CrossRef]

6.   Alinia, P.; Samadani, A.; Milosevic, M.; Ghasemzadeh, H.; Parvaneh, S. Pervasive Lying Posture Tracking. *Sensors* **2020**, *20*, 5953. [CrossRef] [PubMed]

7.   Saenz-Cogollo, J.; Pau, M.; Fraboni, B.; Bonfiglio, A. Pressure Mapping Mat for Tele-Home Care Applications. *Sensors* **2016**, *16*, 365. [CrossRef] [PubMed]

8.   Li, E.; Lin, X.; Seet, B.-C.; Joseph, F.; Neville, J. Low Profile and Low Cost Textile Smart Mat for Step Pressure Sensing and Position Mapping. In Proceedings of the 2019 IEEE International Instrumentation and Measurement Technology Conference (I2MTC), Auckland, New Zealand, 20–23 May 2019; pp. 1–5.

9.   Zhu, Y.; Qiu, S.; Li, M.; Chen, G.; Hu, X.; Liu, C.; Qu, X. A Smart Portable Mat That Can Meausre Sitting Plantar Pressure Distribution with a High Resolution. In Proceedings of the 2019 IEEE 6th International Conference on Industrial Engineering and Applications (ICIEA), Tokyo, Japan, 12–15 April 2019; pp. 141–144.

10. Suprapto, S.S.; Setiawan, A.W.; Zakaria, H.; Adiprawita, W.; Supartono, B. Low-Cost Pressure Sensor Matrix Using Velostat. In Proceedings of the 2017 5th International Conference on Instrumentation, Communications, Information Technology, and Biomedical Engineering (ICICI-BME), Bandung, Indonesia, 6–7 November 2017; pp. 137–140.

11. Pizarro, F.; Villavicencio, P.; Yunge, D.; Rodríguez, M.; Hermosilla, G.; Leiva, A. Easy-to-Build Textile Pressure Sensor. *Sensors* **2018**, *18*, 1190. [CrossRef] [PubMed]

12. Vehec, I.; Livovsky, L. Flexible Resistive Sensor Based on Velostat. In Proceedings of the 2020 43rd International Spring Seminar on Electronics Technology (ISSE), Demanovska Valley, Slovakia, 14–15 May 2020; pp. 1–6.

13. Hopkins, M.; Vaidyanathan, R.; Mcgregor, A.H. Examination of the Performance Characteristics of Velostat as an In-Socket Pressure Sensor. *IEEE Sens. J.* **2020**, *20*, 6992–7000. [CrossRef]

14. Tihak, A.; Boskovic, D. Experimental evaluation of challenges in designing a resistive pressure sensors. In Proceedings of the IEEE EUROCON 2019—18th International Conference on Smart Technologies, Novi Sad, Serbia, 1–4 July 2019; pp. 1–6.

15. Lin, X.; Seet, B.-C. A Linear Wide-Range Textile Pressure Sensor Integrally Embedded in Regular Fabric. *IEEE Sens. J.* **2015**, *15*, 5384–5385. [CrossRef]

16. Hou, B.; Qian, K.; Li, L.; Shi, Y.; Tao, L.; Liu, J. MongoDB NoSQL Injection Analysis and Detection. In Proceedings of the 2016 IEEE 3rd International Conference on Cyber Security and Cloud Computing (CSCloud), Beijing, China, 25–27 June 2016; pp. 75–78.

17. Hillar, G.C. *MQTT Essentials—A Lightweight IoT Protocol*; Packt Publishing: Birmingham, UK, 2017; ISBN 9781787285149.

18. Dirolf, M.; Chodorow, K. *MongoDB: The Definitive Guide*; O'Reilly: Beijing, China, 2010; ISBN 9781449381561.

19. MongoDB Atlas. Deploy a Fully Managed Cloud Database in Minutes. Available online: www.mongodb.org (accessed on 20 November 2020).

20. Celesti, A.; Fazio, M.; Villari, M. A Study on Join Operations in MongoDB Preserving Collections Data Models for Future Internet Applications. *Future Internet* **2019**, *11*, 83. [CrossRef]

21. Krizhevsky, A.; Sutskever, I.; Hinton, G. ImageNet Classification with Deep Convolutional Neural Networks. *Neural Inf. Process. Syst.* **2012**, *25*. [CrossRef]

22. Phung, V.H.; Rhee, E.J. A High-Accuracy Model Average Ensemble of Convolutional Neural Networks for Classification of Cloud Image Patches on Small Datasets. *Appl. Sci.* **2019**, *9*, 4500. [CrossRef]

23. Szegedy, C.; Liu, W.; Jia, Y.; Sermanet, P.; Reed, S.; Anguelov, D.; Erhan, D.; Vanhoucke, V.; Rabinovich, A. Going deeper with convolutions. In Proceedings of the 2015 IEEE Conference on Computer Vision and Pattern Recognition (CVPR), Boston, MA, USA, 7–12 June 2015; pp. 1–9.

24. Han, X.; Zhong, Y.; Cao, L.; Zhang, L. Pre-Trained AlexNet Architecture with Pyramid Pooling and Supervision for High Spatial Resolution Remote Sensing Image Scene Classification. *Remote Sens.* **2017**, *9*, 848. [CrossRef]

25. Samir, S.; Emary, E.; El-Sayed, K.; Onsi, H. Optimization of a Pre-Trained AlexNet Model for Detecting and Localizing Image Forgeries. *Information* **2020**, *11*, 275. [CrossRef]

26. Kamencay, P.; Benco, M.; Mizdos, T.; Radil, R. A New Method for Face Recognition Using Convolutional Neural Network. *Adv. Electr. Electron. Eng.* **2017**, *15*, 663–672. [CrossRef]

Article

Which Digital-Output MEMS Magnetometer Meets the Requirements of Modern Road Traffic Survey?

Michal Hodoň [1,*], Ondrej Karpiš [1], Peter Ševčík [1] and Andrea Kociánová [2]

[1] Department of Technical Cybernetics, Faculty of Management Science and Informatics, University of Žilina, 010 26 Žilina, Slovakia; karpis@pd.uniza.sk (O.K.); peter.sevcik@fri.uniza.sk (P.Š.)
[2] Department of Highway Engineering, Faculty of Civil Engineering, University of Žilina, 01026 Žilina, Slovakia; andrea.kocianova@uniza.sk
* Correspondence: michal.hodon@fri.uniza.sk; Tel.: +421-415134355

Abstract: Present systems for road traffic surveillance largely utilize MEMS magnetometers for the purpose of vehicle detection and classification. Magnetoresistive sensing or LR oscillation circuitry are technologies providing the sensors with the competitive advantage which lies in the energy efficiency and low price. There are several chip suppliers on the market who specialize in the development of these sensors. The aim of this paper is to compare available sensors from the viewpoint of their suitability for traffic measurements. A summary of the achieved results is given in the form of the score for each sensor. The introduced sensor chart should provide the audience with knowledge about pros and cons of sensors, especially if intended for the purposes of road traffic surveillance. The authors in this research focused on the specific situation of road traffic monitoring with magnetometers placed at the roadside.

Keywords: magnetometer; traffic; vehicle; classification; measurement; detection

check for
updates

Citation: Hodoň, M.; Karpiš, O.; Ševčík, P.; Kociánová, A. Which Digital-Output MEMS Magnetometer Meets the Requirements of Modern Road Traffic Survey?. *Sensors* **2021**, *21*, 266. https://doi.org/10.3390/s21010266

Received: 30 November 2020
Accepted: 30 December 2020
Published: 3 January 2021

Publisher's Note: MDPI stays neutral with regard to jurisdictional claims in published maps and institutional affiliations.

1. Introduction

At present, non-intrusive automatic traffic counters are mainly used for short-term road traffic surveys. The counters are located mostly next to the road (e.g., cameras and microwave radars), across the road (pneumatic counters), or directly on the road surface in the middle of the traffic lane (magnetic traffic counters). In recent years, research and development have focused on counters based on magnetometers, which are already commonly used as a replacement for induction loops built into the road pavement. The possibility to use magnetometers placed next to the road is verified, which is very advantageous from the point of view of short-term surveys. However, it brings several challenges that need to be solved. One of the important ones is that in such a location the response from passing vehicles is much lower than when the sensor is located directly in the middle of the lane. Moreover, the amplitude of the record decreases significantly as the distance increases. Therefore, it is necessary to choose a suitable magnetometer that will be sufficiently sensitive and reliable, especially under real traffic conditions.

Currently, magnetometers based on micro-electro-mechanical systems (MEMS) technology are mainly used for vehicle detection. The situation on the MEMS market is evolving and several sensors (e.g., the HMC5983, Honeywell, Charlotte, NC, USA and the LSM303DLHC, STMicroelectronics, Geneva, Switzerland), which we have used in the past [1], are no longer available. Our intention is to compare the currently available magnetometers in terms of their suitability for vehicle detection if the sensor is located next to the road. Recently we compared 10 different sensors in the laboratory [2,3] from which we selected the four best. Now we are mainly interested in realistically achievable vehicle detection results.

Most vehicles are still based on internal combustion engines, which do not generate a significant magnetic field of their own. Detection of vehicles by magnetometers is based on

111

the effect of ferromagnetic materials contained in vehicles on the Earth's magnetic field. As the magnitude of the Earth's magnetic field is approximately 50 μT, it is necessary to focus on sensors with the highest possible sensitivity. Sensitivity is usually expressed in terms of the number of quantization steps per μT (LSB/μT).

The paper is organized as follows: Section 2 is focused on the state-of-the-art in the area of magnetometers used for traffic survey. In Section 3, basic parameters of selected sensors are presented. Section 4 contains a description of hardware used in all experiments. Section 5 is devoted to the laboratory experiments. In Section 6, the results of real-world measurements are presented and discussed. Detection algorithm and results are described in Section 7. Section 8 summarizes results of the sensor evaluation. Finally, Section 9 contains brief conclusions and a description of future research plans.

2. Related Work

The intelligent transportation systems (ITS) of the 21st century demand reliable, real-time vehicle volume and classification information. Different systems for different purposes integrate digital anisotropic magnetometers in their designs, as for example in parking lots [4], for stop detection at signalized intersections [5], for real-time traffic surveillance [6], etc. However, most magnetometer sensors applied in the field of traffic monitoring and classification are low-cost and energy-efficient substitutes of other technologies, such as for example inductive loops or cameras. Scenarios of traffic monitoring and vehicle classification were also the intended application areas of the sensors investigated throughout the paper. An extensive body of research is still carried out in this field, whilst findings in following articles were considered during our measurements.

The authors in [7] focused on the utilization of magnetometer sensors for length-based vehicle classification, where through their computationally efficient classification model reached classification accuracy of 97.70% by using of the anisotropic magnetoresistance (AMR) effect.

In [8], the authors through the usage of a HMC1502 AMR magnetometer (Honeywell) presented an efficient approach to the modeling and classification of vehicles using their magnetic signatures. They proposed a sensor-dependent approach for modeling the obtained magnetic signature of each vehicle. The orientation of the used magnetometer was towards the Y and Z-axis components of the magnetic field.

The utilization of cost-effective solution for on-road traffic monitoring based on the usage of RM3100 magnetometers (PNI Sensor Corporation, Santa Rosa, CA, USA), was introduced in [9]. The authors, through modelling of the local magnetic field perturbations caused by moving vehicles, extracted the magnetic waveform characteristics for vehicle identification and speed estimation. They equipped their system with wireless connectivity to broadcast the information about vehicle types, volume and speeds.

The authors in [10] also used a cheap AMR magnetometer, installed roadside, for road vehicle recognition and classification. Their system was used for measuring magnetic field changes for the detection of passing vehicles, and for recognition of vehicle types. Mel frequency cepstral coefficients were introduced to analyze vehicle magnetic signals and extract them as vehicle features with the representation of cepstrum, frame energy, and gap cepstrum of magnetic signals. According to this analysis they presented a special algorithm for the classification of the magnetic features of four typical types of vehicles—sedans, vans, trucks and buses.

The authors in [11] proved the advantages of using of AMR magnetometers over Hall sensors, giant magnetoresistance (GMR) sensors, and tunneling magnetoresistance (TMR) sensors as a low cost as well as low power solution for vehicle detection sensing. In their research, they used two AMR sensor nodes spaced 1 m apart based on HMC5883L magnetometers (Honeywell) to measure vehicle speeds on the road. According to the sampling frequency limit their system could measure vehicle speeds up to 100 km/h.

Research in [12] described the possibility of adding another sensor to magnetometers for vehicle tracking on roadways to build a low-cost, low-complexity vehicle tracking sensor platform for highway traffic monitoring. Their approach was based on multirate particle filtering that fused the measurements from two different sensors. The sensors were an accelerometer and a magnetometer, and they operated with different sampling rates.

The authors in [13] utilized a FXOS8700 magnetometer as the basis of the presented smart wireless sensor for traffic monitoring with efficient and reliable algorithms for vehicle detection, speed and length estimation and classification. They introduced this AMR sensor as a suitable alternative for inductive loop sensors. Their system was portable, reliable, and cost-effective with an affordable price of 50 USD. The authors claimed 99.98% detection accuracy, 97.11% speed estimation accuracy, and 97% length-based vehicle classification accuracy.

Detection of vehicles based on HMC5883L magnetometers was presented in [14]. The sensors were placed roadside and measured traffic in the adjacent lane. The authors proposed adapting a threshold state machine algorithm to detect vehicles. Their sensor system is wireless, compact, and cost-effective while achieving high accuracy and viability in urban environments.

A comprehensive analysis of traffic surveillance based on magnetic technology and the corresponding wireless sensor networks, pointing out vehicle detection and counting, speed estimation and vehicle classification applications was presented in [15]. The authors developed a low-cost and energy-efficient type of multi-function wireless traffic magnetic sensor for vehicle detection at the jam flow conditions. Honeywell HMC1001 and HMC1002 magnetic sensors were used for this purpose.

The advantages of magnetic detector-based sensors compared to other technologies were also presented in [16]. The authors there presented a single magnetic detector system based on a Honeywell HMC5843 magnetometer. They presented a technique for false detection filtering where the vehicle classes are estimated using a feedforward neural network which was implemented in the detector control unit. For the training of the neural network the back-propagation algorithm was used with different training parameters.

A three axis digital HMR2300 AMR magnetometer (Honeywell) was used for the road vehicle classification in [17]. The vehicles were classified into four groups—hatchbacks, sedans, buses, and (MPVs). Authors developed classification algorithm based on analysis of time domain and frequency domain features in combination with three common classification algorithms in pattern recognition.

Magneto-inductive RM3100 sensors were used in [18] for road vehicles velocity estimation. The developed magnetic sensor system employed wireless connectivity, while it was cost-effective, and environmental-friendly. Through modelling of local magnetic field perturbations caused by a moving vehicle, the authors extracted the characteristics of magnetic waveforms for speed estimation.

HMC2003 three-axis magnetic sensor boards with HMC100x AMR sensing chips were used in the system presented in [19]. The authors built a roadside magnetic sensor system for vehicle detection.

The authors in [20] built a vehicle detection system as a wireless sensor network composed of a collection of sensor nodes put in the center of a lane with access point box used for the data collection.

In [21] a vehicle detection state machine for magnetometer sensors for n-motorway lanes with multiple lane changes is presented. The proposed method can be used for suppressing the interference from a vehicle in an adjacent lane and lane changing.

QMC5883L modules, based on Honeywell HMC5883L AMR magnetometers, were used for the vehicle detection in [22] and could reliably detect the presence of a vehicle in a parking spot when placed under the front or rear axle of the vehicle.

LIS3MDL AMR magnetometers (STMicroelectronics) were used for the purposes of vehicle presence detection in [23]. The authors in this paper introduced a self-powered and autonomous sensing node equipped with supercapacitors, solar-based energy harvester and wake-up trigger prototype together with a Bluetooth Low-Energy (BLE) radio. The developed triggering system consumes only 150 nA.

Different AMR magnetometers were discussed in [24]—HMC1001, HMC1021 (both Honeywell), KMZ51 (NXP Semiconductors, Eindhoven, The Netherlands) and AFF755B (Sensitec GmbH, Wetzlar, Germany). According to the analysis, a new construction of sensors intended for vehicle detection experiments was presented.

The use of the magnetometers found in smartphones for the purposes of vehicle detection was presented in [25]. The system was used for the locating of street parking places by pedestrians.

From the analysis above is evident that the usage of AMR magnetometers for the purposes of road vehicle detection is very common, especially due to their relatively high accuracy which is in the contrast with low price and energy-efficiency which these sensors provide. After application of specific algorithms, these sensors can be easily used for almost full traffic surveillance, which involves vehicle classification, estimation of vehicle speed or traffic jam detection, eventually as a part of specific sensor systems [26]. After the implementation of appropriate software, magnetometer sensors could also provide a value-added contribution into the area of traffic surveillance, where other technologies take the role, as for example in sensing drunken drivers [27], as a part of driving assistance systems [28], for the edge traffic flow detection [29], as energy-efficient substitution of cameras for the detection and classification of road vehicles [30], or for the traffic abnormality detection [31] etc.

Other low-cost technologies which could be used for vehicle detection were summarized in [32]. The authors summarized the progress in the area to help identify the sensing technologies with relatively high detection accuracy together with cost effectiveness and ease of installation. Special attention was paid to wireless battery-powered detectors of small dimensions that can be quickly and effortlessly installed alongside traffic lanes without any additional supporting structures. The methods of collecting traffic flow data were described in [33]. The authors tried to establish a low-cost wireless sensor network for providing data to advanced intelligent transportation system. The authors in [34] investigated a low-cost sensor network architecture for temporary installation on city streets as an alternative to commonly used rubber hoses. They presented the low-cost, low energy sensor together with the sensor location model. A case study with the installation of a set of proposed devices was presented to demonstrate its viability.

Different AMR magnetometers, as for example RM3100 (PNI Sensor Corporation), LIS3MDL (STMicroelectronics) or FXOS8700 sensors (NXP Semiconductors) have been used in some of the above articles. However, a direct comparison of the properties and performance of these sensors is lacking. The aim of this article is to compare these sensors and select the most suitable one for the implementation of the road traffic sensors that can be placed at the roadside.

3. Description of Sensors

The design of a road traffic sensor is a complex task. One of the most important steps is to select a suitable sensor. In [2,3] we tested 10 magnetometers in the laboratory. One of the main requirements when choosing magnetometers was their commercial availability. During testing, we focused on the size of the noise and the repeatability of measurements at different magnitudes of the magnetic field. For an analysis of magnetometers accuracy in terms of vehicle detection when placed by roadside, we selected the three best magnetometers (the RM3100, FXOS8700, and LIS3MDL or LSM303C). We also added the MLX90393 sensor, which is designed mainly for low-power devices. The next section lists the basic parameters of each selected sensor.

3.1. RM3100

This sensor manufactured by the PNI Sensor Corporation is exceptional in all respects. It is only tested sensor that does not use magneto-resistive technology, but rather is based on a LR oscillation circuit. It uses the property that the effective inductance of the coil is directly proportional to the magnitude of the magnetic field parallel to the orientation of the coil. The sensor uses three external coils connected to the control chip. Sampling frequency, scan sensitivity, and noise size are all related to the cycle count (CC) parameter, which can be set in the range 0-65535. Low CC values allow a high sampling rate to be used, but the resolution is lower. The situation is reversed for higher CC values. The manufacturer recommends using CC values in the range of 30–400. A different CC value can be set for each channel. The number of sensed channels affects the maximum sampling frequency. For CC = 50, the maximum sampling frequency is 1600/(number of channels). Magnetic field measurement range of the sensor is ±800 µT and the sensitivity is 75 LSB/µT for the default value of CC (200). This sensor is the only one of our selection to encode outputs using 24 bits. Other sensors are 16-bit. In addition to its advantages (high sampling frequency and high sensitivity), this sensor also has disadvantages: due to the need for external coils, the sensor is relatively large and also relatively expensive—especially compared to other sensors (see Table 1).

Table 1. Important parameters of sensors.

Sensor	Range [µT]	Sensitivity [LSB/µT]	Sampling Frequency [Hz]	Unite Price [€]
RM3100	±800	>100 [1]	1600/n [1]	12.75
LIS3MDL/LSM303C	±400	68.42	80/155	1.37
FXOS8700	±1200	10	800	3.41
MLX90393	±4800	6.21	717	1.65

[1] Depends on Cycle Count setting.

3.2. LSM303C and LIS3MDL

These are representatives of the magnetometers manufactured by STMicroelectronics. In addition to the magnetometer, the LSM303C also includes an accelerometer, both of which are completely independent. The magnetometers of both sensors have very similar properties. In terms of management registers, they are almost identical. It can be said that the LIS3MDL is an improved version of the LSM303C magnetometer. The main difference is that the LIS3MDL supports the ranges ±4, ±8, ±12 and ±16 Gauss (±400 to ±1600 µT) and the "FAST" mode with support for a sampling frequency of 155 to 1000 Hz (depending on the required output quality). Interestingly, although the LSM303C has a single ±16 Gauss range according to the datasheet it is also possible to use (undocumented) ±4, ±8 and ±12 Gauss settings. The main advantage of these sensors is their higher sensitivity, which is for the range ±4 Gauss at the level of 6842 LSB/Gauss (or 68.42 LSB/µT). A certain limitation is the relatively low sampling frequency—for the LSM303C only 80 Hz and for the LIS3MDL 155 Hz (at maximum quality). The configuration of the sensors is relatively simple and consists in the selection of the range, sampling frequency and quality.

3.3. FXOS8700

The FXOS8700 from NXP Semiconductors includes an accelerometer in addition to the magnetometer. The range of the sensor is quite large: ±1200 µT. This is associated with a lower sensitivity of 10 LSB/µT. The main advantage of the sensor is the high sampling frequency of 800 Hz, which does not depend on the number of measured channels. However, if we want to use an accelerometer at the same time as the magnetometer, the maximum sampling frequency will be halved, i.e., 400 Hz. The amount of noise can be affected by the over sample ratio (OSR) setting, the maximum size of which depends on the sampling frequency.

3.4. MLX90393

This sensor from Melexis is designed for low-power applications. The sampling frequency of the sensor can be up to 700 Hz and depends on the over sample ratio setting and the way the output is filtered, with 8 different levels of filtration available. The sensitivity of the sensor is higher in the XY plane than in the Z axis and can reach a maximum of 6.211 LSB/µT for the X and Y axes and 3.406 LSB/µT for the Z axis. The sensitivity depends on the gain of the analog part and the method of selecting the 16 bits of output from the internal 19-bit analog-to-digital converter, with each channel having its own settings.

The main parameters of all the sensors, including average prices from most common shops dedicated to electronic components (we compare prices from the supplier mouser.com), are summarized in Table 1.

4. Hardware Platform

To be able to test all sensors under the same conditions, particular break-out boards of the respective sensors were purchased. A break-out board makes it easy to use a single electrical component when adding the pins to the small package of magnetometer what allows connecting the board to a higher circuit. This makes it relatively easy to use. We decided to use RaspberryPi 3 Model B+ as the control board for setting up the sensor parameters, to start/end measurements and to store measured values in SD card. For this purpose, a special shield was designed and developed for RaspberryPi (see Figures 1 and 2).

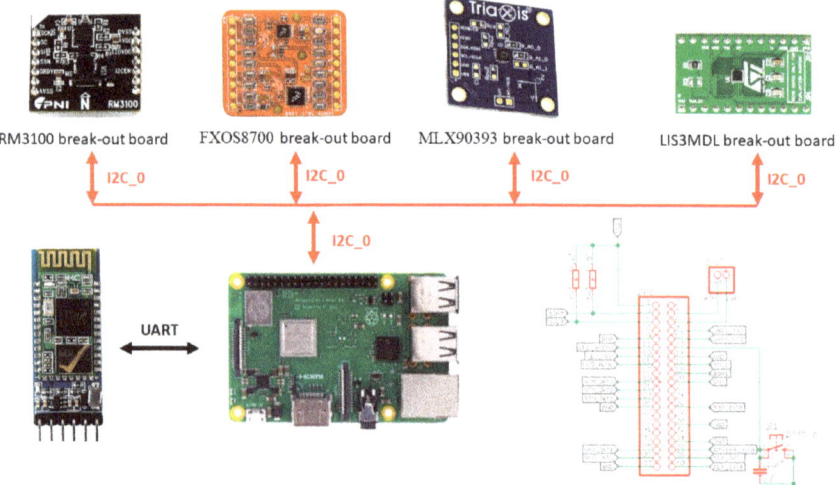

Figure 1. Block schematic of the developed measurement board.

Figure 2. Completed measurement board with all magnetometer break-out boards installed in the top and Bluetooth module installed in the bottom (all attached to the developed shield).

All selected sensors support serial peripheral interface (SPI) and inter-integrated circuit (I2C) communication interfaces. During our experiments, we used I2C in FAST mode (400 kHz). It can be seen also in the figures above, where all magnetometer breakout boards communicate with RaspberryPi via I2C interface. The Bluetooth module is connected through universal asynchronous receiver-transmitter (UART) interface. The measurement board also contains one indicating RGB LED diode and one development button for starting/stopping and resetting the measurements. External connectors allow connection of other possible sensors. Power supply was provided through standard 10 Ah Li-Ion Mini USB power bank, what was sufficient for the measurements lasting. Later on a developed Android application, which allowed an Android smartphone to connect to the measurement board, was used for the remote control of measurement and data download through Bluetooth. After all necessary testing procedures, the measurement board was further used for the sensors' performance evaluation.

5. Laboratory Measurements

The real environment test of the sensors took place on the two-lane road I/64 in the First, we performed measurements in the laboratory to determine the effect of RaspberryPi (RPi) on the sensors. We tested two configurations: 1—placement of the expansion board directly on the RPi, 2—expansion board on the cable, approx. 40 cm from the RPi. For both configurations, two types of measurements were performed: scanning by each sensor separately and scanning by all sensors at once. During the measurements, the sensors were placed min. 2 m aside from sources of interference (computers, wiring). The length of each measurement was at least 20 seconds so that the number of readings was at least 2000 for each sensor. The measured values were stored in SD card located on the RPi and evaluated offline.

The settings of sensors were adjusted to maximize their sensitivity, while the sampling frequency was approximately 100 Hz. The main parameters of the sensors were set as follows (in parentheses is the actual sampling frequency—fs):

- RM3100: Cycle Count = 300 (fs = 104 Hz)
- LIS3MDL: range ±400 µT, Ultra-high-performance mode, FAST mode (fs = 157 Hz)
- FXOS8700: OSR = 8 (fs = 103 Hz)
- MLX90393: DIC_FILT = 2, OSR = 3, GAIN_SEL = 7 (fs = 96 Hz).

For each measurement, we calculated the variance, which reflects the magnitude of the noise. The measured noise is the sum of the sensor's own noise and the noise induced from the environment. The results of measurements performed for each sensor separately are given in Table 2.

Table 2. Variance of noise for individual measurements [μT^2].

Axis X	RM3100	LIS3MDL	FXOS8700	MLX90393
Board on RPi	0.01885	0.061643	0.187634	0.863626
Board on cable	0.015285	0.062874	0.16698	0.845773
Difference [%]	−18.9	+2.0	−11.0	−2.1
Axis Y	**RM3100**	**LIS3MDL**	**FXOS8700**	**MLX90393**
Board on RPi	0.00279	0.05997	0.158713	0.729022
Board on cable	0.002567	0.05807	0.152333	0.736557
Difference [%]	−8.0	−3.2	−4.0	+1.0
Axis Z	**RM3100**	**LIS3MDL**	**FXOS8700**	**MLX90393**
Board on RPi	0.004791	0.12119	0.374178	1.942289
Board on cable	0.003306	0.1206965	0.369923	1.768549
Difference [%]	−31.0	−0.4	−1.1	−8.9

If we sort the sensors according to the size of the noise (from the smallest), the following order applies: RM3100, LIS3MDL, FXOS8700, MLX90393. The same order applies to all axes.

We expected that the measurement with sensors on the cable would contain the least noise, as the noise sources on the RPi will be more distant from the sensors. This has also been confirmed. With two minor exceptions, the amount of noise is lower for sensors located on a cable. However, the differences are relatively small, within a few percent. The only exception is the RM3100 sensor, which has very low intrinsic noise and at the same time high sensitivity. Therefore, it was most significantly affected by the noise generated by RPi. Nevertheless, even in the worst case (axis X), the amount of noise of the RM3100 is more than 3 times lower than that of the second-best sensor—LIS3MDL.

From a practical point of view, we are most interested in the X-axis, which is oriented towards the road if the sensors are located directly on the RPi and it is placed on the ground (parallel to the road). Differences between measurements of up to 19% were found in this axis.

In the second measurement, the magnetic field was sensed by all sensors at once. This means more current consumption and more frequent communication via the I2C bus. Therefore, we expected that the measured noise would be higher than in the previous measurement. The measurement results are shown in Table 3.

Table 3. Variance of noise for joint measurements [μT^2].

Axis X	RM3100	LIS3MDL	FXOS8700	MLX90393
Board on RPi	0.012109	0.071062	0.241074	0.907603
Board on cable	0.023884	0.065095	0.216764	0.890775
Difference [%]	+97.2	−8.4	−10.1	−1.8
Axis Y	**RM3100**	**LIS3MDL**	**FXOS8700**	**MLX90393**
Board on RPi	0.002546	0.074101	0.195486	0.721353
Board on cable	0.002911	0.059963	0.160871	0.762524
Difference [%]	+14.3	−19.1	−17.7	+5.7
Axis Z	**RM3100**	**LIS3MDL**	**FXOS8700**	**MLX90393**
Board on RPi	0.005866	0.185112	0.438575	1.896881
Board on cable	0.003518	0.126429	0.447737	1.861972
Difference [%]	−40.0	−31.7	+2.1	−1.8

This measurement is more important to us because it corresponds to a situation of measuring vehicle records simultaneously with all sensors. The order of the sensors in terms of noise remained unchanged. When comparing the results with the previous measurement, we see that in almost all cases there was an increase in the measured noise. In the X-axis, which we are most interested in, the biggest percentage difference was with the FXOS8700 sensor—a change from 0.16698 (Table 2, board on cable) to 0.216764 (Table 3) represents an increase of almost 30%.

As in the first measurement, better results are obtained with the sensor board on the cable. The most notable exception is the RM3100 sensor, which has almost twice the noise in the X-axis compared to the placement of the sensors on the board. The X-axis was oriented parallel to the cable, and this apparently caused higher measured noise with this most sensitive sensor.

It should be noted that the comparison of sensors is not perfect. The differences in the measured noise are certainly also influenced by the mutual position of the sensor and RPi. However, this cannot be avoided, as we want to measure the deformation of the earth's magnetic field by vehicles in real traffic with all sensors at once. The sensors are therefore necessarily differently oriented with respect to the individual noise sources.

After considering the results, we decided that due to the much simpler manipulation, we will use an expansion board located directly on the RPi during real measurements. Although this placement of expansion board increases the amount of measured noise (usually by a few percent) it should not significantly affect the performance of the sensors in detecting vehicles.

6. Real Traffic Measurements

The real environment test of the sensors took place on the two-lane road I/64 in the village of Porúbka (Slovakia) with daily traffic of 27,228 veh/day and rush-hour traffic of 2,051 veh/h (14% of trucks) measured by a Sierzega SR4 radar during a testing day. We performed two measurements at different distances of the sensors from the lane. In the first case, the sensor was placed on the outer edge of the road line and in the second case, it was at a distance of 0.5 m from the road line. In the previous measurements in [2], we evaluated the effect of sensor placement—we tested the placement directly on the ground and at a height of 30 cm above the ground. We found that the difference between the measured values is not significant. In these measurements, we decided to place the sensor directly on the ground. We wanted the sensor to be inconspicuous because we had found in the past that drivers tended to bypass the sensor when it was clearly visible and marked with a traffic cone.

Measurements were taken between 16:45 and 17:30. We set the duration of both measurements so that the number of captured vehicles is approximately 100. For evaluation, passing vehicles were also recorded by a camera (with a frame rate of 24 fr/s). Figure 3 shows the location of the sensors during the measurements, the orientation of the axes relative to the road, and the location of the camera. The picture also shows a view of the measuring set.

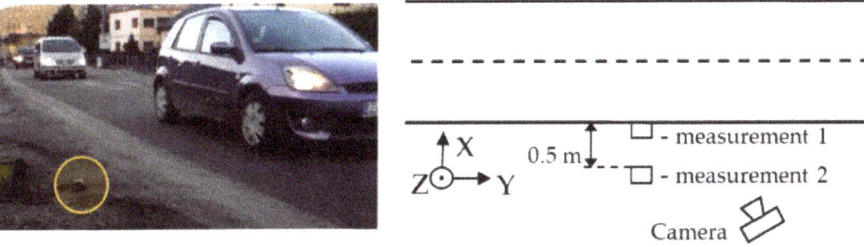

Figure 3. Sensor placement and view of the measuring set.

During the first measurement, 88 vehicles were recorded, of which 74 were cars, nine vans, three buses and two trucks. In the second measurement, there were 94 vehicles, of which 86 were cars, seven vans and one truck. Based on the camera recording, each vehicle was assigned a type and time of passage (accurate to 1/24 s).

First, we evaluated the amount of noise from the measured data. According to the camera recording, we found a section in which no vehicles passed, and we calculated the variance. The length of the section was 20 s (comparable to noise measurements in the laboratory). The results are shown in Table 4.

Table 4. Amount of noise in real conditions [μT^2].

Sensor	Measurement 1			Measurement 2		
	X	Y	Z	X	Y	Z
RM3100	0.0028	0.0011	0.0104	0.0089	0.0007	0.0228
LIS3MDL	0.0899	0.0650	0.0935	0.0720	0.0692	0.1019
FXOS8700	0.1939	0.1740	0.4627	0.1823	0.1482	0.4200
MLX90393	0.6430	0.5899	1.7458	0.6419	0.6464	1.6755

Approximately the same level of noise was recorded in both measurements. The biggest differences are with the most sensitive sensor RM3100. If we compare a similar measurement performed in the laboratory (Table 3—joint measurement, placement of the expansion board on RPi), we find that in most cases slightly lower noise was measured in the exterior than in the interior. This result can be explained by stronger sources of interfering electromagnetic noise in the interior.

A much more important indicator of sensor quality is the achievable signal-to-noise ratio (SNR). Assuming a constant noise level, this ratio will depend on the distance of the sensor from the vehicle and the size of the passing vehicle. Based on the camera record, we found records of ten passenger cars and calculated the average SNR. The results are shown in Table 5. We used Equation (1) to calculate the SNR:

$$SNR = 10log\frac{var(CAR)}{var(NOISE)} \tag{1}$$

where *var*() represents the variance of a given signal and corresponds to its power.

Table 5. Mean SNR [dB] of a passenger car.

Sensor	Measurement 1			Measurement 2		
	X	Y	Z	X	Y	Z
RM3100	30.0	33.1	14.7	22.5	27.9	11.7
LIS3MDL	11.7	10.2	5.9	8.4	6.8	2.3
FXOS8700	10.9	9.1	3.2	6.9	5.0	1.2
MLX90393	6.4	4.2	1.1	3.5	1.6	0.3

This measurement fully showed the capabilities of the sensors, especially the sensitivity to relatively small changes in the Earth's magnetic field caused by the passage of vehicles. The worst is again the MLX90393 sensor. This result was to be expected due to the low sensitivity of this sensor and at the same time its relatively high intrinsic noise. The RM3100 sensor achieved the best result, but the LIS3MDL provided good results too. This measurement also indicated the importance of placing the sensor as close as possible to the lane. Increasing the distance by 0.5 m resulted in a significant decrease in SNR (depending on the axis, the difference is from 3 to 8 dB for the RM3100 sensor). We assumed that the best results would be achieved in the X axis, which is oriented perpendicular to the road axis, and this was confirmed. An exception is the RM3100 sensor, which achieved the best SNR ratio in the Y axis (3.1–5.4 dB higher than in the X axis). It should be possible to use the values measured in both axes for the detection and eventual classification of vehicles. The Z axis at this sensor location contains the smallest information content.

The different SNR level for the individual sensors is also visible in Figure 4, which shows the record of the Ford Focus combi with all sensors in the X-axis and in Figure 5, which shows a short part of recorded data by all sensors in the X-axis during both measurements.

From the records in Figure 5, it is possible to observe a significant influence of the quality of the used sensor (sensitivity and intrinsic noise) and the distance of sensors from the road (measurement 1 versus measurement 2). Significantly higher deformation of the Earth's magnetic field caused by real passage of vehicle was recorded by RM3100 and LIS3MDL sensors, and it is about 10 times higher in comparison with deformations obtained by FXOS8700 a MLX90393 sensors. The recorded deformation of magnetic field is reduced about half by moving all sensors by 0.5 m. Displayed results confirm that the RM3100 sensor is the best and the MLX90393 sensor is the worst of the tested magnetometers. The red dots in the figure mark the passing vehicle.

The most important test is to evaluate the success of vehicle detection by individual sensors. As part of pre-processing, it is necessary to remove noise and the DC component (offset) of the signal from the measured signals. The DC component of the signal depends on the size of the Earth's magnetic field and is generally different at each place on Earth. A low-pass filter was used to suppress noise. After frequency analysis of the measured signals, we found that the useful signal contains frequency components up to about 2 Hz. Therefore, we chose the frequency of the low-pass filter at 2.5 Hz. The attenuation of the higher frequency components was 60 dB per decade. The DC component of the signal was calculated as the arithmetic mean of the values in that part of the signal where no vehicles passed. After removing the DC component, we found that the signals in some sensor axes still exhibited a certain offset that varied linearly over time. This linear offset was identified and removed. Only the RM3100 did not contain a linear offset in any axis. The worst in this respect was the LIS3MDL sensor, whose offset sometimes seemed to "float". Note that in real operation an algorithm for continuous offset detection and removal must be used.

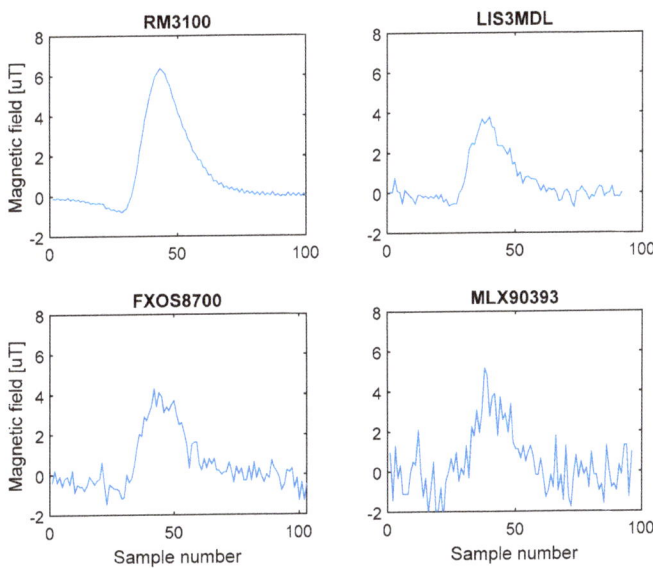

Figure 4. Record of Ford Focus combi in X axis.

We used two different approaches to detect vehicles—in the first case we evaluated only the signal in the most important X-axis and in the second case we also used data measured in other axes. In both cases, we intentionally used a simple detection algorithm to highlight the influence of the sensor properties (especially intrinsic noise and sensitivity) on the results obtained. A sophisticated detection algorithm could partially erase the differences between the individual sensors.

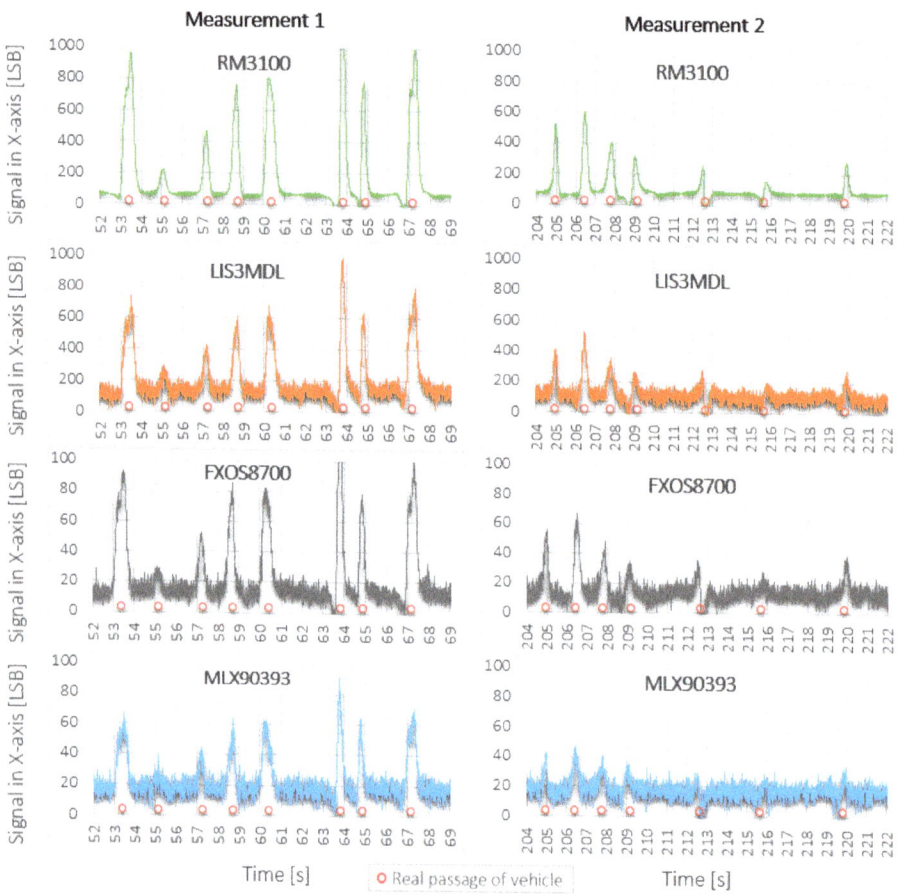

Figure 5. Comparison of recorded data by all sensors during both test measurements.

7. Detection Algorithm

The algorithm is based on the detection of the signal crossing over one threshold value. Therefore, the input signal must be non-negative (e.g., signal energy). When evaluating the signal, we considered the real properties of the vehicles and the traffic itself, namely the length of the vehicle and the gap between the vehicles. The length of vehicles is usually greater than 4 m. This, at a speed of 50 km/h (the municipal speed limit in Slovakia) and a sampling frequency of 100 Hz, represents approximately 29 samples per vehicle. The same goes for the gap between vehicles. We tested different settings for both parameters and selected the settings that achieved the best results. In one case the minimum vehicle length was 14 samples and the sample gap 21, in the other case the values 30 and 60 were used. The basic principle of the detection algorithm is shown in Figure 6. The algorithm assumes input signal with removed noise and zero offset.

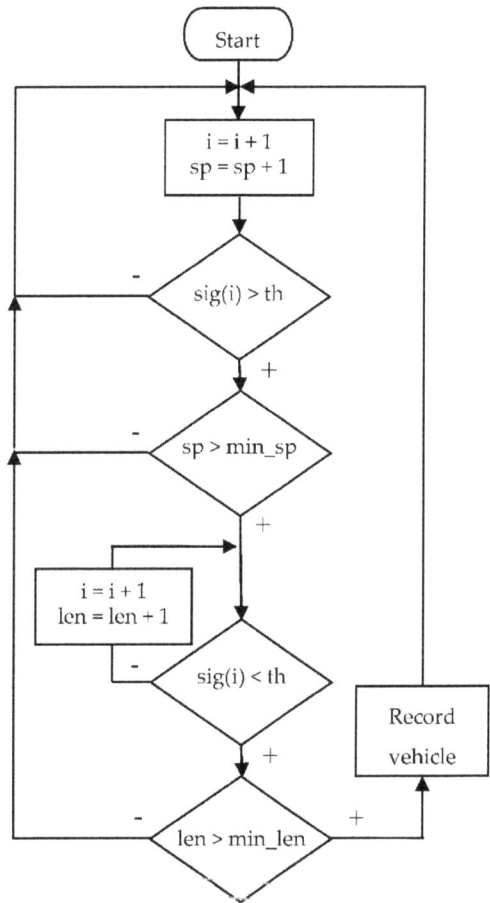

sig(i) – actual sample, th – threshold, sp – space between vehicles, min_sp – minimal space
len – length of vehicle, min_len – minimal length

Figure 6. Detection algorithm principle.

The algorithm successively compares all samples with the threshold. After exceeding the threshold, the length of the gap between the vehicles is checked. If the gap is sufficient, we assume that this is the beginning of the new vehicle record. If the gap is too small, we consider the record to be a continuation of the previous vehicle's record. This part of the algorithm is not shown in Figure 6 for the sake of clarity. After detecting the vehicle, the algorithm waits for the signal to drop below a threshold value. The length of the vehicle is given by the number of samples that are above the threshold. The length must be greater than the given minimum value. In Figure 7 is an example of a gap that is too short and a gap that is long enough.

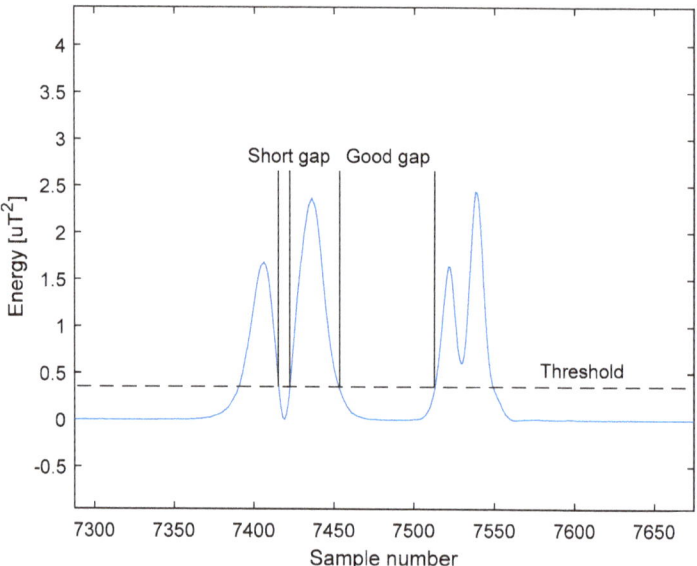

Figure 7. Example of gap length evaluation.

7.1. Application Scenario No.1—The Detection Based on the Single Signal

The energy of the most significant component of the signal (X-axis), which is proportional to the square of the signal, was used as the input signal for the detection algorithm. Example of the signal energy for the best sensor RM3100 and the worst sensor MLX90393 is shown in Figure 8. An important fact is that the input signal from the RM3100 sensor remains almost three times larger than the input signal from the MLX90393 due to its higher sensitivity and low level of intrinsic noise. This has a direct effect on the success of the detection, especially in cases of very low response from the passing vehicle (e.g., if the vehicle passed in the measuring profile at a greater distance from the sensors). This case can be observed from the detection results of both sensors, for both measurements in the graphs in Figure 8, where the results of detection by a given sensor are displayed (green and blue dots), as well as the actual vehicle crossings determined from the camera recording (real passage of vehicle, red dots). The method of evaluation and the results of the detection itself for all sensors are given below for both measurements.

The vehicle detection results based on the input signal are highly dependent on the specific value of the threshold. When choosing it, a compromise must be made between the number of undetected vehicles and the number of false positives. The lower the threshold, the more vehicles we can detect. However, at the same time, the algorithm is more prone to exceeding the threshold value due to noise or offset change, which is a false positive. Since we do not know in advance which threshold is the best, we performed detection for different thresholds. Figure 9 shows the dependence of the number of undetected vehicles on the size of the threshold value for all sensors.

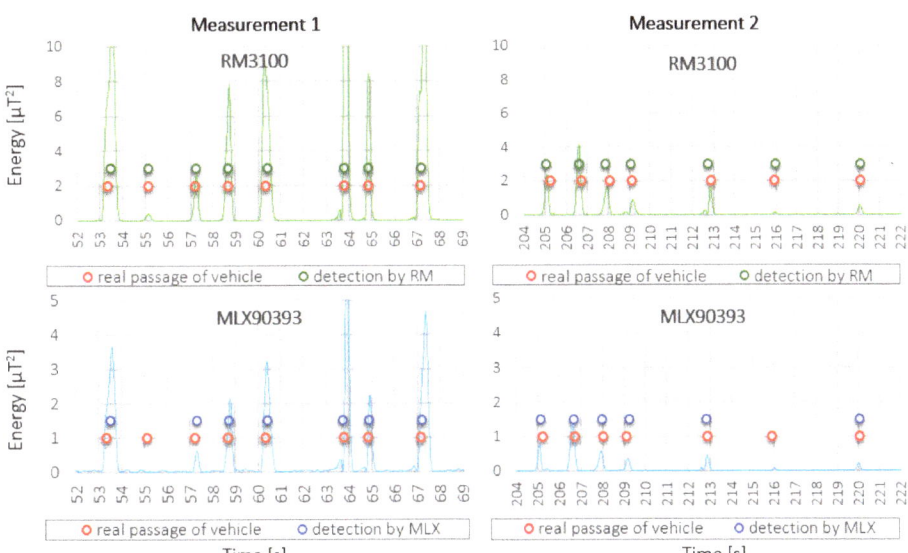

Figure 8. Comparison of the change of the input signal for detection at measurement 1 and measurement 2 for two selected sensors—RM3100 and MLX90393.

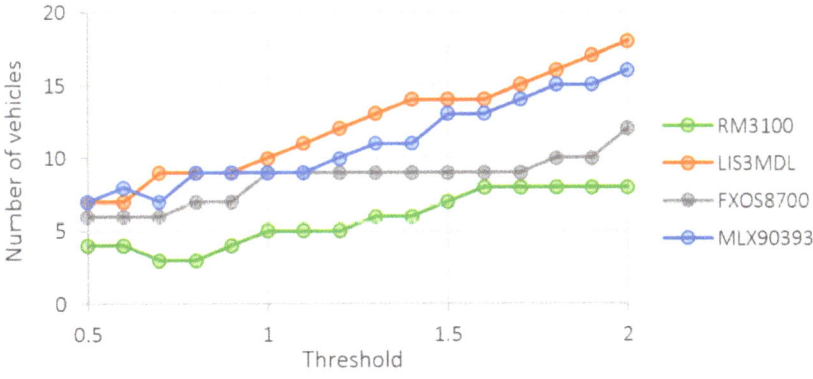

Figure 9. Number of undetected vehicles at different threshold level.

The number of undetected vehicles is expected to increase with increasing threshold size. This does not only apply to very low threshold levels, when several records are "merged" into one, especially for sensors with higher intrinsic noise. The best result was achieved by the RM3100 sensor. It is followed by FXOS8700 and at the end LIS3MDL with MLX90393 were placed. Given the proclaimed, relatively high sensitivity of the LIS3MDL sensor and the amount of noise and SNR compared to the FXOS8700 sensor, this result is quite surprising.

Figure 10 shows the dependence of the number of false positives on the size of the threshold value. Due to the higher noise of the LIS3MDL, FXOS8700 and MLX90393 sensors, frequent false detections occur at low thresholds.

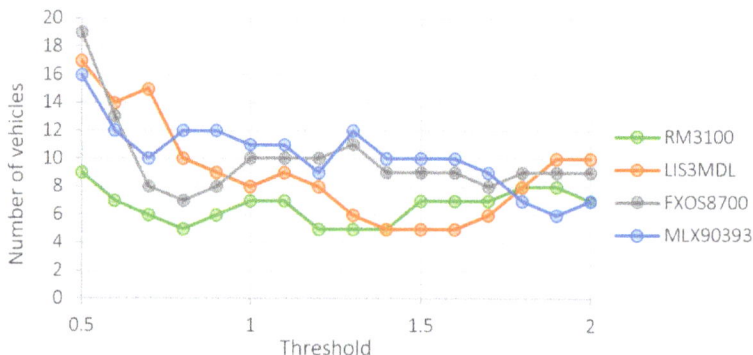

Figure 10. Number of false positives at different threshold level.

Figure 11 shows the total number of errors—the sum of undetected vehicles and false positives.

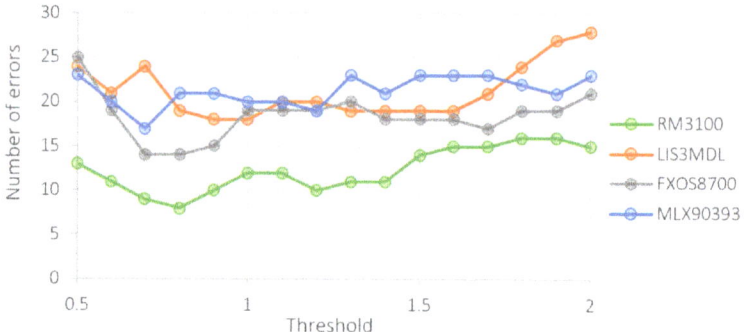

Figure 11. Total number of errors at different threshold level.

All three last images were obtained for parameter settings 14/21 (minimum vehicle length and minimum gap). For the 30/60 setting, the number of undetected vehicles increases, and the number of false positives decreases. In both cases, the reason is the tightening of requirements.

The best sensor is the RM3100, which can keep false positives low over a wide range of threshold levels. This is due to the very low noise of this sensor. Upon closer examination of the reasons of false positives for the RM3100 sensor, we found that they were all caused by the passage of trucks in the opposite direction. It is a "tax" for its high sensitivity.

Comparing Figures 9 and 10, we see that sensors achieve the best results at different threshold levels. A trade-off needs to be made between the sensor's ability to detect vehicles and the number of false positives. In this respect, the RM3100 sensor is again the best. The detection ability of this sensor is not as sensitive to the level of the threshold as it is for other sensors. This allows to choose a threshold value that is optimal in both respects.

Table 6 shows the optimal threshold level for each sensor together with the achieved results. We determined the optimal threshold level by taking the minimum of the sum of undetected vehicles and false positives.

Table 6. Optimal threshold level and detection results for measurement 1.

Detection Parameters	Observed Characteristics	RM3100	LIS3MDL	FXOS8700	MLX90393
14/21	Threshold	0.8	0.9	0.8	0.7
	Undetected	3 (3.4%)	9 (10.2%)	7 (8.0%)	7 (8.0%)
	False	8 (9.1%)	9 (10.2%)	7 (8.0%)	10 (11.4%)
	Errors	11	18	14	17
30/60	Threshold	1.2	0.9	0.9	0.7
	Undetected	8 (9.1%)	12 (13.6%)	10 (11.4%)	11 (12.5%)
	False	3 (3.4%)	2 (2.3%)	3 (3.4%)	2 (2.3%)
	Errors	11	14	13	13

For all sensors, the best results were obtained for detection parameters 30/60. In this case, there are more undetected vehicles and a low number of false positives. If we require a lower number of undetected vehicles, it is better to use the 14/21 setting.

The results of the second measurement, with the sensor located at a distance of 0.5 m from the lane, are shown in Table 7.

Table 7. Optimal threshold level and detection results for measurement 2.

Detection Parameters	Observed Characteristics	RM3100	LIS3MDL	FXOS8700	MLX90393
14/21	Threshold	0.5	0.3	0.8	0.8
	Undetected	1 (1.1%)	1 (1.1%)	5 (5.3%)	10 (10.6%)
	False	5 (5.3%)	9 (9.6%)	3 (3.2%)	3 (3.2%)
	Errors	6	10	8	13
30/60	Threshold	1.4	0.3	0.8	0.8
	Undetected	7 (7.4%)	9 (9.6%)	5 (5.3%)	11 (11.7%)
	False	2 (2.1%)	9 (9.6%)	2 (2.1%)	2 (2.1%)
	Errors	9	18	7	13

Despite the greater distance of the sensor from the road, the sensors achieved better results than in the first measurement. This result may seem paradoxical, but it cannot be generalized. The change in magnetic field caused by large vehicles in the opposite direction can be detected by sensors and usually manifests as false positive but can also cause the records of several vehicles to be combined into one. Of course, the composition of the vehicles in both directions was not the same in both measurements, so different number of false positives and/or combined records were generated. The influence of oncoming vehicles can be reduced by using several sensors placed parallel to the road. Exploring this option is beyond the objectives of this article.

7.2. Application Scenario No.2—The Detection Based on the Multiple Signals

In this section, we focused on identifying opportunities to improve detection through the use of signals measured in different axes. We examined all combinations of signals measured in two axes, while we used the following relations to combine two signals into one: $A^2 + B^2$, $(A + B)^2$, abs(A) + abs(B) and arctan(A/B) (according to [19]). For the sensors RM3100, FXOS8700 and MLX90393, the best results were obtained with the sum of the signal energies in the X and Y axes, i.e. $X^2 + Y^2$. Only the LIS3MDL sensor shows the best results for the combined signal $X^2 + Z^2$. Table 8 shows the best results obtained for the first measurement.

Table 8. Detection parameters and results for measurement 1.

Observed Characteristics	RM3100	LIS3MDL	FXOS8700	MLX90393
Detection parameters	14/21	14/21	14/21	14/21
Axes	$X^2 + Y^2$	$X^2 + Z^2$	$X^2 + Y^2$	$X^2 + Y^2$
Threshold	0.9	1.4	1.3	0.9
Undetected	3 (3.4%)	5 (5.7%)	6 (6.8%)	8 (9.1%)
False	3 (3.4%)	3 (3.4%)	4 (4.5%)	5 (5.7%)
Errors	6	8	10	13
Change in%	45	33	23	0

The use of values from two axes led to significantly better, or at least the same, results as when using one axis (comparison with Table 6). This time, better results were obtained for detection parameters 14/21. This is because adding the energies of the two signals increases the width of the vehicle's recording and decreases the gap between vehicles. If a longer gap is required (60 vs. 21), the vehicle records are removed more frequently. Adding the two signals also requires increasing the size of the threshold. The LIS3MDL sensor is the only one to achieve the best results for the combination of X and Z axes. For other sensors, the combination of X and Y axes is the best.

We evaluated the second measurement in the same way. For all sensors, the best results were obtained for the combined signal $X^2 + Y^2$. Table 9 shows the achieved results.

Table 9. Detection parameters and results for measurement 2.

Observed Characteristics	RM3100	LIS3MDL	FXOS8700	MLX90393
Detection parameters	14/21	14/21	14/21	14/21
Axes	$X^2 + Y^2$	$X^2 + Y^2$	$X^2 + Y^2$	$X^2 + Y^2$
Threshold	0.6	1.0	1.2	0.9
Undetected	1 (1.1%)	1 (1.1%)	7 (7.4%)	8 (8.5%)
False	5 (5.3%)	10 (10.6%)	2 (2.1%)	2 (2.1%)
Errors	6	11	9	10
Change in%	0	−10	−28	23

Unlike the first measurement, the results have now only been improved for the MLX90393 sensor. The results of the RM3100 did not improve and the results of the other two sensors were even worse. The percentage of deterioration looks significant, but in reality, it was only an increase in the number of errors by one and two (respectively LIS3MDL and FXOS8700).

8. Summary of Results

To determine the real properties of the sensors (RM3100, LIS3MDL, FXOS8700, and MLX90393), measurements were performed in the laboratory and under real conditions. Measurements in the laboratory were aimed at determining the amount of noise that can be expected when measuring with the sensors. The magnitude of the measured noise depends on the sensor's own noise, the noise generated by the sensing device and the ambient noise. We minimized the ambient noise mainly by increasing the distance of the sensors from the main sources of interference (computers and electrical wiring). The effect of the sensing device itself, which is based on the RPi, was tested in two ways—by placing the expansion board with sensors directly on the RPi and by distancing the expansion board from the RPi with a cable.

The first measurement was performed for each sensor separately. The measurement results showed that the magnitude of the measured noise is lower when placing the expansion board on the cable. The differences of noise level were small, within a few percent. Significant differences were recorded only for the RM3100 sensor, which is the most sensitive of all tested sensors.

In the second measurement, the noise was measured simultaneously by all sensors. Simultaneous sensing by all sensors causes increased current consumption and also more frequent communication via the I2C bus, which is reflected in an increase in the measured noise. The largest percentage difference compared to the first measurement was recorded for the FXOS8700 sensor (almost 30% for the X-axis). As in the first measurement, lower noise was measured when the expansion board was placed on the cable. The exception was the RM3100 sensor, which recorded in the X-axis almost twice as much noise on the cable as on the board. This anomaly was caused by the orientation of the cable parallel to the X-axis of the sensor and its high sensitivity.

In both measurements in the laboratory, the order of the sensors according to the amount of noise was as follows (sorted from the smallest noise to the largest): RM3100, LIS3MDL, FXOS8700 and MLX90393.

Despite the higher measured noise value (usually by a few percent), we decided to use sensors placed directly on the expansion board in further measurements. The decisive factor was the much simpler handling of the sensing device.

The performance of sensors in vehicle detection was tested in two measurements performed on a local two-lane road. In the first case, the sensor was placed on the outer edge of the road line and in the second case, it was at a distance of 0.5 m from the road line. First, we evaluated the amount of noise, which was slightly lower than in the laboratory measurements. This is due to the smaller number of sources of interfering electromagnetic noise in the exterior.

The ability of the sensors to detect the vehicle is largely dependent on the magnitude of the signal-to-noise ratio, i.e., the SNR. Therefore, for both measurements, we calculated the average SNR value from the records of ten passenger cars. This measurement showed how important it is to place the sensor as close to the lane as possible. Increasing the distance by 0.5 m results in a significant decrease in SNR (depending on the axis, the difference is from 3 to 8 dB for the RM3100 sensor). The highest SNR values were recorded by the RM3100 sensor. This test also showed that the highest SNR is achieved in the X and Y axes.

In order to compare the performance of sensors in vehicle detection, an algorithm based on the evaluation of the measured signal energy transition over a threshold value was used. The X-axis signal was used for evaluation. During preprocessing the DC component was removed from the measured signal and the noise was suppressed by a low-pass filter. Only the RM3100 sensor has not any offset. The worst in terms of preprocessing is the LIS3MDL sensor, whose offset seems to "float". For the other sensors, the offset was a linear function of time.

The performance of the detection algorithm depends on the level of the threshold. Therefore, we evaluated each sensor for different threshold levels. In addition to the size of the threshold, we tested various settings for the minimum length of the vehicle and the minimum gap between vehicles. When comparing sensor performance, we used the best settings found for each sensor separately. We evaluated the number of undetected vehicles and the number of false positives. The RM3100 sensor achieved the best results in both measurements. The high sensitivity of the RM3100 sensor causes a low number of undetected vehicles (3.4% and 1.1% in the first and second measurements) but on the other hand a higher number of false positives, which were caused by the detection of vehicles moving in the far lane. This sensor is also the least sensitive to the specified threshold level. The increased sensitivity of other sensors to the size of the threshold in practice means higher demands on the processing of input data, as well as on the detection algorithm itself. From this point of view, the RM3100 sensor offers a certain stability during detection, even in the most unfavorable detection conditions (e.g., greater distance of the vehicle from the sensor when passing through the measuring profile, lower volume of ferromagnetic parts in the vehicle, etc.).

We also tested the possibility of improving detection by using signals measured in multiple axes. The results obtained are ambiguous. In the first measurement, the detection was improved for three sensors, but in the second measurement only for one sensor and for the other two, the results were even worsened. From this point of view, the RM3100 sensor was again the best, which achieved an improvement of 45% in the first measurement and in the second there was neither improvement nor deterioration of the results.

A summary of the achieved results is given in Table 10 in the form of the score. We determined the order of individual sensors for each evaluated area. When evaluating the success of the detection, we took into account the average of the results of both measurements.

Table 10. Summary of the achieved results.

Parameter	RM3100	LIS3MDL	FXOS8700	MLX90393
Sensitivity	1	2–3	2–3	4
Noise level	1	2	3	4
SNR	1	2	3	4
Offset	1	4	2	3
Detection—one axis	1	3–4	2	3–4
Detection—two axes	1	3	2	4
Size	4	1	3	2
Price	4	1	3	2
Energy consumption [1]	4	3	1	2

[1] Based on datasheet values.

For the overall evaluation, we considered only the first six criteria. Size, price, and energy consumption are not very important for the development of a sensor for short-term traffic survey.

The RM3100 sensor was the best in all important areas. Its high sensitivity and low noise allow the best detection of vehicles, even at a greater distance of the sensor from the road. The disadvantage of high sensitivity is the higher susceptibility to errors caused by the passage of vehicles in the opposite direction, which, however, can be eliminated by a more sophisticated detection algorithm. In second place is FXOS8700, closely followed by LIS3MDL. The MLX90393 sensor was placed last, which is mainly due to its higher noise combined with lower sensitivity. However, even its results are not unusable, especially when measuring near the lane. At longer distances (more than 1.0 m), there is a significant increase in the risk that the response from a passing vehicle will be literally "buried" in the sensor's own noise.

9. Conclusions

Our goal was to compare selected magnetometers in terms of the possibility of their use to detect vehicles when placing the sensor next to the road. An expansion board for the RaspberryPi was designed for simultaneous measurement with all sensors. With the created sensing device, initial tests were performed under laboratory conditions, while we evaluated the amount of noise measured by the sensors at different configurations of the measuring device.

The most important were the measurements made on the road with real traffic. We performed two measurements at different distances from the road. We evaluated the measured signals using an algorithm for vehicle detection based on signal energy. We found the best settings of the detection algorithm parameters for each sensor. We also investigated the possibility of vehicle detection based on the evaluation of signals from several axes of the magnetometer.

The order of the sensors was as follows: RM3100, FXOS8700, LIS3MDL and MLX90393. The RM3100 sensor achieved the best results in all tests. This sensor has the highest sensitivity and the lowest intrinsic noise. These features allow the sensor to be placed at greater distances from the road, which is very important due to the possibility of

Sensors **2021**, *21*, 266

placing automatic traffic counters during traffic surveys. A good feature of the RM3100 is also the possibility of increasing its sensitivity at lower sampling frequency and/or a smaller number of scanned axes. The main disadvantages of the RM3100 include its larger dimensions and by far the highest price.

These results are only the first stage in designing a suitable sensor for the magnetic traffic counter to be placed at the roadside.

The analysis presented in the paper will serve to the future research when the special sensor node for traffic surveillance will be designed. With respect to the paper findings, magnetometer RM3100 will be used as the main sensing unit for this node. According to the SoA analysis in Section 2, it is expected that magnetometer pair spaced by the exact distance of min. 10 cm will provide sufficient performance for accurate road vehicle detection even in if vehicle will pass during traffic jam. For detection purposes, bandpass filter together with local maxima detection on correlated signals from both magnetometers should be applied. Vehicle classification will be then based on the convolutional neural network applied to the recorded detections. For this purpose, the building of robust dataset belongs to one of the most important tasks of our future research.

Author Contributions: M.H. and P.Š. designed HW platform and realized measurements, O.K. implemented software for measurements and together with A.K. evaluated the results. All authors have read and agreed to the published version of the manuscript.

Funding: This research together with the APC was funded by the Interreg V-A SK-CZ Cross-border Cooperation Program grant number ITMS 304011P777-Innovative monitoring and analysis of traffic on the cross-border road network.

Institutional Review Board Statement: Not applicable.

Informed Consent Statement: Not applicable.

Data Availability Statement: The data presented in this study are available on request from the corresponding author.

Acknowledgments: This contribution is the result of the project Innovative monitoring and analysis of traffic on the cross-border road network, ITMS 304011P777 supported by the Interreg V-A SK-CZ Cross-border Cooperation Program.

Conflicts of Interest: The authors declare no conflict of interest.

References

1. Karpis, O. Sensor for vehicles classification. In Proceedings of the Federated Conference on Computer Science and Information Systems (FedCSIS), Wroclaw, Poland, 9–12 September 2012; pp. 785–789.
2. Hodon, M.; Karpis, O.; Sevcik, P.; Micek, J.; Sarafin, P.; Hudik, M.; Kocianova, A. Methodology for the choice of a right digital magnetometer for the vehicle detection purposes. *Sens. Transducers* **2019**, *238*, 57–63.
3. Hodon, M.; Karpis, O.; Sevcik, P.; Micek, J.; Kocianova, A. An overview of magnetometer sensors performance for the purposes of traffic flow monitoring. In Proceedings of the 5th International Conference on Sensors and Electronic Instrumentation Advances (SEIA '2019), Adeje, Spain, 25–27 September 2019; IFSA Publishing: Barcelona, Spain, 2019; pp. 195–199.
4. Paidi, V.; Fleyeh, H.; Håkansson, J.; Nyberg, R.G. Smart parking sensors, technologies and applications for open parking lots: A review. *IET Intell. Transp. Syst.* **2018**, *12*, 735–741. [CrossRef]
5. Yang, J.J.; Zuo, B. Performance of Wireless Magnetometers for Stop Bar Detection at Signalized Intersections. *Transp. Res. Rec. J. Transp. Res. Board* **2018**, *2672*, 55–63. [CrossRef]
6. Balid, W.; Tafish, H.; Refai, H.H. Intelligent Vehicle Counting and Classification Sensor for Real-Time Traffic Surveillance. *IEEE Trans. Intell. Transp. Syst.* **2018**, *19*, 1784–1794. [CrossRef]
7. Balid, W.; Refai, H.H. Real-time magnetic length-based vehicle classification: Case study for inductive loops and wireless magnetometer sensors in Oklahoma state. *Transp. Res. Rec. J. Transp. Res. Board* **2018**, *2672*, 102–111. [CrossRef]
8. Prateek, G.V.; Nijil, K.; Hari, K.V.S. Classification of Vehicles Using Magnetic Field Angle Model. In Proceedings of the 4th International Conference on Intelligent Systems, Modelling and Simulation, Bankok, Thailand, 29–31 January 2013. [CrossRef]
9. Feng, Y.; Mao, G.; Cheng, B.; Li, C.; Hui, Y.; Xu, Z. MagMonitor: Vehicle Speed Estimation and Vehicle Classification through a Magnetic Sensor. *IEEE Trans. Intell. Transp. Syst.* **2020**, 1–12. [CrossRef]
10. Chen, X.; Kong, X.; Xu, M.; Sandrasegaran, K.; Zheng, J. Road Vehicle Detection and Classification Using Magnetic Field Measurement. *IEEE Access* **2019**, *7*, 52622–52633. [CrossRef]

11. Santoso, B.; Yang, B.; Ong, C.H.L.; Yuan, Z. Traffic Flow and Vehicle Speed Measurements using Anisotropic Magnetoresistive (AMR) Sensors. In Proceedings of the International Magnetics Conference (INTERMAG), Singapore, 23–27 April 2018. [CrossRef]
12. Wahlström, N.; Hostettler, R.; Gustafsson, F.; Birk, W. Rapid classification of vehicle heading direction with two-axis magnetometer. In Proceedings of the International Conference on Acoustics, Speech and Signal Processing (ICASSP), Kyoto, Japan, 25–30 March 2012. [CrossRef]
13. Hostettler, R.; Djurić, P.M. Vehicle Tracking Based on Fusion of Magnetometer and Accelerometer Sensor Measurements with Particle Filtering. *IEEE Trans. Veh. Technol.* **2015**, *64*, 4917–4928. [CrossRef]
14. Balid, W.; Tafish, H.; Refai, H.H. Cost effective Vehicle Classification using a single wireless magnetometer. In Proceedings of the International Wireless Communications and Mobile Computing Conference (IWCMC), Paphos, Cyprus, 5–9 September 2016; pp. 194–199. [CrossRef]
15. Bao, X.; Li, H.; Xu, D.; Jia, L.; Ran, B.; Rong, J. Traffic Vehicle Counting in Jam Flow Conditions Using Low-Cost and Energy-Efficient Wireless Magnetic Sensors. *Sensors* **2016**, *16*, 1868. [CrossRef] [PubMed]
16. Sarcevic, P.; Plet, S. Vehicle Classification and False Detection Filtering using a Single Magnetic Detector based Intelligent Sensor. In Proceedings of the 2018 IEEE 16th International Symposium on Intelligent Systems and Informatics (SISY), Subotica, Serbia, 13–15 September 2018. [CrossRef]
17. Xu, C.; Wang, Y.; Bao, X.; Li, F. Vehicle Classification Using an Imbalanced Dataset Based on a Single Magnetic Sensor. *Sensors* **2018**, *18*, 1690. [CrossRef] [PubMed]
18. Feng, Y.; Mao, G.; Cheng, B.; Huang, B.; Wang, S.; Chen, J. MagSpeed: A Novel Method of Vehicle Speed Estimation through a Single Magnetic Sensor. In Proceedings of the IEEE Intelligent Transportation Systems Conference (ITSC), Auckland, New Zealand, 27–30 October 2019. [CrossRef]
19. Wang, Q.; Zheng, J.; Xu, H.; Xu, B.; Chen, R. Roadside Magnetic Sensor System for Vehicle Detection in Urban Environments. *IEEE Trans. Intell. Transp. Syst.* **2018**, *19*, 1365–1374. [CrossRef]
20. Haoui, A.; Kavaler, R.; Varaiya, P. Wireless magnetic sensors for traffic surveillance. Transportation. *Transp. Res. Part. C Emerg. Technol.* **2008**, *16*, 294–306. [CrossRef]
21. Guilbert, D.; Bastard, C.L.; Leng, S.; Wang, Y. State Machine for Detecting Vehicles by Magnetometer Sensors. *IEEE Sens. J.* **2016**, *16*, 5127–5128. [CrossRef]
22. Floris, A.; Girau, R.; Porcu, S.; Pettorru, G.; Atzori, L. Implementation of a Magnetometer based Vehicle Detection System for Smart Parking applications. In Proceedings of the IEEE International Smart Cities Conference (ISC2), Piscataway, NJ, USA, 28 September–1 October 2020. [CrossRef]
23. Solic, P.; Leoni, A.; Colella, R.; Perkovic, T.; Catarinucci, L.; Stornelli, V. IoT-Ready Energy-Autonomous Parking Sensor Device. *IEEE Internet Things J.* **2020**. [CrossRef]
24. Fura, V.; Petrucha, V.; Platil, A. Construction of an AMR magnetometer for car detection experiments. In Proceedings of the IOP Conf. Series: Materials Science and Engineering, 5th International Conference on Materials and Applications for Sensors and Transducers, Mykonos, Greece, 27–30 September 2015. [CrossRef]
25. Arab, M.; Nadeem, T.; Park, M. Locating On-Street Parking Spaces Using Magnetometer-Based Pedestrians' Smartphones. In Proceedings of the 14th Annual IEEE International Conference on Sensing, Communication, and Networking (SECON), San Diego, CA, USA, 12–14 June 2017. [CrossRef]
26. Bikku, T.; Narayana, V.L.; Gopi, A.P.; Khadherbhi, S.R. Sensors Systems for Traffic Congestion Reduction Methodologies. In Proceedings of the Third International conference on I-SMAC, Palladam, India, 12–14 December 2019. [CrossRef]
27. Moin, A.S.; Tanuja, C.; Senthil Kumar, N.C.; Nallakaruppan, M.K.; Senthilkumaran, U. Sensing Drunken Drivers Using Data Science. In Proceedings of the 5th International Conference on Advanced Computing & Communication Systems (ICACCS), Coimbatore, India, 15–16 March 2019. [CrossRef]
28. Leng, S.; Briand, P. Infrastructure and Vehicle Communication for Speed Limitation Based on Magnetic Markers. In Proceedings of the IEEE Intelligent Vehicles Symposium, Tokyo, Japan, 13–15 June 2006. [CrossRef]
29. Chen, C.; Liu, B.; Wan, S.; Qiao, P.; Pei, Q. An Edge Traffic Flow Detection Scheme Based on Deep Learning in an Intelligent Transportation System. *IEEE Trans. Intell. Transp. Syst.* **2020**, 1–13. [CrossRef]
30. Tsai, C.; Tseng, C.; Tang, H.; Guo, J. Vehicle Detection and Classification based on Deep Neural Network for Intelligent Transportation Applications. In Proceedings of the Asia-Pacific Signal and Information Processing Association Annual Summit and Conference (APSIPA ASC), Honolulu, HI, USA, 12–15 November 2018. [CrossRef]
31. Sreelatha, R.; Roopalakshmi, R.; Bharadwaj, K.A. An Enhanced Traffic Abnormality Detection System for Vehicle Characteristics Tracking using Radar Signals. In Proceedings of the 2nd International Conference on Innovative Mechanisms for Industry Applications (ICIMIA), Bangalore, India, 5–7 March 2020. [CrossRef]
32. Bernas, M.; Płaczek, B.; Korski, W.; Loska, P.; Smyła, J.; Szymała, P. A survey and comparison of low-cost sensing technologies for road traffic monitoring. *Sensors* **2018**, *18*, 3243. [CrossRef] [PubMed]
33. Handscombe, J.; Yu, H.Q. Low-cost and data anonymised city traffic flow data collection to support intelligent traffic system. *Sensors* **2019**, *19*, 347. [CrossRef] [PubMed]
34. Álvarez-Bazo, F.; Sánchez-Cambronero, S.; Vallejo, D.; Glez-Morcillo, C.; Rivas, A.; Gallego, I. A low-cost automatic vehicle identification sensor for traffic networks analysis. *Sensors* **2020**, *20*, 5589. [CrossRef] [PubMed]

Article

BLE-Based Indoor Tracking System with Overlapping-Resistant IoT Solution for Tourism Applications

Radosław Belka *, Roman Stanisław Deniziak , Grzegorz Łukawski and Paweł Pięta

Faculty of Electrical Engineering, Automatic Control and Computer Science, Kielce University of Technology, Al. Tysiąclecia P.P.7, 25-314 Kielce, Poland; s.deniziak@tu.kielce.pl (R.S.D.); g.lukawski@tu.kielce.pl (G.Ł.); p.pieta@tu.kielce.pl (P.P.)
* Correspondence: r.belka@tu.kielce.pl; Tel.: +48-41-342-4369

Abstract: In this paper, an overlapping-resistant Internet of Things (IoT) solution for a Bluetooth Low Energy (BLE)-based indoor tracking system (BLE-ITS) is presented. The BLE-ITS is a promising, inexpensive alternative to the well-known GPS. It can be used in human traffic analysis, such as indoor tourist facilities. Tourists or other customers are tagged by a unique MAC address assigned to a simple and energy-saving BLE beacon emitter. Their location is determined by a distributed and scalable network of popular Raspberry Pi microcomputers equipped with BLE and WiFi/Ethernet modules. Only simple triggered messages in the form of login records (LRs) are sent to a server, where the so-called path vectors (PVs) and interest profile (IPr) are set. The authors implemented the prototype and demonstrated its usefulness in a controlled environment. As it is shown in the paper, the solution is highly overlap-resistant and mitigates the so-called multilocation problem.

Keywords: Internet of Things; Bluetooth; indoor tracking; mobile localization

Citation: Belka, R.; Deniziak, R.S.; Łukawski, G.; Pięta, P. BLE-Based Indoor Tracking System with Overlapping-Resistant IoT Solution for Tourism Applications. *Sensors* **2021**, *21*, 329. https://doi.org/10.3390/s21020329

Received: 26 November 2020
Accepted: 2 January 2021
Published: 6 January 2021

Publisher's Note: MDPI stays neutral with regard to jurisdictional claims in published maps and institutional affiliations.

1. Introduction

Innovation in the tourism sector is linked to modern solutions such as Internet of Things (IoT), distributed sensor networks (DSN), cloud computing, mobile communication, and machine learning [1]. Smart tourism should provide tour information and tour guidance services before, during, and after the trip. Thus, it requires the implementation of additional solutions to support the process of their development. Two main groups of requirements for smart tourism solutions can be distinguished. The first group is related to customers (visitors). They should be able to remotely plan a specific date and route of the tour and to obtain proposed paths of seeing and basic information about expositions, as well as weather forecasts or free parking places. Moreover, tourists want to receive information about his/her current position, propositions for further routes, and additional information about a given object. An appropriate tour report including the tourist's profile of interest and related information would also be appreciated after a finished visit.

The second group of functionalities is addressed to the management. They usually want to monitor the number of visitors in a given period, free places for given exhibition routes, and information about critical situations (overloads, emergencies, etc.). Some solutions such as automated pedestrian counters make it possible to understand how and when such facilities are being used. Unfortunately, existing solutions have many drawbacks: they are expensive, they do not provide information either about the sequence of visits (tracking functionality) or the individual preferences of the visitor, and they do not deliver personalized feedback.

This article focuses on one of the basic and very useful new functionalities, which is obtaining reliable statistical data about the degree of interest in each specific attraction—point of interest (POI)—both from a global and individual point of view. Gathering data about the level of interest in individual POIs allows park managers to better adapt the tourist offer and have more appropriate staff management. In addition, obtaining information about

133

the individual interest of a person (so-called interest profile—IPr) significantly supports the targeting process, i.e., customizing the individual offer. For this reason, it would be expedient to develop a solution that allows anonymous estimation of profiles of interest for individual clients. This becomes possible thanks to the use of IoT solutions and a location method based on Bluetooth Low Energy technology.

2. IoT/BLE-Based Positioning and Tracking Systems

The Internet of Things concept is currently one of the fastest growing ICT technologies, which has a significant impact on and benefits science and the economy. These solutions are based on the idea of linking everyday objects into a computer network, mainly for the exchange, processing, and analysis of data [2]. The IoT has been functioning in global solutions for many years, although not directly under the current name. According to the IoT analytics report [3], the concept of the Internet of Things usually covers areas of the so-called smart city and connected industry and building, but also appears in the areas of smart sales or agriculture.

One of the most important components of the IoT architecture is the distributed sensor network (DSN). In the considered case, the DSN should primarily provide information about the customer's location at a given time. There are many methods for locating and tracking a person or an object. The predominant mechanisms for tracking humans involve the use of video surveillance systems. These systems require a human operator to monitor the CCTV images at a central location. Loss of concentration usually occurs when fatigue sets in [4]. Vehicles and other objects are usually tracked using trackers whose implementation is based on the Global Positioning System (GPS). These systems display the location of a vehicle within a specified time frame. GPS, however, supports outdoor navigation since it requires line-of-sight operation with at least three satellites [5]. Another technique for implementing a tracking system is by using radio frequency identification (RFID). RFID uses either passive or active tags to track objects [6]. Passive RFID tracking is widespread in shops and libraries where tags are attached to products and are checked as they leave the shop by passing through receivers near the doors. Active RFID is popularly used in warehouses and locations such as airports where a larger range is needed. RFID tracking uses ultra-low power and there is no need for line-of-sight operation. While RFID tags are very cheap, small, and suitable for tracking objects, the sensors are considerably more expensive and require extensive configuration and software installation [7]. RFID signals are easily blocked by objects and other radio waves. One more method for tracking objects is based on GSM communication technology. The GSM equipment communicates with the GSM network through relay stations. The time at which the signals arrive, together with the angle of arrival from at least three stations, allows location detection through triangulation [8]. The main problem with GSM is the inaccuracy in location due to its limited coverage in densely populated areas [9].

The global navigation satellite system (GNSS) is the dominating technology for global positioning systems (GPSs), but since the GNSS signals are not able to penetrate buildings, other technologies should be used for indoor positioning systems (IPS). Methods using WiFi, ultra-wideband (UWB) [10], Zigbee [11], or visible light communication (VLC) were proposed. WiFi is often used for coarse urban localization with accuracy of tens of meters, but some methods for IPS were also developed [12]. The recent developments in Bluetooth technology have created new opportunities for IPS. Especially, Bluetooth Low Energy (BLE) supports low-cost, low-power beacons [13,14] that can be easily distributed. Moreover, BLE is available in all recent smartphones and many other mobile devices. However, BLE-based localization brings new challenges caused by the unique properties of BLE signals.

Indoor localization systems (ILSs) are based on measuring signals sent by transmitters. Various techniques are used for this purpose: time of arrival (TOA), time difference of arrival (TDOA), angle of arrival (AOA), and received signal strength indication (RSSI). Among them, only RSSI may be applied without additional hardware for existing wireless technologies. The most commonly used RSSI-based methods of localization are: trilateration, fingerprinting, and triangulation. Trilateration (or multilateration) [15–17] is based on measuring the signal strength by computing the distance between a client device and three (or more) access points with known positions. This method is simple, but since RSSI tends to fluctuate, the accuracy is low (about 2–4 m.). Fingerprinting is performed in two phases. During the first step (the offline phase), for each position the RSSI from several access points is recorded and stored in the fingerprint database. During the second step (online tracking phase), the current RSSI is compared with the values stored in the database and the closest match returns the position. This method provides acceptable accuracy (0.6–1.3 m), but in case of any changes, the database has to be updated. In the case of the triangulation method, the position is determined by measuring angles of signals received from at least three access points.

A lot of ILSs are applying the fingerprinting method. In [18], BLE was applied in offline training as well as online locating phases of the ILS. In this method, a Gaussian filter is used for the preprocessing of the signals received from BLE beacons. An ILS based on fingerprinting which uses various densities of beacons was presented in [19]. In [20], a method reducing the effort required for creating the fingerprinting map and determining the beacon positions was proposed. The method is based on graph-based optimization and uses the pedestrian dead reckoning method. Based on RSSI readings collected by a user walking in a region, the constraints for adjacent poses are generated. Then, the optimal set of poses constructing the fingerprinting map as well as the estimated positions of beacons is generated.

Since fingerprinting is known as not efficient due to the long-time location learning phase, some improvements enhancing the location accuracy were proposed. A hybrid approach based on fingerprinting and trilateration [21] uses a gradient filter for RSSI estimation. In weighted centroid localization (WCL) [22], a weight is assigned to each beacon for computing the distance. The weight is the inversed distance applied to a given degree. Thus, the beacon nearest to the location has the highest weight. In [23], a method based on fingerprinting and WCL was presented.

To achieve higher accuracy in trilateration-based methods, the inter Ring Localization Algorithm (iRingLA) was proposed [24]. Instead of one circle representing the distance from the beacon, in IRingLA, rings are used. The width of the ring corresponds to the RSSI measurement error. Then, the position is estimated as the most probable position from the intersection of at least three rings. Since the value of RSSI may depend on many factors other than the distance between devices, in [25], a method using more parameters was proposed. Instead of one instantaneous value for the RSSI/distance ratio, the reference RSSI and path lost index as well as error are computed as average values from experimental measurements of the RSSI. This way, the accuracy of 0.4 m was obtained.

Kalman-based fusion of trilateration and dead reckoning [26] enabled achieving a position accuracy of less than one meter. Dead reckoning estimates the client position assuming that the start position is known. The final position is estimated as a function of the step length and the total number of steps. An accelerometer, magnetometer, and orientation sensor are used in the localization process. A Kalman filter is used as a fusion center to compute the final position by merging positions obtained by the two fused methods. Another approach applying trilateration and Kalman filtering was proposed in [27]. In this method, the channel diversity is used to mitigate the effect of fast fading and the effect of interference during RSSI measurements. Kalman filtering is used for reducing the error caused by wrong RSSI measurements.

An example of a BLE-based localization system for smart home power management is given in [28]. The ILS is used for identification of the user location and power management using mobile devices. In [29], a system based on BLE beacons and dongles was used for user monitoring. To improve the accuracy, a machine learning algorithm was used. InLoc [30] is a system based on beacons and smartphones, which may be used for monitoring, tracking, guiding, emergency evacuation, and meeting planners. In [31], the Monte Carlo localization (MCL) method was presented. MCL is a technique for indoor localization using mobile phones with an accelerometer, compass, and BLE beacons. Some of the recent reviews of indoor localization systems and technologies are given in [32,33].

3. Sensor Network for Tourist Path—General Description

The preliminary concept of the system, general data structures, and some simulation analyses were presented in our previous works [34–36]. The presented system is primarily developed for collecting information on so-called interest profiles (activity profiles) for people visiting various types of indoor tourist attractions, such as museums or exhibitions. This means that for each client, a sequence of specific data denoted as a path vector (PV) should be obtained. The PV represents which attractions were visited, in what order, and how much interest they aroused for the visitor.

It should be noted that individual attractions (POIs—points of interest) can be located relatively close to each other, in particular several exhibitions can be placed in one museum room. Analysis of available indoor location methods indicates that the most advantageous solution is the BLE technology. In the related literature, the basic parameter subject to optimization is the position accuracy. As mentioned, positioning techniques based on BLE can be divided into range-based method (RbM) using triangulation (trilateration), and fingerprint-based methods (FbM) using a predefined reference fingerprint map (RFM). The disadvantage of the RbM approach is primarily the unreliability and inadequacy of the propagation models used in distance estimation. The location of the signal detector and the features of the POI objects (i.e., size and electrical conductivity) have a key impact on signal attenuation. This requires individual calibration of the propagation models to effectively estimate the position. Such activities are tedious and time-consuming and indicate that an RFM would be a better approach. However, in this case, the problem may be the instability of Bluetooth emitters, which requires obtaining an RFM for each of them.

This article focuses on the most important requirement of the developed system, which is obtaining information describing the interest profile of a particular visitor. It is worth noticing that, due to the spatial size of the POI, typically from several to tens of meters, the location accuracy has low importance. This means that the appearance of a specific person near a given POI may be dichotomous. Taking into account the specificity of distributed amusement parks, in the proposed system architecture, only one scanner could be associated with one POI. The possibility of using multiple scanners is being considered to improve the system's reliability and fault tolerance; however, this solution raises system costs. In the further part of the research, it was assumed that only one Bluetooth signal scanner/receiver is connected to one POI. Another assumption is to locate the signal detectors at a fixed position associated with the POI, while the visitors should be equipped with mobile signal transmitters. In the other proposed solutions, the role of the transmitter is often played by the client's personal mobile device, but such a solution threatens the anonymity of visitors. In order to ensure good privacy, it is recommended to equip visitors with portable emitting devices such as dedicated battery-powered beacons. In the presented solution, beacons equipped with the CSR101x series chipset (for BT 4.1) or the CSR102x series (for BT 5.0) were proposed.

The scheme of the system is shown in Figure 1. The BLE signal detection can be based on a popular single-board Raspberry Pi microcomputer typically equipped with 802.15.4 BLE 4.1 modules and proper 802.3 and 802.11 network interfaces. The devices are connected to an IPv4 network capable of carrying information to the server. For the purposes of demonstration, the role of the network may be a dedicated VLAN, separated from the university network infrastructure. The prototype server was based on the influxDB solution.

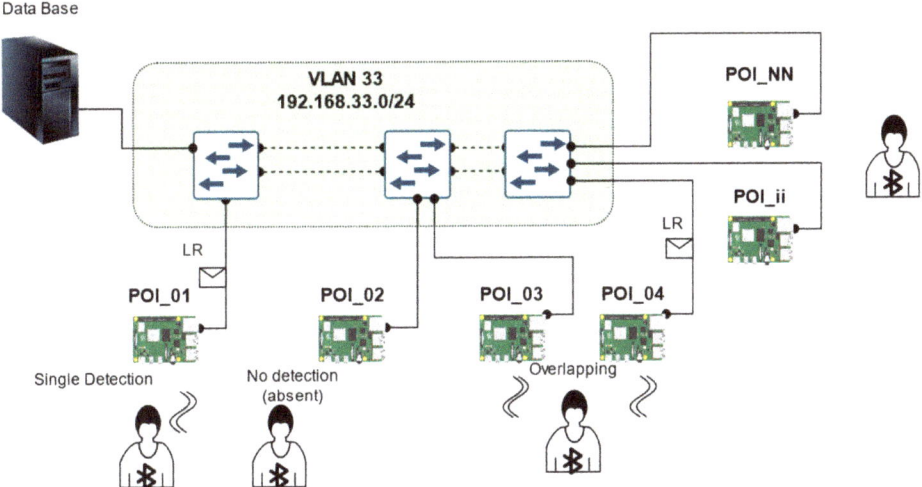

Figure 1. General diagram of the sensor network for a tourist path.

Areas of the detector's range (detection area—DA) should cover the whole POI. In typical variants known from other similar solutions, the emitters are located in fixed points near each attraction. This allows modifying the DA size using the Tx Power parameter setting option. In the proposed system, the emitters are located on the mobile client side, thus DAs will have rather comparable ranges. Meanwhile, the actual POIs in the park may be of different sizes. This will require a different approach to determining the parameter denoted as the interest level (IL), which represents the degree of interest in an attraction. Initially, this value can be related to the period of time that a visitor spent near a given attraction. Then, the key issue is to correctly recognize the moment of entry to the DA (so-called login time in—LTin) and the moment of definitive leave from the DA (LTout). However, this is not the only option. An alternative method of determining the IL parameter not directly related to the LTin and LTout timestamps will also be proposed.

The basic version of the system assumes that the individual POIs are so far apart that the corresponding DAs do not overlap. This is an assumption that may or may not be fulfilled, despite the specificity of the tourist facilities as theme parks. A client visiting individual attractions will leave behind a characteristic trace in the form of a so-called path vector (PV), which is a sequence of ILs. Basing on the PVs, information about the individual interest profile (IP) can be easily obtained. However, it should also consider situations where two or more DAs are overlapped, i.e., emitter signals are received simultaneously by two or more POI detectors. This is primarily a result of short proximity of attractions and may result in acquisition of false or uncertain statistical data. In contrast to the RbM and FbM methods, where it is a normal and desirable state, in the presented concept, it leads to an unacceptable phenomenon of multilocation. An additional assumption of the solution is to assign a given person to one and only attraction at a given time. The problem can only be slightly mitigated by adjusting the power level of Tx emitters. The goal is therefore to develop a method that can allow identifying the visitor's position as accurately as possible. For this reason, the development and testing of a proper data processing algorithm became necessary. Implementation of the algorithm should take place on scanning devices (in the SBC RPI 4B default), and the software was further called middleware.

4. Measurement Methodology

4.1. Experimental Procedures

The development of a prototype solution was preceded by a number of localization experiments. These experiments were divided into two phases. The main goal of the first phase was to develop a localization algorithm and choose its parameters for assuring the best localization consistency in a controlled laboratory environment. During this phase, a proprietary application for the Android 7+ operating system was used. The prototype application, called BleSkaner+, was run on smartphones. The application uses the Bluetooth 4.0+ interface for scanning nearby Bluetooth Low Energy (BLE) devices using a standard Android API [37]. For receiving as many beacon signals as possible, it uses the lowest latency mode available (ScanSettings.SCAN_MODE_LOW_LATENCY). Although the low latency mode is the most energy-consuming one, the application seems to have minimal influence on the total device battery life. For most of the devices used in the experiment, the BLE scan was automatically stopped by the operating system after about 30 min. For assuring a continuous measurement, the scan process is automatically restarted every 25 min. Research results show that the loss of signals during the restart may be neglected. The application stores scan results in CSV files in the device's file system. These files may also be synchronized with an FTP server. The raw data were then analyzed in PTC Mathcad and free statistic software PAST 3.21 [38].

First, basic tests of the reliability of the scanning process were carried out (A experiment). The research included the influence of beacon interval (BI) values on basic signal statistics. Then, the focus was on analyzing the position agreements. In the B and C experiments, 4 POIs (areas 1–4) and one client were included in the research model. Since the network data transmission was not fully implemented in the application, BleSkaner+ was run on the mobile side, and Bluetooth emitters (B1–B4) were stationary. Experiments were conducted in two variants: multiroom (weak overlapping) and single room (strong overlapping). Figure 2 shows the arrangement of POIs in the room.

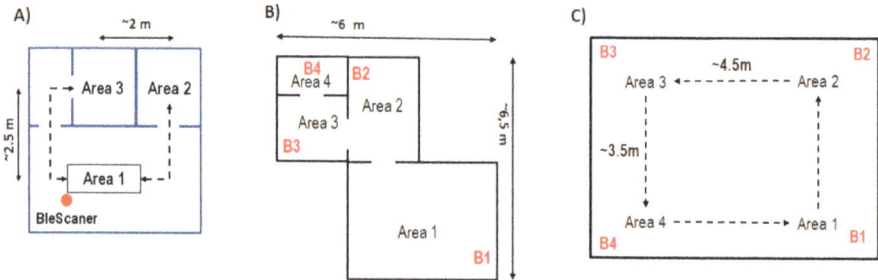

Figure 2. Beacon arrangement during the first phase of the experiment: (**A**) scanning process reliability; (**B**) multiroom with weak overlapping; (**C**) single room with strong overlapping.

The second phase of the experiment focused on obtaining data in an environment similar to real-life conditions. For making it possible, a prototype sensor network was built, where models of attractions (POIs) were included. Multimedia presentations displayed on 17″ screen notebooks were considered as attractions. Presentations were focused on tourism and entertainment, and each was 3 to 5 min long. Initially, 12 attractions were prepared, and 9 of them were included in the experiment. The POIs were located in the halls of a two-story building, and they were separated by at least 10 m of distance. The precise location of POIs is given in Table 1. Every POI was supplemented with an Android device, which was stationary during the experiment. As previously, the BleSkaner+ application was used for scanning mobile Bluetooth beacons carried by visitors. The collected raw data were processed according to the developed algorithm and supported by the *middleware* software described in Section 4.3.

Table 1. 3D position of points of interest (POIs) (attractions) used in the second stage of the experiment. The number of stair steps is used for the Z coordinate.

POI	X [m]	Y [m]	Z [step]
START/FINISH	0	24	27
01	1	14	27
02	0	2	30
03	10	0	30
05	32	1	30
06	46	1	30
07	51	0	0
08	39	0	0
11	4	0	0
12	2	10	3

During the research, Bluetooth iNode tags were used as beacon emitters. These tags use the Qualcomm® CSR1011 QFN chip and are powered by CR2032-type batteries. The tag's beacon interval (BI) may be freely changed in a wide range from 320 ms to 10.24 s, and the Tx power of each tag is adjustable in a range from −18 to +8 dBm. For making sure the results are as precise as possible, for each tag, the Tx power was set to the maximum of +8 dB, and the BI was set to a minimal span of 0.32 s.

The model included 9 POIs and 15 different beacons. Full sequences of visiting for 32 persons were recorded. Visitors were mostly university students. One PV was not fully registered (only two of nine attractions), probably due to the emitter malfunction. Thus, the reliability of beacon emitters reached about 97.5%. Visiting time was in the range from 6 to 37 min, 13.5 min on average, and the median was 9 min. Average time spent for visiting one attraction was about 60 s.

4.2. Sensor Data Processing

A prototypical sensor network should be capable of estimating the interest profile data based on RSSI signals from BLE emitters. Due to the variability and unpredictability of Bluetooth signal propagation conditions, individual interpretation of the received values is required. Moreover, the radio wave interference phenomena due to the simultaneous operation of many devices result in an asynchronous and incomplete RSSI acquisition. In particular, many of the data packets sent by an emitter will not be correctly received and interpreted by a receiver. Therefore, the first step was to develop and test the aggregation and smoothing algorithm, which would compute a synchronized and smoothed waveform from the asynchronous time series of raw RSSI values. This conversion allowed the missing signal to be represented by a value of 0 instead of null. Additionally, as the RSSI value is an interval variable, we decided to convert it into a ratio variable named Vout. In other words, the input RSSI data series are smoothed and scaled to more intuitive values in the range 0–100.

The next step is to define a decision algorithm that would qualify a moving object as present in the DA (DA presence). As a result, it became possible to obtain information about the object's LTin and LTout. As the last element of the data processing, a special converter was designed. It accepts Vout and DA presence variables as the input and converts them to a login record whose structure was presented by the authors in [34,35]. Summarizing, the gathered data were processed according to the developed algorithm presented in Figure 3.

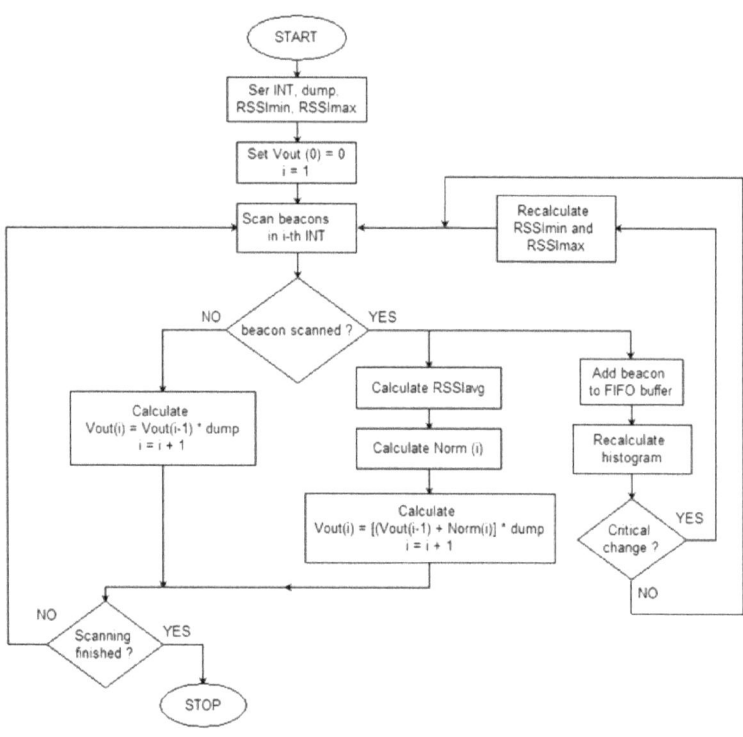

Figure 3. Smoothing-aggregation algorithm.

The variables used in the algorithm are: RSSI (in dBm), Norm(i)—scaled value for the i-th interval, and Vout(i)—output value for the i-th interval. The algorithm parameters are:

- INT—aggregation interval for a time series;
- dump—smoothing factor (blanking), number in the range 0–1;
- RSSImin and RSSImax—cut-off thresholds for RSSI values, determined based on the RSSI percentile distribution.

The algorithm is as follows:

1. Set INT, dump, RSSImin, RSSImax, and Vout (0) = 0.
2. For the given i-th INT interval, obtain the corresponding RSSI values.

   If no RSSI, then calculate

$$\text{Vout}(i) = [\text{Vout}(i-1)]\cdot\text{dump},\tag{1}$$

otherwise, calculate the average value of the corresponding RSSI (RSSIavg), scale it to Norm(i) by Formula (1b), and calculate the actual Vout value (1c):

$$\text{Norm}(i) = 100\cdot\frac{1-\text{dump}}{\text{dump}}\cdot\begin{cases}0 & \text{if RSSIavg}(i) < \text{RSSImin} \\ \frac{\text{RSSIavg}-\text{RSSImin}}{\text{RSSImax}-\text{RSSImin}} & \text{if RSSImin} < \text{RSSIavg}(i) < \text{RSSImax} \\ 1 & \text{if RSSIavg}(i) > \text{RSSImax}\end{cases}\tag{2}$$

$$\text{Vout}(i) = [\text{Vout}(i-1) + \text{Norm}(i)]\cdot\text{dump}\tag{3}$$

and go to the next INT (increment i).

The process of scaling raw RSSI values essentially came down to using a look-up table (LUT) mapping RSSI(i) values to Norm(i) values. The general linear threshold shape of the transformation function is depicted in Figure 4.

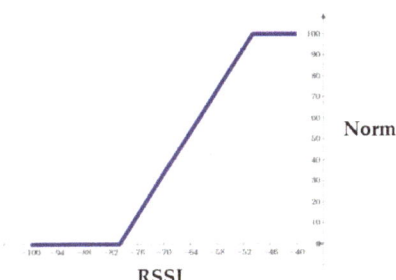

Figure 4. Piece-wise linear normalizing function for received signal strength indication (RSSI) to Norm transform.

The key issue encountered while using the LUT in working conditions was the problem of setting the right values for the RSSImin and RSSImax cut-off thresholds. The assumption was made that the thresholds should represent certain values from the RSSI centile distribution. This hypothesis arose from the fact that the distribution of RSSI values usually does not have the feature of normality, which was also demonstrated by other authors [39]. For this reason, three possible approaches were considered:

- Static approach—threshold values are constant over time and identical for each emitter–scanner pair. This approach is the simplest to implement and the fastest in operation. The accuracy of the results raises doubts, given that the propagation conditions, the power of the transmitters, and the sensitivity of the receivers need not be constant.
- Dynamic approach—constant over time, but each emitter–scanner pair is assigned an individual threshold value. This approach is simple to implement and it is the most reliable; however, it can only be realized a posteriori, i.e., when all tourists have finished visiting the park. The complete state of the park would be determined, e.g., at the end of the day, which, due to the purpose of this research, turns out to be the best solution. This approach was applied to the results of phase I and phase II experiments.
- Adaptive approach (self-learning)—the threshold values are adjusted for each emitter–scanner pair during the scanning process. This approach allows self-correcting the cut-off thresholds using the historical data of recorded RSSI signals, which are stored in the form of cumulative histograms. Such histograms allow determining specific RSSI percentiles with ease.

Another important issue was the selection of the decision threshold for the Vout value, which was used to determine the tourist's presence in the DA. In the basic variant, the discrimination algorithm assumes no overlapping. In this situation, a simple decision rule has been proposed, which tests whether the Vout signal exceeds the threshold value. The discrimination algorithm qualifies a beacon (person) as present in the DA (detection area) based on the value of Vout; in particular, it allows determining LTin and LTout information.

The proposed fixed threshold method performs simple discrimination with a threshold value proportional to max (Vout) for each emitter–scanner pair. The proposed formula is as follows:

$$\text{Thresh\_value} = \eta \cdot \max(\text{Vout}) \tag{4}$$

where the η coefficient is chosen experimentally.

For the phase 1 experiment data, the decision whether an object has entered or left the DA was made when the Vout value, respectively, exceeded or dropped below the threshold of 20% of the maximum value. The disadvantage of this method is quite significant—it can be properly realized only after the end of the tourist's sightseeing.

Characteristics of the adaptive approach applied to the aggregation-smoothing algorithm suggest that a constant Thresh_value may be sufficient because the Vout values are already normalized. However, it turns out that short-term signal loss becomes a problem because it results in unusually long intervals between two received packets. During the experiments, it was observed that the length of a critical signal break is a period of 2 to 6 s. RSSI values received after the critical break were called break-RSSI. In this case, due to the qualities of the smoothing algorithm, the Vout reaches much lower maximum values. For this reason, it becomes necessary to propose an additional correction algorithm.

Suppose that for each emitter–scanner pair, TimeBreaks stores the values of time intervals between two consecutive receiving RSSI values. By default, the values of TimeBreaks should be equal to the aggregation interval. Higher values signify disturbances in the process of obtaining location data. They should also be accompanied by rather low RSSI values, although for each scanner, the situation may be different. If higher TimeBreaks values are accompanied by stronger RSSI signals, this becomes a problem because it negatively affects Vout values. It can easily be observed that if the RSSI signal is registered every N intervals, then the Vout may approach the following limit:

$$\max(\text{Vout}) = \frac{\text{dump}}{1 - \text{dump}^N} \cdot \max(\text{Norm}) \tag{5}$$

Therefore, the recommended formula for calculating the decision threshold is given as follows:

$$\text{Thresh\_value} = \eta \cdot \max(\text{Vout}) \cdot \frac{1 - \text{dump}}{1 - \text{dump}^N} \tag{6}$$

The value of N can be determined adaptively based on the distribution of those TimeBreaks values that correspond to break-RSSIs. The following formula for calculating the N was proposed:

(a) Determine the median (med) of a subset of TimeBreaks values such that 1 s < TimeBreak < 6 s;
(b) Select the larger value from max (1, med −2).

If the signals are received frequently enough, then N = 1 and Formula (6) comes down to (4). In critical situations when N > 1, the decision threshold value will be lowered, compensating the potential error.

4.3. Prototype Middleware Implementation

Prototype middleware algorithms, described in the previous subsection, were implemented in Python programming language. In order for the application to be able to efficiently utilize multiple cores of RPi's System on a Chip (up to four cores in the case of RPi 3B+ or RPi 4), the program logic has been divided into several processes that were designed using the consumer–producer software design pattern. The communication between processes is carried out using synchronized FIFO (First In, First Out) queues (the Queue class from the Python multiprocessing module).

The first process, named BLEScanner, is responsible for scanning BLE devices. RSSI acquisition is performed using the commonly recognized bluepy library. However, during the middleware's development process, one shortcoming of the library's scanner class was discovered, and for this reason a custom scanner class derived from the default one was implemented. BLEScanner can be configured to use bluepy's active scanning, as well as a passive mode. Furthermore, the scan's timeout can be adjusted. Moreover, RSSI measurements can be optionally filtered by MAC addresses of the scanned devices (a list of allowed MACs can be provided).

Experiments conducted with the use of iNode tags showed that a scan timeout closely matching the advertisement time (beacon interval, BI) of tags should be avoided because in such a situation, the longest signal breaks were observed (up to several seconds). Based on the outcomes of the experiments, and because the shortest BI that can be set for iNode tags is 0.32 s, the decision was made to use active scanning with a timeout of 200 ms. This configuration provided the best results regarding the average number of acquired RSSI values per MAC per second (2.65), with relatively short and rare maximum signal breaks (1.2 s).

The second middleware process, named VoutProducer, receives raw RSSI measurements from the BLEScanner and converts them to Vout using the smoothing-aggregation algorithm described in Section 4.2:

- The aggregation interval (INT) was set to 1 s;
- The dump smoothing factor was set to 0.8 (it is configurable);
- For adjusting RSSImin and RSSImax cut-off thresholds for RSSI values, an adaptive (self-learning) approach was implemented, which uses cumulative histograms.

In order for the self-learning algorithm to adapt the cut-off thresholds dynamically and accurately even for the shortest tourist visits in POIs, it was decided to update the RSSImin and RSSImax every time 10 new RSSI values accumulated in a histogram. This computation was performed separately for each scanned BLE device because cumulative histograms are associated with individual MACs.

The third middleware process, named LRProducer, analyzes Vout signals, determines tourists' presence in the DA, and converts Vout to login records. Vout values are aggregated individually for each BLE device in intervals named time slots (TSs). By default, a TS lasts 5 s, but its duration can be adjusted (also in real time). Time slots are synchronous— this means that each RPi calculates login records (LRs) in the same intervals. Moreover, LRProducer computes LRs only when the Vout signal reaches a certain threshold level (lower signals are discarded).

Since each of the previously described processes should be able to process (consume) some input data, as well as output (produce) some other data, to unify this behavior, an abstract ProcessWithIOQueues class was implemented. Most middleware processes are derived from this abstract class, which greatly simplifies the communication between them. Moreover, this solution also provides an easy way to configure many different consumers for data produced by a particular process, e.g., the BLEScanner can output scan data simultaneously to the VoutProducer and to some other process that transmits raw RSSI values to the central server, where they are saved in the InfluxDB database.

The nature of this research led to a strong need for conducting many comprehensive and thorough application tests. For this reason, the software was equipped with a sophisticated logging subsystem:

- Each process can log its own messages to a separate file;
- Root-level logging aggregates messages from all processes, sorts them by a timestamp using a heap queue, and outputs them to a single file (it is mainly used for reporting abnormal situations, i.e., warnings and errors);
- Messages can also be sent to syslog, which is the standard logging solution for Unix-like operating systems.

To supplement the application with the logging capabilities described above, an additional ProcessWithLogger class was implemented, which became the parent class for the ProcessWithIOQueues class. To better utilize RPi's SoC, the final stage of logging (the interaction with the file system and syslog) is conducted in a separate process named LoggerProcess, which communicates with other middleware processes using a dedicated synchronized FIFO log queue.

The main application process is responsible for managing the middleware's configuration, starting individual processes, and stopping them when a shutdown request is received.

5. Results and Discussion

5.1. Phase 1A Experiment—Reliability of the Scanning Process

Using the tools presented in Section 4, the RSSI values for the case shown in Figure 2A were collected. The sequence of changes was (1–2–3–2–) × 10, with 30 s presence in each area. Thus, the total scanning time was 4 × 10 × 30 s = 20 min, whereby 25% of the total time was spent in AREAs 2 and 3 and 50% in AREA 1. The measurement was repeated for three different BIs: 0.32 s (2690 analyzed RSSI values), 1.28 s (672 analyzed RSSI values), and 5.12 s (180 analyzed RSSI values). Basic statistical measures were calculated, along with the distribution of numerical data (histograms). The base for the analysis was primarily RSSI values in the typical range: −100 to −30 dBm. Moreover, unexpected interruptions (so-called breakTime) were taken into account. Interruption was assumed critical if its time span was longer than ceil(3·BI).

Table 2 presents three representative parameters of a set of RSSI values: packet processing efficiency (PPE), RSSI median, and RSSI interquartile range (IQR). PPE is computed as a ratio of the number of received packets to the theoretical number of packets sent by a packet emitter, resulting from the presupposed BI. Due to the observation that the distribution of data was skewed instead of normal, median and IQR statistical measures were used.

Table 2. Basic statistical parameters of "A" scanning experiment.

	BI [s]	ALL	AREA1	AREA2	AREA3
	0.32	71.72	82.51	45.44	76.48
PPE. [%]	1.28	72.27	78.93	53.19	78.51
	5.12	77.57	87.07	61.44	75.09
	0.32	−73	−71	−79	−75
Median	1.28	−73	−71	−76	−74
	5.12	−72	−66	−77	−72
IQR	0.32	8	10	5	5
	1.28	9	10	7	6
	5.12	12	13.5	6.5	5

The PPE reliability factor reached 70% and more, which means that, e.g., for BI = 0.32 s, ~two independent signal strength measurements per second are anticipated. As expected, the average signal strength for AREA 1 was the highest, as was the PPE. In AREAs 2 and 3, more but comparably separated, the signal strength is noticeably weaker. Particularly, it was noticed that the signal from AREA 2 is weaker due to a metal locker placed in the room, which reduced propagation of the signal. Different signal parameters are reflected in the distribution (histograms) of the measurements, with a decrease in PPE from 80% to a mere 45% and an exceptionally high rate of critically weak signals (RSSI < −80 dBm), as shown in Figure 5.

The results show a slight improvement in the signal quality for longer beacon intervals. This indicates that in less dynamic scenarios, the BI could be increased, not only for the sake of energy savings, but also due to the improved reliability of the data transmission.

With respect to the *breakTime*, it was verified that for BI = 0.32 s, less than 2% of received packets were preceded by critical interruptions longer than 1 s, whereby the maximum interruption was 3 s for AREAs 1 and 3 and up to 8 se for AREA 2. For BI = 1.28, the share of critical interruptions (>4 s) was about 4.4%, whereby the maximum interruption was 12 s for AREAs 1 and 3 and up to 27 s for AREA 2. For BI = 5.12 s, no maximum interruption was longer than 20 s, whereby about 3.3% lasted longer than 15 s.

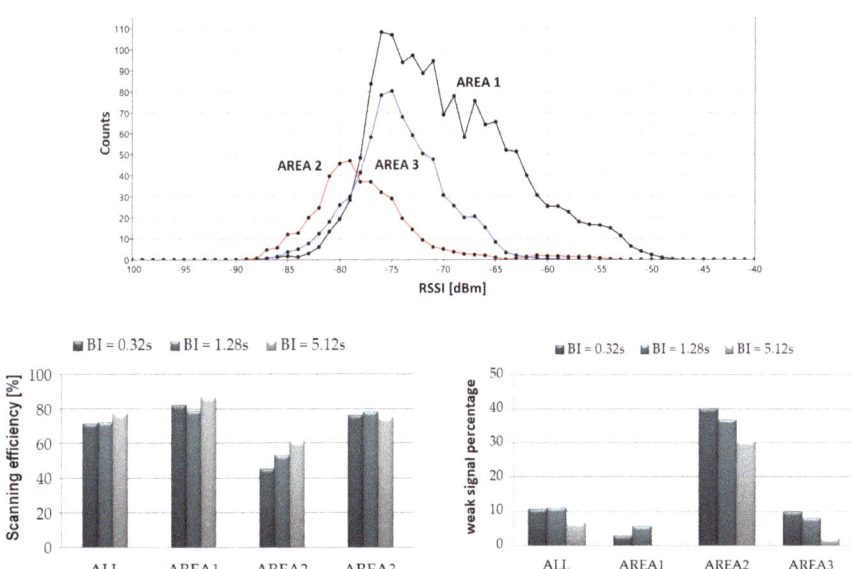

Figure 5. Statistical parameters of Bluetooth Low Energy (BLE) signals for different values of the beacon interval.

5.2. Phase 1B Experiment—Position Agreement Test for Multiroom Weak Overlapping Case

In this part of the experiments, the RSSI values for the case shown in Figure 2B were recorded. The sequence of changes was (1–2–3–4–3–2–) × 5, with 30 s presence in each area. Thus, the total scanning time was 5 × 6 × 30 s = 15 min, whereby ~16.7% of the total time was spent in AREAs 1 and 4 and ~33.3% in AREAs 2 and 3.

Figure 6 shows the processed time series. The values INT = 1 s and dump = 0.65 were adopted, while RSSImin and RSSImax were estimated from the percentile distribution of RSSI values for levels 0.4 and 0.95, respectively.

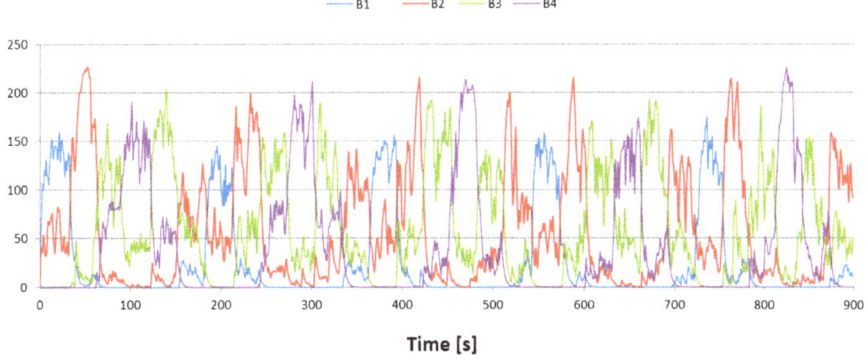

Figure 6. Processed Vout time series.

Next, the processed data were classified according to the "Winner Takes All" (WTA) principle. This means that the classification was based only on the highest Vout value criterion. An additional condition was introduced—the ratio of the highest Vout value to the second one must exceed the given threshold *h*. Otherwise, the algorithm will return 0, indicating that the person is outside of any DA. The algorithm is as follows:

1. For a given aggregation interval INT, create a so-called fingerprint vector (FV) containing the corresponding Vout values;
2. Sort the FV in descending order -> FVsort;
3. Check if (FVsort [0] < Thresh_value) or (FVsort[0]/FVsort[1] < h):

    if the condition is true, then positions [INT] = 0;

    otherwise, positions [INT] = index + 1, where the index should satisfy formula: FV [index] = FVsort [0].

The result of the algorithm is a time-dependent relationship representing the belonging of a given person to a particular DA. This time series has been named the decision function (DF). It is assumed below that individual POIs are identified by natural numbers from 1, whereas 0 denotes a position outside of any DA. The results are shown in Figure 7. The h value was assumed to be 1.

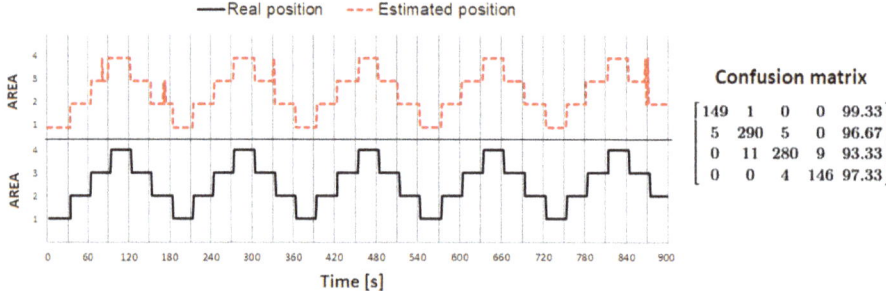

Figure 7. Graph showing the real position (solid line) vs. the estimated decision function (DF—dashed line) determined in phase 1B experiments using the proposed algorithms.

In order to objectively estimate the accuracy of the positioning, the following numerical measures were proposed:

- Position agreement (PA)—percentage of compliance of relevant values in real position and DF time series;
- Visit period error (VP error)—the relative difference between the real and estimated time spent in the area.

The highest PA, ~96.1%, was obtained for dump = 0.65 and low_perc = 0.4. As expected in the extreme positions (Area 1 and Area 4), the PA is greater, in the order of 98–99%. In addition, a location error often occurs during crossing area boundaries, which is a normal and acceptable situation. The VP error for individual positions was 2.7% for AREA1, 0.7% for AREA2, 3.7% for AREA3, and 3.3% for AREA4, and the total average error was ~ 2.4%.

5.3. Phase 1C Experiment—Position Agreement Test for Single Room Strong Overlaping Case

In this phase, the RSSI values for the case shown in Figure 2C were recorded. The sequence of changes was (1–2–3–4–) × 6, with 30 s presence in each area. Thus, the total scanning time was 4 × 6 × 30 s = 12 min, whereby ~25% of the total time was spent in AREAs 1–4. In addition, the experiment was carried out in two variants: the more favorable—back to the room, facing the emitter (best case), and the less favorable—front facing the room, back to the emitter (worst case). This is due to the fact that the beacon emitter was placed in the form of a necklace, located at the front at the level of the chest. It was to be expected that the propagation conditions along the emitter–scanner path would be different, mainly due to the wave absorption by the human body. This way, the effect of either the translational or rotational position was studied. Similarly, to experiment B, the position agreement was determined—Figure 8.

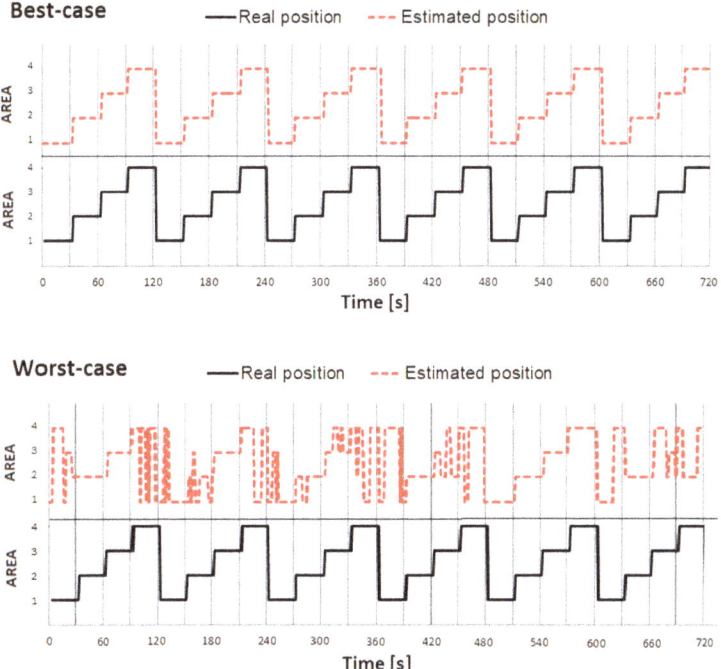

Figure 8. Graph showing the real position (solid line) vs. estimated decision function (DF) (dashed line) determined in phase 1C experiments using the proposed algorithms.

Despite the relatively close location of the emitters and strong overlapping, the best-case variant achieved the PA value at 97.9%. However, in the worst-case variant, as expected, the compliance was unacceptably low and estimated to a maximum of ~ 73%. The average RSSI values recorded from the emitter, appropriate for a given position in individual positions for best-case and worst-case scenarios, were also compared. The differences were from 4 to even 10 dBm, depending on a particular location. This points to the unreliability of FRM-based localization methods, suggesting the need for a higher number of detectors.

5.4. Discriminant Analysis vs. WTA Approach

An effective way of assessing the ability to discriminate profiles is to perform a linear discriminant analysis (LDA). The objective of the LDA is to estimate discriminant functions that are a linear combination of independent variables that will discriminate between the categories of the dependent variable in the most effective manner. It also evaluates the accuracy of the classification. In the considered case, the canonical variate analysis (CVA) method was used [38]. Results for phase 1C experiments are presented in Figure 9.

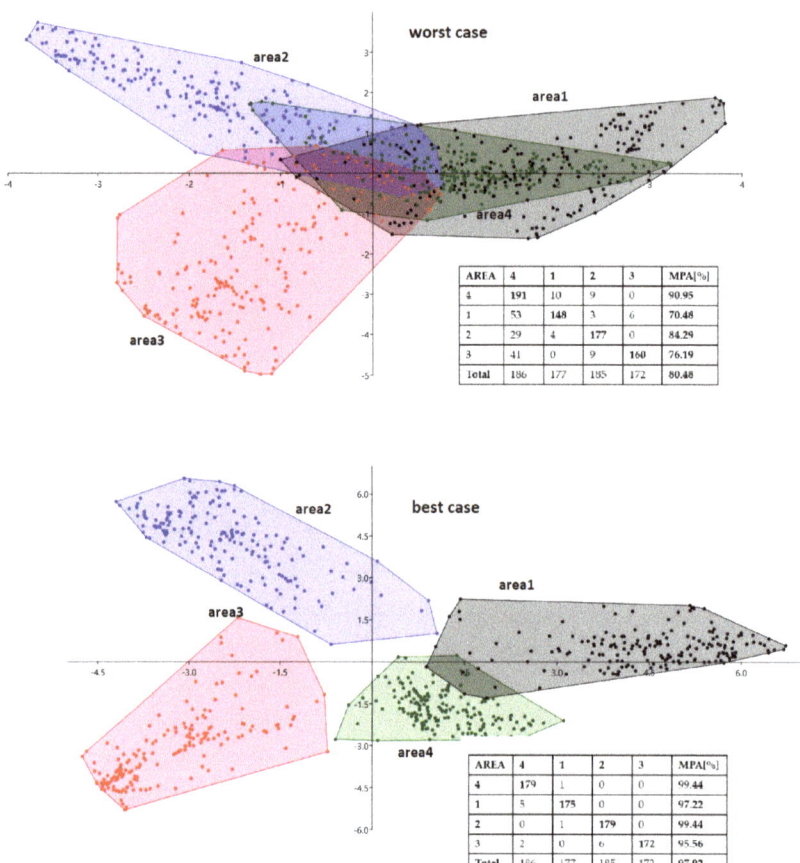

Figure 9. Linear discriminant analysis using the CVA method for worst-case and best-case variants of phase 1C experiments (confusion matrices included).

The number of samples in the considered case was 720 and corresponded to the signal measurements for every second from four scanners. The classes correspond to four locations (scanners) and there should be 180 observations in each of them. As shown in the inset table in Figure 9, the number of classified samples presented in a diagonal position for each class slightly differs from 180.

In the best-case scenario, the discriminatory effectiveness of the CVA method and the method based on the WTA criterion was similar. On the other hand, in the worst-case scenario, the discriminatory effectiveness was theoretically improved from around 73% to around 80%, which unfortunately is still low. This means that when all four values are taken into account during the discrimination analysis, the system's locational capability can only improve slightly. Moreover, the conducted experiments led to an interesting observation. People who were close to an attraction, but were facing the opposite direction, were more often qualified as absent (position 0). This may have a positive impact on the resulting statistics of interest profile measurements.

5.5. Phase 2 Experiment—Results

During the experiment, a total of 96,502 packets were analyzed, with an average of 715 per minute. Only one emitter out of 32 was temporarily inactive (for seven out of nine POIs). The reliability level has been estimated at 97.5%, which is acceptable from a practical point of view. Median value of beacons registered for one client for one POI was 182, interquartile range: (IQ: 97—356). On average, the system processed approximately three beacons/s, which is a similar value to the number of beacons sent by one emitter. An important element of the solution developed in phase 2 (middleware) is the Vout and DA presence converter to record login, as conversion to an LR is an important element of the IoT architecture. A login record is a structured unit of information, representing one event, i.e., the presence of an emitter (tourist) in a given DA (attraction). During the experiment, a total of 1093 LRs were registered, i.e., on average ~ 34 per visitor. About 52% of LRs had a time shorter than 5 s. On the other hand, the number of LRs with a VT of 10 s or more was 379 (~ 12 per visitor). In further analysis, only LRs with a time of 5 s or longer were accepted. The average number of accepted LRs generated by one scanner was 1.44 per minute, where for visitors who devoted more than 1 minute to one attraction (11 people known as long-term visitors), this parameter was 1.2 per minute, while for the other visitors (21 people known as short-term visitors), this parameter was 1.57 per minute. It can be assumed that in a situation where ~20 people would be present at the same time in the DA, the related scanner will generate an average of ~ 30 LRs per minute, which should enable their smooth transfer to the central server even when using low-bandwidth technology such as LoRaWAN.

An example of the Vout time series for one of the visitors is shown in Figure 10. There is a clear signal overlap which leads to the problem of multilocation.

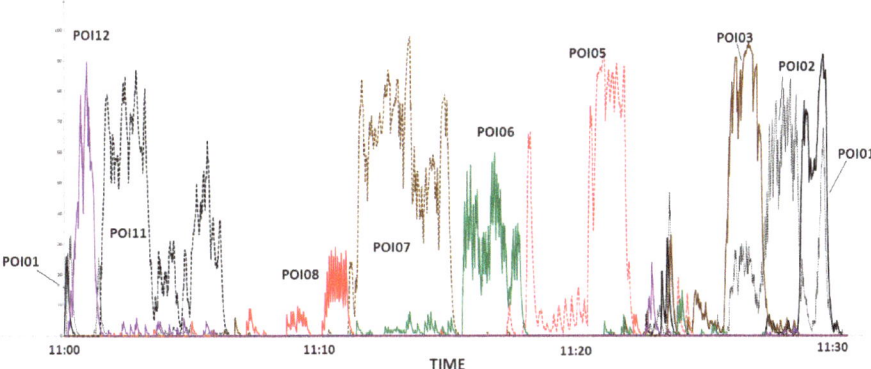

Figure 10. Vout time series for a representative visitor.

The overlapping factor has been introduced as the ratio of the overlap time to the total visiting time. This coefficient was determined for each visitor independently, in two variants:

- Vout overlapping (Voverlap)—a situation where the Vout value is nonzero for at least two scanners simultaneously. It is an indicator of the physical signal overlap;
- LR overlapping (LRoverlap)—a situation where the time intervals of two or more LRs collide with each other, interpreted as an unacceptable multilocation situation (being simultaneously in two or more DAs).

First of all, it is advised to minimize LRoverlap equal to 0, while Voverlap can be greater than 0. Note that in the absence of the proposed analytical solutions, the LRoverlap value is equal to Voverlap. The average value of the Voverlap coefficient for 32 PVs was approximately 68% (mean = 0.6826, stdev = 0.1632). This means that only in ~ 32% of the visit time would the location be unambiguous. Moreover, the degree of multilocation for Voverlap was found to be 3 to 7 (i.e., in some cases, a maximum of seven scanners simultaneously generated a nonzero Vout signal). Such low efficiency is unacceptable from a practical point of view.

Thanks to the implementation of middleware algorithms, the average LRoverlap value was clearly lower: average ~ 0.1455, stdev = 0.0595, max 0.375. This means that, on average, the visitor's location is practically undefined due to multilocation only for ~1/7 of the visiting time. Furthermore, the degree of multilocation was not greater than 3.

The research also suggests that the value of the overlapping factor depends on the time of the visit. The average Voverlap values turned out to be slightly lower (~0.6) for long-time visitors compared to short-time visitors (~0.72); however, the differences are at the border of statistical significance (*t*-test for CI = 0.95, p ~ 5.9%). A stronger difference was observed for LRoverlap, where 0.115 vs. 0.161 values were estimated, respectively.

5.6. IoT Architecture vs. LR Overlapping

As mentioned above, a login record (LR) is a structured unit of information representing the event characterized by the presence of a particular emitter (tourist) in a given DA (attraction). The Vout to LR conversion performed by the scanner is optional, as it is possible to send Vout data directly to the central server. However, sending just login records can significantly reduce the amount of information being transmitted. In the basic version of the system, it is required to send one information frame per second per MAC. Meanwhile, the conducted experiments demonstrated that the average number of information frames sent by a scanner can be as low as 1.5 frames per minute per MAC, which is about 40 times less than the theoretical number. This observation makes the idea of using dedicated network technologies such as LoRaWAN very plausible.

Each login record contains the following information:

- POI (point of interest, attraction) identifier;
- Beacon (tourist) identifier (MAC, beaconId, etc.);
- The moment in time of entering the DA (LTin, short for login time in);
- Visit time (VP, short for visit period) or equivalent information about the moment at the time of leaving the DA (LTout, short for login time out), where VP = LTout-LTin+1;
- Additionally, the level of tourist interest in the attraction (IL, short for interest level).

The value of the IL parameter is calculated as the Vout cumulative value in a period of time determined by the LTin and LTout timestamps. To be more precise, this calculation requires knowledge of the discriminant function corresponding to the Vout values, and then the whole formula can be written as follows:

$$IL(POI) = \int_{T_{IN}}^{T_{OUT}} Vout(t) \cdot [DF(t) = POI\_Id] \cdot dt \tag{7}$$

It should be noted that IL can also be represented as information about the average signal strength. However, the original representation as cumulative signal strength allows a simple aggregation of LRs in a situation when a particular tourist has visited a given DA several times.

Login records can be synchronous or asynchronous. Synchronous LRs are calculated in specific moments in time, e.g., once every 5 s, 10 s, or 30 s. Additionally, an LR will not be sent by the scanner if the Vout value is below the decision threshold level, which makes it easier to tackle the problem of overlapping. Asynchronous LRs are sent the moment the LTin and LTout parameters have been determined—this approach was used during the research stage. However, with asynchronous LRs, there is always a risk of system starvation when the VP is very long. In such a situation, it is recommended to segment the LRs into shorter fragments (periodic LRs).

In the context of the topics discussed so far, a certain issue of great practical significance emerges—the problem of multilocation. The simplest solution to the overlapping problem involves comparing the value of Vout signals and choosing the strongest one at any moment in time. Based on this information, a decision about the tourist current location should be made, as was done during the phase 1 experiments. However, it requires a centralized approach which necessitates sending raw RSSI data, or at least Vout values, to the server where the decision will be determined. This solution reduces beacon scanners to the role of signal retransmitters and is not conformable to the concept of edge computing and IoT.

The IoT approach assumes that the server receives data only in the form of LRs, i.e., without the Vout values. Despite that, the authors devised a solution to the overlapping problem. As a comparative criterion, a simple parameter was proposed, calculated as the ratio of IL to VP, representing the average value of Vout. The analysis of data acquired during the experiment allowed comparing both methods and assessing the consistency of the results produced by the IoT approach with the results computed by the theoretically more effective centralized approach. The average effectiveness of the IoT approach (IoT agree) compared to the central one was about $96.7 \pm 1.8\%$. For long-term visitors, the effectiveness was even higher—about $98 \pm 1\%$. This means that the decisions made only on the basis of LRs data are almost identical to those determined with the centralized approach. Detail information for all 32 visitors is presented in Table 3.

Table 3. Voverlap vs. LRoverlap values for observed visitors—details.

Client_Id	Total Visit Time [min]	Scanned Beacons /min	Number of LRs	LR Density [LR/min]	Vout Overlap [%]	MaxOverlap for Vout	LR oVerlapping [%]	IoT_Agree [%]
C01	10	270.5	11	1.10	74.33	5	12.00	97.33
C02	9	243.1	12	1.33	72.22	4	14.81	95.19
C03	12	192.6	18	1.50	81.25	5	15.97	97.36
C04	8	323.1	10	1.25	92.08	5	15.83	96.25
C05	9	53.9	17	1.89	33.89	3	14.26	99.63
C06	7	214.4	9	1.29	72.86	4	14.76	96.19
C07	8	172.8	11	1.38	53.96	5	13.33	97.71
C08	7	207.3	11	1.57	65.24	5	14.76	94.29
C09	8	205.1	14	1.75	73.75	5	13.75	97.50
C10	6	227.3	11	1.83	77.50	4	17.50	94.72
C11	9	291.2	13	1.44	81.85	7	21.67	96.30
C12	8	222.4	15	1.88	71.04	6	17.92	93.75
C13	8	174.1	13	1.63	76.67	5	13.33	95.83
C14	8	259.1	10	1.25	78.33	5	14.38	95.63
C15	8	228.1	13	1.63	68.54	5	11.04	97.08
C16	25	264.4	23	0.92	77.67	5	9.87	97.87
C17	30	235.3	28	0.93	52.44	5	10.89	98.61
C18	12	234.0	32	2.67	80.69	6	37.50	90.83
C19	8	294.1	15	1.88	79.79	5	18.33	95.42
C20	8	237.1	11	1.38	79.58	4	15.42	95.21
C21	7	163.1	14	2.00	48.57	3	20.48	96.43
C22	8	234.6	11	1.38	77.92	4	12.92	97.29
C23	13	186.8	24	1.85	72.14	3	23.33	97.18
C24	18	232.1	32	1.78	65.93	5	18.61	95.65
C25	31	257.7	21	0.68	58.76	4	7.47	99.14
C26	37	75.4	60	1.62	27.03	3	13.15	97.57
C27	15	200.4	17	1.13	76.67	5	11.11	97.22
C28	15	217.5	20	1.33	64.11	5	9.00	98.44
C29	14	167.4	13	0.93	28.45	4	3.57	98.69
C30	12	257.4	12	1.00	75.69	5	9.03	97.22
C31	28	318.9	25	0.89	92.08	5	9.64	98.99
C32	25	315.0	29	1.16	53.13	6	9.93	98.27

The basic innovation of the described solution concerns transferring a significant part of the decision-making process from the central server to intermediate devices—IoT gateways, built on the basis of SBCs (Single Board Computers). In the proposed solution, a set of special packets called LRs is sent instead raw packets. The most visible advantage concerns increasing the involvement of intermediary scanning units in the location detection process, limiting data transfer to the most important ones (see scanned beacons/min vs. LR density/min in Table 3), relieving the central server and database, and making the architecture more flexible. At the same time, as shown in the IoT_agree parameter in Table 3, the level of localization accuracy is only from ~1 to ~5% worse than in traditional, centralized solutions. It should also be noted that the IoT approach in its current state does not require communication between RPis. This makes the proposed solution less complex and, at the same time, satisfactorily effective.

6. Conclusions

This article presents the concept and pilot implementation of an indoor tracking system, whose main purpose is acquiring relevant information about the behavior of visitors. The concept of this work was to create a tourist service system, but it may be more widely used. The precise position of a person is not so important in this case (unlike in GPS-like systems), but rather the interest level of a person for each POI is, which is represented by an integrated value of a properly scaled RSSI rather than the duration of the visit. Such an approach makes the process of acquiring the most important data concerning a visit easier. The problem, however, is the strong overlapping of signals, especially in the case of short proximity to other POIs. This leads to the multilocation problem, which makes neither the proper recognition of a path nor computing the correct values of the interest level parameter possible. In the paper, a solution to this problem was proposed, where properly prepared signals in individual time windows are compared and the WTA (Winner Takes All) principle is applied. Conducted experiments show that such an approach gives satisfactory results.

Currently, the proposed system is run as a distributed sensory network built on the basis of popular Raspberry Pi 4B SBCs. Raw RSSI data are retrieved with the help of the widely known bluepy library and then it can be processed using the middleware presented in this article. It is intended that the output in the form of integrated LR packets is delivered to the InfluxDB database system, dedicated to retrieving and processing time series. In the centralized system, decisions concerning the identification of location and computing IL parameters for each POI are taken. Further plans include creating software for collecting ILs sequences (so-called behavior vector) and their statistical analysis. It is worth mentioning that the architecture of the proposed solution allows for integration of the system with alternative solutions using, e.g., tracking with the use of GPS technology.

Author Contributions: Formal analysis, R.B.; investigation, R.B., P.P. and G.Ł.; methodology, R.S.D.; software, P.P. and G.Ł.; supervision, R.S.D.; writing—original draft, R.B., P.P. and G.Ł.; writing—review and editing, R.S.D. All authors have read and agreed to the published version of the manuscript.

Funding: This research was founded by the European Union's Smart Growth Operational Programme 2014–2020, under grant agreement no POIR.04.01.02-00-0041/17-00.

Institutional Review Board Statement: Not applicable.

Informed Consent Statement: Not applicable.

Data Availability Statement: Data is contained within the article.

Conflicts of Interest: The authors declare no conflict of interest. The funders had no role in the design of the study; in the collection, analyses, or interpretation of data; in the writing of the manuscript, or in the decision to publish the results.

References

1. Gretzel, U.; Sigala, M.; Xiang, Z.; Koo, C. Smart tourism: Foundations and developments. *Electron Mark.* **2015**, *25*, 179–188.
2. Zeinab, K.A.M.; Elmustafa, S.A.A. Internet of things applications challenges and related future technologies. *World Sci. News* **2017**, *67*, 126–148.
3. Global Industry Analysts, Inc. Internet of Things (IoT) Analytics-Market Analysis, Trends, and Forecasts; Report. Available online: https://www.mordorintelligence.com/industry-reports/iot-analytics-market (accessed on 17 October 2020).
4. Antic, B.; Castaneda, J.O.N.; Culibrk, D.; Pizurica, A.; Crnojevic, V.; Philips, W. Robust Detection and Tracking of Moving Objects in Traffic Video Surveillance. *ACIVS* **2009**, *5807*, 494–505.
5. Bajaj, B.; Ranaweera, S.L.; Agrawal, D.P. GPS: Location-Tracking Technology. *Computer* **2002**, *35*, 92–94. [CrossRef]
6. Want, R. An Introduction to RFID Technology. *IEEE Pervasive Comp.* **2006**, *5*, 25–33. [CrossRef]
7. Muzhir, S.; Al-Ani, M.S. Packages Tracking Using RFID Technology. *Int. J. Buss ICT* **2015**, *1*, 12–20.
8. Kivimaki, A.; Fomin, V. What Makes a Killer Application for the Cellular Telephony Services? In Proceedings of the 2nd IEEE SIIT Conference, Boulder, CO, USA, 3–6 October 2001; pp. 25–37.
9. Ghribi, B.; Logrippo, L. Understanding GPRS: The GSM Packet Radio Service. *Comp. Net.* **2000**, *34*, 763–779. [CrossRef]

10. Delamare, M.; Boutteau, R.; Savatier, X.; Iriart, N. Static and Dynamic Evaluation of an UWB Localization System for Industrial Applications. *Science* **2019**, *1*, 62. [CrossRef]
11. Blumenthal, J.; Grossmann, R.; Golatowski, F.; Timmermann, D. Weighted Centroid Localization in Zigbee-based Sensor Networks. In Proceedings of the 2007 IEEE International Symposium on Intelligent Signal Processing, Alcala de Henares, Spain, 3–5 October 2007; pp. 1–6.
12. He, X.; Badiei, S.; Aloi, D.; Li, J. WiFi iLocate: WiFi based indoor localization for smartphone. In Proceedings of the Wireless Telecommunications Symposium 2014, Washington, DC, USA, 9–11 April 2014; pp. 1–7.
13. Dawson, C. Device Tracking on a Scattered Bluetooth-Enabled Network. Bachelor's Dissertation, Faculty of Engineering, University of Bristol, Bristol, UK, 2005.
14. Sheng, Z.; Pollard, J.K. Position Measurement using Bluetooth. *IEEE Trans Cons. Electr.* **2006**, *52*, 555–558.
15. Jeon, K.E.; She, J.; Soonsawad, P.; Ng, P.C. BLE Beacons for Internet of Things Applications: Survey, Challenges, and Opportunities. *IEEE Iot J.* **2018**, *5*, 811–828.
16. Yang, J.; Chen, Y. Indoor Localization Using Improved RSS-Based Lateration Methods. In Proceedings of the IEEE Global Telecommunications Conference GLOBECOM 2009, Honolulu, HI, USA, 30 November–4 December 2009; pp. 1–6.
17. Jianyong, Z.; Haiyong, L.; Zili, C.; Zhaohui, L. RSSI Based Bluetooth Low Energy Indoor Positioning. In Proceedings of the IPIN Conference, Busan, Korea, 27–30 October 2014; pp. 526–533.
18. Faragher, R.; Harle, R. Location Fingerprinting With Bluetooth Low Energy Beacons. *IEEE J. Sel. Areas Commun.* **2015**, *33*, 2418–2428. [CrossRef]
19. Zuo, Z.; Liu, L.; Zhang, L.; Fang, Y. Indoor Positioning Based on Bluetooth Low-Energy Beacons Adopting Graph Optimization. *Sensors* **2018**, *18*, 3736. [CrossRef] [PubMed]
20. Subhan, F.; Hasbullah, H.; Rozyyev, A.; Bakhsh, S. Indoor positioning in Bluetooth networks using fingerprinting and lateration approach. In Proceedings of the ICISA Conference, Jeju Island, Korea, 26–29 April 2011; pp. 1–9.
21. Subedi, S.; Kwon, G.; Shin, S.; Hwang, S.; Pyun, J.-Y. Beacon based indoor positioning system using weighted centroid localization approach. In Proceedings of the Icufn Conference, Vienna, Austria, 5–8 July 2016; pp. 1016–1019.
22. Subedi, S.; Pyun, J.-Y. Practical Fingerprinting Localization for Indoor Positioning System by Using Beacon. *J. Sens.* **2017**, *2017*, 16. [CrossRef]
23. Dalce, R.; Van den Bossche, A.; Val, T. Indoor SelfLocalization in a WSN, based on Time of Flight: Propositions and Demonstrator. In Proceedings of the IEEE IPIN 2013 Conference, Montbeliard-Belfort, France, 28–31 October 2013; pp. 28–31.
24. Thaljaoui, A.; Val, T.; Nasri, N.; Brulin, D. BLE Localization using RSSI Measurements and iRingLA. In Proceedings of the IEEE ICIT 2015 Conference, Seville, Spain, 17–19 March 2015.
25. Röbesaat, J.; Zhang, P.; Abdelaal, M.; Theel, O. An Improved BLE Indoor Localization with Kalman-Based Fusion: An Experimental Study. *Sensors* **2017**, *17*, 951. [CrossRef] [PubMed]
26. Cantón Paterna, V.; Calveras Augé, A.; Paradells Aspas, J.; Pérez Bullones, M.A. A Bluetooth Low Energy Indoor Positioning System with Channel Diversity, Weighted Trilateration and Kalman Filtering. *Sensors* **2017**, *17*, 2927. [CrossRef] [PubMed]
27. Ke, C.; Wu, M.; Chan, Y.; Lu, K. Developing a BLE Beacon-Based Location System Using Location Fingerprint Positioning for Smart Home Power Management. *Energies* **2018**, *11*, 3464. [CrossRef]
28. Torii, H.; Ibi, S.; Sampei, S. Indoor Positioning and Tracking by Multi-Point Observations of BLE Beacon Signal. In Proceedings of the 15th Workshop on Positioning, Navigation and Communications (WPNC), Bremen, Germany, 25–26 October 2018; pp. 1–5.
29. Chandel, V.; Ahmed, N.; Arora, S.; Ghose, A. InLoc: An end-to-end robust indoor localization and routing solution using mobile phones and BLE beacons. In Proceedings of the IPIN 2016 Conference, Alcala de Henares, Spain, 4–7 October 2016; pp. 1–8.
30. Hou, X.; Arslan, T. Monte Carlo localization algorithm for indoor positioning using Bluetooth low energy devices. In Proceedings of the ICL-GNSS 2017 Conference, Nottingham, UK, 27–29 June 2017; pp. 1–6.
31. Kárník, J.; Streit, J. Summary of available indoor location techniques. *Ifac-Pap.* **2016**, *49*, 311–317.
32. Zafari, F.; Gkelias, A.; Leung, K.K. A Survey of Indoor Localization Systems and Technologies. *IEEE Commun. Surv. Tutor* **2019**, *21*, 2568–2599. [CrossRef]
33. Samama, N. *Indoor Positioning: Technologies and Performance*; Wiley–IEEE: Hoboken, NJ, USA, 2019.
34. Belka, R. An indoor tracking system and pattern recognition algorithms as key components of IoT-based entertainment industry. *Proc. Spie* **2019**, *11176*, 1–10.
35. Belka, R.; Deniziak, R.S.; Płaza, M.; Hejduk, M.; Pięta, P.; Czekaj, P.; Wołowiec, P.; Ludwinek, K.; Płaza, M. Integrated visitor support system for tourism industry based on IoT technologies. *Proc. Spie* **2018**, *10808*, 447–454.
36. Pięta, P.; Deniziak, R.S.; Belka, R.; Płaza, M.; Płaza, M. Multi-domain model for simulating smart IoT-based theme parks. *Proc. Spie* **2018**, *10808*, 867–878.
37. Android API Reference: BluetoothLeScanner Class. Available online: https://developer.android.com/reference/android/bluetooth/le/BluetoothLeScanner (accessed on 17 November 2020).
38. Hammer, O.; Harper, D.A.T.; Ryan, P.D. PAST: Paleontological statistics software package for education and data analysis. *Palaeontol. Electron.* **2001**, *4*, 9.
39. Pei, L.; Chen, R.; Liu, J.; Kuusniemi, H.; Tenhunen, T.; Chen, Y. Using Inquiry-based Bluetooth RSSI Probability Distributions for Indoor Positioning. *J. Glob. Position. Syst.* **2010**, *9*, 122–130.

sensors

MDPI

Article

WON-OCDMA System Based on MW-ZCC Codes for Applications in Optical Wireless Sensor Networks

Saleh Seyedzadeh [1], Andrew Agapiou [1], Majid Moghaddasi [2], Milan Dado [3] and Ivan Glesk [1,*]

[1] Faculty of Engineering, University of Strathclyde, Glasgow G1 1XQ, UK; saleh.seyedzadeh@strath.ac.uk (S.S.); andrew.agapiou@strath.ac.uk (A.A.)
[2] TBA Group, 2623 AP Delft, The Netherlands; majid.moghaddasi@tba.group
[3] Faculty of Electrical Engineering and Information Technology, University of Žilina, 010 26 Žilina, Slovakia; milan.dado@uniza.sk
*   Correspondence: ivan.glesk@strath.ac.uk

Abstract: The growing demand for extensive and reliable structural health monitoring resulted in the development of advanced optical sensing systems (OSS) that in conjunction with wireless optical networks (WON) are capable of extending the reach of optical sensing to places where fibre provision is not feasible. To support this effort, the paper proposes a new type of a variable weight code called multiweight zero cross-correlation (MW-ZCC) code for its application in wireless optical networks based optical code division multiple access (WON-OCDMA). The code provides improved quality of service (QoS) and better support for simultaneous transmission of video surveillance, comms and sensor data by reducing the impact of multiple access interference (MAI). The MW-ZCC code's power of two code-weight properties provide enhanced support for the needed service differentiation provisioning. The performance of this novel code has been studied by simulations. This investigation revealed that for a minimum allowable bit error rate of 10^{-3}, 10^{-9} and 10^{-12} when supporting triple-play services (sensing, datacomms and video surveillance, respectively), the proposed WON-OCDMA using MW-ZCC codes could support up to 32 simultaneous services over transmission distances up to 32 km in the presence of moderate atmospheric turbulence.

Keywords: optical sensors; vibration sensing; quality of service differentiation; wireless optical networks; free space optics; multiwavelength laser; optical code division multiple access (OCDMA)

check for updates

Citation: Seyedzadeh, S.; Agapiou, A.; Moghaddasi, M.; Dado, M.; Glesk, I. WON-OCDMA System Based on MW-ZCC Codes for Applications in Optical Wireless Sensor Networks. *Sensors* **2021**, *21*, 539. https://doi.org/10.3390/s21020539

Received: 28 November 2020
Accepted: 11 January 2021
Published: 13 January 2021

Publisher's Note: MDPI stays neutral with regard to jurisdictional claims in published maps and institutional affiliations.

1. Introduction

Optical sensors have found their application in structural health monitoring (SHM) thanks to their small size, high accuracy and immunity to electromagnetic noise [1]. The use of optical multiplexing techniques has advanced the capacity, capabilities and performance of sensor networks in terms of the number of sensing points while lowering system complexity and cost [2]. Optical fibres that carry sensor signals have also been used as sensing elements themselves. The successful application of optical sensing in the construction industry has been reported for different monitoring purposes including gas leakage [3], temperature [4], strain [5], structure vibration [6], reinforced concrete beams [7] and building cladding systems [8].

It is essential to monitor civil structures to appraise the structural condition to be able to predict the internal damages at an early stage [9,10]. Several fibre-optic methods and tools have been developed for vibration monitoring. In 2001, a fibre Bragg gratings (FBG) coupled with a broadband light source were exploited to detect vibrations based on the light intensity modulation produced by vibrating FBG [11]. The feasibility of a fully distributed vibration sensing was evaluated based on a fibre diversity detection sensor [12]. An intensity-modulated fibre-optic accelerometer was also developed for vibration monitoring of wind turbine blades [13].

Collecting and transporting data from optical sensors for their processing is the role of the optical sensor network (OSN). Optical multiplexing techniques including time and wavelength division multiplexing [14] and optical code division multiple access (OCDMA) have been adopted to connect distributed sensing points [15]. In wavelength division multiplexing, each sensor is assigned a single wavelength from the source optical spectrum [16]. Time division multiplexing dedicates different time slots to individual sensors. For OCDMA sensor networks both, synchronous and asynchronous architectures have been proposed [17] with focus on exploring different coding techniques. For example, a spectral amplitude coding (SAC) offers a reasonable multiple access interference (MAI) cancellation, simplicity of implementation [18] and the ability to support a differentiated quality of service (QoS) by varying code-weight [19]. Using the variable-weight SAC (VW-SAC) coding an efficient OCDMA communication system for supporting the vibration sensing of unequally distributed points has been proposed [6].

Most research has focused on equally distributed sensor points, where the received optical power (ROP) by each sensor should be similar. However, in SHM, most structures are distributed with different distances, and therefore it is not possible to set up an equidistant sensor network. This leads to a near-far problem. It should be noted that the use of optical amplifiers to compensate for losses is possible but increases the system noise as well as the cost of the network. To resolve this problem and support the vibration sensing of unequally distributed points, an SAC-OCDMA system was developed and proposed [20]. Similarly, for the VW-SAC system, different code families [18,19,21,22] and detection techniques [23] have been proposed. A successful experimental proof of concept for its use in optical communication has been already reported [24].

Optical fibres have a large bandwidth. This provides a temptation to extend the already existing fibre infrastructure to support SHM. However, it might not be the most cost-effective to install optical fibre for monitoring hard-to-reach places. Wireless optical networks (WON) are an elegant solution where the implementation of fibre is impractical or not cost-effective [25]. The integration of OCDMA and WON systems can provide the desired solution [26,27]. Wireless OCDMA systems have already been deployed to support healthcare monitoring applications [28]. However, the majority of developed OCDMA codes have too high cross-correlation thus not suitable for WON and SHM applications. Inspired by ZCC [29] and MDW [30], this paper proposes a Multi-Weight-Zero Cross-Correlation (MW-ZCC) code for use in WON-OCDMA systems that is capable of carrying simultaneously SHM, including video surveillance data.

The paper is organised as follows. Section 2 describes the MW-ZCC code construction, Section 3 the architecture of WON-OCDMA for a sensor system and explains the code detection and design. Section 4 focuses on the main results, and Section 5 presents analytical results; this is followed by Sections 6 and 7.

2. Code Construction

The novel MW-ZCC code for SAC-OCDMA system is matrix-based, and its construction follows a series of simple steps described below.

Step 1: The code is based on an $X \times N$ matrix where a number of lines N represents a number of codes (i.e., users or sensors $\cdots$) and a number of columns N represents a number of chips, respectively. Thus the base matrix produces X code sequences with code length N. The cornerstone of each matrix is a matrix, H_0 where:

$$H_0 = \begin{bmatrix} 0 & 1 & 1 \\ 1 & 0 & 0 \end{bmatrix} \tag{1}$$

This matrix is utilised for increasing the number of users and weights using a simple replacement technique.

Step 2: A new matrix H_j can be generated from the existing $H_{(j-1)}$ matrix using a replacement technique as follows:

$$H_j = \begin{bmatrix} 0 & H_{(j-1)} & H_{(j-1)} \\ H_{(j-1)} & 0 & 0 \end{bmatrix} \tag{2}$$

Step 3: When the replacement $(H_{(j-1)})$ is done, there will be blank spaces in the newly generated matrix H_j which are filled in by a series of '0's according to the matrix size; therefore, all the created matrices are symmetrical.

For example, in the earlier substitution, $R = 1$, we have:

$$
\begin{aligned}
H_j &= \begin{bmatrix} 0 & H_0 & H_0 \\ H_0 & 0 & 0 \end{bmatrix} \\
&= \begin{bmatrix} 0 & 0 & 0 & 0 & 1 & 1 & 0 & 1 & 1 \\ 0 & 0 & 0 & 1 & 0 & 0 & 1 & 0 & 0 \\ 0 & 1 & 1 & 0 & 0 & 0 & 0 & 0 & 0 \\ 1 & 0 & 0 & 0 & 0 & 0 & 0 & 0 & 0 \end{bmatrix}
\end{aligned}
\tag{3}
$$

Step 4: To generate higher code weights and users, another replacement is required. Now we use $R = 2$:

$$
\begin{aligned}
H_j &= \begin{bmatrix} 0 & H_1 & H_1 \\ H_1 & 0 & 0 \end{bmatrix} \\
&= \begin{bmatrix} 0 & 0 & 0 & 0 & H_0 & H_0 & 0 & H_0 & H_0 \\ 0 & 0 & 0 & H_0 & 0 & 0 & H_0 & 0 & 0 \\ 0 & H_0 & H_0 & 0 & 0 & 0 & 0 & 0 & 0 \\ H_0 & 0 & 0 & 0 & 0 & 0 & 0 & 0 & 0 \end{bmatrix}
\end{aligned}
\tag{4}
$$

If W is the code weight, X is the number of codewords (i.e., the number of users), and N will be the length of the constructed code. The described code generation procedure produces multiple weight codes all with code-weights of power of 2:

$$W_i = 2^i \qquad 0 \leq i \leq R+1 \tag{5}$$

The highest achievable code-weight, W_{max} for the proposed code is, therefore, $2^R + 1$. From this, the number of the required replacement, R can be calculated:

$$R = Log_2 W_{max} - 1 \tag{6}$$

Similarly, a number of the generated codes (signature), X (i.e., users) is obtained by $2^R + 1$, and the code length can be calculated as $N = 3^{R+1}$.

Step 5: To achieve code-weights increments without increasing the number of users, the matrix can simply be multiplied horizontally. For example, a double code weight and double code length can be achieved as

$$W_i' = 2W_i \tag{7}$$

and

$$N_i' = 2N \tag{8}$$

Step 6: If it is only desired to increase the number of users without the code-weight increase, the mapping technique is applied to double the number of users.

In Equation (9) matrix H' illustrates the increment of the code-weight while in Equation (10), matrix $\hat{H}$ denotes the increase in the number of users, as was explained in steps 5 and 6 respectively. Here, the the code-weight which were initially 4, 2 and 1 had been increased to 8, 4 and 2 while the number of users has been maintained as 4:

$$H' =$$

$$
\begin{bmatrix}
0 & 0 & 0 & 0 & 1 & 1 & 0 & 1 & 1 & 0 & 0 & 0 & 0 & 1 & 1 & 0 & 1 & 1 \\
0 & 0 & 0 & 1 & 0 & 0 & 1 & 0 & 0 & 0 & 0 & 0 & 1 & 0 & 0 & 1 & 0 & 0 \\
0 & 1 & 1 & 0 & 0 & 0 & 0 & 0 & 0 & 1 & 1 & 0 & 0 & 0 & 0 & 0 & 0 & 0 \\
1 & 0 & 0 & 0 & 0 & 0 & 0 & 0 & 1 & 0 & 0 & 0 & 0 & 0 & 0 & 0 & 0 & 0
\end{bmatrix}
\tag{9}
$$

$$\hat{H} =$$

$$
\begin{bmatrix}
0 & 0 & 0 & 0 & 1 & 1 & 0 & 1 & 1 & & & & & & & & & \\
0 & 0 & 0 & 1 & 0 & 0 & 1 & 0 & 0 & & & & & & & & & \\
0 & 1 & 1 & 0 & 0 & 0 & 0 & 0 & 0 & & & & & & & & & \\
1 & 0 & 0 & 0 & 0 & 0 & 0 & 0 & 0 & & & & & & & & & \\
& & & & & & & & & 0 & 0 & 0 & 0 & 1 & 1 & 0 & 1 & 1 \\
& & & & & & & & & 0 & 0 & 0 & 1 & 0 & 0 & 1 & 0 & 0 \\
& & & & & & & & & 0 & 1 & 1 & 0 & 0 & 0 & 0 & 0 & 0 \\
& & & & & & & & & 1 & 0 & 0 & 0 & 0 & 0 & 0 & 0 & 0
\end{bmatrix}
\tag{10}
$$

All empty spaces are filled by "0"s. Thus, the number of users has increased from four to eight while the number of code-weight is maintained as four. The total length of the resulting code, N_T after the mapping is dependent on the number of mapping, M, and can be attained by $N_T = M \times N$, where N is the length of the matrix before mapping. M can be attained by X_T/W. Here X_T is the total number of users.

3. System Description

Figure 1 illustrates the layout of the combined OCDMA and WON system. The OCDMA utilises a multiwavelength laser source based on [31]. This multiwavelength laser generates 90 wavelengths λ_1 to λ_M spectrally separated by 20 GHz into so-called wavelength chips. Set of k wavelength is then distributed towards V video surveillance transmitters while a set of p wavelengths is distributed towards B transmitters used for structural vibration sensing. Note $V \times k + B \times p = M$ were the number of generated wavelength by the laser.

Video surveillance data from each transmitter are carried by a dedicated MW-ZCC code with a code weight of k. Each code uses the assigned subset of wavelengths i to $(i + k)$ from a dedicated $k \times 1$ array waveguide grating (AWG). A Mach-Zehnder modulator that follows performs NRZ on-off keying modulation of the Video surveillance signal on the code. Finally, signals from all video transmitters are combined by a $(V + B) \times 1$ power coupler and send for optical amplification before being broadcasted into free space towards the receiver. On a reception side, a $1 \times (V + B)$ power coupler sends a copy of the received spectrum to each decoder. The code detection is handled by fibre Bragg gratings (FBGs). Decoded data are sent to a user photodetector (PIN) for optical to electrical conversion. Finally, data are analysed. In this experiment, a bit error rate (BER) analyser is used to assess the quality of received signals in order to evaluate the system performance.

For vibration sensing, a set of B $(p \times 1)$ AWGs is used to form a unique code with the code-weight of p at each vibration sensing point. (see Figure 1). There, a collimator mounted on the sensing box works as a code modulator to imprint the vibrations. In conducted simulations, a Mach-Zehnder modulator has been utilised to imitate the detrimental behaviour of the collimator used in vibration sensors. Three different frequencies of 70, 140 and 210 MHz were used to represent low, medium and high vibration, which are adopted from previous experimental research [6]. In the real world, the vibration intensity is not the discrete number; its range depends on the physical nature of the monitored structure and variations of the quiver. Before broadcasting, data from all vibration sensors are sent to an $(V + B) \times 1$ power coupler followed by an optical amplifier. On the receiving side, FBGs are used to filter out the individual codes. The decoded codes carrying vibration data are then converted into electrical domain by PIN photodetectors and sent for analyses; this experiment uses an oscilloscope with fast Fourier transform module.

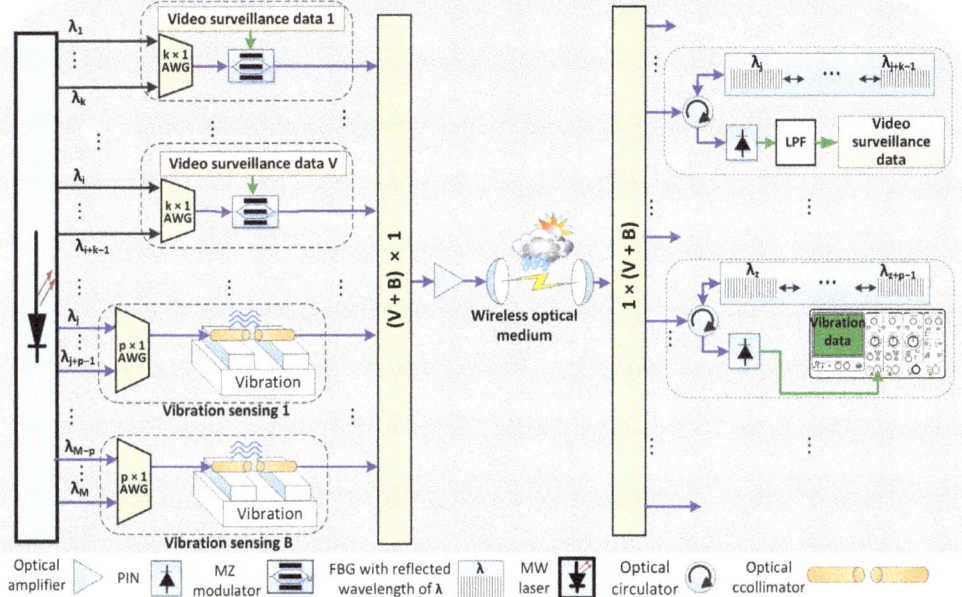

Figure 1. Diagram of WON-OCDMA hybrid system for video surveillance and vibration sensing monitoring.

4. Simulation Results

During the simulation, it was assumed there are four communication data channels coexisting with two video surveillance transmitters and two sensing points transmitters. Based on the MW-ZCC codes, code-weights of 4, 2, and 1 were assigned for video, data and sensing services, respectively. Used codes and associated wavelength code carriers are presented in Figure 2. The system performance was simulated using OptiSystem version 12 software, and default values were used for the optical and electrical components.

Weight	Code #	192.2	192.25	192.3	192.35	192.4	192.45	192.5	192.55	192.6	192.65	192.7	192.75	192.8	192.85	192.9	192.95	193	193.05
4	C_1	0	0	0	0	1	1	0	1	1	0	0	0	0	0	0	0	0	0
	C_2	0	0	0	0	0	0	0	0	0	0	0	0	0	1	1	0	1	1
2	C_3	0	0	0	1	0	0	1	0	0	0	0	0	0	0	0	0	0	0
	C_4	0	1	1	0	0	0	0	0	0	0	0	0	0	0	0	0	0	0
	C_5	0	0	0	0	0	0	0	0	0	0	0	0	1	0	0	1	0	0
	C_6	0	0	0	0	0	0	0	0	0	0	1	1	0	0	0	0	0	0
1	C_7	1	0	0	0	0	0	0	0	0	0	0	0	0	0	0	0	0	0
	C_8	0	0	0	0	0	0	0	0	0	1	0	0	0	0	0	0	0	0

Figure 2. Codes composition for the proposed WON-OCDMA system for video surveillance, data and vibration services.

Three different vibration frequencies (see Table 1) monitored by two sensor nodes N1 and N2 were used to demonstrate the performance of the proposed system shown in Figure 1.

Table 1. Vibration frequencies monitored by nodes N1 and N2.

Node	Exp1	Exp2	Exp3
N1	70 MHz	0 MHz	210 MHz
N2	0 MHz	210 MHz	140 MHz

The bit rate for data and video services was set to 1.25 Gbps to follow the ANSI T1.105 standard of OC-24. The lasers power for each wavelength chip was set to 0 dBm. The bandwidth for AWGs at the vibration sensing points and FBGs at the monitoring side was considered as 50 GHz. The Mach-Zehnder modulator extinction ratio was 30 dB, and the noise figure for the optical amplifier was 4 dB. The WON transmitter and receiver aperture diameter were set to 5 and 20 cm, respectively. The PIN photodetectors were used with responsivity was 1 A/W and thermal noise of 10^{-22} W/Hz. In the WON channel, the assumed attenuation was set constant at 4 dB/km. The performance of the system was evaluated for WON affected by moderate turbulence (case when atmosphere index refraction structure is 10^{-14} m$^{-2/3}$ [32]). The received power from sensing nodes N1 and N2 in Experiments 1 to 3 is shown in Figure 3a–c, respectively. The plotted RF signals are photodetector responses to received optical signals from two vibrations sensing nodes after 2 km transmission in WON under medium turbulence. Data represent weak, medium and high-level vibrations with frequencies of 68.1, 140.4 and 208.2 MHz, respectively. Figure 3a,b are related to scenarios in which only one sensor is affected by vibrations, while in Figure 3c both sensors are simultaneously affected (i.e., modulated). In all three scenarios, video data transmissions were active. By comparing those three plots, it can be seen that the signals from other sensors and video surveillance data have a negligible effect on the quality of retrieved signal for individual vibration sensors.

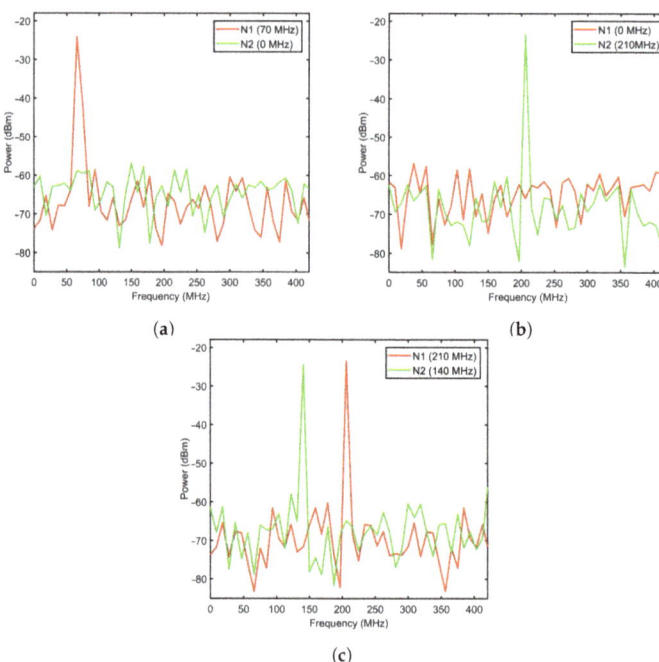

Figure 3. RF signal received from nodes N1 and N2 in experiments 1–3 (**a**–**c**) indicated in Table 1.

Example of SNR of the signal s from a sensing node N2 under conditions depicted in Figure 3c received over WON as a function of transmission distance is shown in Figure 4. The green line is the detectability limit. Maintaining an SNR of 15 dB, which is considered as the minimum recoverable value [6].

Example of received vibration signal (210 MHz and 140 MHz) from two sensing nodes N1 and N2, respectively after 3.2 km transmitted in WON with moderate turbulence is depicted in Figure 5. The eye diagrams for the worst-case scenario data and surveillance video are shown in Figure 6. After 3.2 km transmission, the BER values for data and video are 10^{-9} and 10^{-13}, respectively. The signals from the vibration sensing were also retrievable at this distance with SNR of 15.4 and 16.1 dB for node N1 and N2, respectively.

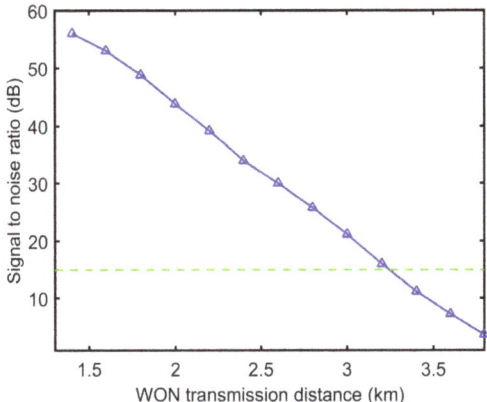

Figure 4. Example of SNR of the received signal from sensing none N2 as a function of transmission distance. The green line is the detectability limit.

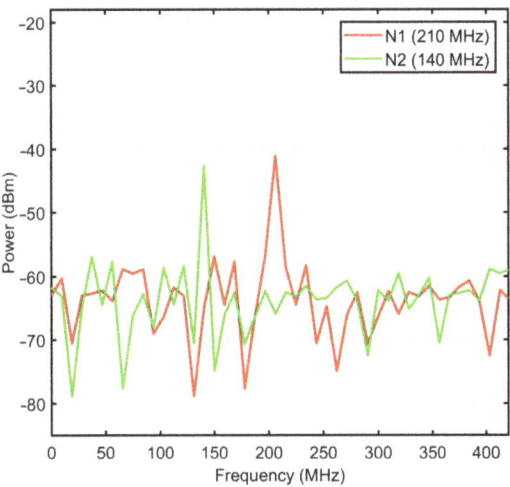

Figure 5. Example of received RF signal from sensing nodes N1 and N2 after 3.2 km transmitted in WON with moderate turbulence.

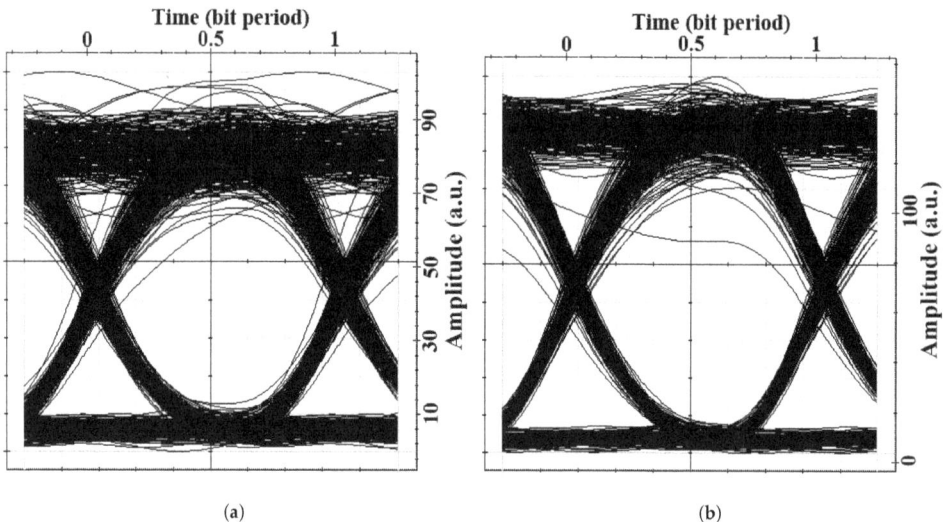

Figure 6. Eye diagram of signals related to (**a**) data service and (**b**) video surveillance data after 3.2 km propagation in atmosphere.

5. Theoretical Analysis

To analyse the results obtained, we assume each sensing point acts as a data transmitter operating at the same data rate and using OOK modulation. This analysis aims to provide a lower bound of the system capacity.

The SNR of a consecutive fibre optic communication system is attained as [23]:

$$SNR = \frac{\langle I \rangle^2}{\langle I^2 \rangle} = \frac{I_b^2}{i_{nb}^2} \tag{11}$$

where i_{nb}^2 is the power of noise sources that exist in the photocurrent and I_b is the mean acquired photocurrent at the receiver. It can be determined as:

$$I_b = RbW_h P_r \tag{12}$$

where P_r is the achieved optical power per wavelength, R is the photodiode responsivity, b is a bit value and is equal to 1, and where the specified subscriber transmit bit "1", elsewhere it is zero. W_h is the count of wavelengths for the users in group h which are retrieved by the photodetector. Their values depend on the detection technique and the coding technique. For complementary subtraction $W_h = W$ because all frequencies of the users are received by the photodetector. Nevertheless, in the direct decoding, that is the technique used for decoding the MW-ZCC, the W_h figure is reliant on the used coding technique. For example, W_h is equal to 1 when the utilised code has a modified quadratic congruence, 2 for MDW code and W for ZCC.

In addition, parameter i_{nb}^2 represents the variance of the total noise power, and for the SAC-OCDMA set-up which employs a multiwavelength laser, it is attained by [33,34]:

$$i_{nb}^2 = i_{RINb}^2 + i_{shb}^2 + i_{th}^2 \tag{13}$$

where i_{RINb}^2, i_{th}^2 and i_{shb}^2 are the variance of the noises incidental to the relative intensity noise (RIN), thermal noise and shot noise. i_{shb}^2 is expressed as:

$$i_{shb}^2 = 2EbW_hP_rB_e \tag{14}$$

B_e denotes the electrical bandwidth, where E represents the electron's charge. With the assumption that the number of disturbing signal transmitting bit "1" at every wavelength for all the users are the same, the mean value for x is:

$$x = \frac{W_h^2(K-1)}{2N} \tag{15}$$

Since RIN occurs at the transmitter and all other interfering users cause crosstalk with the desired user signal, it is concluded that $W_h = W$ and

$$i_{RINb}^2 = RIN(bWP_r + xP_c)^2B_e \tag{16}$$

where RIN is the noise factor. The thermal noise can be achieved by:

$$i_{th}^2 = \frac{4K_BTB_e}{R_L} \tag{17}$$

where T is temperature, K_B is the Boltzmann constant, and R_L is the load resistor. Then the power variance of the total noise is calculated as:

$$i_n^2 = i_{RIN}^2 + i_{sh}^2 + i_{th}^2 \tag{18}$$

To obtain the SNR, considering that the probability of sending bit '1' by every user is $1/2$, then the RIN, as well as the shot noise, must be divided by 2. Therefore, the total SNR can be achieved by:

$$SNR = \frac{R^2W_h^2P^2|_r}{\frac{RIN}{2}(WP_r)^2B_e + EW_hP_rB_e + \frac{4K_BTB_e}{R_L}} \tag{19}$$

where P_r in a SAC-CDMA operating in WON is obtained as:

$$P_r = \frac{P_tD^2e^{-\Omega L}}{N(\theta L)^2} \tag{20}$$

Here, P_t is the total sent power into the free space medium, D is the diameter of the utilised receiver aperture, N denotes the code length, Ω represents the attenuation coefficient, L is the total length of WON medium, and the θ is the beam divergence. To achieve BER as the system performance parameter, the air turbulence effect should be taken into account. The intensity of the turbulences is measured by a Rytov variance, which is attained by:

$$\sigma_R^2 = 1.23C_n^2K_{own}^{7/6}L^{11/6} \tag{21}$$

here C_n^2 is the refractive index structure coefficient and $K_{own} = 2\pi/\lambda$ is the optical wave number.

The system behaviour and reliability are denoted by the probability density function (PDF) of the randomly fading irradiance. Utilising $Gamma - Gamma$ distribution, the pdf of the terms of normalised irradiance I is given by [35]

$$P_G(I) = \frac{2(\alpha\beta)^{\frac{(\alpha+\beta)}{2}}}{\Gamma(\alpha)\Gamma(\beta)}I^{\left[\frac{(\alpha+\beta)}{2}-1\right]}K_{\alpha-\beta}(2\sqrt{\alpha\beta I}) \tag{22}$$

Sensors **2021**, *21*, 539

where $\Gamma(.)$ is the Gamma function, and $K_{(\alpha-\beta)}$ is the qualified Bessel function of the second kind of order $\alpha - \beta$. The α and β factors represent the effective number of small and large-scale twists of the scattering atmosphere and are calculated as

$$\alpha = \left\{ exp \left[\frac{0.49\sigma^2}{\left(1 + 1.11\sigma_R^{\frac{12}{5}}\right)^{\frac{7}{6}}} \right] - 1 \right\}^{-1} \tag{23}$$

and

$$\beta = \left\{ exp \left[\frac{0.51\sigma^2}{\left(1 + 0.69\sigma_R^{\frac{12}{5}}\right)^{\frac{5}{6}}} \right] - 1 \right\}^{-1} \tag{24}$$

The BER of an optical signal which has been transmitted in the *Gamma~Gamma* distributed medium can be obtained as [36]:

$$BER = \int_0^\infty BER_0(I)P_G(I)dI \tag{25}$$

where $BER_0(I)$ represents the BER of the signal conveyed in the additive white Gaussian noise (*AWGN*) channel and is calculated as

$$BER_0(I) = Q\left(\sqrt{\frac{I^2\hat{\gamma}}{2}}\right) \tag{26}$$

where

$$Q(\gamma) = \frac{1}{2}erfc(\frac{y}{\sqrt{2}}) \tag{27}$$

Here, $\hat{\gamma}$ is the average electrical SNR and $erfc(y)$ is the complementary error function.

5.1. Obtained Results

The values for the exploited parameters in the investigation were selected to allow for comparison with previous research and are summarised in Table 2.

Table 2. Summary of the parameters used for system investigation.

Symbol	Parameter	Value
θ	Beam divergence	0.5 mrad
λ	Operating wavelength	1550 nm
D	Receiver aperture diameter	8 cm
B_e	Electrical bandwidth	2.5 GHz
σ_R^2	Rytov variance	1
Ω	Weather attenuation	3 dB/km
P_c	Crosstalk power	−30 dBm
P_t	Total transmitted power	20 dBm

Figure 7 illustrates the performance of WON-OCDMA system with 8 MW-ZCC code words as a function of the received optical power (ROP) per chip. As can be observed, users with higher code-weights provide greater performance.

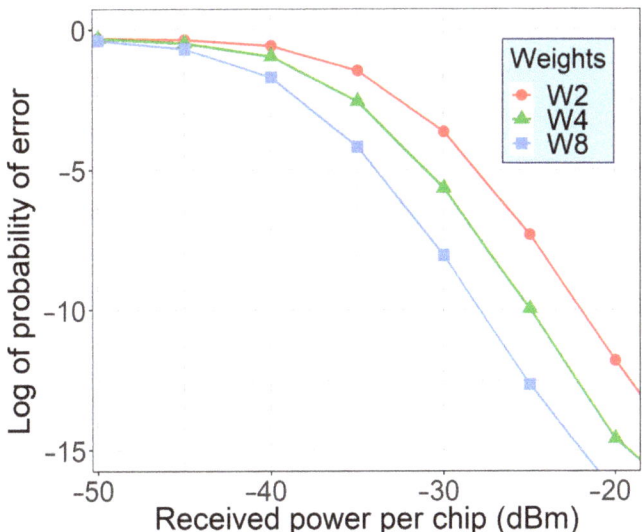

Figure 7. Probability of error versus ROP per code for concurrently transmitting users using code weight W of 2, 4 and 8.

The calculated number of simultaneous users (data services and vibration point sensors) using MW-ZCC codes as data carriers is shown in Figure 8. It was assumed that services are evenly represented in the systems. Assuming the minimum allowable BER of 10^{-3}, 10^{-9} and 10^{-12} to support triple-play services, WON-OCDMA employing novel MW-ZCC codes can support up to 32 simultaneous subscribers. In the OOK modulation, a BER of 10^{-3} is equivalent to an SNR of 15 dB.

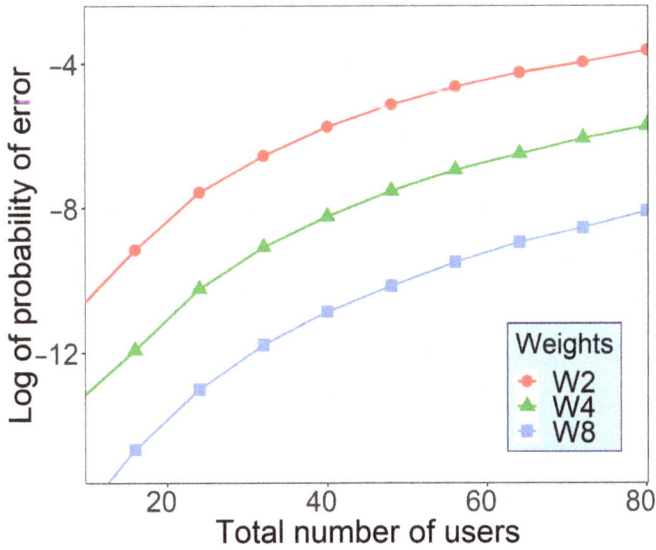

Figure 8. Probability of error versus total number of users as a function of code weight W of 2, 4, 8.

The performance degradation due to increased transmission distance in the atmosphere under moderate turbulence with 32 simultaneous users' (including transmission from 10 sensing points) was investigated using simulation set-up in OptiSystem software. The result is illustrated in Figure 9, indicating a successful transmission up to 2 km.

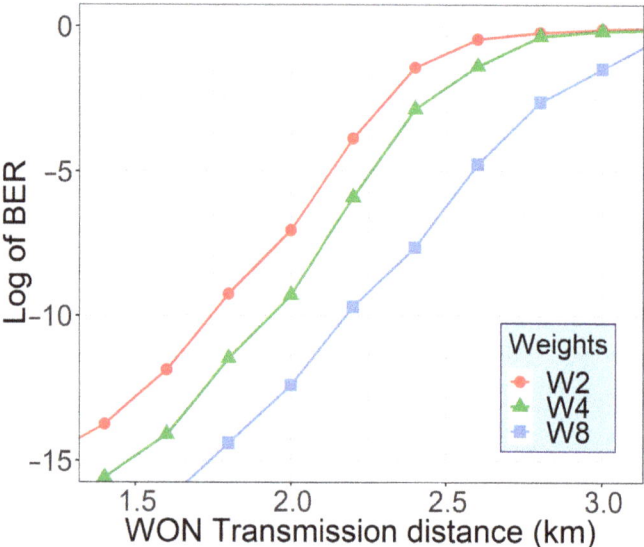

Figure 9. Probability of error versus transmission distance in moderate turbulence for concurrently transmitting users with weights 2, 4 and 8.

6. Discussion

The research presented in this study addresses the functionality gap between emerging optical sensor networks and urban SHM in order to leverage efficient remote vibration sensing of constructed sites. Despite the broad adoption of optical sensing in SHM, there are several challenges when it comes to monitoring various structures located in hard-to-reach areas. To address the needs, this paper proposes a new family of MW-ZCC codes for use in advanced monitoring systems for carrying information collected by optical sensors monitoring structural vibration. The proposed codes were investigated in WON-OCDMA system that does not require any traffic management or synchronisation.

It was shown that the proposed approach could also be effectively implemented without any undesirable interference or crass talk on other simultaneous communication services, including remote video surveillance. The novel family of MW-ZCC codes can support high-performance optical transmission systems that need to provide QoS differentiation in free space applications. As shown, MW-ZCC codes are well suited for use in WON-OCDMA systems even when used as single-weight codes because of their low cross-correlation properties. Since they are easy to convert into codes with the power of two code-weigh, they are well suited to support the desired QoS differentiation.

7. Conclusions

This paper proposes a novel MW-ZCC coding scheme with a low cross-correlation function for WON-OCDMA system. Codes are easy to convert into multiweight power of two codes, thus suitable for supporting a variety of QoS services in WON, including sensing, datacomms and video surveillance applications.

The effect of a free space transmission with medium turbulence on the signal transmission and received optical power was analysed. The simulations results revealed that for a minimum allowable BER of 10^{-3}, 10^{-9}, when supporting triple-play services (sensing, datacomms and video surveillance), the proposed WON-OCDMA employing MW-ZCC codes could carry up to 32 services simultaneously at a distance of 32 km in the presence of moderate turbulence in the atmosphere.

The research results presented in this paper thus offer conceptual approaches for engineering of future OCDMA-based wireless optical networks supporting triple-play services.

Author Contributions: Conceptualisation, S.S. and M.M.; methodology, S.S., M.M., M.D. and I.G.; software, S.S. and M.M.; validation, S.S. and A.A.; formal analysis, S.S., M.D. and I.G.; investigation, S.S., A.A., M.M., M.D. and I.G.; resources, A.A. and I.G.; writing—original draft preparation, S.S. and M.M.; writing—review and editing, S.S., A.A., M.M., M.D. and I.G.; supervision, I.G.; project administration, I.G.; funding acquisition, I.G., A.A. and M.D. All authors have read and agreed to the published version of the manuscript.

Funding: This research was funded by the European Union's Horizon 2020 Research and Innovation Program under the Marie Skłodowska-Curie under Grant 734331, the Slovak Research and Development Agency under the project APVV-17-0631, and supported by Construction Scotland Innovation Centre under the Collaborative Programme of Funding Support i-Con Platform.

Institutional Review Board Statement: Not applicable.

Informed Consent Statement: Not applicable.

Data Availability Statement: Not applicable.

Acknowledgments: We would like thank the University of Strathclyde, Robert Gordon University and Sublime Digital Ltd. for supporting this research project.

Conflicts of Interest: The authors declare no conflict of interest.

References

1. Majumder, M.; Gangopadhyay, T.K.; Chakraborty, A.K.; Dasgupta, K.; Bhattacharya, D.K. Fibre Bragg gratings in structural health monitoring-Present status and applications. *Sens. Actuators A Phys.* **2008**. [CrossRef]
2. Li, H.N.; Li, D.S.; Song, G.B. Recent applications of fiber optic sensors to health monitoring in civil engineering. *Eng. Struct.* **2004**, *26*, 1647–1657. [CrossRef]
3. Shabaneh, A.; Girei, S.; Arasu, P.; Rahman, W.; Bakar, A.; Sadek, A.; Lim, H.; Huang, N.; Yaacob, M. Reflectance response of tapered optical fiber coated with graphene oxide nanostructured thin film for aqueous ethanol sensing. *Opt. Commun.* **2014**, *331*, 320–324. [CrossRef]
4. Woyessa, G.; Nielsen, K.; Stefani, A.; Markos, C.; Bang, O. Temperature insensitive hysteresis free highly sensitive polymer optical fiber Bragg grating humidity sensor. *Opt. Express* **2016**, *24*, 1206. [CrossRef]
5. Li, C.; Zhao, Y.G.; Liu, H.; Wan, Z.; Zhang, C.; Rong, N. Monitoring second lining of tunnel with mounted fiber Bragg grating strain sensors. *Autom. Constr.* **2008**, *17*, 641–644. [CrossRef]
6. Rahimian, F.P.; Seyedzadeh, S.; Glesk, I. OCDMA-based sensor network for monitoring construction sites affected by vibrations. *J. Inf. Technol. Constr.* **2019**, *24*, 299–317.
7. Lu, S.W.; Xie, H.Q. Strengthen and real-time monitoring of RC beam using "intelligent" CFRP with embedded FBG sensors. *Constr. Build. Mater.* **2007**, *21*, 1839–1845. [CrossRef]
8. Unzu, R.; Nazabal, J.A.; Vargas, G.; Hernández, R.J.; Fernández-Valdivielso, C.; Urriza, N.; Galarza, M.; Lopez-Amo, M. Fiber optic and KNX sensors network for remote monitoring a new building cladding system. *Autom. Constr.* **2013**, *30*, 9–14. [CrossRef]
9. Dawood, N.; Rahimian, F.; Seyedzadeh, S.; Sheikhkhoshkar, M. *Enabling the Development and Implementation of Digital Twins: Proceedings of the 20th International Conference on Construction Applications of Virtual Reality*; Teesside University: Middlesbrough, UK, 2020; p. 389.
10. Pour Rahimian, F.; Seyedzadeh, S.; Oliver, S.; Rodriguez, S.; Dawood, N. On-demand monitoring of construction projects through a game-like hybrid application of BIM and machine learning. *Autom. Constr.* **2020**, *110*, 103012. [CrossRef]
11. Takahashi, N.; Yoshimura, K.; Takahashi, S. Fiber Bragg grating vibration sensor using incoherent light. *Jpn. J. Appl. Phys. Part 1 Regul. Pap. Short Notes Rev. Pap.* **2001**, *40*, 3632–3636. [CrossRef]
12. Zhang, Z.; Bao, X. Continuous and damped vibration detection based on fiber diversity detection sensor by Rayleigh backscattering. *J. Light. Technol.* **2008**, *26*, 832–838. [CrossRef]
13. Ge, Y.; Kuang, K.S.; Quek, S.T. Development of a low-cost bi-axial intensity-based optical fibre accelerometer for wind turbine blades. *Sens. Actuators A Phys.* **2013**, *197*, 126–135. [CrossRef]
14. Udd, E.; Spillman, W.B., Jr. *Fiber Optic Sensors: An Introduction for Engineers and Scientists*; John Wiley & Sons: Hoboken, NJ, USA, 2011; pp. 451–462.
15. Taiwo, A.; Seyedzadeh, S.; Taiwo, S.; Sahbudin, R.K.Z.; Yaacob, M.H.; Mokhtar, M. Performance and comparison of fiber vibration sensing using SAC-OCDMA with direct decoding techniques. *Opt. Int. J. Light Electron Opt.* **2014**, *125*, 4803–4806. [CrossRef]

16. Noura, A.; Seyedzadeh, S.; Anas, S.B. Simultaneous vibration and humidity measurement using a hybrid WDM/OCDMA sensor network. In Proceedings of the 4th International Conference on Photonics (ICP 2013), Melaka, Malaysia, 28–30 October 2013; pp. 163–165. [CrossRef]
17. Taiwo, A.; Taiwo, S.; Sahbudin, R.K.Z.; Yaacob, M.H.; Mokhtar, M. Fiber vibration sensor multiplexing techniques for quasi-distributed sensing. *Opt. Laser Technol.* **2014**, *64*, 34–40. [CrossRef]
18. Seyedzadeh, S.; Rahimian, F.P.; Glesk, I.; Kakaee, M.H. Variable weight spectral amplitude coding for multiservice OCDMA networks. *Opt. Fiber Technol.* **2017**, *37*, 53–60. [CrossRef]
19. Anas, S.B.A.; Seyedzadeh, S.; Mokhtar, M.; Sahbudin, R.K.Z. Variable weight Khazani-Syed code using hybrid fixed-dynamic technique for optical code division multiple access system. *Opt. Eng.* **2016**, *55*, 106101. [CrossRef]
20. Seyedzadeh, S.; Glesk, I.; Pour Rahimian, F.; Kwong, W.C. Variable weight code division multiple access system for monitoring vibration of unequally distributed points. In Proceedings of the International Conference on Transparent Optical Networks, Angerrs, France, 9–13 July 2019; pp. 1–4. [CrossRef]
21. Kwong, W.; Yang, G.C. Multiple-Length Multiple-Wavelength Optical Orthogonal Codes for Optical CDMA Systems Supporting Multirate Multimedia Services. *IEEE J. Sel. Areas Commun.* **2004**, *22*, 1640–1647. [CrossRef]
22. Liang, W.; Yin, H.; Qin, L.; Wang, Z.; Xu, A. A new family of 2D variable-weight optical orthogonal codes for OCDMA systems supporting multiple QoS and analysis of its performance. *Photonic Netw. Commun.* **2008**, *16*, 53–60. [CrossRef]
23. Seyedzadeh, S.; Moghaddasi, M.; Anas, S. Variable-weight optical code division multiple access system using different detection schemes. *J. Telecommun. Inf. Technol.* **2016**, *2016*, 50–59.
24. Seyedzadeh, S.; Mahdiraji, G.A.; Sahbudin, R.K.Z.; Abas, A.F.; Anas, S.B.A. Experimental demonstration of variable weight SAC-OCDMA system for QoS differentiation. *Opt. Fiber Technol.* **2014**, *20*, 495–500. [CrossRef]
25. Cvijetic, N.; Wilson, S.G.; Brandt-Pearce, M. Receiver optimization in turbulent free-space optical MIMO channels with APDs and Q-ary PPM. *IEEE Photonics Technol. Lett.* **2007**, *19*, 103–105. [CrossRef]
26. Sahbudin, R.K.Z.; Kamarulzaman, M.; Hitam, S.; Mokhtar, M.; Anas, S.B.A. Performance of SAC OCDMA-FSO communication systems. *Opt. Int. J. Light Electron Opt.* **2013**, *124*, 2868–2870. [CrossRef]
27. Moghaddasi, M.; Taiwo, A.; Seyedzadeh, S.; Boroon, M.; Hitam, S.; Anas, S. Performance analysis of spectral amplitude coding-optical code division multiple access (SAC-OCDMA) in free space optical networks with a multi-wavelength laser source. *Lasers Eng.* **2017**, *38*, 67–80.
28. Alyan, E.; Aljunid, S. Development of wireless optical CDMA system for biosignal monitoring. *Optik* **2017**, *145*, 250–257. [CrossRef]
29. Anuar, M.S.; Aljunid, S.; Saad, N.M.; Hamzah, S.M. New design of spectral amplitude coding in OCDMA with zero cross-correlation. *Opt. Commun.* **2009**, *282*, 2659–2664. [CrossRef]
30. Ahmed, N.; Aljunid, S.; Fadil, A.; Ahmad, R.; Rashid, M. Performance enhancement of OCDMA system using NAND detection with modified double weight (MDW) code for optical access network. *Opt. Int. J. Light Electron Opt.* **2013**, *124*, 1402–1407. [CrossRef]
31. Mamdoohi, G.; Sarmani, A.R.; Abas, A.F.; Yaacob, M.H.; Mokhtar, M.; Mahdi, M.A. 20 GHz spacing multi-wavelength generation of Brillouin-Raman fiber laser in a hybrid linear cavity. *Opt. Express* **2013**, *21*, 18724. [CrossRef] [PubMed]
32. Mahdieh, M.H.; Pournoury, M. Atmospheric turbulence and numerical evaluation of bit error rate (BER) in free-space communication. *Opt. Laser Technol.* **2010**, *42*, 55–60. [CrossRef]
33. Moghaddasi, M.; Mamdoohi, G.; Noor, A.S.M.; Mahdi, M.A.; Anas, S.B.A. Development of SAC–OCDMA in FSO with multi-wavelength laser source. *Opt. Commun.* **2015**, *356*, 282–289. [CrossRef]
34. Matem, R.; Aljunid, S.; Junita, M.; Rashidi, C.; Ahmed, I.S. Photodetector effects on the performance of 2D Spectral/Spatial code in OCDMA system. *Optik* **2019**, *178*, 1051–1061. [CrossRef]
35. Rodrigues, G.K.; Carneiro, V.G.A.; da Cruz, A.R.; Giraldi, M.T.M.R. Evaluation of the strong turbulence impact over free-space optical links. *Opt. Commun.* **2013**, *305*, 42–47. [CrossRef]
36. Wang, Z.; Zhong, W.D.; Fu, S.; Lin, C. Performance comparison of different modulation formats over free-space optical (FSO) turbulence links with space diversity reception technique. *IEEE Photonics J.* **2009**, *1*, 277–285. [CrossRef]

Article

Energy-Efficient Clustering Multi-Hop Routing Protocol in a UWSN

Nhat-Tien Nguyen [1,2], Thien T. T. Le [2], Huy-Hung Nguyen [2] and Miroslav Voznak [1,*]

[1] Department of Telecommunications, VSB-Technical University of Ostrava, 708 00 Ostrava, Czech Republic; tien.nn@sgu.edu.vn

[2] Faculty of Electronics and Telecommunications, Sai Gon University, Ho Chi Minh City 700000, Vietnam; thien.lett@sgu.edu.vn (T.T.T.L.); nghhung@sgu.edu.vn (H.-H.N.)

* Correspondence: miroslav.voznak@vsb.cz

Abstract: Underwater wireless sensor networks are currently seeing broad research in various applications for human benefits. Large numbers of sensor nodes are being deployed in rivers and oceans to monitor the underwater environment. In the paper, we propose an energy-efficient clustering multi-hop routing protocol (EECMR) which can balance the energy consumption of these nodes and increase their network lifetime. The network area is divided into layers with regard to the depth level. The data sensed by the nodes are transmitted to a sink via a multi-hop routing path. The cluster head is selected according to the depth of the node and its residual energy. To transmit data from the node to the sink, the cluster head aggregates the data packet of all cluster members and then forwards them to the upper layer of the sink node. The simulation results show that EECMR is effective in terms of network lifetime and the nodes' energy consumption.

Keywords: underwater wireless sensor network; energy-efficient; clustering; depth-based routing

Citation: Nguyen, N.-T.; Le, T.T.T.; Nguyen, H.-H.; Voznak, M. Energy-Efficient Clustering Multi-Hop Routing Protocol in a UWSN. *Sensors* **2021**, *21*, 627. https://doi.org/10.3390/s21020627

Received: 29 November 2020
Accepted: 13 January 2021
Published: 18 January 2021

Publisher's Note: MDPI stays neutral with regard to jurisdictional claims in published maps and institutional affiliations.

1. Introduction

The ecosystem on Earth mainly consists of water, which covers more than 75% of its surface. Water covers the Earth in many forms as rivers, lakes, and oceans and plays a crucial role in human life and for other animals. Technological developments have allowed sensors to be deployed for the exploration of nature's forest, river, and lake environments. These sensors are embedded with smart sensing and intelligent computing and are capable of communicating with each other. Underwater wireless sensor networks (UWSNs) consist of many autonomous sensor nodes, which are considered homogeneous nodes and limited in energy [1,2]. These underwater sensor nodes are deployed in rivers or seas to detect the characteristics present in the water environment, such as temperature, current flow, pressure, and water quality. This type of data is aggregated at a data processing station according to different types of applications. From observation of the environment, humans gain many benefits for many applications, such as environmental monitoring, disaster forecasting, military surveillance, and assisted navigation. In particular, detailed examination of the underwater environment assists humans in the observation of marine life, disaster forecasting, water pollution monitoring, and sea exploration [3,4]. The hardware architecture of underwater sensor nodes is described in [5]. The internal architecture of an underwater sensor node consists of several modules: memory, an acoustic modem, a sensor, sensor interface circuitry, a control processor unit (onboard controller), and a power supply. The underwater sensor node can be used to measure underwater characteristics such as temperature, density, acidity, chemicals, conductivity, pH, hydrogen, dissolved methane gas, and turbidity.

Figure 1 depicts the network model of UWSNs [1–3]. The UWSN consists of underwater sensor nodes, a sink node, and an onshore base station. In Figure 1, the nodes located near the sink directly transmit data to the sink, while the other nodes form clusters.

169

The underwater sensor nodes transmit their data to the sink at the surface. The sink then forwards the aggregated data to the nearest base station on the mainland. The sink node is equipped with two types of transceivers: (1) a radio transceiver, which can communicate with the base station by radio frequency; and (2) an acoustic transceiver for communication with the sensor nodes. The underwater node is embedded with an acoustic transceiver for transmission between nodes. The transmission medium of the underwater environment is different to that of a terrestrial wireless sensor network (TWSN) with respect to channel modeling, path loss, and topology [2,3]. The underwater wireless sensor nodes are moved by currents with velocities of around 1–3 m/s. The acoustic channel is modeled differently from the radio propagation channel.

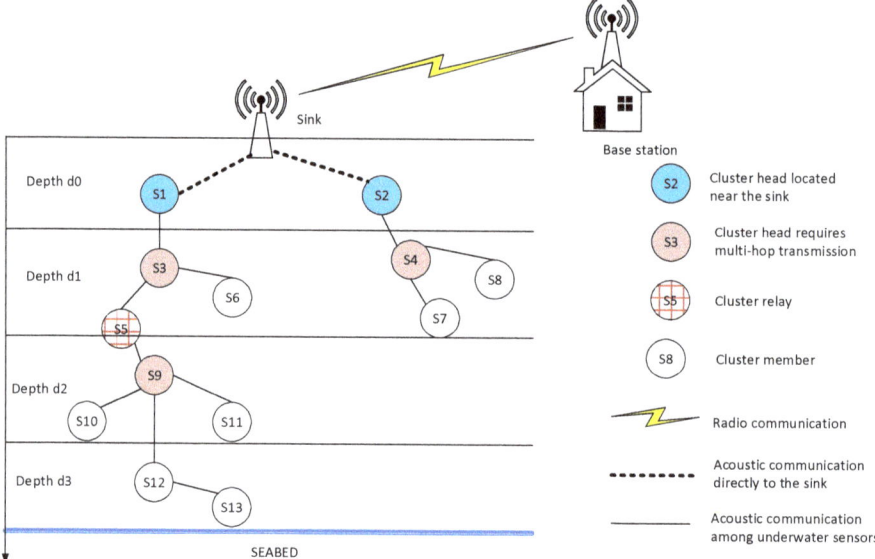

Figure 1. Underwater wireless sensor network (UWSN) model.

In both TWSNs and UWSNs, data packets are sent from a sensor node to the base station via either a one-hop path or a multi-hop path. It is necessary to route the data packet from one node to another node without loss. Since each sensor node is equipped with a battery, which may be difficult to replace or charge, the re-transmission of data packets may consume high energy, which results in a short network lifetime or many dead nodes. In TWSNs, many clustering protocols have been developed to minimize the energy consumption of sensors while successfully transmitting data packets to the destination. In TWSNs, all nodes are homogeneous and energy-constrained, and a low-energy adaptive clustering hierarchy (LEACH) successfully reduces the energy consumption of nodes while maintaining their network lifetime [6]. In [7], a clustering protocol for UWSNs was reviewed, demonstrating that the clustering protocol is suitable for underwater transmission. As with clustering in TWSNs, the clustering protocol is designed to reduce the control information, resulting in a reduction in the overall energy consumption, extended node lifetime, and greater network reliability. However, as a result of the effect of the current on the underwater sensor node, the cluster protocol should maintain connectivity to the network to ensure full coverage. In [8], a depth-based routing protocol (DBR) was developed to route a packet from any sensor to the sink node according to the node's depth level. The DBR allows nodes to forward data to the node at a higher layer near the sink.

In the present paper, we develop a clustering protocol with regard to the location of nodes and residual energy of nodes. We propose an energy-efficient clustering multi-hop routing protocol (EECMR) for UWSNs so that each node can maintain its transmission link to the sink node at the surface and its neighbor sensor nodes. Our contribution through this work is as follows:

- The underwater sensor nodes update the routing path and cluster to connect to the sink without disruption. The sink collects data, which are then transmitted to an onshore gateway.
- Three types of node: cluster head (CH), cluster member (CM), and cluster relay (CR). If a node is the cluster head, the role of the node can be an aggregation node. If a node is the cluster relay, the node forwards data from two clusters at two depth levels. Otherwise, nodes are designated as a cluster member and only send data to the cluster head.
- The underwater sensors calculate the weight according to the node's depth and residual energy to elect to become the cluster head.
- The routing protocol takes into account the number of cluster members and load balancing parameters so that the node selects the best route to the destination.

The remainder of the paper is organized as follows: Section 2 reviews the existing clustering routing protocols for UWSNs; Section 3 introduces and analyzes the energy-efficient clustering multi-hop routing protocol; Section 4 presents an evaluation of network performance in comparison to the LEACH protocol and DBR routing protocol; Section 5 concludes the paper.

2. Related Works

UWSNs have attracted many researchers over the last decade because of their enormous variety of application. Many literature reviews of routing protocols for UWSNs categorizing the routing protocols in terms of the routing strategy have been presented [9]. The routing protocol for UWSNs has two types: localization-based and localization-free protocols. The localization-based routing protocol requires the location of nodes to find the routing path from the node to the sink. Despite this, the localization-free protocol uses the depth measurement of the sensor node to establish the routes to the sink. The depth of the sensor node is measured by the pressure sensors equipped on the node. The localization-free protocol has more advantages than the other in terms of scalability. Due to the mobility of nodes, the routes can be constructed by using the depth if the network topology changes.

In [7], several cluster protocols for UWSNs are reviewed in terms of cluster stability, delay efficiency, load balancing, and energy efficiency. The network requires a capability of 100% coverage due to the long transmission range and high node mobility. The clustering protocols in UWSNs select the cluster heads and cluster members depending on the location of nodes, types of generated packets, priority of nodes, the energy consumption, and the latency of data. A clustering protocol should achieve high network performance with respect to a high packet delivery ratio, low latency, and a long network lifetime. Some clustering protocols are reviewed in detail in this section.

In [10], a clustered-based routing protocol allows the sensors to form clusters according to their depth and energy. The localization-free routing protocol, which is called the energy-efficient routing protocol based on layers and unequal clusters (EERBLC), selects the routing path according to the link quality and residual energy. It presumes that each sensor node does not need its location to set up a cluster. A node calculates a cost according to its residual energy and forwarding ratio. In this protocol, the header nodes selection procedure does not consider the duration of the cluster head and the location of nodes according to the sink. If nodes play the role of the cluster head for a long duration of time, it may become a hot spot, causing a dead node.

Another study applied LEACH in UWSNs to establish a cluster [11]. The study also improved LEACH, providing Controlled-LEACH (C-LEACH). C-LEACH deploys a control node at the center of a network's topology, and the control nodes process the clustering protocol, resulting in a longer network lifetime compared to LEACH. The C-LEACH protocol may take a long time to process the cluster algorithm because the control nodes should transmit to all nodes in the network.

In [12], the authors developed an adaptive node clustering routing protocol for smart ocean UWSNs based on an optimization technique. The network is divided into a cluster in which the cluster head is selected according to the available energy in the sensor node. The re-transmission may cause high latency or duplicated packets at the receiver while selecting the cluster members.

In [13], network deployment is divided into layers in which each layer has a fixed depth value and area width. The multi-layer cluster-based energy-efficient (MLCEE) routing protocol increases network lifetime while reducing the end-to-end delay of a packet. The MLCEE protocol allows the node to calculate its layer; the node then commences broadcasting messages to form a cluster. Since the network is divided into many depth layers, the node adopts the role of forwarder depending on its residual energy and probability.

In [14], a topology control energy balance protocol (TCEB) was implemented for UWSNs. The protocol considers the node's energy and path loss as the factors to select a cluster head. The topology control protocol is represented as a non-cooperative game. Each node can become the cluster head depending on the set of strategies and set of payoffs for the game. The pay-off function is denoted as the function of residual energy and the path loss of one-hop distance and aims to balance the energy consumption of all nodes.

In [15], another clustering protocol scheme was applied for multi-hop routing in UWSNs. The scheme allows nodes to change energy consumption while maintaining excellent network performance. The energy optimization clustering algorithm (EOCA) requires a node to communicate to neighbors within the effective communication range. Each node calculates the total transmission delay between the node and the sink and then elects to become a cluster head according to the value of the total transmission delay. The depth of each node was also used to find a forwarder before sending the packet to the sink. The nodes send data packets to the cluster head or directly to the sink; therefore, the energy consumption at the nodes can be balanced.

In [16], an energy-balanced unequal layering clustering (EULC) algorithm was designed for UWSNs to reduce energy consumption in inter-cluster communications. The EULC creates clusters of varying size within the same layer to solve the "hot spot" issue. The depth of network deployment is divided into layers based on the communication radius. The sensor nodes calculate the weight with respect to the residual energy of the node, the distance to the sink node, and the node degree. The node with the highest weight elects to become the cluster head. The node stores the information of the neighbor cluster head and then calculates the routing selected function to all the neighbor cluster heads according to the distance between the node and the residual energy. The node selects the next-hop cluster head with the smallest selected routing function value.

In [17], the author implemented a simplified balanced energy adaptive routing (S-BEAR) based on a dynamic cluster K-means algorithm. The cluster heads are selected randomly. The nodes join the cluster with the minimum Euclid distance to the cluster head. The cluster head then transmits data to the sink using multi-hop communications.

In [18], autonomous unmanned vehicles (AUVs) were deployed underwater for cluster formation, cluster head selection, and scheduling the transmission and wake-up sleep cycle. Since the cluster heads have to wait for the AUVs to collect data, packet delay may increase as a result of the waiting time at the cluster head.

In [19], a clustering vector-based forwarding algorithm (CVBF) performed clustering with the assistance of a virtual sink for each cluster. The network space is divided into equal cuboids, each cuboid being considered a cluster in which the node near the sink adopts the role of virtual sink.

In [20], the authors presented an energy-optimized path unaware layered routing protocol (E-PULRP) for UWSNs. The network is divided into layers, forming a layered structure around the central sink node. A potential relay node is identified from each layer.

The transmission around the sink is divided into a set of concentric shells which produce the layered structure. Communication from the node to the sink follows a multi-hop path through the relay node at each layer. Therefore, the E-PULRP protocol preserves energy consumption.

There remains some issues and challenges of clustering protocols in UWSNs. The type of nodes and the depth of nodes should be considered because the nodes may generate different types of data such as temperature, density, acidity, chemicals, conductivity, pH, and hydrogen which are categorized into different types of priority level. Therefore, nodes which generate high traffic priority should have higher priority and higher reliability to transmit data to the sink. In addition, the nodes located near the sink always aggregate data from other nodes which may cause a hot spot and dead nodes. Therefore, nodes should change the cluster head role after some time.

In [21], the authors reviewed and compared the routing protocols to select the forwarding node in a UWSN. Most of the routing protocols are multi-hop localization-free protocols which are energy-efficient and reliable. Therefore, the routing protocols for UWSNs should consider the depth of the node, energy consumption, and multi-hop routes in order to develop an efficient, reliable routing protocol. In addition, the clustering protocol for UWSNs shows the benefits in terms of high network coverage, high connectivity, and adaptivity to the dynamic environment. It should be noted that the existing routing protocols have some limitations. However, it is necessary to consider the role of the cluster relay and cluster head duration in minimizing energy consumption. The longer the nodes are at the cluster head, the more energy the nodes consume. In the paper, we propose a clustering protocol which takes into account the residual energy and the depth of nodes. The proposed protocol is described in the following section. A qualitative comparison of the clustering protocols is presented and discussed in Section 3.

3. Energy-Efficient Clustering Multi-Hop Routing Protocol

3.1. Network Model

The network scenario consists of N dynamic nodes which are randomly and sparsely deployed in a three-dimensional scenario $L \times L \times L$. Figure 1 illustrates the network. The data source is the sensed data in the water medium. The data are collected by the underwater sensor nodes. The sensed data are temperature, current flow, and pressure [1–4]. Underwater sensor nodes are equipped with acoustic modems to communicate with other nodes in the water medium. The sink node is deployed at the center of the surface and equipped with both acoustic and radio frequency (RF) modems; the sink's acoustic modems receive data from the underwater sensor nodes, and the RF modem transmits data to the base station on the shore. We assumed that our network scenario was similar to the networks in [8–10]. The underwater sensor nodes are mobile due to water currents with velocities of around 1–3 m/s; therefore, the topology changes rapidly. A table of notations is listed in Table 1. The assumptions of the network can be described as follows:

- The node knows its location and the location of the sink node upon first deployment.
- Nodes can become either the cluster head, cluster relay, or cluster member.
- The cluster head is rotated between the sensor nodes to conserve energy.

Table 1. Table of notations.

Notations	Description
N	Number of nodes
S_0	Sink node
S_i	Sensor node index i, $1 \leq i \leq N$
$L \times L \times L$	Three-dimensional network deployment
Tx	Transmission range of node
n_{depth}	Number of layers

Table 1. *Cont.*

Notations	Description
$Nei(S_i)$	List of neighbors of node S_i
D_m	Depth layer index m, $0 \leq m \leq n_{depth}$
$Lst(D_m)$	List of sensor nodes at depth D_m
TL	Transmission loss of acoustic signal
$\alpha_{TL}(f)$	Absorption coefficient for the medium
W_i	Weight of sensor node S_i
$d(i,j)$	Distance between node S_i and node S_j
$d(i,S_0)$	Distance between node S_i and the sink

The depth of deployment can be divided into layers, where each layer is defined by the transmission range of the node or sink, as given in (1):

$$n_{depth} = \frac{L}{Tx},$$ (1)

where L is the depth of network deployment and Tx is the transmission range of the node or sink.

In the paper, we divide the depth of the network, as shown in Figure 1. The depth of the network is divided into four cases: (1) the sink node at the surface, denoted D_0; (2) nodes stay near the surface, whose depth is D_1; (3) nodes stay in the water, whose depth is D_2; (4) nodes stay near the seabed, whose depth is D_3, where $D_3 > D_2 > D_1 > D_0$. The role of the nodes can be explained as follows:

- Each layer has several clusters, each cluster having one cluster head and a cluster member. For example, node S_3 is the cluster head at depth D_1 and node S_9 is the cluster head at depth D_2.
- Nodes located at the border of two layers can adopt the role of cluster relay, which forwards the data of the deeper layer to the sink. For example, node S_5 becomes a cluster relay which forwards the data of cluster S_9 to cluster S_3 and then transmits to the sink node.
- Node S_{13} located at the seabed takes the multi-hop routing path to the sink via clusters of S_{12}–S_9–S_5–S_3–S_1–sink. The propagation loss model of the underwater acoustic channel is assumed, as in [3]. Since the signals propagate vertically, attenuation increases, which is proportional to increasing distance. The transmission loss is calculated as follows:

$$TL = k_{TL} \times 10 \lg r + \alpha_{TL} r \times 10^{-3},$$ (2)

where TL represents the transmission loss in dB; k_{TL} is the spreading factor, which indicates the spreading loss, its value depending on the water depth and corresponding to the propagation geometry; $k_{TL} = 1$ in shallow water and cylindrical spreading; $k_{TL} = 2$ for deep water and spherical spreading; α_{TL} represents the absorption coefficient of the medium, which depends on the frequency, its unit being dB/km; r is the distance between the receiver and transmitter. The absorption coefficient for the medium is measured in dB/km for f in kHz; the equation for calculation is as follows:

$$\alpha_{TL}(f) = 0.11 \frac{f^2}{1+f^2} + 44 \frac{f^2}{4100+f^2} + 2.75 \times 10^{-4} f^2 + 0.003,$$ (3)

The absorption coefficient increases with increasing frequency. In UWSNs, the frequency is approximately 30 kHz; the absorption coefficient is less than 10 dB/km. The absorption coefficient is derived for chemical absorption in seawater in terms of acoustic frequency, pressure, acidity, temperature, and salinity. The constant values are calculated using Thorp's expression, which denotes the relaxation frequency for different chemical absorptions, the value of the acidic component and pH of the seawater, and the depth pressure of the seawater. Interested readers can refer to [22] for more details.

Based on the energy consumption model presented in [3,8,9], the least transmission power required at the transmitter to achieve power level P_0 at the receiver can be expressed by

$$P_{tx} = P_0 \times d^2 \times 10^{(\alpha_{TL}(f)/10)}, \tag{4}$$

where P_0 is the received power, d is the distance between the transmitter and receiver, and $\alpha_{TL}(f)$ is the absorption coefficient, which is shown in Figure 2.

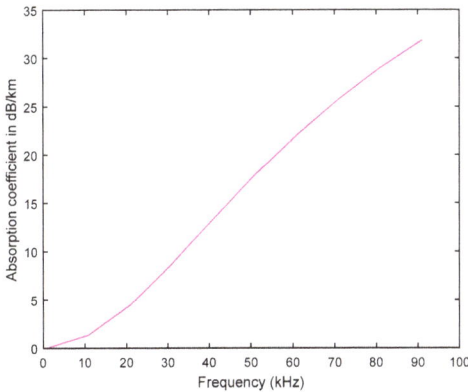

Figure 2. Absorption coefficient for the medium.

Since the characteristic of an acoustic wave in an underwater transmission medium is different from that of a radio wave, the energy consumption of wireless sensor networks cannot be applied to UWSNs. In the present paper, we apply the energy consumption model of the underwater acoustic channel as adopted in [3,12]. To transmit k bits of data over distance d with a data rate R, the energy consumed is defined as follows:

$$E_{Tx}(k,d) = k \times E_{elec} + \frac{k}{R} P_{tx}, \tag{5}$$

where E_{elec} is the energy consumption to route 1 bit of data, and P_{Tx} is the transmitted power, which is shown in equation (4).

To receive k bits of data, the receiver radio energy consumption can be expressed as

$$E_{Rx}(k) = k P_r, \tag{6}$$

where P_r is a constant dependent on the device.

To fuse k bits of data, the energy consumption can be defined as

$$E_{DA}(k) = k \times E_{DA0} \tag{7}$$

where E_{DA0} is the energy consumed by fusing one bit of data, which can be taken as 5 nJ/bit.

Since nodes are mobile due to the water current, we deploy random movement for nodes during the operating time. The current velocity is 1–3 m/s.

3.2. Energy-Efficient Clustering Multi-Hop Routing Protocol

The proposed energy-efficient clustering multi-hop routing protocol (EECMR) consists of two phases: a set-up phase and a steady-state phase. Cluster formation consists of sub-phases: broadcast information, cluster head selection, cluster formation, and scheduling transmission.

In EECMR, the node becomes a CH, CM, or CR. For example, the node becomes a CH in the first round, the node becomes a CR in the second round, and the node may become a CM in the third round. Each node calculates a weight value based on the residual energy and distance to the sink. The weight of each node is used to decide whether or not to become a cluster head for the current round. The weight of S_i is calculated as follows:

$$W_i = \frac{\Delta t}{T} + \alpha \frac{d(i, S_0)}{L} + \beta \frac{E_{Res}}{E_{Init}} \tag{8}$$

where $d(i,S_0)$ denotes the distance between node S_i and the sink, E_{Res} denotes the residual energy, E_{Init} denotes the initial energy, α and β denote the coefficient such that $\alpha + \beta = 1$, Δt denotes the time for which the nodes adopt the role of cluster head, and T is the total operating time.

The EECMR protocol is described in Algorithm 1. At the start t_0, the node does not have information about the surrounding environment. In State 1 from lines 3 to 7, each node broadcasts a "*HELLO*" message to the neighbors. The message includes information of the location and estimated distance to the sink. According to the successfully received "*HELLO*" message, nodes store their neighbors' information in order to select the cluster, which is shown in lines 8 to 11. To prevent a long waiting time, the timeout value is set to the maximum propagation delay of one hop, as in [8]. The maximal propagation delay is calculated as $\tau = Tx/v_0$, where Tx is the maximum transmission range and $v_0 = 1.5 \times 10^3$ m/s is the speed of sound propagation in the water.

Each node can elect to become a cluster head according to the weight compared to that of its neighbors, as in State 2 in Algorithm 1. If the node has the highest weight compared to that of its neighbors, the node will broadcast the "*JOIN*" message to its neighbors in order to form a cluster, as indicated in lines 14 to 17. Otherwise, the node will wait for the "*JOIN*" message; if the node receives only one message, it will become a cluster member of the cluster. If the node receives many "*JOIN*" messages, it will select the sender node with the highest received power or the node with the nearest distance.

We assume that the cluster can be formed between the nearby nodes to reduce energy consumption and transmission time. However, because the nodes at depth D_2 and D_3 may not transmit data directly to the sink due to the limited transmission range, we assume that some nodes will become the CR to forward data to the sink.

State 3 of Algorithm 1 shows the steps in the selection of the relay node. Assumed nodes which are not the CH will become a CR or CM. From lines 24 to 26, if the node receives the "*JOIN*" message from both D_m and D_{m-1}, which are broadcasted by nodes of upper and lower depths, the node elects to become a CR, which will be a forwarder in the routing path. From lines 28 to 29, the nodes only receive a "*JOIN*" message from the CHs at the same depth. The nodes send a "*RESPONSE*" message to the CH to confirm the cluster ID.

State 4 of Algorithm 1 and its multi-hop routing path creation show how the cluster at the deeper layer can forward the packet to the sink via the forwarders or the CR. In line 33, if the CH S_i receives a "*RELAY*" message from S_k, node S_i checks the depth of S_k. From lines 34 to 35, if node S_k is located near the surface, then node Si or $D_m(S_k) < D_m(S_i)$, and node S_i adds S_k as a relay node.

The cluster head schedules the transmission of all cluster members as a time division multiple access (TDMA). The data will be transmitted in the steady phase. The cluster head is selected at the beginning of each superframe in order to balance the load and energy for each node.

Algorithm 1. Energy-Efficient Clustering Multi-Hop Routing Protocol.

Input: node ID, position, initial energy, generated packets
Output: cluster {cluster ID, CH, CM}, CRs

1.   State 1: Network Initialization
2.   **For** each node S_i
3.   Calculate weight W_i as in (8)
4.   Broadcast $HELLO$ = {node ID, position, D_m, W_i, residual energy, history of cluster head}
5.   **End For**
6.   **While** $t < timeout$ do
7.   Receive $HELLO$ from other nodes
8.   Create list of neighbors at each node $Nei(S_i) = \{Nei(S_i) \cup S_j \mid d(i,j) < R\}$
9.   **End While**
10. State 2: Nodes elect to become cluster head
11. **For** each node S_i
12. $\{Sk, Max(W_k)\} = \max\{(W_i, W_j), S_j \in Nei(S_i)\}$
13.   **If** S_i has the $Max(W_k)$
14.   Broadcast $JOIN$ = {Cluster ID, maximum number of cluster member, D_m}
15.   Elect to become cluster head
16.   **Else**
17.   Wait for $JOIN$ message from the cluster head
18.   **End If**
19. **End For**
20. **State 3. Relay node selection**
21. **For** All nodes are not assigned as CH
22.   **If** S_j receives $JOIN$ messages from two nodes at D_m and D_{m-1}, respectively
23.   Broadcast $RELAY$ = {node ID, D_m, Cluster ID(D_m), Cluster ID(D_{m-1})}
24.   Become a relay node which can coordinate the routing path
25.   **Else**
26.   Send the $RESPONSE$ message to the CH
27. $RESPONSE$ = {node ID, cluster ID, D_m}
28.   **End If**
29. **End For**
30. State 4. Multi-hop routing path creation
31. **For** all nodes that receive RELAY message
32.   Find D_m and node ID S_k of RELAY message
33.   **If** node S_i is the CH and $D_m(S_k) < D_m(S_i)$
34.   Add node S_k as the relay node of S_i
35.   **End If**
36. **End For**

3.3. Qualitative Comparison of Clustering Protocols

In this subsection, we provide a qualitative comparison of the clustering protocols for UWSNs with different aspects.

The clustering protocols can take into account many metrics which describe the network topology, such as distance to the sink or other nodes, number of neighbors, path loss, location of the node, and residual energy. Even though each protocol uses different metrics to select the cluster head, they mostly focus on the residual energy of the node and the distance between the node to the sink. To increase network reliability, some clustering protocols select an assisted node which can assume the role of the sink [9,12,18] or the control node [10]. The assisted node can receive data from the sensor node or control the network topology. As a result, the energy consumption of the nodes may be reduced by conserving the node's energy. However, some clustering protocols are only presented and evaluated in two-dimensional (2D) deployment, whereas in the network scenarios of UWSNs, the deployment is three-dimensional (3D). To investigate the clustering protocol with an assisted node in 3D, our proposed EECMR protocol groups the sensor nodes with regard to the residual energy, cluster head duration, and distance to the sink. Among the clustering protocols, only EECMR considers the duration of the cluster head and cluster relay or assisted node in 3D, whereas the others do not consider the duration of the cluster head. A qualitative comparison of the clustering protocols is presented in Table 2.

Table 2. Qualitative comparison of clustering protocols.

Protocols	Parameters to Select the Cluster Head	Network	Assisted Node	Energy
LEACH [5]	Random value	2D	None	Yes
DBR [7]	Depth-based, holding time of packets	3D	None	Yes
EERBLC [9]	Residual energy, random value, number of layers	3D	Two sinks	Yes
C-LEACH [10]	Distance, location of the node	2D	Control node	Yes
MLCEE [12]	Fitness value, small Hop_ID and low number of layers	3D	Two sinks	Yes
TCEB [13]	Residual energy, number of neighbors, path loss	2D	None	Yes
EOCA [14]	Number of neighbor nodes, residual energy, distance to the sink node	2D	None	Yes
EULC [15]	Residual energy, distance to the sink node	3D	None	Yes
S-BEAR [16]	Distance to the sink	2D	None	Yes
CVBF [18]	Residual energy, vector-based routing	3D	Virtual sink	Yes
EECMR	Residual energy, duration of the cluster head, distance to the sink	3D	Cluster relay	Yes

4. Performance Evaluation

We implemented the EECMR protocol and compared it to LEACH [5], DBR [7], and EERBLC [9] in terms of network lifetime and residual energy. DBR, LEACH, and EERBLC were selected for performance comparison since the three protocols consider the clustering and depth of the routing protocol. Network performance was compared using the MATLAB simulation tool. The simulation parameters were set up as in [10,12].

4.1. Simulation Environment

The network scenario consists of dynamic nodes deployed sparsely in a three-dimensional environment. The water current causes node movements, which change the topology rapidly. The sink is located at the center of the surface, as shown in Figure 1. The simulation parameters are shown in Table 3. According to the sensed data, the node can generate one or two packets for transmission. The transmission range of each node varies from 150 to 200 m [10,12]. The underwater sensor nodes are mobile, with the current at 1–3 m/s, which causes changes in the network deployment [10]. In the study, the network deployment was changed after every 100 rounds in order to evaluate the network's mobility. The transmission range of nodes was varied in order to evaluate different network scenarios.

Table 3. Simulation parameters.

Simulation Parameters	Value
Network deployment area	$500 \times 500 \times 500$ m
Number of nodes	50 to 450
Generated packets at each node	1 or 2 data packets
Transmission range	150 m, 200 m
Acoustic frequency	30 kHz
Transmit power	2 W
Receive power	0.1 W
Initial node energy	5 Joules
Number of sink nodes	1
Data packet size	200 bits
Rounds	1000

An example of a network after the implementation of EECRM is shown in Figure 3. Each node is represented as a CM, CH, or CR. The sink is located at the surface, which is represented as a red star in the figure. In order to easily visualize the cluster, we deployed 50 nodes in a volume of $100 \times 100 \times 100$ m. We assumed that the nodes nearest to the sink would become the main forwarder for other nodes, the nodes at the seabed would select the cluster to join, and some nodes at the border of two depth layers would act as the relay which connects the cluster head of the deeper cluster to the sink.

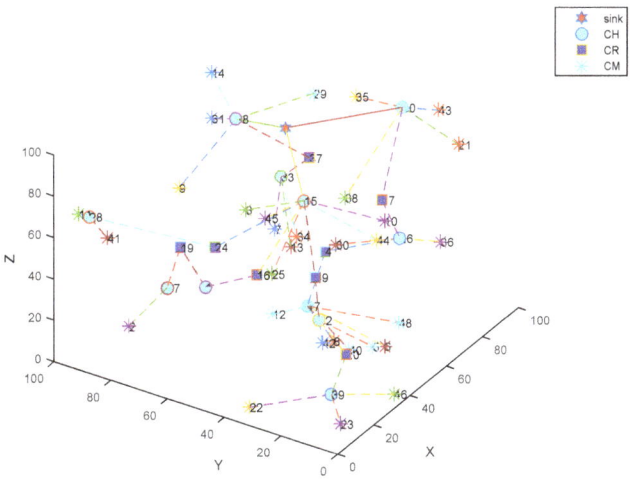

Figure 3. Network deployment after clustering.

4.2. Simulation Results

4.2.1. Network Lifetime

In this work, the network lifetime is defined as the total time that the nodes are alive, which can be considered the number of rounds. When the residual energy of a node decreases to zero, the node is considered a dead node. In our simulation, we compared three protocols to evaluate the network lifetime while varying the number of nodes in 1000 rounds, as shown in Figure 4. In Figure 4a, we consider a network of 450 nodes in 1000 rounds with a transmission range at 200 m; the results show that nodes began to run out of energy at round 300 for LEACH, DBR, EEBLC, and EECMR. The number of dead nodes of the proposed protocol was the lowest compared to the other protocols.

In Figure 4b, we varied the number of nodes in 1000 rounds with the transmission range at 200 m. The LEACH protocol had the highest number of dead nodes compared to the DBR, EEBLC, and EECMR. Since EECMR allows the nodes to form a cluster according to their depth level, nodes only communicate with the nodes at the same depth level in the same cluster. However, nodes in the LEACH protocol became cluster heads in turns according to the generated random number. The nodes may have consumed high energy as a result of increasing the number of transmissions during cluster formation. In EEBLC, the clustering allows unequal clusters in the networks in which nodes can elect to become cluster head considering the number of neighbors and its residual energy. As a result, the number of dead nodes in EEBLC is lower than that of DBR and LEACH, as in Figure 4. In the case of DBR, instead of forming into clusters, the nodes sent data to the sink via a multi-hop routing path according to their depth level. The node would send packets to the forwarder node at the upper depth level without considering the number of neighbors sending packets to the same destination. The forwarder node may have had a high load, which causes high energy consumption while sending packets.

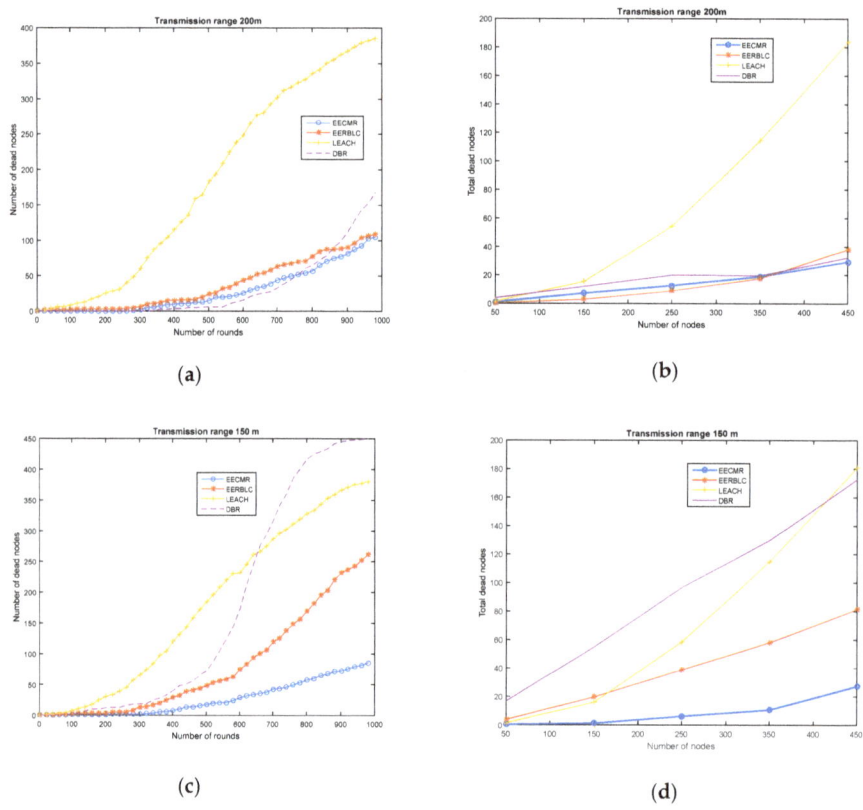

Figure 4. Number of dead nodes: (**a**) Transmission range 200 m, 450 nodes in 1000 rounds; (**b**) Transmission range 200 m, nodes 50 to 450; (**c**) Transmission range 150 m, 450 nodes in 1000 rounds; (**d**) Transmission range 150 m, nodes 50 to 450.

In Figure 4c,d, we evaluate the network performance when the transmission range was 150 m. It is clear that the network performance depended on the transmission range of the node. The number of dead nodes of the three protocols was higher when the transmission range decreased. However, the network performance of clustering protocols of LEACH, EEBLC, and EECMR was similar, which was better than DBR. Therefore, the clustering protocol showed better performance than the multi-path routing protocol.

4.2.2. Residual Energy at the Nodes

In Figure 5, the residual energy of the nodes is shown in different network scenarios. At each round, the nodes generated packets and then forwarded them to the sink node. In Figure 5a, the residual energy of the node decreased according to the timeline, while the number of rounds increased. It is clear that our EECMR performed better in terms of conserving energy; the residual energy in EECMR was higher than that of DBR, LEACH, and EEBLC. DBR was developed for routing protocols in underwater wireless sensor networks, so DBR performed better than LEACH. EEBLC allows nodes to become the cluster head in turns according to their location and residual energy, and the nodes can save energy when varying the number of nodes and transmission range.

In Figure 5b, we varied the number of nodes in the network, while three protocols decreased the residual energy. Despite this, the residual energy in EECMR was higher than in EEBLC, LEACH, or DBR. However, the residual energy of the nodes in LEACH declined quickly compared to EECMR. This can be explained as follows. In a dense network deployment, the nodes consume higher energy to perform more communication tasks, such as transmitting and receiving packets to the larger number of nodes. The nodes in EECMR can act as a cluster head or cluster relay; therefore, the cluster head has the information of its cluster member, which reduces the number of transmissions between nodes. As noted in the previous section, the number of dead nodes in EECMR is less because the nodes conserve energy while sending packets. EEBLC performs better than the others in the case of a low transmission range which ensures a long network lifetime. In LEACH, the node that elects to become a cluster head broadcasts information to the three-dimensional area network; as a consequence, the node consumes more energy. In DBR, the node selects the upper-level depth to become its forwarder. If the number of nodes increases, the forwarder may receive more packets, and then it sends these to the upper-level depth before reaching the sink. More transmission at the nodes and forwarders leads to high energy consumption, as shown in Figure 5.

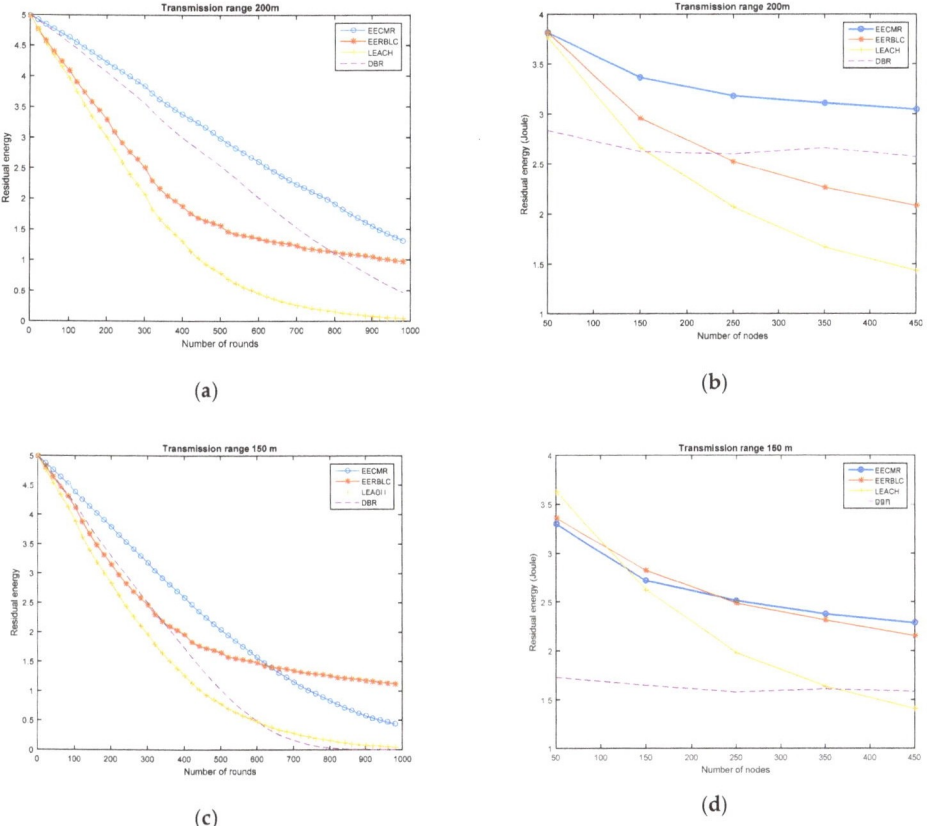

(a)

(b)

(c)

(d)

Figure 5. Average residual energy of a node: (**a**) Transmission range 200 m, 450 nodes in 1000 rounds; (**b**) Transmission range 200 m, nodes 50 to 450; (**c**) Transmission range 150 m, 450 nodes in 1000 rounds; (**d**) Transmission range 150 m, nodes 50 to 450.

In Figure 5c,d, the decrease in the transmission range led to higher energy consumption in EECMR, EEBLC, LEACH, and DBR. These protocols gradually diminished the residual energy with respect to the number of rounds. When increasing the number of rounds with a low transmission range, EERBLC performs better than EECMR. When the number of nodes increases, LEACH and EEBLC perform better than EECMR in the case of a low number of nodes; EECMR performs better than LEACH in the case of dense deployment.

In a comparison of the residual energy performance with different transmission ranges in EECMR, the residual energy for a 200 m transmission distance was higher than a 150 m transmission range. This can be explained as follows. The cluster heads in EECMR aggregate the data of all cluster members and then forward these to the cluster relay which belongs to another cluster. Since the number of data packets is re-transmitted via multi-hop, the amount of energy consumption increases. In addition, the change in the network topology causes the re-established cluster to consume energy-transmitting and -receiving control packets. However, the total received packets at the sink should be considered. This is presented in the next section.

4.2.3. Received Packets at the Sink Node

We assume that all the sensed data of nodes will be received at the sink. In the network deployment, the network topology changes every 100 rounds, which may cause a failure to receive packets at the cluster head and cluster relay. This is because the distance from a cluster member to the cluster head is greater than the transmission range and the received packets at the cluster head or cluster member may fail as a result of a low level of received power. Therefore, the cluster must be re-established, and a new cluster head, cluster member, and cluster relay must be selected. In Figure 6, the total received packets at the sink are evaluated in four cases. In Figure 6a,c, despite different transmission ranges, the received packets in EECMR are higher than in LEACH, EEBLC, or DBR. It is noted that the received packets at the sink increase when the transmission range increases. The number of total received packets in the EECMR scheme is occasionally different, which causes high jitters. Despite this, the increase in transmission range leads to a lower residual energy at the node, as shown in Figure 5. This can be considered a pay-off with respect to the transmission range and network performance.

In Figure 6b,d, the received packets at the sink are shown according to the number of rounds. Due to the number of packets at the sensor node or the number of clusters at each round, the results in the timeline fluctuate. In total, the received packets at the sinks in EECMR are higher than other protocols, which results in high throughput and a more reliable network.

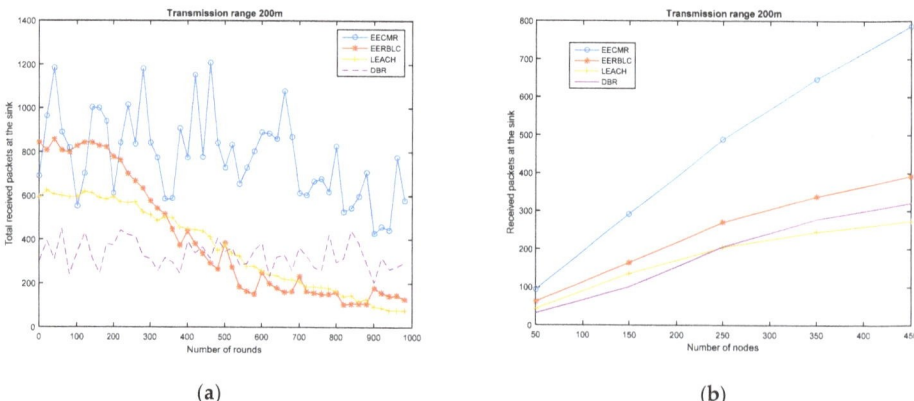

(a)   (b)

Figure 6. *Cont.*

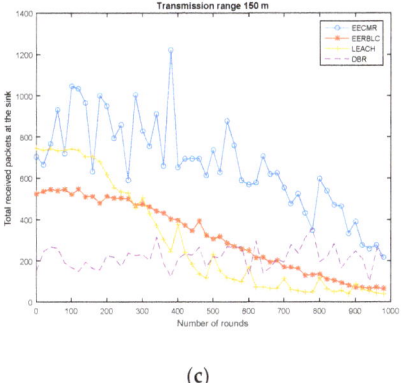
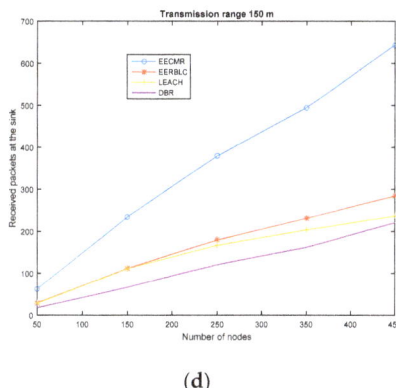

(c)   (d)

Figure 6. Received packets at the sink: (**a**) Transmission range 200 m, 450 nodes in 1000 rounds; (**b**) Transmission range 200 m, nodes 50 to 450; (**c**) Transmission range 150 m, 450 nodes in 1000 rounds; (**d**) Transmission range 150 m, nodes 50 to 450.

5. Conclusions

In this work, we propose the energy protocol EECMR for routing data packets in UWSNs. EECMR is a depth-based clustering protocol that uses the depth level of the node to select cluster head nodes and forwarder nodes for multi-hop routing. EECMR considers the residual energy of the node which elects cluster heads in turns. The nodes can change roles as cluster head, cluster member, and cluster relay. The cluster relay node forwards data from a deeper level to the sink. With the aid of a cluster relay, the energy consumption for transmission is decreased, leading to fewer dead nodes. The simulation results showed that EECMR achieves better performance in terms of higher residual energy, longer network lifetime, and higher received packets at the sink. Although the proposed protocol can properly select the cluster head and cluster relay according to the depth level and residual energy, the high energy consumption at the cluster relay between different depth levels may result in re-clustering or frequent re-clustering. However, the clustering protocol may cause high latency due to the multi-hop routing path. The different types of sensor nodes will have different data priorities, an issue which must be addressed in future work.

In addition, several issues remain open for future work, including optimization of the network topology and implementation of the clustering protocol in firmware to support UWSN application in oceans. In our future work, we will implement the clustering protocols into firmware to investigate the practical performance.

Author Contributions: The main contributions of N.-T.N. and T.T.T.L. were creation of the main ideas and performance evaluation through extensive simulations. H.-H.N. contributed to the manuscript preparation and designed the theoretical analysis. M.V. served as consultant of N.-T.N. to discuss, create, and advise the main ideas and performance evaluations together. All authors have read and agreed to the published version of the manuscript.

Funding: The research leading to these results received funding from the Czech Ministry of Education under grant No. SP2020/65, conducted at the Technical University of Ostrava and partially by The Ministry of Education, Youth and Sports from the Large Infrastructures for Research, Experimental Development and Innovations project "e-Infrastructure CZ–LM2018140". This work was also supported by Saigon University, Vietnam, grant No. TĐ2020-17.

Institutional Review Board Statement: Not applicable.

Informed Consent Statement: Not applicable.

Data Availability Statement: Data is contained within the article.

Conflicts of Interest: The authors declare no conflict of interest.

Sensors **2021**, *21*, 627

References

1. Felemban, E.; Shaikh, F.K.; Qureshi, U.M.; Sheikh, A.A.; Qaisar, S.B. Underwater sensor network applications: A comprehensive survey. *Int. J. Distrib. Sens. Netw.* **2015**, *11*, 896832. [CrossRef]
2. Awan, K.M.; Shah, P.A.; Iqbal, K.; Gillani, S.; Ahmad, W.; Nam, Y. Underwater wireless sensor networks: A review of recent issues and challenges. *Wirel. Commun. Mob. Comput.* **2019**, *2019*, 6470359. [CrossRef]
3. Jouhari, M.; Ibrahimi, K.; Tembine, H.; Ben-Othman, J. Underwater wireless sensor networks: A survey on enabling technologies, localization protocols, and internet of underwater things. *IEEE Access* **2019**, *7*, 96879–96899. [CrossRef]
4. Xu, G.; Shen, W.; Wang, X. Applications of wireless sensor networks in marine environment monitoring: A survey. *Sensors* **2014**, *14*, 16932–16954. [CrossRef] [PubMed]
5. Akyildiz, I.F.; Pompili, D.; Melodia, T. Underwater acoustic sensor networks: Research challenges. *Ad Hoc Netw.* **2005**, *3*, 257–279. [CrossRef]
6. Heinzelman, W.R.; Chandrakasan, A.; Balakrishnan, H. Energy-efficient communication protocol for wireless microsensor networks. In Proceedings of the 33rd Annual Hawaii International Conference on System Sciences, Maui, HI, USA, 4–7 January 2000; p. 10.
7. Sandeep, D.N.; Kumar, V. Review on clustering, coverage and connectivity in underwater wireless sensor networks: A communication techniques perspective. *IEEE Access* **2017**, *5*, 11176–11199. [CrossRef]
8. Yan, H.; Shi, Z.J.; Cui, J.H. DBR: Depth-based routing for underwater sensor networks. In Proceedings of the International Conference on Research in Networking, Dalian, China, 12–17 October 2008; Springer: Berlin/Heidelberg, Germany, May 2008; pp. 72–86.
9. Khan, A.; Ali, I.; Ghani, A.; Khan, N.; Alsaqer, M.; Rahman, A.U.; Mahmood, H. Routing protocols for underwater wireless sensor networks: Taxonomy, research challenges, routing strategies and future directions. *Sensors* **2018**, *18*, 1619. [CrossRef] [PubMed]
10. Zhu, F.; Wei, J. An energy efficient routing protocol based on layers and unequal clusters in underwater wireless sensor networks. *J. Sens.* **2018**, *2018*, 5835730. [CrossRef]
11. Li, Y.; Wang, Y.; Ju, Y.; He, R. Energy efficient cluster formulation protocols in clustered underwater acoustic sensor networks. In Proceedings of the 2014 IEEE 7th International Conference on Biomedical Engineering and Informatics, Dalian, China, 14–16 October 2014; pp. 923–928.
12. Durrani, M.Y.; Tariq, R.; Aadil, F.; Maqsood, M.; Nam, Y.; Muhammad, K. Adaptive node clustering technique for smart ocean under water sensor network (SOSNET). *Sensors* **2019**, *19*, 1145. [CrossRef] [PubMed]
13. Khan, W.; Wang, H.; Anwar, M.S.; Ayaz, M.; Ahmad, S.; Ullah, I. A Multi-Layer Cluster Based Energy Efficient Routing Scheme for UWSNs. *IEEE Access* **2019**, *7*, 77398–77410. [CrossRef]
14. Hong, Z.; Pan, X.; Chen, P.; Su, X.; Wang, N.; Lu, W. A topology control with energy balance in underwater wireless sensor networks for IoT-based application. *Sensors* **2018**, *18*, 2306. [CrossRef] [PubMed]
15. Yu, W.; Chen, Y.; Wan, L.; Zhang, X.; Zhu, P.; Xu, X. An Energy Optimization Clustering Scheme for Multi-Hop Underwater Acoustic Cooperative Sensor Networks. *IEEE Access* **2020**, *8*, 89171–89184. [CrossRef]
16. Hou, R.; He, L.; Hu, S.; Luo, J. Energy-balanced unequal layering clustering in underwater acoustic sensor networks. *IEEE Access* **2018**, *6*, 39685–39691. [CrossRef]
17. Wang, M.; Chen, Y.; Sun, X.; Xiao, F.; Xu, X. Node Energy Consumption Balanced Multi-Hop Transmission for Underwater Acoustic Sensor Networks Based on Clustering Algorithm. *IEEE Access* **2020**, *8*, 191231–191241. [CrossRef]
18. Khan, M.T.R.; Ahmed, S.H.; Kim, D. AUV-Aided Energy-Efficient Clustering in the Internet of Underwater Things. *IEEE Trans. Green Commun. Netw.* **2019**, *3*, 1132–1141. [CrossRef]
19. Ibrahim, D.M.; Eltobely, T.E.; Fahmy, M.M.; Sallam, E.A. Enhancing the vector-based forwarding routing protocol for underwater wireless sensor networks: A clustering approach. In Proceedings of the International Conference on Wireless and Mobile Communications, Seville, Spain, 17–22 June 2014; pp. 98–104.
20. Gopi, S.; Govindan, K.; Chander, D.; Desai, U.B.; Merchant, S.N. E-PULRP: Energy optimized path unaware layered routing protocol for underwater sensor networks. *IEEE Trans. Wirel. Commun.* **2010**, *9*, 3391–3401. [CrossRef]
21. Khasawneh, A.; Latiff, M.S.B.A.; Kaiwartya, O.; Chizari, H. Next forwarding node selection in underwater wireless sensor networks (UWSNs): Techniques and challenges. *Information* **2017**, *8*, 3. [CrossRef]
22. Domingo, M.C. Overview of channel models for underwater wireless communication networks. *Phys. Commun.* **2008**, *1*, 163–182. [CrossRef]

Article

A Portable Electromagnetic System Based on mm-Wave Radars and GNSS-RTK Solutions for 3D Scanning of Large Material Piles

Humberto Fernández Álvarez *, Guillermo Álvarez-Narciandi , María García-Fernández , Jaime Laviada , Yuri Álvarez López and Fernando Las-Heras Andrés

Area of Signal Theory and Communications, University of Oviedo, 33203 Gijón, Spain; alvareznguillermo@uniovi.es (G.Á.-N.); garciafmaria@uniovi.es (M.G.-F.); laviadajaime@uniovi.es (J.L.); alvarezyuri@uniovi.es (Y.Á.L.); flasheras@uniovi.es (F.L.-H.A.)
* Correspondence: fernandezhumberto@uniovi.es

Abstract: In this paper, a portable three-dimensional (3D) scanning system for the accurate characterization of large raw material (e.g., cereal grain, coal, etc.) stockpiles is presented. The system comprises an array of high resolution millimeter-wave radars and a cm-level accuracy positioning system to accurately characterize large stockpiles by means of a high-resolution 3D map, making it suitable for automation purposes. A control unit manages the data received by the sensors, which are sent to a computer system for processing. As a proof of concept, the entire sensor system is evaluated in a real environment for electromagnetically scan a scaled stockpile of coal, used in the industry for handling raw materials. In addition, a highly efficient processing adaptive algorithm that may reconstruct the scanned structure in real-time has been introduced, enabling continuous dynamic updating of the information. Results are compared with those from a photogrammetry-like technique, revealing an excellent agreement.

Keywords: mm-wave radars; GNSS-RTK positioning; wireless technology; electromagnetic scanning; point cloud

Citation: Fernández Álvarez, H.; Álvarez-Narciandi, G.; García-Fernández, M.; Laviada, J.; Álvarez López, Y.; Las-Heras Andrés, F. A Portable Electromagnetic System Based on mm-Wave Radars and GNSS-RTK Solutions for 3D Scanning of Large Material Piles. *Sensors* **2021**, *21*, 757. https://doi.org/10.3390/s21030757

Academic Editor: Ali Khenchaf
Received: 13 December 2020
Accepted: 21 January 2021
Published: 23 January 2021

1. Introduction

Industry 4.0 entails the full interconnection between systems and devices and the employment of massive amounts of data to make predictive decision models. These new challenges are of vital importance to the development of the fourth industrial revolution and settle the basis to the full automation of industrial processes. The machine to machine (M2M) communication is a key challenge to be faced in this context, being crucial for avoiding collisions among machines or with surrounding obstacles and hence, it has attracted the interest of many researchers [1,2]. It should be noticed that there is a large amount of contributions that deal with collision avoidance among vehicles [3–6]. These systems are usually based on detecting objects or structures in a certain perimeter and emitting signals to the machine, so that it can dodge them. However, this bare detection is not enough to fully automatize certain processes, nor to provide an instantaneous decision based on the gathered data. Consequently, additional information is sometimes required, such as the shape and/or volume of certain structures or areas, whose constant update is usually needed, as it may be subjected to continuous changes. Moreover, industrial environments are usually exposed to hazardous conditions, which have to also be taken into account.

Accordingly, the searching of non-invasive techniques to retrieve the actual topography of different areas has been widely pursued during the recent years, as it has a great number of applications not only for industrial solutions, but also for analyzing dense forested terrains [7] or ever-changing river surfaces [8].

185

The information regarding space availability and stored material in certain areas such as docks, industrial plants and/or warehouses is of vital importance for planning and managing processes. An interesting case of use is the analysis of the available stockpile of raw materials in the mining, agriculture, construction and energy industries. The information about these stockpiles is crucial for adjusting different processes such as buffering, blending, stacking, reclaiming and transporting procedures, as well as for achieving a homogeneous stockpile, which would be useful for optimizing the storage space.

The material from these stockpiles is placed by stackers from above and it is withdrawn by means of reclaimers. Reclaimers have only two degrees of freedom (longitudinal position and angle of incline), so if they are not commanded to a place with enough material they are very inefficient, resulting in a low extraction rate with the subsequent cost. For this reason, profiling stockpiles with robust sensors is very relevant as it enables to optimize the performance of the overall system. Currently, the longitudinal position and angle of incline of the reclaimer is chosen manually, requiring workers and being prone to error.

Mathematical and geometrical models have been recently developed for estimating the stockpile shape [9,10]. However, they take certain assumptions or consider ideal geometries that prevent accurately predicting the real stockpile topography [11]. An out-of-date or erroneous information about the current state of the stockpile can lead to overfilling or empty spaces (**rat holing**), which may cause damage to the equipment [12] and/or an inaccurate managing of the available material, both causing long production downtimes. Moreover, the continuous stacking and reclaiming processes conducted at irregular intervals may lead to unpredictable shapes of the stockpile and prevent the fully automation of the processes. Therefore, the continuous dynamic monitoring of the stockpile is crucial for avoiding the aforementioned issues and optimizing the production costs.

The methods employed to experimentally determine the shape of stockpile raw materials have evolved during the last years, starting from the well-known Yo-Yo technique, which consisted of tying a weight to a rope for determining the stockpile height, to the deployment of different systems based on ultrasonic, radar and laser technologies [13].

There are several factors that define the most suitable technology for analyzing stockpile raw materials: material type and characteristics, environmental conditions, budget, maintenance, ease of use and installation, accuracy, external requirements (such as electrical power supply) and safety. Considering the aforementioned factors, it can be concluded that the most appropriate technology for determining the geometrical properties of the stockpiles, relies on non-invasive time-of-flight sensors [12].

Ultrasonic sensors, such as acoustic solid scanners, with wavelengths ranging from 1000 m to 100 m, have fallen into disuse as the measurements are affected by machinery noises, nearby structures, temperature, smoke and wind, as well as by other particles in the air. Moreover, they offer a slow updating rate (long latency) and low coverage [14]. Until the last few years, infrared sensors (with wavelengths ranging from 100 μm to 1 μm) have been the preferred devices for scanning stockpiles. Then, the topographic micro pulse light detection and ranging (LiDAR) technology, which provides a surface map, became of great importance for industrial companies, since it is currently moving towards the full automation of processes [11–16]. However, this technology is not suitable for areas with dense dust, smoke or gas, as the emitted signals suffer a high diffraction on these particles and it also requires permanent cleaning and maintenance [14]. In addition, the LiDAR technology may be affected by the ambient light and hence, brightness or darkness has a great impact on the detected light, which varies depending on the material surface colour (darker colour materials provide lower reflectivity), affecting the ability of the sensor to determine distances accurately [12,16].

Up to now radar technology has been underestimated, primarily due to its high manufacturing costs. However, the reduction of production costs, due to the mass-production of mm-wave radars, makes it a promising alternative to attain high resolution scanners. This technology is more suitable to work under harsh conditions, as it is robust against dust as well as independent of light or atmospheric conditions, in contrast to ultrasonic and infrared technologies. Moreover, it requires minimal maintenance, which is vital as the sensors are usually installed in emplacements with difficult access [14].

Geo-referencing the radar measurements during the scanning process is essential for post-processing the retrieved data and reconstructing the stockpile shape. In this context, encoders as well as Global Navigation Satellite System (GNSS) solutions have been adopted [15–19]. However, the former one, which is the most widely used in the literature, usually provides a relatively low resolution for imaging purposes, as it is designed to provide a coarse estimation of the position and its information is not always prepared to be read from external systems. Moreover, it usually entails moving the sensor through fixed paths (normally rails). Regarding the GNSS, it is very flexible, but the raw positioning accuracy is in the order of several tenths of centimeters.

Aiming at developing a versatile and portable solution, the scanner movement should not be restricted to a predefined path and, hence, a precise technique for geo-referencing the radar measurements is required. Consequently, Real-Time Kinematic (RTK) solutions, which are based on differential GNSS measurements, are ideal for determining the sensors position, as they provide cm-level accuracy position data [20]. Indeed, this geo-referring accuracy is in agreement with the degree of precision provided by the radars.

There are several commercial solutions, provided by companies such as Indurad [14] and ION [21], which use different sensors to scan, model and reconstruct stockpiles. However, these companies employ strategically positioned radars, minimizing the amount of sensors, but at the expense of a precise measurement, above all when the target is at grazing angles. Moreover, the companies do not unveil much information about the employed sensors, scanning processes and post-processing techniques, as they develop profitable *ad-hoc* solutions, which are highly customized according to the client specifications, as mentioned in [11]. Therefore, these *ad-hoc* solutions usually result in high costs (in the order of tens of thousands of euros [12]) and external maintenance.

Other works deal with simulated [17] or extremely small scaled laboratory experiments [11,12,17,18,22,23]. Hence, they did not consider real measured data, which is affected by more complex features such as noise, weather conditions and reflectivity from surrounding elements. Indeed, the measured data in a real environment can be formed by an unstructured point cloud which can be noisy, sparse and incomplete [11] and several methods have to be used to discard unwanted data, such as segmentation, noise filters and/or boundary detector techniques.

In addition, the multiple issues that usually appear during the installation and adjustment of the final system are not taken into account in these simple and limited-scope experiments.

In this paper, a robust and highly precise radar-based system to continuously scan large areas and reconstruct their topography, also suitable for managing and planning processes, is presented. Contrary to most systems described in literature, such as LiDAR, radar technology is employed, taking advantage of its performance under hazardous environmental conditions (e.g., dust, moisture) or in the absence of light. In addition, a highly precise positioning system, with an accuracy in the order of that of the radar subsystem, is deployed, allowing the merger of the point clouds of all the radars acquired at different positions, enhancing the accuracy of the resulting topography of the stockpile and enabling the scanning through irregular paths. Geo-referred radar measurements are processed, resulting in a dynamic reconstruction of the scanned structure in real-time and, hence, allowing the system to make instantaneous decisions. Consequently, the proposed system also targets improving the automation level of stockpile-related industry processes. As a proof of concept, the entire sensor system has been tested in a simulated environment for scanning a stockpile-alike model, as well as in a realistic environment for scanning a scaled coal stockpile.

2. Materials and Methods

2.1. Three-Dimensional (3D) Profiling of Stockpiles

In order to determine the profile of stockpiles, the sensor fusion scheme shown in Figure 1 is proposed. In this setup, several radar sensors are placed along the crane bridge that is part of the stockpile management system, and which can be moved arbitrarily through a rail system. In contrast to conventional systems, the proposed setup takes advantage of this movement to provide a high resolution three-dimension image of the stockpile with centimeter accuracy. In addition, positioning modules are used to track the position of the radars. Position and radar data are broadcasted to a laptop in order to compose the stockpile image. Thus, three subsystems are considered: (i) radar subsystem, (ii) positioning subsystem and (iii) communication and control subsystem.

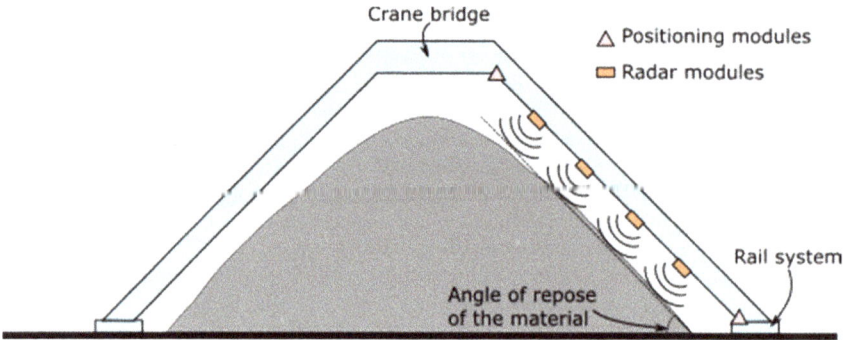

Figure 1. Side-view of the proposed system embedded into the crane-bridge of a stockpile management system.

In this setup, radar modules are in charge of detecting the range to the target and, therefore, they can be considered as the core sensors of the setup. In conventional setups, two options are typically used. In the first one, radars are placed on fixed positions in order to monitor the stockpile from above. Nonetheless, this kind of setup has several drawbacks. First, the view angle of each radar is limited as the stockpile or other mechanical elements could block the signal, preventing imaging some areas. As a consequence, several radars must be strategically placed in order to provide full coverage. These positions must be optimized for each stockpile facility, entailing a higher development time and increasing the cost of the solution. Moreover, the distance between the radars and the stockpile is larger in this setup, and hence the image resolution worsens [24]. The second option places one or two radars over the stockpile, typically in the top of the mobile crane bridge. This type of setup is very effective to calculate the height of the stockpile, but it is not able to provide images with grazing angles.

In the proposed solution, multistatic radar modules are placed along the crane bridge, which is typically designed with an angle close to the angle of repose of the materials. This disposal allows to achieve improved image resolutions (as the radars are usually closer to the stockpile) and avoids losing information at grazing angles. Additionally, the use of multistatic radars enables calculating a point cloud of scatterers by means of synthetic aperture radar [24]. The distance between the radars is chosen so that the overall coverage covers the entire stockpile. It is relevant to note that the distance from the stockpile to the radar modules has an impact in the point cloud resolution, as it is inversely proportional to such a distance [24].

Regarding the positioning subsystem, it is in charge of measuring the positions, so that the point clouds taken from different arbitrary positions can be merged. Since mm-wave radars can provide a resolution in the order of a few centimeters, it is important to use a positioning system with a similar accuracy, since the final stockpile resolution is dominated by the worst case. For this reason, a GNSS-RTK system is used because its accuracy is in the order of 1 cm.

Regarding the number of positioning modules, since the radars are expected to lay along a virtual line, two positioning modules are enough in order to track this line. These tracking modules should be as separated as possible in order to minimize potential alignment errors.

It is interesting to observe that radar data could be merged to create a synthetic aperture radar from arbitrary positions [25,26]. This kind of processing is very powerful as it enables very high resolution images such as the one used for people screening [27]. However, this kind of data fusion requires a spatial data sampling much smaller than the working wavelength (less than 1 cm) [28] and, consequently, it is discarded in this work.

The last subsystem is designed to perform communication and control duties, using a control unit attached to the crane bridge. This subsystem is in charge of controlling the data flow among the subsystems, synchronizing the data retrieved from the radar and positioning subsystems and sending the data to a processing unit, which is basically a standard computer. A workflow of the proposed system and the aforementioned interconnection between the subsystems is presented in Figure 2.

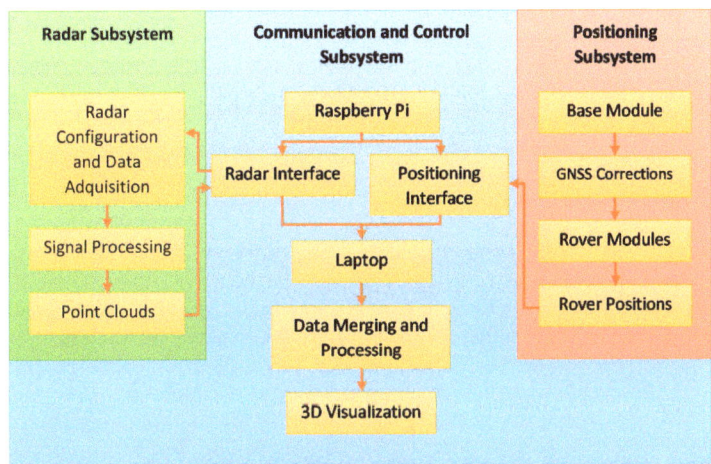

Figure 2. Workflow of the proposed system.

The retrieved information from the radars and rover modules is merged on the laptop for processing and visualization purposes (as it is indicated in Figure 2). However, the point clouds provided by the radars at each measurement position are defined according to the local coordinate system (LCS) of each radar, which is neither fixed (as the radars will be moved during the scan process) nor common for all radars. Therefore, these point clouds should be manipulated to refer them to a global coordinate system (GCS), which is fixed and common to all the radars and the whole system, forming a unified point cloud. For this purpose, several coordinate system transformations, which are explained in Appendix A, are performed.

2.2. Components

In the demonstrator used in this paper (see Figure 3), two platforms with wheels are built to accommodate a foldable ladder mimicking a piece of the crane bridge. The radar modules are fixed using *ad-hoc* 3D printed structures and the control unit consists of a laptop.

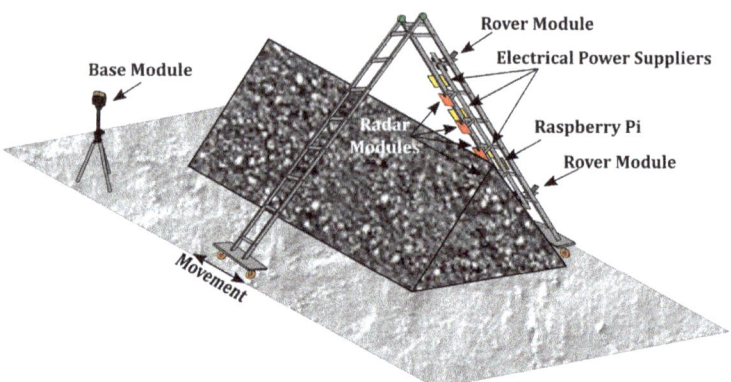

Figure 3. Scheme of the proposed system.

After analyzing the commercial off-the-shelf sensors, the *IWR1443* radar modules, operating in the frequency band from 76 to 81 GHz and manufactured by Texas Instruments [29] were selected for several reasons: integration of the radiofrequency elements on the board, easily control through a USB to UART interface and maximum range between 150 to 200 m (much larger than the maximum typical ranges in the order of 30–40 m commonly required [12,30]). In addition, they can be configured to provide not only the detected objects using a point cloud representation, but also the intensity of each point, which will be useful for spatial filtering unwanted echoes.

Each module comprises three transmitting and four receiving channels, allowing us to create a virtual array of twelve receiving channels and hence, improving the angular resolution. Each transmitting and receiving channel is composed of an array of three series fed patches with a 3dB-beamwidth of $28° \times 56°$.

The radar modules are directly connected to the control unit using USB to micro USB cables (which is the radar interface in Figure 3) and they are configured to provide a point cloud as their output data. The configuration of the radar parameters has to be conducted taking into account the deploying environment. Indeed, employing a proper configuration, it is possible to filter some spurious and undesired points, mainly caused by different factors: double reflections happening close to the radars, channel coupling or any other unwanted reflections. An *ad-hoc* GUI application running on the control unit, which sends configuration commands to the radars, was developed to configure the radars in the field. The main adjustable configuration commands are: the constant false alarm rate (CFAR), direct current (DC) and static clutter removal and peak grouping (which groups points by range and/or velocity).

Among the available GNSS-RTKs on the market, the ones manufactured by Emlid were chosen, because at the time they were acquired they offered one of the best performance-price ratio. A *Reach RS2* module [31] is intended to act as a base station, sending correction data to two *Reach M2* modules [32] that will work as rovers and will be placed on the ladder, providing a 7 to 14 mm positioning accuracy.

The GNSS-RTK communication with the control unit is based on a client-server architecture and a text protocol for acquiring latitude, longitude and height information. A Wi-Fi network is deployed to enable interchanging information between the GNSS-RTKs modules among them and with the control unit (positioning interface in Figure 3).

A portable dual band router TP-Link M7450 is used to establish the wireless communications between the subsystems, using the standard 802.11b/g/n and allowing to manage the control unit remotely through a laptop. For the proposed application, a Raspberry Pi 4 is used as the control unit of the system. However, it should be highlighted that the software implemented to manage and receive information from the sensors using the

Raspberry Pi 4, can be adapted to any other control unit device, such as a programmable logic controller (PLC).

Finally, the commercial software Matlab is chosen to run the code in charge of processing the data and reconstructing and rendering the surface on the laptop.

3. Results

Two measurement set-ups have been considered. In the first one, the stockpile of material is simulated using air bubble aluminum laminations supported by adjustable photography background supports. This set-up, hereinafter referred to stockpile-alike model, has been deployed in the outdoors of the research group laboratory, and has been primarily devoted to analyzing and debugging the system performance, as well as for calibrating the sensors. It has also allowed us to adjust the data processing technique for reconstructing the structure.

The second set-up, which will be called a real environment, is composed of a scaled stockpile of coal deposited on the Gijón seaport.

3.1. Stockpile-alike Environment

This section presents the measurement results obtained with the stockpile-alike environment. Once the required programs to control the sensors and fetch the measured data have been developed, the sensors arrangement on the ladder was set. After several tests, it was found that the best configuration for the radars and the rover modules on the ladder corresponds to the one presented in Figure 4a, where the rover modules are placed on the top and bottom of the ladder, being the radars on the middle. Each sensor is placed in the middle of each rung, being separated by 30 cm from each other, and no empty rung is left among the sensors. Taking into account that the distance from the ladder to the material is in the order of 70 cm, this setup provides a proper coverage of the scanned structure with an adequate sensors signal footprint, avoiding uncovered areas.

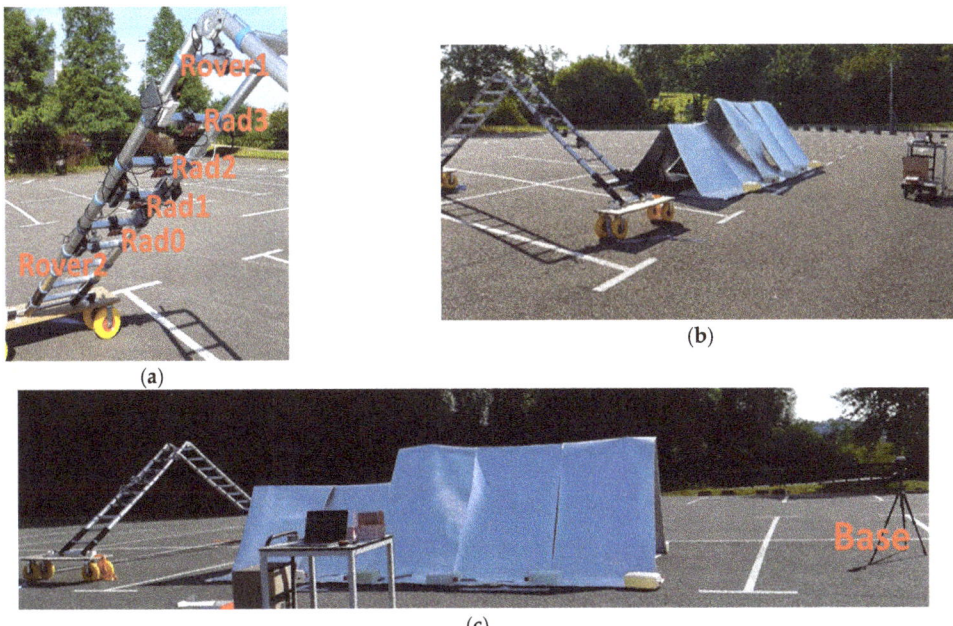

Figure 4. (**a**) Scheme of the sensors arrangement on the ladder; (**b**) lateral and (**c**) front views of the stockpile-alike model.

The stockpile-alike is disposed in two differentiating heights, as illustrated in Figure 4b,c, placed at 1.2 m and 1.5 m height, being the longitudinal dimensions of each section of 2 m and 3.4 m, respectively. Before starting the measurements, a calibration of the system should be performed to determine the relative position of the radars with respect to the rover modules. This is crucial to map the point cloud provided by each radar in its LCS to the defined GCS.

The measurements are conducted in continuous mode, setting the system to take an acquisition every half a second. Aiming at controlling the data acquisition process, several software tools have been developed, such as the continuous checking of the correct sensor operation (including the saturation level of the radar receiving chain or any communication interruption) and the monitoring of the GNSS-RTK positioning accuracy (mainly reduced due to weak signal to noise ratio reception or high dilution precision rates).

The measurements are carried out by longitudinally moving the system along the stockpile-alike model. The radars are configured with a CFAR threshold of 5 dB, so that they provide a dense point cloud. This is useful for not missing any information from the scanned structure, but it contains a large amount of undesired points (mainly from the floor and multi reflection paths). The latter is partially reduced by grouping the points by range.

The point cloud retrieved from each radar at each measurement instant is manipulated to refer it to the GCS (following the process described on Appendix A). It is worth mentioning that though the structure is designed to be linearly moved along an almost straight direction, it may suffer certain deviations that can also be corrected using the method described in the Appendix A.

In Figure 5a, the scanning area is presented. The positions of the GNSS-RTK rover modules at each measurement instant are depicted in Figure 5b (rover1 and rover2 dots in red and blue, respectively). Moreover, the retrieved filtered point cloud corresponding to a round trip scanning path, i.e., moving the system from the beginning of the scanned structure to the end and back to the beginning (Figure 5c), is also shown. The point cloud in blue corresponds to the one retrieved during the first part of the scanning acquisition (moving the system from the beginning to the end of the scanned structure, along the $\hat{x}_v$ direction), whereas the one in red corresponds to the data obtained during the second part of the acquisition (moving the system from the end to the beginning of the scanned structure, along the $-\hat{x}_v$ direction). From the point cloud results, it can be noticed a clear overlap of both point clouds (blue and red), indicating the robustness of the proposed system and method (on Appendix A) for fusing the information provided by the radars and rover modules.

Besides a proper configuration of the radars, several filters have to be employed to remove spurious and unwanted points. Therefore, a spatial filter is used to remove those points whose signal level lies below a certain threshold level. Moreover, a linear regression is applied for discarding other noisy points, coming from unwanted reflections (see Appendix A). This filtering procedure allows us to highly automatize the removal of unwanted points, even when the spatial filter is not properly adjusted. As it can be seen from Figure 5c, just a few points of the cloud are caused by spurious reflections and, therefore, it can be concluded that the filtering processes proposed are efficient. Moreover, the few unwanted remaining points lie in dispersed areas, far away from the ones caused by the scanned structure and hence, they do not result in confusing information.

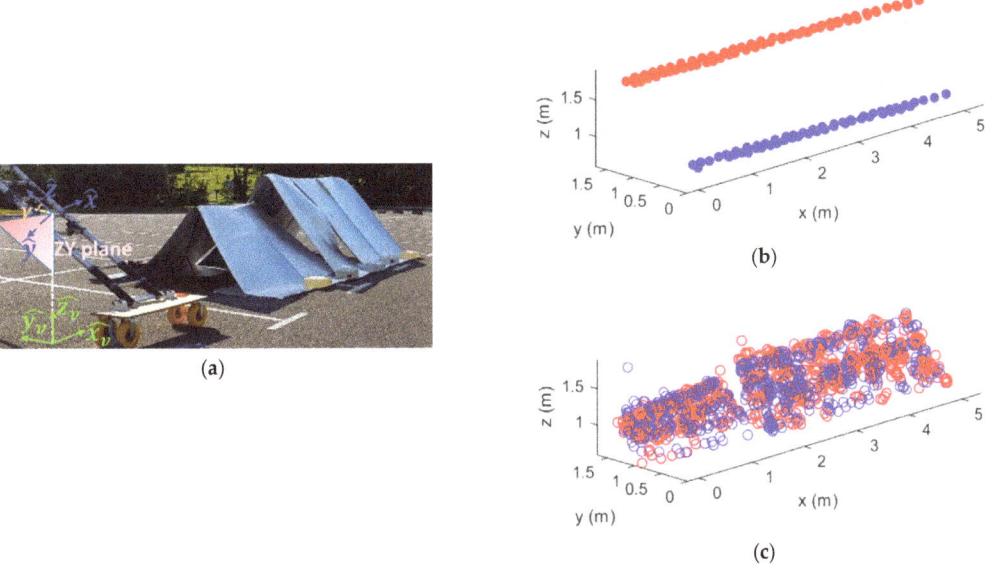

Figure 5. (**a**) Scanning area; (**b**) rover modules positions and (**c**) point cloud retrieved from a round trip scanning path.

There are several techniques for reconstructing the surface of the structure from a point cloud. In this paper, although conventional Delaunay triangulation, used in [33], has been evaluated, additional *ad-hoc* techniques have also been investigated. The first one is based on a piecewise cubic interpolation and a surface reconstruction using fitting functions to adjust the surface to the retrieved point cloud. The results are presented in Figure 6a and this procedure is called *proc1*.The second technique involves a smoothing, triangle linear interpolation and the use of the spring model, which allows us to accurately connect the points on the cloud [34]. The reconstructed surface, after applying this technique, is presented in Figure 6b and this procedure is called *proc2*. From both reconstructions, the shape and the height variations of the stockpile-alike model are clearly observed, with the height of the first and second sections of the stockpile respectively being 1.25 m and 1.53 m and their longitudinal lengths being 2 m and 3.4 m, which closely fit the true dimensions of the stockpile-alike model, as shown in Table 1. The slight discrepancies may be due to calibration errors and/or inaccuracies when acquiring the stockpile-alike model dimensions.

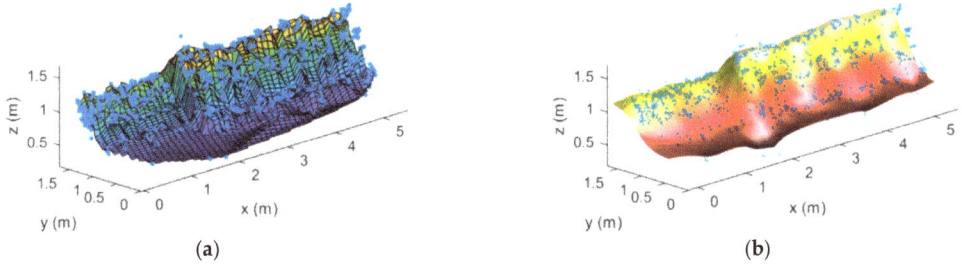

Figure 6. Surface reconstruction of the stockpile-alike model following (**a**) *proc1* and (**b**) *proc2* procedures.

Table 1. Real and reconstructed dimensions of the stockpile.

	Section 1		Section 2	
	Height (m)	Length (m)	Height (m)	Length (m)
Real dimensions	1.20	2	1.50	3.4
Reconstructed Stockpile	1.25	2	1.53	3.4

3.2. Real Environment

Once the system was adjusted and a precise reconstruction of the stockpile-alike model was achieved, it was tested in a more realistic environment. For this purpose, a real stockpile of coal was deployed. However, in contrast to real stockpiles with heights in the order of tenths of meters, the considered model was scaled, being equivalent to a local measurement of a complete stockpile. The considered scaled-stockpile has three clear sections with different heights (see Figure 7). The first section, with a maximum height of 1.58 m, is followed by an almost flat middle area and then, a final section, slightly higher than the previous one, completes the stockpile.

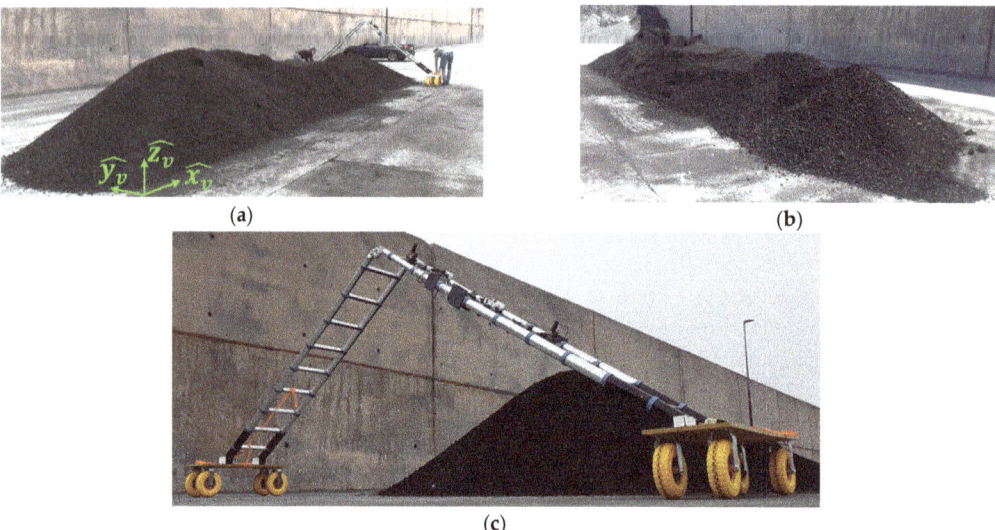

(a)

(b)

(c)

Figure 7. (a,b) Scaled stockpile from two different perspectives; (c) the ladder with the sensors prior to conducting the stockpile scanning.

The scanning procedure is identical to the one described for the stockpile-alike model. As the real stockpile has similar height dimensions as the previous stockpile-alike model and the distance from the radars to the stockpile is similar, the sensors on the ladder are placed at the same positions.

Although the stockpile was located close to a high wall, as can be seen in Figure 7, the rover modules could receive a strong enough signal from the satellites to solve their position in their fix mode and hence, a high positioning accuracy was provided.

Regarding the radars configuration, the optimum CFAR threshold has been proved to be between 5 and 13 dB, so that a dense point cloud can be obtained and no information from the scanned structure is missed.

The data processing technique and the filtering applied to the point cloud are identical to the ones employed for the stockpile-alike model (see Appendix A for further information about data processing). Once again, a visualization coordinate system has to be defined, which is represented in Figure 7a.

In Figure 8a, the rover modules positions at each measurement instant are depicted (red and blue dots, respectively for rover1 and rover2). The retrieved point cloud corresponding to a round trip scanning path is shown in Figure 8b. Once again, the points corresponding to each movement direction are represented with a different color, with both point clouds being similar and again demonstrating the robustness of the proposed method for referring the point cloud to the defined GCS.

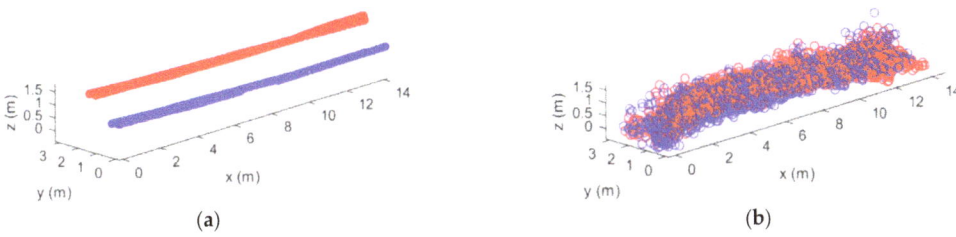

Figure 8. (**a**) Rover modules positions and (**b**) point cloud retrieved from a round trip scanning path.

Then, the surface is reconstructed using both *proc1* and *proc2* and the results are shown in Figure 9. From this reconstruction, the three sections of the stockpile are clearly distinguishable, having the first one a height of 1.52 m (almost the same as the actual one, 1.58 m). The reconstructed stockpile length (14.2 m) is slightly smaller than the length of the true stockpile, as there is certain information of the stockpile base that is lost, due to the lack of an additional radar on the bottom of the ladder. However, the latter is not critical, as stockpiles are commonly uniform on its base and, consequently, no relevant information is missing.

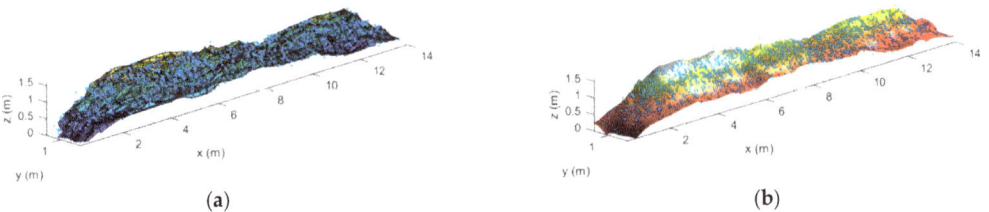

Figure 9. Surface reconstruction of the real stockpile following (**a**) *proc1* and (**b**) *proc2* procedures.

3.3. Complete Reconstruction of the Real Stockpile

Once the real stockpile has been properly scanned and its lateral surface accurately reconstructed, a complete model of the stockpile may be desired. For estimating such model, the stockpile should be scanned from both sides. As the proposed system is a prototype, including the sensors that are only on a single side, the ladder was flipped so that same sensors are used for conducting the scanning at both sides. Therefore, a round trip scanning for each side of the stockpile can be performed to fully model the stockpile.

Since both side scans can be referred to the GCS, the retrieved data can be merged and the point cloud is referred to the same visualization coordinate system. The rover modules positions at each measurement instant along with the retrieved point cloud are presented in Figure 10. For the sake of compactness, Figure 11 just shows the reconstruction results obtained when applying *proc2* from three different perspectives. From these results, the three different sections that constitute the stockpile can be clearly observed, concluding that a complete model of the stockpile can be retrieved using the proposed technique.

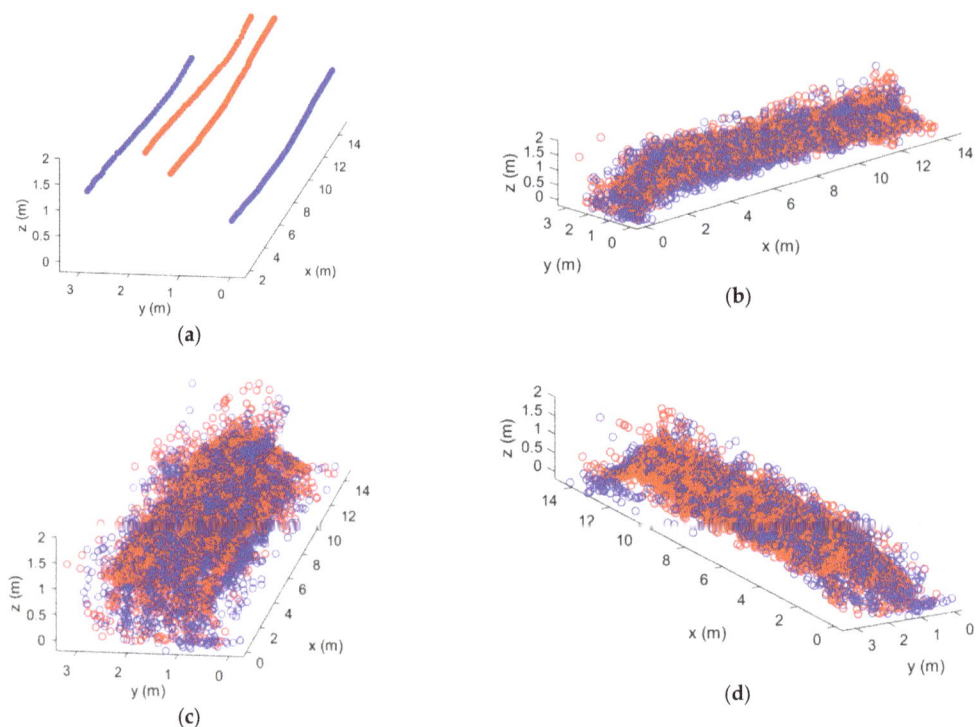

Figure 10. (**a**) Rover modules positions and (**b,c,d**) different perspectives of the point cloud retrieved from a round trip scanning path from both sides.

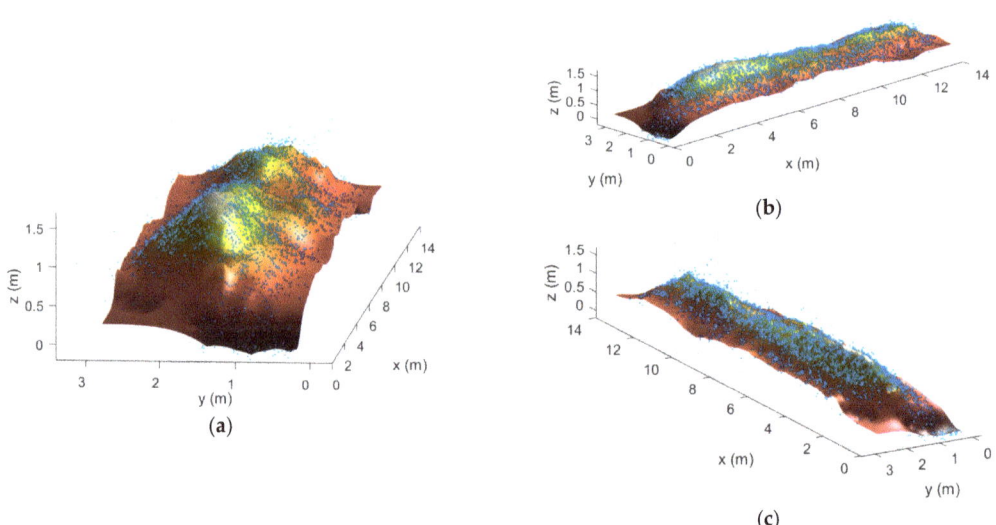

Figure 11. Surface reconstruction of the real stockpile from different perspectives.

In order to evaluate the robustness of the proposed system, the stockpile was modified, with the new one having a height and length of 1.5 m and 11.6 m, respectively (see Figure 12), and a new scan was conducted. In Figure 12b the results obtained after reconstructing the scanned data are shown. It can be seen that the reconstruction closely follows the changes of the stockpile geometry, confirming the robustness of the proposed system and the suitability of the applied methods.

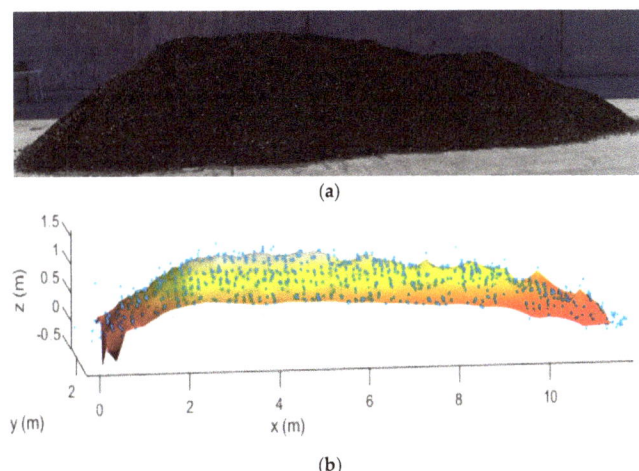

Figure 12. (**a**) Picture and (**b**) surface reconstruction of the stockpile.

Aiming at assessing the accuracy of the proposed system, a photogrammetry-like technique is employed to compare the profiles of both the real and reconstructed stockpile. The true profile of the stockpile was extracted from a picture took during the measurements, which corresponds to the yellow line in Figure 13. This profile is compared with the one obtained after the reconstruction (green line in Figure 13). It can be noticed the correlation between both curves, being almost identical on the middle section and having slight deviations on the lateral sections, which can be attributed to other scattering sources, as the scanner arrives at the ends of the stockpile.

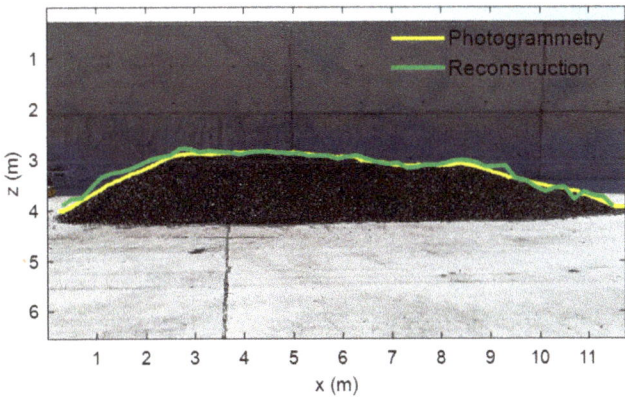

Figure 13. Picture of the stockpile, with the profile being recovered using a photogrammetry-like technique shown in yellow and the profile obtained from the reconstruction in green.

Analyzing the previous results, it has been found that the mean absolute error on predicting the stockpile profile height is 6.4 cm and the root mean square deviation is 8.6 cm. These errors are mainly due to the sensors precision and resolution, as well as due to the employed calibration and positioning methods. However, it has been shown that the system provides high precision to retrieve the stockpile profile. Indeed, the agreement between the outline and shape of the real and reconstructed stockpiles is very good. Moreover, the errors are much smaller than the ones presented in other works [15–35], always being much less than 20 cm, which is an acceptable level [12].

Real-Time Reconstruction

In this section, a viability analysis for reconstructing the stockpile in real-time is conducted. Therefore, only the data retrieved until a given instantaneous measurement position is used for reconstructing the stockpile. As the radars have the capability of scanning the stockpile in three dimensions, the point cloud retrieved at each measurement instants contains points not only in the scanning plane (ZY plane shown in Figure 5a), but also from previous and forward stockpile parts. This allows us to redefine the reconstructed image with the information provided from successive measurement acquisitions, making the method adaptive in a certain way. The results of this real-time reconstruction are shown in Figure 14 for the two real stockpiles previously analyzed at two different instants. Consequently, it can be concluded that the proposed system and the employed methods are suitable for real-time scanning and reconstruction applications.

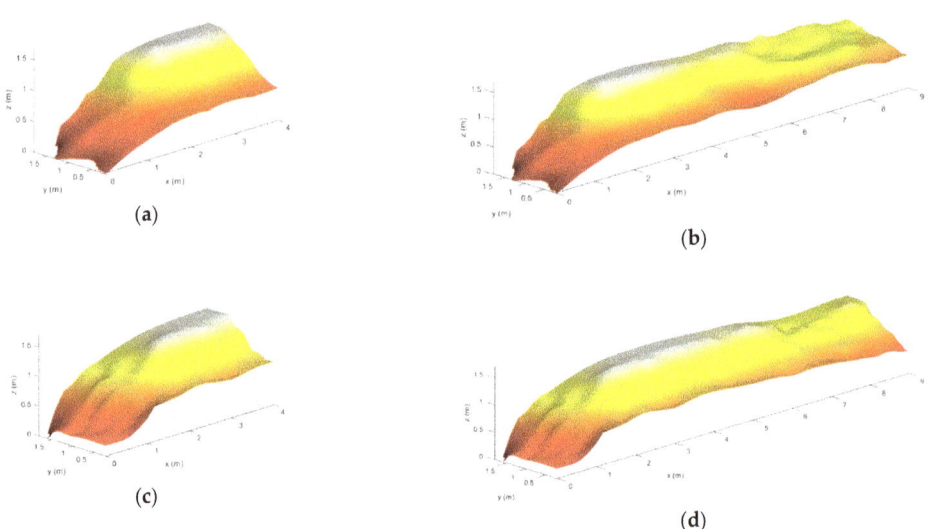

Figure 14. Reconstruction of the two real stockpiles when the scanner system is at (**a,c**) 4 m and (**b,d**) 9 m from the beginning of each stockpile.

4. Discussion

The electromagnetic scanning system presented in this article gathers most of the requirements demanded by the Industry 4.0, regarding the connection between systems and the management of data. In this article, a new system to estimate the topography of stockpiles has been fully developed, from the selection and arrangement of their core components to the managing and processing of the acquired data. Moreover, the system does not rely on mathematical or geometrical models used in the literature to predict the initial shape of stockpiles, which cannot continuously monitor the structure, causing inefficient handling of the industrial processes [9–11].

A robust and highly accurate technique for managing the sensors data and reconstructing the stockpile topography from the obtained point cloud has been presented. It is worth noting that it avoids the usage of other models that cannot provide a continuous dynamic monitoring of the scanned structure and/or other time consuming and less reliable techniques that greatly depend on the selected algorithm [11].

The proposed system is cost-effective, mainly thanks to the use of commercial off-the-shelf components, whose prices are dropping due to their mass production.

In contrast to other works that propose alternatives that are only assessed in laboratory conditions, the solution presented in this article has been tested in a realistic environment, obtaining highly precise reconstructions of the scanned structure.

It should be noticed that it is not easy to analyze the accuracy of the obtained results when scanning large structures, as the true shape and dimensions of such structures are not known. Indeed, there are not many works in the literature that quantitatively compare the obtained results from the scanning process with the actual structure. Nonetheless, in this article two techniques have been proposed to perform such comparisons. The first one relies on the measurements of the structure dimensions taken in the field, whereas the other one uses a photogrammetry-like technique to extract the profile of the scanned structure. From both methods, a high accuracy on the structure reconstruction has been clearly obtained. In fact, the proposed system performs better in terms of accuracy than other works proposed in the literature [15,35].

Finally, it should be noted that although the data retrieved from the sensors is downloaded after the scanning process, the viability of reconstructing the surface in real-time has been verified.

5. Conclusions

In this article, a new and highly precise system has been presented for electromagnetically scanning large structures. The system combines the range information provided, as point clouds, by an array of mm-wave radars with the highly accuracy positioning data provided by GNSS-RTK modules, forming a sensor-fusion system that enables to merge the point clouds taken from different arbitrary positions. Moreover, communication and control components have been employed to send and receive data from the sensors and to manage the system status. A laptop has been also used for fusing the geo-referred data and properly reconstructing the scanned structure. Therefore, a new methodology to achieve 3D images of any large structure, object or group of objects, even when dust or heavy smoke are present and regardless of the ambient light, is introduced. As a proof of concept, the system has been tested on a stockpile-alike model and in a realistic environment at a seaport with a scaled coal stockpile, obtaining accurate results in both cases.

The reconstructed model has been compared with the true scanned structure dimensions, giving small errors (on the order of centimeters). For further verification of the system accuracy, a photogrammetry-like technique is used to compare the reconstructed profile with the true one, showing also small discrepancies. Therefore, the precision on the reconstruction of the structure has been validated, as well as the proper performance of the sensors that comprise the system.

In addition, the system and the proposed reconstruction method have been tested under real-time conditions, showing an excellent performance.

It should be noticed that although the proposed system is a proof-of-concept for scanning reasonably large structures, it can be easily scaled. Moreover, it can be used in other outdoor applications involving the retrieving of an electromagnetic image of large structures.

Author Contributions: Conceptualization, all authors; methodology, all authors; software, H.F.Á.; hardware, all authors; validation, all authors; formal analysis, H.F.Á.; investigation, H.F.Á.; resources, H.F.Á.; data curation, H.F.Á.; writing—original draft preparation, H.F.Á.; writing—review and editing, all authors; visualization, H.F.Á.; supervision, F.L.-H.A.; project administration, H.F.Á. and F.L.-H.A.; funding acquisition, G.Á.-N., M.G.-F., J.L., Y.Á.L. and F.L.-H.A. All authors have read and agreed to the published version of the manuscript

Funding: This research was funded by Ministerio de Ciencia, Innovación y Universidades of Spain Government under project MILLIHAND RTI2018-095825-B-I00, by the Gobierno del Principado de Asturias and European Union (FEDER) under Project GRUPIN-IDI-2018-000191 and by the TSK company under its Open Innovation Program.

Data Availability Statement: The data presented in this study are available in the article figures and tables.

Acknowledgments: Special thanks to the TSK company for the provided material and environment to conduct the measurements.

Conflicts of Interest: The authors declare no conflict of interest.

Appendix A

The point cloud provided by each radar on each measurement position is related to its own local coordinate system (LCS). Aiming at reconstructing the scanned surface, the aforementioned point clouds should be referred to a global common fixed coordinate system (GCS). This system is defined by three orthonormal vectors $(\hat{x}, \hat{y}, \hat{z})$, which are determined from the positioning data provided by the GNSS-RTK modules as follow:

- $\hat{x}$ vector → obtained by computing the mean of the retrieved positions provided by the rover modules along the longitudinal scanning of the stockpile (from the beginning to the end of the stockpile).
- $\hat{z}$ vector → defined by the vector connecting the two rover module positions.
- $\hat{y}$ vector → cross product between $\hat{x}$ and $\hat{z}$ vectors.

The advantages of using the aforementioned coordinate system is that their constituent vectors (blue triple $(\hat{x}, \hat{y}, \hat{z})$ in Figure A1) are almost parallel to the local systems ones of the radars (brown triple $(\hat{x}_r, \hat{y}_r, \hat{z}_r)$ in Figure A1). Once the point clouds of the radars are defined with respect to the GCS, an additional transformation has to be conducted to refer them to the visualization coordinate system (green triple $(\hat{x}_v, \hat{y}_v, \hat{z}_v)$ in Figure A1). The latter provides a better representation of the structure, so that the $\hat{z}_v$ vector points to the sky, whereas the $\hat{x}_v$ and $\hat{y}_v$ vectors are parallel to the ground.

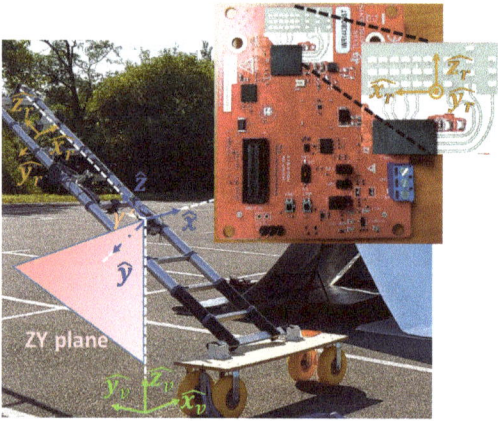

Figure A1. Coordinate system representation.

The positioning information is given by the rover modules on the ECEF (*Earth-centered, Earth-fixed*) coordinate system. Therefore, a coordinate system transformation is firstly required for referring this positioning information to the GCS.

Figure A2 shows the data processing flow chart followed in this article. Firstly, the global coordinate system is defined (as previously indicated) and the positioning data provided by the rover modules are referred to the GCS. Then, the data from the radars are processed for each measurement instant by following the steps described below (blocks in yellow in Figure A2):

- Computation of an instantaneous coordinate system (ICS), which is defined by the auxiliary vectors $(\hat{x}_i, \hat{y}_i, \hat{z}_i)$. These vectors are computed in a similar way as the GCS previously defined, except for $\hat{x}_i$ that is calculated from several consecutive measurement positions (four in this case). These ICS allows to determine the radars orientation on each measurement instance and, hence, its LCS.
- The correction angles that determine the orientation of the ICS (and hence the LCS) regarding the GCS (see Figure A3) are calculated as follows:
  - α_x is extracted by projecting the vector $\hat{z}_i$ on the ZY plane (obtaining $\hat{z_{pi}}$) and computing the angle between $\hat{z_{pi}}$ and the XZ plane. After applying the rotation by an angle α_x around the $\hat{x}$ axis to the vectors $(\hat{x}_i, \hat{y}_i, \hat{z}_i)$, the triad $(\hat{x_{ir1}}, \hat{y_{ir1}}, \hat{z_{ir1}})$ is obtained.
  - α_y will be the angle between the $\hat{z_{ir1}}$ and the YZ plane.
  - α_z will be the rotation angle required to make the triad $(\hat{x_{ir1}}, \hat{y_{ir1}}, \hat{z_{ir1}})$ and $(\hat{x}, \hat{y}, \hat{z})$ coincident.

Once the correction angles are extracted, the rotation matrices are applied to transform the ICS, so that its triad vectors $(\hat{x}_i, \hat{y}_i, \hat{z}_i)$ have the same orientation as the ones of the GCS $(\hat{x}, \hat{y}, \hat{z})$.

- A filtering based on the range and reflected power is firstly applied to the point clouds provided by each radar at each measurement instant for discarding unwanted points. These points are detected with a low power or far away from the radars and in dispersed areas, so they cannot be attributable to the scanned structure.
- The translation matrix from the ICS of each radar to the GCS is determined using the relative positions of the radars regarding the rover modules defined by an initial calibration. Using both the translation matrices and the rotation ones, it is possible to refer the point clouds provided by the radars at each measurement instant in the GCS.

Once all the data is processed, a linear regression is applied to the final point cloud (which is defined regarding the GCS). For doing so, the points on the cloud that lies at a certain distance from the ZY plane (see Figure A1) are selected for computing a lineal regression, discarding the points that lie far away from this lineal regression. Although the latter filtering process is computed at each measurement instant, it can be conducted at any other interval.

Finally, an additional transformation is applied to represent the point cloud in the visualization coordinate system (green triad vectors $(\hat{x}_v, \hat{y}_v, \hat{z}_v)$ in Figure A1). The latter transformation is obtained by rotating the point cloud $\beta = 90° - \gamma$ degrees around the $\hat{x}$ vector, being γ the angle between $\hat{z}$ and the ground (obtained from the rover modules positioning information), and a translation regarding $\hat{z}_v$ (allowing to refer the point cloud with regards to the ground). This transformation is useful for a better interpretation of the retrieved point cloud.

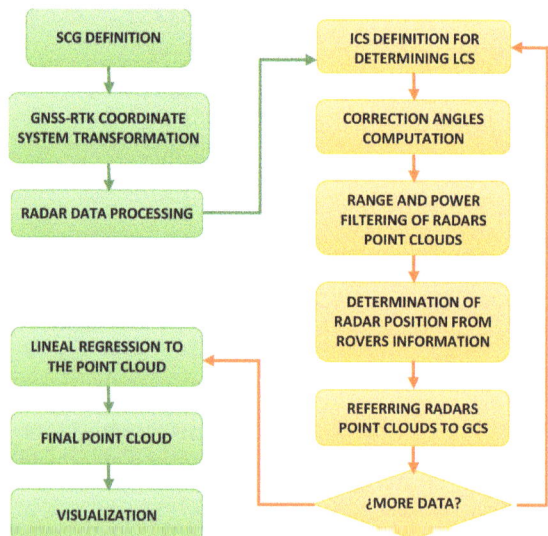

Figure A2. Data processing flow chart.

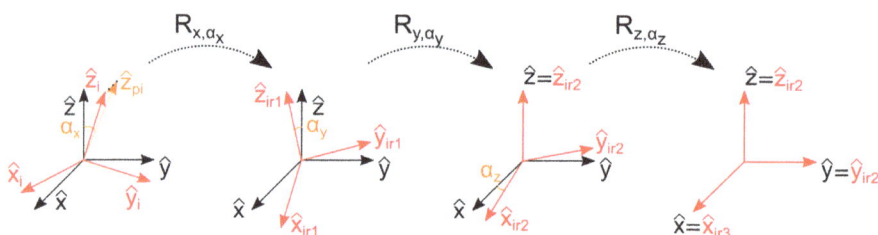

Figure A3. Coordinate system transformation to get the ICS vectors $(\hat{x}_i, \hat{y}_i, \hat{z}_i)$, and hence the LCS of each radar, equally oriented as the GCS ones $(\hat{x}, \hat{y}, \hat{z})$.

References

1. Sun, D.; Hwang, S.; Kim, B.; Ahn, Y.; Lee, J.; Han, J. Creation of One Excavator as an Obstacle in C-Space for Collision Avoidance during Remote Control of the Two Excavators Using Pose Sensors. *Remote Sens.* **2020**, *12*, 1122. [CrossRef]
2. Wei, P.; Cagle, L.; Reza, T.; Ball, J.; Gafford, J. LiDAR and Camera Detection Fusion in a Real-Time Industrial Multi-Sensor Collision Avoidance System. *Electronics* **2018**, *7*, 84. [CrossRef]
3. Graham, J.H.; Meagher, J.F.; Derby, S.J. A Safety and Collision Avoidance System for Industrial Robots. *IEEE Trans. Ind. Appl.* **1986**, *22*, 195–203. [CrossRef]
4. Xiang, X.; Qin, W.; Xiang, B. Research on a DSRC-based rear-end collision warning model. *IEEE Trans. Intell. Transp. Syst.* **2014**, *15*, 1054–1065. [CrossRef]
5. Kusano, K.D.; Gabler, H.C. Safety benefits of forward collision warning, brake assist, and autonomous braking systems in rear-end collisions. *IEEE Trans. Intell. Transp. Syst.* **2012**, *13*, 1546–1555.
6. Mukhtar, A.; Xia, L.; Tang, T.B. Vehicle Detection Techniques for Collision Avoidance Systems: A Review. *IEEE Trans. Intell. Transp. Syst.* **2015**, *16*, 2318–2338. [CrossRef]
7. Kobler, A.; Norbert, P.; Ogrinc, P.; Todorovski, L.; Ostir, K.; Dzeroski, S. Repetitive interpolation: A robust algorithm for DTM generation from Aerial Laser Scanner Data in forested terrain. *Remote Sens. Environ.* **2007**, *108*, 9–23. [CrossRef]
8. Milan, D.J.; Heritage, G.L.; Hetherington, D. Application of a 3D laser scanner in the assessment of erosion and deposition volumes and channel change in a proglacial river. *Earth Surf. Process. Landf.* **2007**, *32*, 1657–1674. [CrossRef]
9. Lu, T.-F.; Myo, M.T.R. Optimal Stockpile Voxel Identification Based on Reclaimer Minimum Movement for Target Grade. *Int. J. Miner. Process.* **2011**, *98*, 74–81. [CrossRef]

10. Robinson, G.K.; Ross, K.A. Blending in the Ends of Chevron Stockpiles. *Bulk Solids Hand.* **1991**, *11*, 595–602.
11. Zhao, S.; Lu, T.F.; Koch, B.; Hurdsman, A. Stockpile Modelling using Mobile Laser Scanner for Quality Grade Control in Stockpile Management. In Proceedings of the 12th International Conference on Control Automation Robotics & Vision (ICARCV), Guangzhou, China, 5–7 December 2012; pp. 811–816.
12. Slipper, K. Research and development of a Rotating Level Sensor: To provide a low-cost alternative for large stockpile profiling in real-time. Ph.D. Thesis, Murdoch University, Perth, Australia, 2017.
13. Level measurement Production overview for applications in liquids and bulk solids. Available online: https://jprsystems.com/wp-content/uploads/EndressHauser-Level-Brochure.pdf (accessed on 24 November 2020).
14. Indurad solutions. Available online: https://indurad.com/ (accessed on 24 November 2020).
15. Zhao, S.; Lu, T.F.; Koch, B.; Hurdsman, A. Dynamic modelling of 3D stockpile for life-cycle management through sparse range point clouds. *Int. J. Miner. Process* **2013**, *125*, 61–77. [CrossRef]
16. Soudarissanane, S.; Lindenbergh, R.; Menenti, M.; Teunissen, P.J.G. Incident Angle Influence on the Quality of Terrestrial Laser Scanning Points. In Proceedings of the ISPRS Workshop Laserscanning, Paris, France, 1–2 September 2009.
17. Zhao, S.; Lu, T.F.; Koch, B.; Hurdsman, A. 3D stockpile modelling and quality calculation for continuous stockpile management. *Int. J. Miner. Process* **2015**, *140*, 32–42. [CrossRef]
18. Lu, T.F.; Zhao, S.; Xu, S.; Koch, B.; Hurdsman, A. A 3DOF system for 3 dimensional stockpile surface scanning using laser. In Proceedings of the 6th IEEE Conference on Industrial Electronics and Applications, Beijing, China, 21–23 June 2011; pp. 1–5.
19. Winkel, R.; Augustin, C.; Nienhaus, K. 2D Radar Technology Increasing Productivity by Volumetric Control and Hopper Car Positioning in Brown Coal Mining. *Górnictwo i Geoinżynieria* **2011**, *35*, 273–289.
20. Garcia-Fernandez, M.; Alvarez-Lopez, Y.; Las Heras, F. Autonomous Airborne 3D SAR Imaging System for Subsurface Sensing: UWB-GPR on Board a UAV for Landmine and IED Detection. *Remote Sens.* **2019**, *11*, 2357. [CrossRef]
21. ION solutions. Available online: https://iongroup.com/ (accessed on 24 November 2020).
22. Lu, T.F.; Xu, S. SPSim: A stockpile simulator for analyzing material quality distribution in mining. In Proceedings of the International Conference on Mechatronics and Automation (ICMA), Xi'an, China, 4–7 August 2010; pp. 299–304.
23. Gerlach, K.-H. Achieving the Right Quality Mix. *Siemens' Customer Magazine Metals & Mining*. 2009, pp. 20–22. Available online: https://www.primetals.com/fileadmin/user_upload/metals-magazine/2009_02/009_Metals-Magazine_2-2009_Cost-Saving_Solutions.pdf (accessed on 24 November 2020).
24. Ahmed, S.S. *Electronic Microwave Imaging with Planar Multistatic Arrays*; Logos Verlag Berlin GmbH: Berlin, Germany, 2014.
25. García Fernández, M.; Alvarez-Lopez, Y.; Arboleya-Arboleya, A.; González-Valdés, B.; Rodríguez-Vaqueiro, Y.; Las-Heras, F.; Pino-García, A. Synthetic Aperture Radar Imaging System for Landmine Detection Using a Ground Penetrating Radar on Board a Unmanned Aerial Vehicle. *IEEE Access* **2018**, *6*, 45100–45112. [CrossRef]
26. Álvarez-Narciandi, G.; López-Portugués, M.; Las-Heras, F.; Laviada, J. Freehand, Agile, and High-Resolution Imaging with Compact mm-Wave Radar. *IEEE Access* **2019**, *7*, 95516–95526.
27. Sheen, D.M.; McMakin, D.L.; Hall, T.E. Three-dimensional millimeter-wave imaging for concealed weapon detection. *IEEE Trans. Microw. Theory Tech.* **2001**, *49*, 1581–1592. [CrossRef]
28. Álvarez-Narciandi, G.; Laviada, J.; Las-Heras, F. Freehand mm-wave imaging with a compact MIMO radar. *IEEE Trans. Antennas Propag.* 2020. Available online: https://ieeexplore.ieee.org/document/9162460 (accessed on 30 November 2020).
29. Texas Instrument solutions. Available online: https://www.ti.com/product/IWR1443 (accessed on 24 November 2020).
30. Xiaowei, P. Online Smart Sensor to Measure Stockpiles used in Mineral Processing. In Proceedings of the International Conference on Mining, Minerals and Metallurgical Engineering (ICMMME'15), Harare, Zimbabwe, 9–10 October 2015.
31. RTK-GNSS Emlid Reach RS2. Available online: https://emlid.com/reachrs2/ (accessed on 24 November 2020).
32. RTK-GNSS Emlid Reach M2. Available online: https://emlid.com/reach/ (accessed on 24 November 2020).
33. Zhang, W.; Yang, D. Lidar-Based Fast 3D Stockpile Modeling. In Proceedings of the International Conference on Intelligent Computing, Automation and Systems (ICICAS), Chongqing, China, 6–8 December 2019; pp. 703–707.
34. Understanding gridfit. Available online: https://svn.oss.deltares.nl/repos/openearthtools/trunk/matlab/general/grid_fun/private/gridfit/doc/gridfit.pdf (accessed on 24 November 2020).
35. Deng, Y.; Liu, X. Electromagnetic Imaging Methods for Nondestructive Evaluation Applications. *Sensors* **2011**, *11*, 11774–11808. [CrossRef] [PubMed]

Article

Algorithm for Dynamic Fingerprinting Radio Map Creation Using IMU Measurements

Peter Brida [1], Juraj Machaj [1,*], Jan Racko [1] and Ondrej Krejcar [2]

[1] Department of Multimedia and Information Communication Technology, Faculty of Electrical Engineering and Information, University of Zilina, Univerzitna 1, 01026 Zilina, Slovakia; peter.brida@feit.uniza.sk (P.B.); jan.racko@feit.uniza.sk (J.R.)

[2] Center for Basic and Applied Research, Faculty of Informatics and Management, University of Hradec Kralove, Rokitanskeho 62, 500 03 Hradec Kralove, Czech Republic; ondrej.krejcar@uhk.cz

* Correspondence: juraj.machaj@feit.uniza.sk

Abstract: While a vast number of location-based services appeared lately, indoor positioning solutions are developed to provide reliable position information in environments where traditionally used satellite-based positioning systems cannot provide access to accurate position estimates. Indoor positioning systems can be based on many technologies; however, radio networks and more precisely Wi-Fi networks seem to attract the attention of a majority of the research teams. The most widely used localization approach used in Wi-Fi-based systems is based on fingerprinting framework. Fingerprinting algorithms, however, require a radio map for position estimation. This paper will describe a solution for dynamic radio map creation, which is aimed to reduce the time required to build a radio map. The proposed solution is using measurements from IMUs (Inertial Measurement Units), which are processed with a particle filter dead reckoning algorithm. Reference points (RPs) generated by the implemented dead reckoning algorithm are then processed by the proposed reference point merging algorithm, in order to optimize the radio map size and merge similar RPs. The proposed solution was tested in a real-world environment and evaluated by the implementation of deterministic fingerprinting positioning algorithms, and the achieved results were compared with results achieved with a static radio map. The achieved results presented in the paper show that positioning algorithms achieved similar accuracy even with a dynamic map with a low density of reference points.

Keywords: localization; IMU; Wi-Fi; positioning; dead reckoning; particle filter; fingerprinting

Citation: Brida, P.; Machaj, J.; Racko, J.; Krejcar, O. Algorithm for Dynamic Fingerprinting Radio Map Creation Using IMU Measurements. *Sensors* **2021**, *21*, 2283. https://doi.org/10.3390/s21072283

Academic Editor: Paolo Bellavista

Received: 15 February 2021
Accepted: 22 March 2021
Published: 24 March 2021

Publisher's Note: MDPI stays neutral with regard to jurisdictional claims in published maps and institutional affiliations.

1. Introduction

With the recent development of location-based services (LBS) in the indoor environment, there is a big demand for the deployment of indoor localization systems [1]. This is mainly because GNSS (Global Navigation Satellite Systems) localization services, which are widely used in the outdoor environment to provide location estimates, cannot provide accurate and reliable localization service in indoor environments. This is mainly related to the properties of GNSS signals that are transmitted from earth orbit and affected by signal attenuation, conditions in the ionosphere as well as multipath propagation. A combination of all these can cause loss of signal or high localization errors in dense urban environments and indoors.

Therefore, alternative positioning solutions have been and are being developed to provide accurate and reliable position estimates in both dense urban and indoor environments. These solutions traditionally utilize data from available enabling technologies to estimate the position of mobile devices or users in the environment. These enabling technologies can be represented by ultrasound [2], cameras [3], light sensors [4], magnetometers [5], MEMS (Micro-Electro-Mechanical Systems) or IMUs (Inertial Measurement Units) [6–8] as well as radio receivers [9]. Each of these technologies has its pros and cons. For example,

205

positioning using cameras can provide high accuracy; however, it can have relatively high computation complexity compared to systems based on radio signals [3]. On the other hand, localization based on measurements of magnetic fields can provide high accuracy for moving users with small complexity; however, it is almost useless for static positioning, as position estimates are based mainly on the classification of changes of the magnetic field when a user moves around the area [10].

When it comes to radio network-based positioning, this can provide position estimates with various levels of accuracy. This is due to the fact that various radio networks use transmit signal on different frequencies with different bandwidths, and thus, allow the collection of different type of data that can be used to estimate position. For example, UWB (Ultra-Wide Band) technology can provide propagation time ToA (Time of Arrival) measurements thanks to the wide bandwidth of the signal, which is transmitted on high frequencies. Therefore, it is possible to use UWB technology to build localization systems based on trilateration and achieve high accuracy even in environments with multipath propagation [11].

An important factor for the deployment of the localization system is the additional cost and complexity required for the operation of the system. The aforementioned UWB localization can provide high performance; however, it requires a dedicated infrastructure, and UWB receivers are not yet commonly implemented in widely used smart devices. Thus, users have to be equipped with tags that are used only for positioning purposes.

The motivation of our work is to build a low-cost positioning system that can provide room-level accuracy without the need for any significant investments into the infrastructure. Therefore, the decision was to set up the localization system on Wi-Fi technology. The main advantage is that Wi-Fi technology can be considered to be ubiquitous and all modern smart devices are able to receive signals from Wi-Fi access points (APs). The localization system is based on fingerprinting framework, since it allows the use of simple Received Signal Strength (RSS) measurements, which does not require any additional modification of devices. Fingerprinting approach has a significant advantage when compared to RSS based trilateration [12] since information about transmit power is not required. Moreover, the effect of shadowing caused by walls and other obstacles as well as multipath fluctuation does not have to be considered when fingerprinting-based localization is implemented.

The main drawback of the localization systems based on fingerprinting framework is the need for radio map measurements [13]. The radio map is basically a database of measurements performed on predefined reference points and is used during the position estimation process. The collection of RSS samples at predefined positions is usually a time-consuming process, especially if localization services are to be provided on a large scale. One way to avoid time-consuming calibration measurements for radio map is to use complex simulation of radio signal propagation, based either on signal modeling or raytracing algorithms [14]. However, these complex simulations still cannot provide realistic estimates of RSS levels in a dynamic indoor environment and can reduce localization performance [15,16].

To overcome the problems related to complexity and time required to collect radio map measurements, in this paper, we propose a solution for dynamic map creation. The proposed solution is based on a collection of data for a radio map while walking around the localization area. It does not require accurate measurement of the position of each reference point, nor doing static measurements at each of the reference points.

The proposed solution is based on the collection of data from IMU and Wi-Fi receiver, which are both implemented in all smart devices currently available on the market. The data from IMU are then processed by a dead reckoning algorithm and particle filter to recover the track of the user. When the track has been successfully recovered the position of reference points with RSS measurements provided by the Wi-Fi receiver can be estimated and stored in the radio map.

The rest of the paper is organized as follows: in Section 2, related solutions used for deployment and experimental evaluation of the systems are described, the proposed dynamic map creation solution is described in Section 3, Section 4 describes the experimental setup and discusses the achieved results and Section 5 concludes the paper.

2. Related Work

2.1. Fingerprinting Localization

Among the localization techniques used for indoor positioning based on Wi-Fi signals, fingerprinting localization has the most attention, with a vast number of modifications proposed by many research teams. This is due to the fact that fingerprinting positioning can estimate the position of the user with the use of easily obtained RSS measurements. While traditional distance-based localization methods that use RSS measurements for distance estimation are negatively affected by fluctuations caused by multipath propagation of wireless signals, the fingerprinting-based positioning systems seem to perform much better in environments with dense multipath propagation.

The operation of fingerprinting localization systems can be divided into two separate parts, usually referred to as offline and online phases. The offline phase is dedicated to calibration measurements of a radio map, while the online phase describes how the system operates during positioning.

During the offline phase, measurements are traditionally performed at predefined reference points distributed in the area of interest, where localization services will be provided, also referred to as the localization area. The measurements on individual reference points are stored in the database widely called a radio map. The principle of the radio map is shown in Figure 1. The radio map consists of reference points identification, the position of each reference point, as well as measured data. The position of the reference point is defined by coordinates [x_{RP}, y_{RP}, z_{RP}], where x_{RP} and y_{RP} represent coordinates in 2D cartesian space and z_{RP} defines the floor of the building. The most important information in the radio map is represented by RSS samples measured from all available APs. All the RSS measurements are linked to MAC addresses of APs that transmitted the signal; these are used as identification of individual transmitters during the position estimation process.

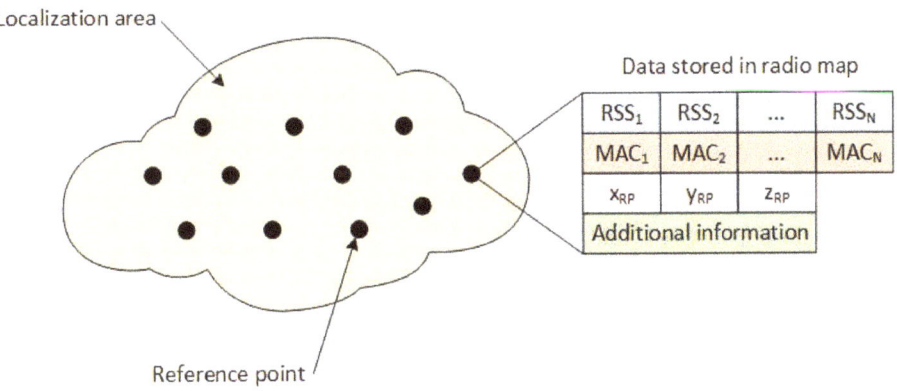

Figure 1. Principle of the radio map.

Additional information can be included in the radio map as well, which can be the identification of a device that was used for measurements, the orientation of the device during the measurement, etc. This information may help to improve the performance of the localization system.

In the online phase, the main goal is to estimate the position of the mobile device based on actual RSS measurements collected at the unknown position. This can be done by algorithms that can be divided into three main categories—deterministic approach, probabilistic approach and based on machine learning techniques.

Recently, machine learning algorithms based on neural networks and support vector machines are becoming extremely popular in different areas of signal processing and data analysis. Therefore, their use in localization systems is gaining a lot of attention as well [17,18].

In the probabilistic approach, the position of the mobile device is assumed to be a random vector [19]. In this case, the localization candidate is commonly chosen based on the highest posterior probability of the location candidates. If RSS measurements are represented by a vector S and γ_i represents position for i-th reference point, then the decision rule based on Bayes' theorem is given as follows:

$$P(\gamma_i|S) = \frac{P(S|\gamma_i)P(\gamma_i)}{P(S)},$$ (1)

where the posterior probability $P(\gamma_i | S)$ is described as a function of likelihood $P(S | \gamma_i)$, the prior probability $P(\gamma_i)$ has uniform distribution if no prior data are available and the observed evidence $P(S)$ given by:

$$P(S) = \sum_i P(S|\gamma_i) P(\gamma_i).$$ (2)

Other likelihood functions can also be used, as can be seen in [20].

Contrarily, in the deterministic framework, the state of the mobile device is assumed to be a non-random vector. The main idea is that the position of the mobile device can be estimated, since RSS values depend on the position of the mobile device. Therefore, the position of the mobile device $\hat{x}$ can be estimated based on a direct comparison of RSS values measured by the mobile device with values stored in the radio map database. In this case, the estimator can be written as:

$$\hat{x} = \frac{\sum_{i=1}^{M} \omega_i \cdot \gamma_i}{\sum_{i=1}^{M} \omega_i},$$ (3)

where M is the number of reference points in the radio map database and ω_i represents nonnegative weight assigned to the i-th reference point with position γ_i. Weights ω_i can be calculated using different metrics [21]; however, the most commonly used metric is the Euclidean distance d_E, given by:

$$d_E = \sqrt{\sum_{k=1}^{N} (a_k - b_k)^2},$$ (4)

where N is the number of elements in the RSS vector, i.e., the number of APs detected by the Wi-Fi receiver, a_k represents k-th element of vector A and b_k represents k-th element of vector B.

The positioning algorithm that uses estimator (3) to estimate the position using K highest weights is called Weighted K-Nearest Neighbors (WKNN) [22]; if K highest weights in the estimator (3) are set to 1 and the other weights are set to 0, it represents the KNN (K-Nearest Neighbors) algorithm. If the position of the mobile device is estimated using only a single highest weight, the algorithm becomes the NN (Nearest Neighbor) algorithm [23].

In general, KNN and WKNN provide more accurate position estimates, especially when K is set to 3 or 4, since it is possible to estimate the position of the mobile device more precisely. However, the NN algorithm can achieve an accuracy similar to KNN and WKNN algorithms when the density of the radio map is high enough [20]. This is due to the fact that the NN algorithm can only estimate positions on reference points; thus, the minimum error is given by the distance between them.

2.2. Improvements of the Radio Map

Since the radio map is required for fingerprinting-based localization, a lot of attention was aimed at modifications of the radio map collection process or dynamic updates of the radio map. Most of the proposed solutions can be divided into two main categories. The first category consists of solutions that help to increase radio map density by the implementation of interpolation algorithms to estimate fingerprints on additional reference points from the manually measured radio map. The second category of solutions is aimed at online radio map updates using measurements taken during the localization phase, either from a localized device or a set of sensors placed in the localization area.

The interpolation methods are used to increase radio map density, these solutions are based on assumption that the smaller distance between reference points the better resolution of the localization system, and thus, it should be possible to achieve higher localization accuracy. The first solutions for interpolation of reference points in sparse radio maps were based on linear interpolation [24], Radial Basis Function (RBF) [25], Kiring interpolation [26] as well as Inverse Distance Weighting (IDW) [27]. A more advanced solution referred to as VORO was proposed by Lee and Han [28] and is based on Log-Distance Path Loss. The interpolation was performed in two phases. In the first phase, the positions of APs were estimated. In the second phase parameters of signal, fading was estimated for each Voronoi cell, while fading of walls and obstacles was taken into the account. The parameters of signal fading were then used to estimate RSS on interpolated reference points. Based on experimental results, the VORO solution achieved significantly better results than IWF and RBF based interpolations.

Another solution for interpolation of radio map was proposed by Khalajmehrabadi et al. in [29]; in this case, interpolation was reformulated as a minimization problem known as the Least Absolute Shrinkage and Selection Operator (LASSO). The main advantage is that the proposed algorithm interpolates signals from randomly selected reference points and new samples are estimated for each AP individually; thus, it seems to be more robust.

Application of the Kiring interpolation technique on radio map re-emerged recently in applications related to 5G communication [30] and V2X (Vehicle to everything) [31] with distributed implementation. In these cases, it is required to estimate the power of the received signal for multiple nodes in the area. Kiring interpolation can achieve reasonably good performance since the implementation is mainly aimed at vehicle communication in the outdoor environment without any significant shadowing caused by obstacles between the transmitter and individual receivers.

On the other hand, algorithms in the second category aimed at online radio map updates are based on the assumption that the radio map changes over time, due to changes in the environment, and thus, by regular updates to the radio map, it will be possible to improve the localization accuracy. The changes in the environment might be caused by variation of temperature, humidity, movement of obstacles or changes in the infrastructure, i.e., furniture and equipment, reconstruction of the building, replacement or upgrade of some transmitters in the area [32]. These solutions are based on machine learning [33] and regression methods [34].

Xu et al. proposed an online radio map update scheme based on the marginalized particle gaussian process in [35]. The proposed solution utilizes crowdsourced fingerprints to update the radio map, while the position of online measurements is estimated using the existing radio map. The advantage of the solution lies in recursive processing of the measurements until the location is aligned with the radio map.

Huang et al. [36] implemented a marginalized particle Gaussian process in combination with pedestrian dead reckoning and Wi-Fi based localization for alignment of measurements with the existing radio map. Results show that implemented solution can provide better localization performance than the Gaussian process regression approach; however, this requires significantly more processing power. Thus, the online update is not automatic but has to be scheduled, so that it will not disrupt localization service.

The online radio map update using measurements of data from the fixed nodes was proposed by Batalla et al. [37]. The authors proposed to use a number of nodes to monitor changes in radio signal propagation. These devices are placed on some of the reference points. Measurements performed by the fixed nodes are used to update the offline radio map. The disadvantage of the system is a requirement for the implementation of fixed nodes and the fact that the number of nodes will increase significantly when the localization area consists of a large number of rooms, since conditions in different rooms will change independently, unlike in large open spaces such as industrial halls, where some correlation between neighboring reference points can be expected without constraints.

All the solutions described above can help to improve the performance of the localization system based on fingerprinting framework. However, all these solutions require initial calibration measurements for the radio map, which are time-consuming. Some of the solutions require additional investment into infrastructure, to collect data for online radio map updates.

The dynamic online calibrated radio map proposed in [38] helps to construct the radio map of the localization area and provide online updates of the radio map database based on the measurements performed by APs implemented in the area. This solution is quite promising; however, it is based on the assumption that most of the APs in the area are capable to perform RSS measurements and send them to the localization server. This might be true in cases when the network in the whole localization area (building) has a single administrator; unfortunately, this is not always the case.

In this paper, we focus on a low-cost solution, focused on the reduction of effort required for initial calibration measurements, which is required for most of the solutions presented above and does not require access to network infrastructure.

2.3. Dead Reckoning with Particle Filter

The dead reckoning positioning using data form low-cost IMU has attracted a lot of attention lately [8]. In a previous work [39], we described the implementation of the dead reckoning algorithm with a particle filter. The dead reckoning algorithm utilizes data from IMU to reconstruct the track of the user. The implementation can be divided into three parts: in the first part, the algorithm for step detection is implemented, the second part consists of an algorithm for heading angle estimation and the third part is represented by a particle filter algorithm that uses map information to improve position estimates. The block diagram of the particle filter pedestrian dead reckoning (PF-PDR) is shown in Figure 2.

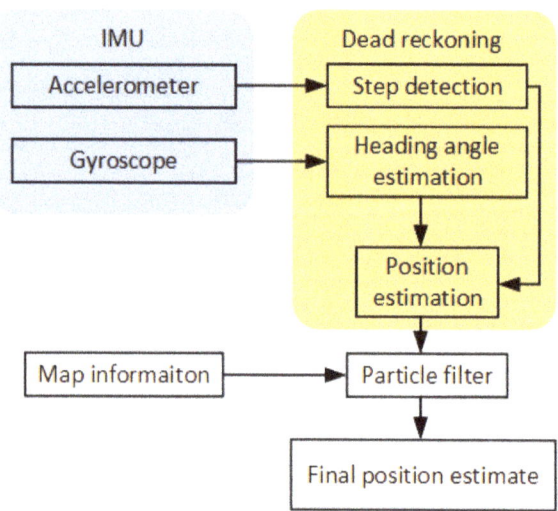

Figure 2. Block diagram of particle filter pedestrian dead reckoning.

In the implemented dead reckoning solution, the first task is to detect the step of the user [40]. For this purpose, data from the accelerometer implemented in IMU are used.

The significant pattern of the step can be found in the vertical axis; therefore, a vertical component of acceleration has to be estimated accurately. This is not always possible, especially when low-cost accelerometers are used for data collection; thus, the norm of acceleration can be used to detect the step. The norm of acceleration is given by:

$$a(t) = \sqrt{a_x^2(t) + a_y^2(t) + a_z^2(t)} - g, \tag{5}$$

where g is gravitational acceleration and a_x, a_y, a_z stand for measured acceleration in all three axes of the accelerometer implemented in IMU [41]. The norm can be used for step detection using either peak detection, frequency analysis of the signal or the zero-crossing method, which was implemented in our case. In theory, each step has a different length, and this should be taken into the account during the implementation of the dead reckoning algorithm; however, in this case, a fixed step length of 0.75 m was used. This setting was tested in [39] and provided reasonably accurate position estimates thanks to the implementation of a particle filter.

The second part of the dead reckoning algorithm is based on heading estimation, which can be done by integration of angular velocity measured by the gyroscope, and is given by:

$$\omega_b(t) = (\omega_x(t), \omega_y(t), \omega_z(t)), \tag{6}$$

where $\omega_x, \omega_y, \omega_z$ are angular rotations measured for each axis in the body frame of the IMU. Then, the attitude of the IMU can be represented by direction cosine matrix C, which is the rotation matrix given by:

$$C = \begin{bmatrix} \cos\theta\cos\Psi & \cos\theta\sin\Psi & -\sin\theta \\ \sin\varphi\sin\theta\cos\Psi - \cos\varphi\sin\Psi & \sin\varphi\sin\theta\sin\Psi + \cos\varphi\cos\Psi & \sin\varphi\cos\theta \\ \cos\varphi\sin\theta\cos\Psi + \sin\varphi\sin\Psi & \cos\varphi\sin\theta\sin\Psi - \sin\varphi\sin\Psi & \cos\varphi\cos\theta \end{bmatrix}, \tag{7}$$

where φ, θ, Ψ represent the Euler angles roll, pitch and yaw, respectively. In order to track the orientation of the IMU, the rotation matrix has to be updated all the time. The updated matrix $C(t + \Delta t)$ can be calculated as follows:

$$C(t + \Delta t) = C(t)\left(I + \frac{\sin\sigma}{\sigma}B + \frac{1 - \cos\sigma}{\sigma^2}B^2\right), \tag{8}$$

where Δt is the sampling interval, I is a 3-by-3 identity matrix, $\sigma = |\Delta t \omega_b|$ and

$$B = \begin{bmatrix} 0 & -\omega_z\Delta t & \omega_y\Delta t \\ \omega_z\Delta t & 0 & -\omega_x\Delta t \\ -\omega_y\Delta t & \omega_x\Delta t & 0 \end{bmatrix}. \tag{9}$$

Afterwards, it is possible to calculate yaw angle Ψ from the updated rotation matrix, which actually represents the heading of the user:

$$\Psi = \arctan(C_{2,1}, C_{1,1}). \tag{10}$$

In the last step of the dead reckoning algorithm, the position of the user can be estimated as follows:

$$\begin{bmatrix} P_{x_k} \\ P_{y_k} \end{bmatrix} = \begin{bmatrix} P_{x_{k-1}} + l_k\sin\Psi_k \\ P_{y_{k-1}} + l_k\cos\Psi_k \end{bmatrix}, \tag{11}$$

where P_{x_k} and P_{y_k} represent a position on the x-axis and y-axis in step k, l_k stands for step length and Ψ_k represents the heading angle in step k.

To achieve the optimal combination of information from various sources, Bayesian filters are widely used; unfortunately, Bayesian filters only work well with linear models. Since the localization process is nonlinear, an approximation of the Bayesian filter must be implemented. A particle filter is a popular approximation, where posterior state distribution is approximated using particles. Moreover, the advantage of the particle filter is that a representation of particles as standalone points can easily be combined with information about the area in the map-matching process [42].

The particle filter is operating in prediction and update steps. During the prediction step, the number of particles $x^{(p)}$, $p = 1, \ldots, N$ is generated from proposal distribution in a time step t:

$$x_t^{(p)} \approx \pi\left(x_t^{(p)} \middle| x_{t-1}^{(p)}, \ y_{1\ldots t-1}\right), \tag{12}$$

where $y_{1\ldots t-1}$ stands for measurements one step before t. It is assumed that states establish a Markov model; the current state x_t depends solely on the previous state x_{t-1}.

During the uprate phase, it is required to recalculate weights according to the likelihood of observation, so the weights are given as follows:

$$w_i^p = w_{i-1}^p \frac{p\left(y_t \middle| x_t^{(p)}\right) p\left(x_t^{(p)} \middle| x_{t-1}^{(p)}\right)}{q\left(x_t^{(p)} \middle| x_{t-1}^{(p)}, y_i\right)}. \tag{13}$$

After the update, the weights are normalized. During the operation of the particle filters, just a few particles will be assigned all calculated weights. Over time, the propagation of particles with low weights has a negative impact on posterior distribution, which is referred to as degradation. In order to avoid degradation, resampling is required [43]. The implemented solution performed resampling when the number of active particles was less than $N/5$.

3. Proposed Solution

In order to remove the biggest drawback of fingerprinting positioning systems, energy and time required for the construction of a radio map, we have proposed a solution for dynamic radio map creation. The proposed solution utilizes IMU data and dead reckoning using the particle filter presented in [39]. In traditional fingerprinting solutions, the radio map is created either by performing measurements on predefined spots or by complex simulations of radio propagation [44]. However, simulations cannot provide realistic results even when a large number of complex factors affecting radio signal levels are considered [45]. Therefore, systems with radio maps based on real-world measurements traditionally outperform systems based on artificial radio maps [16].

Our proposed dynamic map creation solution is aimed at the reduction of radio map measurements complexity, since the solution can provide an automatic collection of RSS fingerprints for radio map. The proposed solution is based on RSS measurements during a walk through the localization area. Data are collected using the developed Sensor Reader app, which allows collecting data from both IMU and Wi-Fi receiver at the defined sampling rates. In the application, the sampling rate for IMU data was set to 100 Hz and for Wi-Fi signals, the measurements of RSS from all surrounding APs were performed every 5 s in order to provide reasonable separation for reference points in the radio map.

In the second step, the data collected by the user during the walk around the area is processed by the dynamic map creation algorithm. The dynamic map creation algorithm use data from IMU, which are processed by the PF-PDR algorithm in order to reconstruct the trajectory of the user. Furthermore, reference points are defined on the trajectory on time steps corresponding to Wi-Fi measurements.

The last step of the proposed solution is the process of reference point merging. This process is used to combine measurements from the reference points with similar position or neighboring reference points with extremely similar RSS values. The flowchart of the dynamic map creation, as well as the Reference Point (RP) and merge process, is shown in Figure 3.

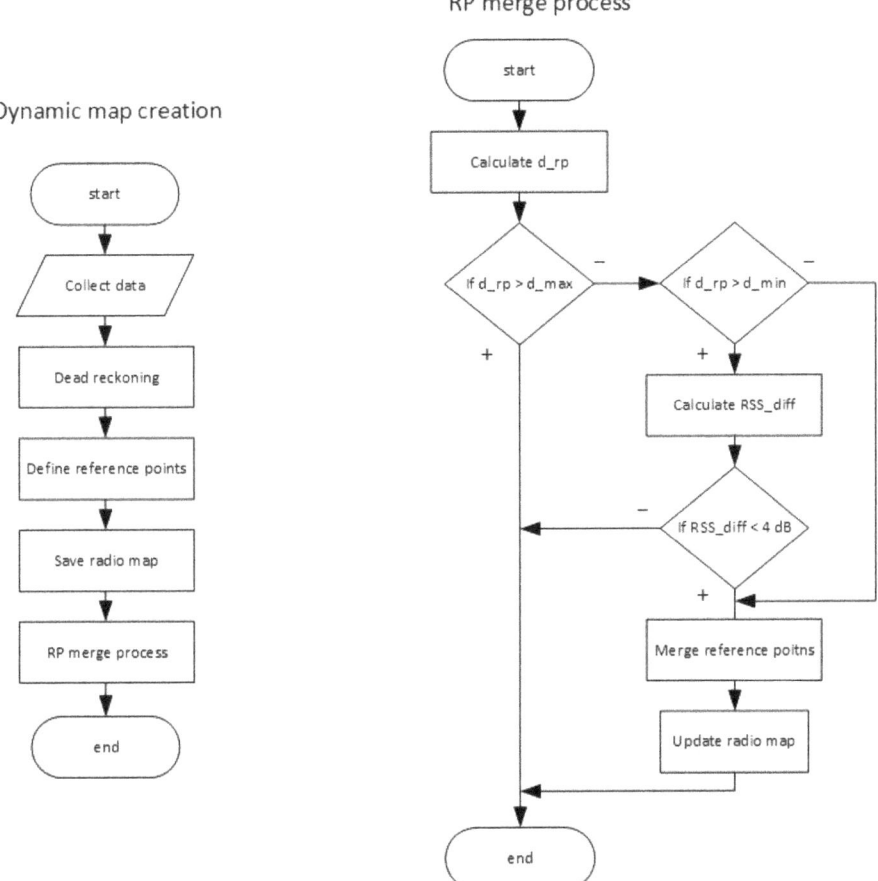

Figure 3. Flowchart of the proposed dynamic map creation solution and RP merge process.

Since the time interval for RSS measurements had a fixed value of 5 s, it is possible to estimate positions of individual reference points on which the radio map measurements were performed. It could happen that RSS measurements were performed during the same period as the user made a step which was detected by a dead reckoning algorithm; in such a case, the measurements are linked to the posterior position of the user.

However, since the user can move freely around the area while performing the radio map measurements, it can happen that some RSS measurements are performed at reference points that are close to each other. In order to achieve an even distribution of reference points in the radio map, the RP merge process was proposed. The process will run for each combination of neighboring reference points and in the first step calculate the physical distance between them. If the distance is smaller than $d\_max = 4$ m, the merging process will continue. The distance is then compared to d_min, and if it is smaller, the neighboring RPs will be merged without a comparison of the RSS values. However, if the distance is between d_max and d_min, the algorithm will continue with a comparison of RSS values on the neighboring reference points in order to decide about merging.

The RSS comparison is based on the computation of the mean RSS difference between the neighboring reference points denoted as RSS_{dif}, the value is given as follows:

$$RSS_{dif} = \frac{1}{n} \sum_{1}^{n} \left| RSS_n^1 - RSS_n^2 \right|, \qquad (14)$$

where n is the number of unique APs detected on both neighboring points, defined by the number of unique MAC addresses and RSS_n^1 and RSS_n^2 represent RSS samples measured from AP with n-th MAC address at the first and the second neighboring node, respectively. The threshold for the merging of neighboring nodes was set to 4 dB. When the RSS_{dif} is higher than the threshold the neighboring nodes are considered to represent significantly different conditions in the radio channel [46]; therefore, the merging of reference points is not performed, and both reference points will be considered in the final radio map database.

In case that all required conditions were met in the algorithm, i.e., the physical distance between RPs is below d_min or the average RSS difference RSS_{dif} is above 4 dB, the merging of reference points will be performed.

In the merging process, the position of the merged reference point is defined as the average of positions of the original reference points. The RSS values for the merged reference point are calculated as average values of RSS samples collected for both original reference points. In the case where some APs are detected on only one of the original reference points, values are considered to be –100 dBm, which represents the sensitivity of a Wi-Fi receiver.

4. Achieved Results and Discussion

4.1. Proof of Concept of Dynamic Radio Map Creation

In order to test and prove the feasibility of our solution, we have performed initial testing of the system for the dynamic radio map construction at the Department of Multimedia and Information-communication technology of the University of Zilina. The walked path recovered from the IMU data processed by particle filter-based dead reckoning algorithm is shown in Figure 4; red circles in the figure represent positions of reference points created by the dynamic radio map creation solution.

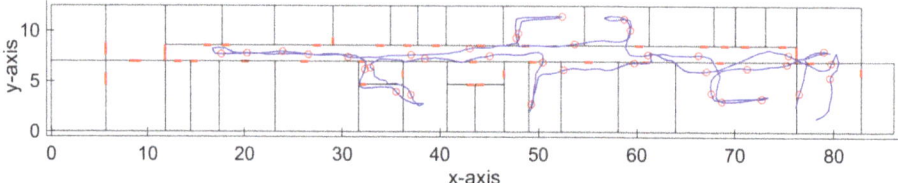

Figure 4. Track recovered by the dead reckoning algorithm with detected reference points.

We have also evaluated the accuracy of the implemented dead reckoning algorithm, which is an important parameter since it has an impact on the accuracy of the reference points' position. The localization error of the dead reckoning algorithm with particle filter is presented in Table 1. The localization error was estimated as a distance between the recovered track and the reference track. The ground truth position was estimated thanks to the time stamps assigned at the known positions; during the experiment, constant movement speed was considered. Therefore, ground truth positions can be defined on a line between two known points with desired time steps. Thus, it was possible to link position estimates in individual time steps with ground truth position estimates and calculate localization error for each time step.

Table 1. Localization error of the dead reckoning algorithm.

Localization Error [m]				
Minimum	Median	Mean	90%	Maximum
0.007	0.43	0.59	1.64	2.44

From the results presented in the table, it can be seen that the average localization error achieved by the implemented algorithm was around 0.6 m. Moreover, it is well known that localization error achieved by the dead reckoning algorithm increases with time due to the integration of error from sensors; therefore, this can be reduced if measurements are performed on multiple shorter tracks starting from a known position. We assume that the average localization error of 0.6 m will not have a significant impact on the localization accuracy, since it is significantly lower than the resolution of the radio map, which in our case is assumed to be 2 m. Therefore, in case the distance between the neighboring dynamic reference points is less than 4 m, the reference points will be processed by the RP merging algorithm described in the previous section. The algorithm will automatically merge points with a distance less than 2 m, and perform a similarity check for neighboring RPs with a distance up to 4 m.

With a further analysis of the achieved results, we have found out that in some cases, the track estimated by the implemented dead reckoning algorithm, although with reasonably small error, still crosses between the rooms through walls, as can be seen in Figure 5.

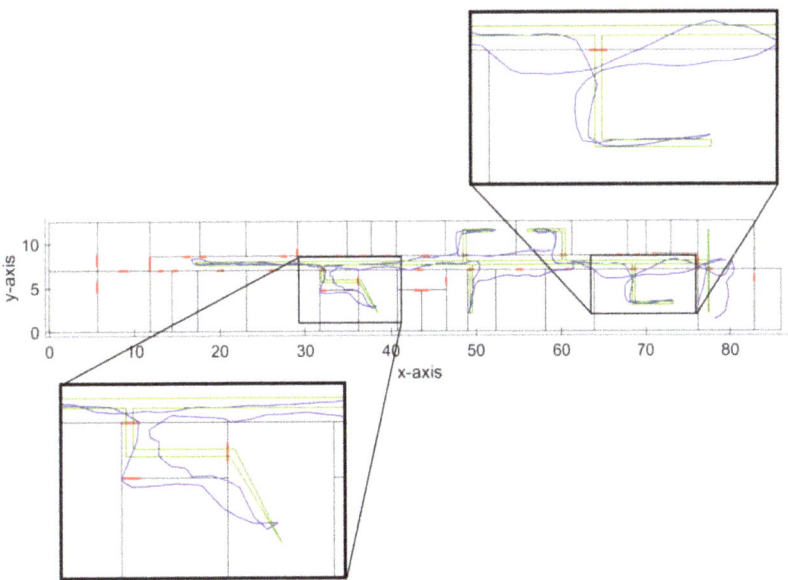

Figure 5. Detailed view of errors of the recovered track.

These localization errors might be a problem in cases when IMU data are used for real-time navigation; however, in an application focused on dynamic radio map construction, this can be neglected, since the localization error introduced by this phenomenon will still be reasonably low. Moreover, these errors mainly occurred when moving through the corridors, where multiple neighboring reference points are expected to be merged. This is because the user usually travels through corridors multiple times; therefore, more reference points are expected to appear in this area. Moreover, if corridors are passed multiple times by the user with different localization error, it can be expected that part of the localization error can be mitigated by the RP merging algorithm. These errors are likely to occur in different directions; therefore, the average position of merged reference points can be corrected. We assume that this problem of the dead reckoning algorithm can be further reduced by the modification of weights in the used particle filter, which will be investigated in the future.

Since in a fingerprinting-based localization system the position is estimated based on RSS comparison, it is important to have accurate RSS measurements for each reference point. Therefore, in order to prove the feasibility of the dynamic map creation, we have performed some static measurements on the positions of reference points and compared the RSS samples. The RSS values in static measurements were averaged from the 20 samples, since this process helps to reduce RSS fluctuations and is used during static radio map measurements. The difference of RSS calculated from static and dynamic measurements at seven reference points for all detected APs is presented in Table 2. The values in the table are based on a comparison of RSS samples from 86 APs, with signals from the same AP detected at different RPs treated as unique samples. The number of APs detected for RPs is not the same across the map; therefore, selected RPs had between 5 and 16 detected signals, representing RPs with poor as well as good coverage.

Table 2. Difference between static and dynamic RSS values.

Difference of RSS Values [dB]				
Minimum	Median	Mean	90%	Maximum
0.024	1.99	2.057	5.123	12.126

From the table, it can be seen that on average, the difference between RSS values from dynamic and static measurements is just above 2 dB, with 90% of differences lower than 5.2 dB, which might be caused by signal fluctuations. However, the maximum difference is above 12 dB, which seems to be high enough to cause localization errors. However, a number of such high RSS differences was less than 10% of all samples. It is important to note here that RSS measurements can also be affected by the orientation of the mobile device as well as attenuation caused by the human body. In some cases, the difference of RSS caused by the human body can be up to 10 dB for signals in the ISM (Industrial, Scientific and Medical) band [47], which is the frequency band used for 802.11b/g/n Wi-Fi signal transmission.

Based on the results we can conclude that the proposed solution for dynamic radio map creation was able to provide RSS measurements with reasonable accuracy, while significantly reduce the time required to perform the measurements required for radio map. When compared to static measurements of the radio map, it was possible to reduce the required time by 90%, therefore making it possible to perform multiple dynamic measurements and still reduce the required effort significantly.

4.2. Localization Performance

We have also evaluated the performance of the localization system with the use of dynamic radio map creation. The radio map used in the experiment was created using the dynamic map creation algorithm; in total, 66 reference points was created. The total number of unique detected APs was 97. The number of APs detected on a single reference point in the radio map was between 5 and 32, with an average of 16 APs per reference point.

To test the feasibility of a dynamic radio map, we have performed 38 position estimates at points that did not correspond to locations of reference points in the radio map. Localization was performed using NN, KNN and WKNN algorithms, and the achieved localization error is presented in Table 3; in this table, results achieved for the static map are presented as well. These results were achieved with the static radio map, with calibration measurements taken at reference points placed in a grid with 2-m separations. In the case of the static map, the position of the mobile device was estimated at 25 positions.

Table 3. Localization error.

		Localization Error [m]			
	Algorithm	Minimum	Mean	Median	Standard Deviation
Dynamic Map	NN	1.01	3.51	3.01	1.97
	KNN	0.43	4.05	3.39	2.64
	WKNN	0.59	3.77	2.9	2.46
Static Map	NN	0	2.91	3	2.28
	KNN	0.33	2.75	2.43	1.33
	WKNN	0.24	2.72	2.42	1.39

The results presented in Table 3 for the KNN and WKNN algorithms were achieved with $K = 3$, as this setting should in theory provide the optimal localization performance. However, when the dynamic radio map was used, it seems to perform worse than the NN algorithm. This is caused by the small density of reference points in the radio map. For further analysis, the CDF of localization errors achieved by localization algorithms with a dynamic radio map is presented in Figure 6.

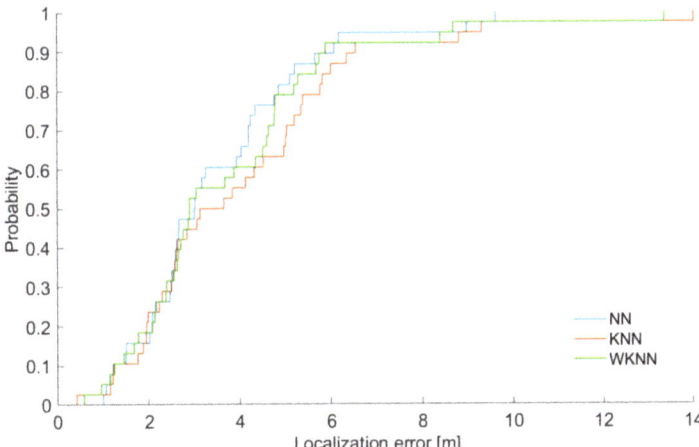

Figure 6. CDF of achieved localization errors.

It is important to note here that all algorithms performed better with the static radio map, which was expected since the radio map had a higher density of reference points. Interestingly enough, there was no significant difference in the median localization error for the NN algorithm, since in both cases, the median error was 3 m, while the difference in the median value was just around 0.5 m for the WKNN algorithm and approximately 0.9 m for the KNN algorithm. On the other hand, the difference in the mean localization error ranges from 0.6 m for the NN algorithm up to 1.3 m for the KNN algorithm.

The lack of difference in the median error, which is given by 50 percentiles of all achieved errors, for the NN algorithm can be caused by the fact that in some localization points, the distance to the nearest reference point in the radio map was similar in both scenarios. However, due to the lower density of the dynamic radio map, the average error of the NN algorithm was negatively affected by higher errors at higher percentiles.

Based on these results, we can conclude that the dynamic radio map can provide reasonably accurate position estimates, while significantly reducing the effort required to set up a fingerprinting localization system.

From the data presented in the figure, it is clear that under the given conditions, the NN algorithm outperformed both KNN and WKNN algorithms. However, it is clear that the difference between the localization results provided by all three algorithms is quite small. Nevertheless, the worst performance was achieved by the KNN algorithm. This is caused by the fact that in KNN algorithms selected K reference points to contribute to the final position estimate with the same weight, which is not ideal in the case when the mobile device is not placed in the center of gravity of the selected reference points.

It can be seen that the minimum error is between 0.4 m and 1 m, which is expected due to the limited resolution of the radio map in the experiment. It can be concluded that in 40% of location estimates, the performance of all algorithms was almost the same. The difference in positioning performance is clearer for 50% error where the KNN algorithm starts to perform significantly worse than other algorithms. It can be concluded that WKNN and NN algorithms achieved localization error below 6 m in 90% of position estimates, while the KNN algorithm achieved an error smaller than 6 m in 85% of estimates.

Since the radio map of the localization area is sparse, and thus, might be causing higher localization errors in the case when a larger number of reference points is used in the position estimation process, we also investigated the impact of the different number of considered reference points, i.e., different K values, on the localization accuracy; the achieved medial localization errors can be seen in Figure 7.

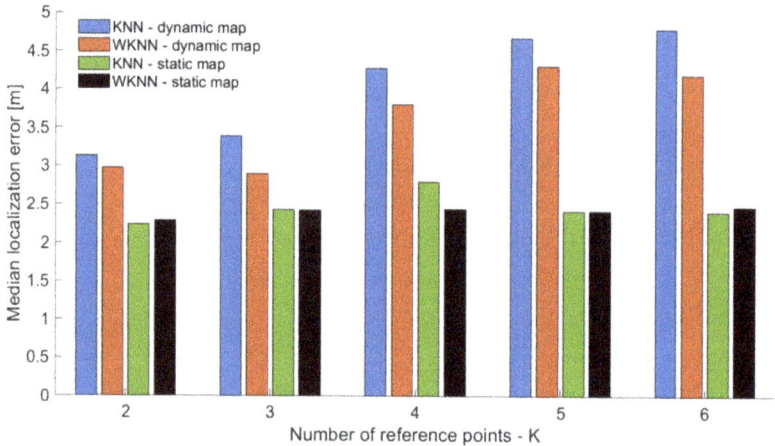

Figure 7. Impact of the number of reference points used for position estimation.

From the results presented in Figure 7, it can be seen that K, representing the number of reference points used in KNN and WKNN algorithms, has an impact on the localization accuracy. This holds for both the static and dynamic map; however, due to the low density of reference points in the dynamic radio map, the effect is different than in localization with a static map. When the dynamic radio map was used, the higher value of K leads to a higher localization error since reference points further from the actual position are selected and considered in the localization process. On the contrary, it can be seen that K has a smaller impact on the localization error with a static radio map.

When the median localization error of KNN and WKNN algorithms with a dynamic radio map is compared to the error achieved by the NN algorithm with a dynamic radio map, it can be concluded that NN outperformed the KNN algorithm for any value of K, since the KNN algorithm achieved the lowest error with $K = 2$ and the error was 3.13 m, while the NN algorithm achieved a median error of 3.02 m. On the other hand, the WKNN algorithm achieved a lower median error than the NN algorithm for both $K = 2$ and $K = 3$.

From the results, it can be seen that the best localization error was achieved for $K = 2$ for both dynamic and static radio maps. This is in contrast with the assumptions and results presented in previously published papers [17,20]. The fact that $K = 2$ achieved the lowest localization error for almost all cases, except WKNN with a dynamic radio map, might be given by the fact that experiments were performed in the building with relatively small offices and narrow corridors; therefore, each room had only two or four reference points. As a consequence, with higher K, some reference points were selected in incorrect rooms, and therefore, they had a negative impact on localization error.

Interestingly enough, the best results for each KNN and WKNN were achieved with a different number of considered reference points. The lowest median error was achieved for $K = 2$ and $K = 3$ for the KNN and WKNN algorithms, respectively. The low optimal value of K is given by the low density of the radio map; however, it is interesting to see that even with sparse reference points in the radio map, the achieved localization accuracy is close to the accuracy achieved with the radio map with reference points in the grid with 2 m spacing, which requires significantly higher effort and consumes significantly more time to perform calibration measurements for the radio map.

5. Conclusions

In the paper, the solution for a dynamic radio map collection was introduced. The proposed solution is based on simultaneous measurements of RSS from Wi-Fi networks and the collection of IMU data. The IMU data are processed by the dead reckoning algorithm with particle filtering, which helps to reduce the localization error of the recovered track. The proposed solution was tested in a real-world environment. The mean localization error of the recovered track was less than 0.6 m with a maximum error of approximately 2.5 m.

The algorithm for reference points merging that helped to process radio map data was introduced since some reference points generated form the PF-PDR algorithm were too close to each other and had too similar RSS measurements. Moreover, generated reference points were compared with static measurements. From the comparison, it can be concluded that the dynamic points had reasonably accurate RSS measurements with a mean RSS difference from static measurements around 2 dB. Therefore, we concluded that the dynamic radio map can be suitable for positioning.

In order to provide a proof of concept, the feasibility of the radio map was tested in the localization system with NN family algorithms. Interestingly enough, the achieved mean localization error was similar to results achieved in our previous experiments with a much denser radio map created using static measurements. Moreover, the NN algorithm achieved the lowest mean localization error and the lowest standards deviation among all three algorithms. This might be caused by the extremely low density of the reference points in the radio map. Therefore, the distance between the reference points selected by KNN or WKNN might have been too high, resulting in higher localization errors. This was also proved by the experiment aimed at the evaluation of the impact of the number of reference points used for position estimation in KNN and WKNN algorithms, where it can be seen that with higher K, the localization error of the KNN algorithm is increasing significantly, which is not the case when a radio map with a higher density of reference points was used.

Author Contributions: Conceptualization, J.M., J.R. and P.B.; methodology, J.M., J.R., P.B. and O.K.; investigation, J.R., J.M. and P.B.; writing and editing, data curation, visualization and formal analysis, J.M.; supervision, P.B.; funding acquisition, P.B., J.M. and O.K. All authors have read and agreed to the published version of the manuscript.

Funding: This work has been partially supported by the Slovak VEGA grant agency, Project No. 1/0626/19 "Research of mobile objects localization in IoT environment", the European Union's Horizon 2020 research and innovation program under the Marie Skłodowska-Curie grant agreement No 734331 and by project (2021/2204), Grant Agency of Excellence, Faculty of Informatics and Management, University of Hradec Kralove.

Institutional Review Board Statement: Not applicable.

Informed Consent Statement: Not applicable.

Data Availability Statement: The data presented in this study are available on request from the corresponding author. The data are not publicly available due to privacy restrictions.

Conflicts of Interest: The authors declare no conflict of interest. The funders had no role in the design of the study; in the collection, analyses or interpretation of data; in the writing of the manuscript, or in the decision to publish the results.

References

1. Basiri, A.; Lohan, E.S.; Moore, T.; Winstanley, A.; Peltola, P.; Hill, C.; Amirian, P.; Figueiredo e Silva, P. Indoor Location Based Services Challenges, Requirements and Usability of Current Solutions. *Comput. Sci. Rev.* **2017**, *24*, 1–12. [CrossRef]
2. Hammoud, A.; Deriaz, M.; Konstantas, D. Robust Ultrasound-Based Room-Level Localization System Using COTS Components. In Proceedings of the 2016 Fourth International Conference on Ubiquitous Positioning, Indoor Navigation and Location Based Services (UPINLBS), Shanghai, China, 2–4 November 2016; pp. 11–19.
3. Jabborov, F.; Cho, J. Image-Based Camera Localization Algorithm for Smartphone Cameras Based on Reference Objects. *Wirel. Pers. Commun.* **2020**, 1–17. [CrossRef]
4. Gligorić, K.; Ajmani, M.; Vukobratović, D.; Sinanović, S. Visible Light Communications-Based Indoor Positioning via Compressed Sensing. *IEEE Commun. Lett.* **2018**, *22*, 1410–1413. [CrossRef]
5. Montoliu, R.; Torres-Sospedra, J.; Belmonte, O. Magnetic Field Based Indoor Positioning Using the Bag of Words Paradigm. In Proceedings of the 2016 International Conference on Indoor Positioning and Indoor Navigation (IPIN), Alcala de Henares, Spain, 4–7 October 2016; pp. 1–7.
6. Mikov, A.; Panyov, A.; Kosyanchuk, V.; Prikhodko, I. Sensor Fusion For Land Vehicle Localization Using Inertial MEMS and Odometry. In Proceedings of the 2019 IEEE International Symposium on Inertial Sensors and Systems (INERTIAL), Naples, FL, USA, 1–5 April 2019; pp. 1–2.
7. Niu, C.; Chang, H. Research on Indoor Positioning on Inertial Navigation. In Proceedings of the 2019 IEEE 2nd International Conference on Computer and Communication Engineering Technology (CCET), Beijing, China, 16–18 August 2019; pp. 55–58.
8. Jimenez, A.R.; Seco, F.; Prieto, C.; Guevara, J. A Comparison of Pedestrian Dead-Reckoning Algorithms Using a Low-Cost MEMS IMU. In Proceedings of the 2009 IEEE International Symposium on Intelligent Signal Processing, Budapest, Hungary, 26–28 August 2009; pp. 37–42.
9. Xiao, J.; Zhou, Z.; Yi, Y.; Ni, L.M. A Survey on Wireless Indoor Localization from the Device Perspective. *ACM Comput. Surv.* **2016**, *49*, 25:1–25:31. [CrossRef]
10. Liu, G.-X.; Shi, L.-F.; Chen, S.; Wu, Z.-G. Focusing Matching Localization Method Based on Indoor Magnetic Map. *IEEE Sens. J.* **2020**, *20*, 10012–10020. [CrossRef]
11. Mayer, P.; Magno, M.; Schnetzler, C.; Benini, L. EmbedUWB: Low Power Embedded High-Precision and Low Latency UWB Localization. In Proceedings of the 2019 IEEE 5th World Forum on Internet of Things (WF-IoT), Limerick, Ireland, 15–18 April 2019; pp. 519–523.
12. Sahin, S.; Ozcan, H.; Kucuk, K. Smarttag: An Indoor Positioning System Based on Smart Transmit Power Scheme Using Active Tags. *IEEE Access* **2018**, *6*, 23500–23510. [CrossRef]
13. He, S.; Chan, S.-G. Wi-Fi Fingerprint-Based Indoor Positioning: Recent Advances and Comparisons. *IEEE Commun. Surv. Tutor.* **2016**, *18*, 466–490. [CrossRef]
14. Tam, W.K.; Tran, V.N. Propagation Modelling for Indoor Wireless Communication. *Electron. Commun. Eng. J.* **1995**, *7*, 221–228. [CrossRef]
15. Deasy, T.P.; Scanlon, W.G. Simulation or Measurement: The Effect of Radio Map Creation on Indoor WLAN-Based Localisation Accuracy. *Wirel. Pers. Commun.* **2007**, *42*, 563–573. [CrossRef]
16. Machaj, J.; Brida, P. Impact of Radio Map Simulation on Positioning in Indoor Environtment Using Finger Printing Algorithms. *ARPN J. Eng. Appl. Sci.* **2015**, *10*, 6404–6409.
17. Liu, H.; Darabi, H.; Banerjee, P.; Liu, J. Survey of Wireless Indoor Positioning Techniques and Systems. *IEEE Trans. Syst. ManCybern. Part C (Appl. Rev.)* **2007**, *37*, 1067–1080. [CrossRef]
18. Chen, Z.; Zou, H.; Yang, J.; Jiang, H.; Xie, L. WiFi Fingerprinting Indoor Localization Using Local Feature-Based Deep LSTM. *IEEE Syst. J.* **2020**, *14*, 3001–3010. [CrossRef]
19. Roos, T.; Myllymäki, P.; Tirri, H.; Misikangas, P.; Sievänen, J. A Probabilistic Approach to WLAN User Location Estimation. *Int. J. Wirel. Inf. Netw.* **2002**, *9*, 155–164. [CrossRef]
20. Honkavirta, V.; Perala, T.; Ali-Loytty, S.; Piche, R. A Comparative Survey of WLAN Location Fingerprinting Methods. In Proceedings of the Navigation and Communication 2009 6th Workshop on Positioning, Hannover, Germany , 19 March 2009; pp. 243–251.

21. Machaj, J.; Brida, P. Performance Comparison of Similarity Measurements for Database Correlation Localization Method. In *Proceedings of the Intelligent Information and Database Systems*; Nguyen, N.T., Kim, C.-G., Janiak, A., Eds.; Springer: Berlin/Heidelberg, Germany, 2011; pp. 452–461.

22. Li, B.; Salter, J.; Dempster, A.G.; Rizos, C. Indoor Positioning Techniques Based on Wireless LAN. In Proceedings of the Lan, First Ieee International Conference on Wireless Broadband and Ultra Wideband Communications, Sydney, NSW, Australia, 13–16 March 2006; pp. 13–16.

23. Bahl, P.; Padmanabhan, V.N. RADAR: An in-Building RF-Based User Location and Tracking System. In Proceedings of the IEEE INFOCOM 2000. Conference on Computer Communications. Nineteenth Annual Joint Conference of the IEEE Computer and Communications Societies (Cat. No.00CH37064), Tel Aviv, Israel , 26–30 March 2000; Volume 2, pp. 775–784.

24. Chai, X.; Yang, Q. Reducing the Calibration Effort for Probabilistic Indoor Location Estimation. *IEEE Trans. Mob. Comput.* **2007**, *6*, 649–662. [CrossRef]

25. Krumm, J.; Platt, J. *Minimizing Calibration Effort for an Indoor 802.11 Device Location Measurement System*; Microsoft Research: Redmond, WA, USA, 2003; p. 8.

26. Li, B.; Wang, Y.; Lee, H.K.; Dempster, A.; Rizos, C. Method for Yielding a Database of Location Fingerprints in WLAN. *IEEE Proc. Commun.* **2005**, *152*, 580. [CrossRef]

27. Kuo, S.; Tseng, Y. Discriminant Minimization Search for Large-Scale RF-Based Localization Systems. *IEEE Trans. Mob. Comput.* **2011**, *10*, 291–304. [CrossRef]

28. Lee, M.; Han, D. Voronoi Tessellation Based Interpolation Method for Wi-Fi Radio Map Construction. *IEEE Commun. Lett.* **2012**, *16*, 404–407. [CrossRef]

29. Khalajmehrabadi, A.; Gatsis, N.; Akopian, D. Structured Group Sparsity: A Novel Indoor WLAN Localization, Outlier Detection, and Radio Map Interpolation Scheme. *IEEE Trans. Veh. Technol.* **2017**, *66*, 6498–6510. [CrossRef]

30. Chowdappa, V.; Botella, C.; Samper-Zapater, J.J.; Martinez, R.J. Distributed Radio Map Reconstruction for 5G Automotive. *IEEE Intell. Transp. Syst. Mag.* **2018**, *10*, 36–49. [CrossRef]

31. Roger, S.; Botella, C.; Pérez-Solano, J.J.; Perez, J. Application of Radio Environment Map Reconstruction Techniques to Platoon-Based Cellular V2X Communications. *Sensors* **2020**, *20*, 2440. [CrossRef]

32. Gallagher, T.; Li, B.; Dempster, A.G.; Rizos, C. Database Updating through User Feedback in Fingerprint-Based Wi-Fi Location Systems. In Proceedings of the 2010 Ubiquitous Positioning Indoor Navigation and Location Based Service, Kirkkonummi, Finland, 14–15 October 2010; pp. 1–8.

33. Sun, Z.; Chen, Y.; Qi, J.; Liu, J. Adaptive Localization through Transfer Learning in Indoor Wi-Fi Environment. In Proceedings of the 2008 Seventh International Conference on Machine Learning and Applications, San Diego, CA, USA, 11–13 December 2008; pp. 331–336.

34. Wu, C.; Yang, Z.; Xiao, C. Automatic Radio Map Adaptation for Indoor Localization Using Smartphones. *IEEE Trans. Mob. Comput.* **2018**, *17*, 517–528. [CrossRef]

35. Xu, Z.; Huang, B.; Jia, B.; Li, W. Online Radio Map Update Based on a Marginalized Particle Gaussian Process. In Proceedings of the ICASSP 2019 - 2019 IEEE International Conference on Acoustics, Speech and Signal Processing (ICASSP), Brighton, UK, 12–17 May 2019; pp. 4624–4628.

36. Huang, B.; Xu, Z.; Jia, B.; Mao, G. An Online Radio Map Update Scheme for WiFi Fingerprint-Based Localization. *IEEE Internet Things J.* **2019**, *6*, 6909–6918. [CrossRef]

37. Batalla, J.M.; Mavromoustakis, C.X.; Mastorakis, G.; Xiong, N.N.; Wozniak, J. Adaptive Positioning Systems Based on Multiple Wireless Interfaces for Industrial IoT in Harsh Manufacturing Environments. *IEEE J. Sel. Areas Commun.* **2020**, *38*, 899–914. [CrossRef]

38. Atia, M.M.; Noureldin, A.; Korenberg, M.J. Dynamic Online-Calibrated Radio Maps for Indoor Positioning in Wireless Local Area Networks. *IEEE Trans. Mob. Comput.* **2013**, *12*, 1774–1787. [CrossRef]

39. Racko, J.; Brida, P.; Perttula, A.; Parviainen, J.; Collin, J. Pedestrian Dead Reckoning with Particle Filter for Handheld Smartphone. In Proceedings of the 2016 International Conference on Indoor Positioning and Indoor Navigation (IPIN), Alcala de Henares, Spain, 4–7 October 2016; pp. 1–7.

40. Khedr, M.E.; El-Sheimy, N. SBAUPT: Azimuth SBUPT for Frequent Full Attitude Correction of Smartphone-Based PDR. *IEEE Sens. J.* **2020**, 1-1. [CrossRef]

41. Kang, W.; Nam, S.; Han, Y.; Lee, S. Improved Heading Estimation for Smartphone-Based Indoor Positioning Systems. In Proceedings of the 2012 IEEE 23rd International Symposium on Personal, Indoor and Mobile Radio Communications - (PIMRC), Sydney, NSW, Australia, 9–12 September 2012; pp. 2449–2453.

42. Kemppi, P.; Rautiainen, T.; Ranki, V.; Belloni, F.; Pajunen, J. Hybrid Positioning System Combining Angle-Based Localization, Pedestrian Dead Reckoning and Map Filtering. In Proceedings of the 2010 International Conference on Indoor Positioning and Indoor Navigation, Zurich, Switzerland, 15–17 September 2010; pp. 1–7.

43. Hol, J.D.; Schon, T.B.; Gustafsson, F. On Resampling Algorithms for Particle Filters. In Proceedings of the 2006 IEEE Nonlinear Statistical Signal Processing Workshop, Cambridge, UK, 13–15 September 2006; pp. 79–82.

44. Ye, Y.; Wang, B. Indoor Radio Map Construction Based on Crowdsourced Fingerprint Splitting and Fitting. In Proceedings of the 2017 IEEE Wireless Communications and Networking Conference (WCNC), San Francisco, CA, USA, 19–22 March 2017; pp. 1–6.

45. Pelant, J.; Tlamsa, Z.; Benes, V.; Polak, L.; Kaller, O.; Bolecek, L.; Kufa, J.; Sebesta, J.; Kratochvil, T. BLE Device Indoor Localization Based on RSS Fingerprinting Mapped by Propagation Modes. In Proceedings of the 2017 27th International Conference Radioelektronika (RADIOELEKTRONIKA), Brno, Czech Republic, 19–20 April 2017; pp. 1–5.
46. Račko, J.; Machaj, J.; Brída, P. Wi-Fi Fingerprint Radio Map Creation by Using Interpolation. *Procedia Eng.* **2017**, *192*, 753–758. [CrossRef]
47. Januszkiewicz, Ł. Analysis of Human Body Shadowing Effect on Wireless Sensor Networks Operating in the 2.4 GHz Band. *Sensors* **2018**, *18*, 3412. [CrossRef] [PubMed]

sensors

MDPI

Article

Wi-Fi-Based Location-Independent Human Activity Recognition via Meta Learning

Xue Ding [1], **Ting Jiang** [1], **Yi Zhong** [2,*], **Yan Huang** [3] and **Zhiwei Li** [1]

[1] School of Information and Communication Engineering, Beijing University of Posts and Telecommunications, Beijing 100876, China; dxue@bupt.edu.cn (X.D.); tjiang@bupt.edu.cn (T.J.); lzw_fire@bupt.edu.cn (Z.L.)

[2] School of Information and Electronics, Beijing Institute of Technology, Beijing 100081, China

[3] Global Big Data Technologies Centre (GBDTC), School of Electrical and Data Engineering, University of Technology Sydney, Sydney, NSW 2007, Australia; Yan.Huang-3@student.uts.edu.au

* Correspondence: yi.zhong@bit.edu.cn

Abstract: Wi-Fi-based device-free human activity recognition has recently become a vital underpinning for various emerging applications, ranging from the Internet of Things (IoT) to Human–Computer Interaction (HCI). Although this technology has been successfully demonstrated for location-dependent sensing, it relies on sufficient data samples for large-scale sensing, which is enormously labor-intensive and time-consuming. However, in real-world applications, location-independent sensing is crucial and indispensable. Therefore, how to alleviate adverse effects on recognition accuracy caused by location variations with the limited dataset is still an open question. To address this concern, we present a location-independent human activity recognition system based on Wi-Fi named WiLiMetaSensing. Specifically, we first leverage a Convolutional Neural Network and Long Short-Term Memory (CNN-LSTM) feature representation method to focus on location-independent characteristics. Then, in order to well transfer the model across different positions with limited data samples, a metric learning-based activity recognition method is proposed. Consequently, not only the generalization ability but also the transferable capability of the model would be significantly promoted. To fully validate the feasibility of the presented approach, extensive experiments have been conducted in an office with 24 testing locations. The evaluation results demonstrate that our method can achieve more than 90% in location-independent human activity recognition accuracy. More importantly, it can adapt well to the data samples with a small number of subcarriers and a low sampling rate.

Keywords: Wi-Fi sensing; human activity recognition; location-independent; meta learning; metric learning; few-shot learning

check for updates

Citation: Ding, X.; Jiang, T.; Zhong, Y.; Huang, Y.; Li, Z. Wi-Fi-Based Location-Independent Human Activity Recognition via Meta Learning. *Sensors* **2021**, *21*, 2654. https://doi.org/10.3390/s21082654

Academic Editor: Peter Brida

Received: 1 March 2021
Accepted: 5 April 2021
Published: 9 April 2021

1. Introduction

Human Activity Recognition (HAR) has been considered as an indispensable technology in many Human–Computer Interaction (HCI) applications, such as smart home, health care, security surveillance, virtual reality, and location-based services (LBS) [1,2]. Traditional human activity sensing approaches are the wearable sensor-based methods [3,4] and the camera (vision)-based methods [5,6]. While promising and widely used, these device-based approaches suffer from respective drawbacks, making them fail to be suitable for all the application scenarios. For instance, the wearable sensor-based method works only if the users are carrying the sensors, such as smartphones, smart shoes, or smartwatches with built-in inertial measurement units (IMUs), including gyroscope, accelerometer, magnetometer, etc. However, it is inconvenient for constant use. In addition, although the camera (vision)-based method could potentially achieve satisfactory accuracy, it is limited by certain shortcomings, such as privacy leakage, line-of-sight (LOS) and light conditions, etc. Moreover, both methods require dedicated devices, which are high cost. In addition, the durability of the devices is another critical factor that should be considered.

223

Recently, Wi-Fi-based human activity recognition has attracted extensive attention in both academia and industry, becoming one of the most popular device-free sensing (DFS) technologies [7,8]. Compared with the other wireless signals, such as Frequency Modulated Continuous Wave (FMCW) [9,10], millimeter-wave (MMW) [11,12], and Ultra Wide Band (UWB) [13–17], Wi-Fi possesses the most prominent and potential advantage, which is that it is ubiquitous in people's daily lives. Leveraging the commercial off-the-shelf (COTS) devices, Wi-Fi-based human activity recognition obviates the need for additional specialized hardware. Beyond this, it also has the same merits as other wireless signals, including the capability to operate in darkness and non-line-of-sight (NLOS) situations while providing better protection of users' privacy in the meantime. As a result, research on Wi-Fi-based human activity recognition has proliferated rapidly over the past decade [18–21].

Previous attempts involving Wi-Fi-based sensing yielded great achievements, such as E-eyes [22], CARM [23], etc. However, the major challenge referring to the generalization performance of the approaches and systems has not been fully explored and solved. For instance, when deployed in a room, the system must work well in each location rather than a specified location. Location-independent sensing is one of the most necessary generalization capabilities. It can also be regarded as the ability of a method to transfer among different locations. Note that this is a crucial factor to determine whether the technology can be commercialized. According to the principle of wireless perception, it is not difficult to find that human activities in different locations have different effects on signal transmission. Specifically, activities conducted by people in different locations will change the path of wireless signal propagation in different ways, leading to diverse multipath superimposed signals at the receiver. It is worth noting that these signals have different data distributions, which can be treated as different domains. Hence, it is clear that the human activity recognition model trained in a specific domain will not work well in the other domains. The most obvious solution is to provide abundant data for each domain to learn the characteristics of activities in the different domains. However, it is labor-intensive, time-consuming, and with poor user experience to obtain a large amount of data in practical applications. Therefore, how to utilize as few samples as possible to solve the problem of location-independent perception to achieve outstanding generalization performance is desired.

Some solutions have been proposed to solve the above problems, and remarkable progress has been made, which lays a solid foundation for realizing location-independent sensing with good generalization ability. The solutions fall into the following four categories: (1) Generate virtual data samples for each location [24], (2) Separate the activity signal from the background [25,26], (3) Extract domain-independent features [27], and (4) Domain adaptation and transfer learning. Some approaches involving other domains (such as environment, orientation, and person) can also be grouped into these four categories. However, they pay less attention to location-independent sensing [28–31]. Although the above methods promote the process of device-free human activity recognition from academic research to industrial application, there are still some limitations. WiAG [24] requires the user to hold a smartphone in hand for one of the training sample collections in order to estimate the parameters. Widar 3.0 [27] is limited by link numbers and complex parameter estimation methods. FALAR [25] benefits from its development of a new Open-Wrt firmware which can get fine-grained Channel State Information (CSI) of all the 114 subcarriers, improving data resolution. Similarly, high transmission rates of the perception signal (such as 2500 packets/s in Lu et al. [26]) can also boost the resolution. As the author described by Zhou et al. [30], a low sampling rate may miss some key information, which accounts for the deterioration in the system performance. However, using shorter packets helps reduce latency and has less impacts on communication. The detailed discussions about the effect of different sampling rates on the sensing accuracy can be found in the evaluation in [27,30]. In summary, a location-independent method that can adapt to data with a small number of antennas and subcarriers as well as a small data transmission rate is required.

This work aims to realize device-free location-independent human activity recognition using as few samples as possible. It means that the model trained with the source domain data samples can perform well on the target domain with only very few data samples. We describe our task as a few-shot learning problem, improving the performance of the model in the unseen domain when its amount of available data are relatively small [32]. The task is also consistent with meta learning, whose core idea is learning to learn [33]. They have been successfully applied in a variety of fields to solve classification tasks. Inspired by the typical meta learning approach matching network, we apply the learning method obtained from the source domain to the target domain by means of metric learning [34,35]. Assuming that, although there is no stable feature that can describe a class of actions well, we can still identify its category through maximizing the inter-class variations and minimizing intra-class differences. Judging the category of a sample by calculating the distance can be regarded as a learning method. To realize location-independent sensing, we expect to learn not only the discriminative features representation specific to our task but also the distance function and metric relationships that can infer the label with a confident margin.

In this paper, we first comprehensively and visually investigate the effects of the same activity at different locations on wireless signal transmission. We also analyze the signal received in different antennas and subcarriers with different sampling rates. Moreover, we discuss how different locations affect signal transmission without any other variable influence factors by utilizing data collected from the anechoic chamber. Then, we propose a device-free location-independent human activity recognition system named WiLiMetaSensing, which is based on meta learning to enable few-shot learning sensing. Convolutional Neural Network (CNN) and Long Short-Term Memory (LSTM) are introduced for feature representation. Unlike the traditional feature extraction process for Wi-Fi signal based on LSTM, in this paper, the memory capacity of LSTM is utilized to retain the valuable information of the samples from all the activities. In addition, an attention mechanism-based metric learning method is used to learn the metric relations of the activity with the same or different categories. Finally, extensive experiments are conducted to explore the recognition performance of the proposed system. The evaluation refers to the property involving single location, mixed locations, and location-independent sensing. Unlike existing evaluations, we reduce the sampling rate, the number of subcarriers, and antennas. Experiments show that WiLiMetaSensing achieves satisfying results with robust performance in a variety of situations.

2. Preliminary

2.1. Channel State Information

The Wi-Fi-based wireless sensing principle is leveraging the influence of perceptual targets on the transmitted signal for recognition. During the transmission from the transmitter (TX) to the receiver (RX), the wireless signal would be refracted, reflected, and scattered when encountering obstacles and objects (dynamic or static), which results in the superposition of multipath signals at the receiver. In a Multiple Input Multiple Output (MIMO) and Orthogonal Frequency Division Multiplexing (OFDM)-based Wi-Fi communication system, this process can be described by fine-grained CSI. In recent years, the physical layer information of some commercial off-the-shelf (COTS) Wi-Fi devices has gradually become available, making it possible to obtain CSI directly [36]. Compared with coarse-grained Received Signal Strength Indicator (RSSI), CSI provides richer channel characteristics.

Letting y and x respectively denote the received signal and transmitting signal, the relation between y and x can be modeled as:

$$y = Hx + N \tag{1}$$

where H is the channel matrix, and N is the noise vector. H completely describes the characteristics of the channel. The process of calculating the channel matrix is called channel estimation. H can be represented in either channel frequency response (CFR) in frequency domain or channel impulse response (CIR) in time domain. The former is given by

$$\left\|H_{ij}(f_k)\right\|e^{j\angle H_{ij}(f_k)}, k \in [1, N_S], i \in [1, N_t], j \in [1, N_r] \qquad (2)$$

where $H_{ij}(f_k)$ is a complex number, which denotes the CSI corresponding to the subcarrier k whose carrier frequency is f_k. $\left\|H_{ij}(f_k)\right\|$ and $\angle H_{ij}(f_k)$ denote amplitude and phase, respectively. i and j are the index of TX and RX antennas, respectively. N_t and N_r stand for the number of antennas at the TX and RX, respectively. N_s represents the number of subcarriers for each pair of transceiver antennas.

2.2. Data Acquisition

To thoroughly analyze the challenges in Wi-Fi-based human activity recognition and evaluate the performance of the method proposed in this paper, we built a dataset in an office environment. The data collection scene is shown in Figure 1. Specifically, Linux 802.11n CSI Tool based on Intel 5300 Network Interface Card (NIC) is leveraged to acquire the raw CSI data [36]. The TX and RX work on 802.11n and operate on a 5 GHz frequency band with a bandwidth of 20 MHz. They are both equipped with three antennas. In addition, 30 subcarriers from each TX-RX pair can be obtained. Thus, there are $3 \times 3 \times 30$ subcarriers in total. We can only use the signal collected from part of the antennas. The data transmission rate is 200 frames/s. We can also subsample the signal measurement to verify the performance of the system at low sampling rates.

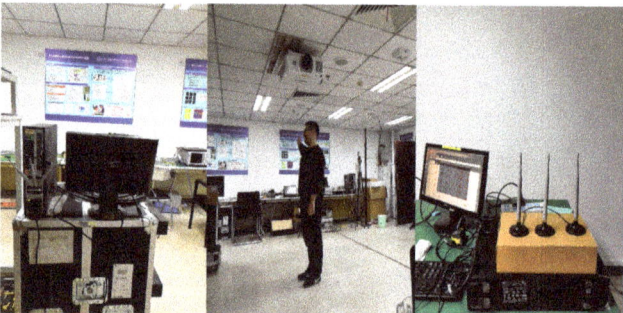

Figure 1. Data collection experimental scene in the office.

Table 1 shows the predefined four activities conducted by six volunteers (five males and one female), whose ages range from 23 to 30. We collected the data in a cluttered office environment with lots of tables, chairs, and experimental facilities. The room size is approximately 6 m $\times$ 8 m. The distance between the antennas of the TX and the RX is 4 m, and the antennas were both fixed at 1.2 m above the floor. The samples are collected at 24 different locations within a region between the transceivers. The specified location layout is given in Figure 2. The distance between adjacent positions is approximately 0.6 m. We collect 50 samples for each activity at each location for each person. Since the initial sampling rate is 200 frames/s, and the actual duration of the actions is 3.5~4 s, namely 700~800 frames, we take 750 frames as a sample.

Table 1. Predefined activities.

Mark	Activity
O	Draw a circle with right hand
X	Draw a cross with right hand
PO	Lift up and lay down two arms
UP	Push and open with two arms

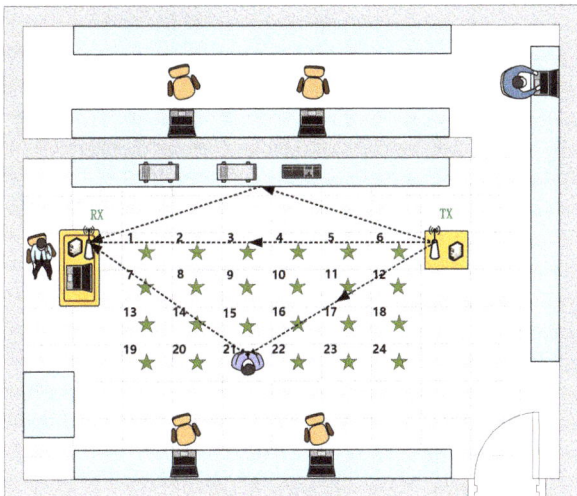

Figure 2. The layout of data collection locations.

To further demonstrate the influence of activities at different locations on the transmitted signal, we also conducted some experiments in a half-wave anechoic chamber. It is a six-sided box with a shielded design, covering the electromagnetic wave absorbing material inside except for the floor. It simulates an ideal open field situation, in which the site has an infinitely large, well conductive ground plane. In a semi-anechoic chamber, since the ground is not covered with absorbent material, the reflected path will be existing, so that the signal received by the receiving antenna will be the sum of the direct and reflected path signals. More importantly, without the influence of the environment and the other same frequency wireless interference, the same activity conducted by the same person at different locations can effectively reflect the characteristics affected by the locations. The data collection scene is shown in Figure 3. Four activities in Table 1 are conducted by one person. The distance between the antennas of the TX and the RX is 3 m, and the antennas were both fixed at 1.1 m above the floor. The samples are collected at five different locations whose coordinates are (0, 0), (0.6 m, 0.6 m), (0.6 m, −0.6 m), (−0.6 m, −0.6 m), (−0.6 m, 0.6 m). (0,0) is the midpoint of the line between the TX and the RX.

2.3. Problem Analysis

To illustrate the issues and challenges of location-independent human activity recognition using Wi-Fi signals, we comprehensively analyze the CSI measurements involving different human activities at distinct locations collected in the office and anechoic chamber.

As shown in Figure 4, at a fixed location in both two environments, CSI amplitudes of the received signal for four different activities own different waveforms, leading to diverse characteristic patterns. Furthermore, it can be observed that the two different samples of the same activity seem to have a very similar variation tendency. These are the fundamentals of wireless sensing.

Figure 3. Data collection experimental scene in the anechoic chamber.

As illustrated in Figure 5, the measured signals possess varying CSI amplitudes for the same activity at different locations. Particularly in the anechoic chamber, other variables were eliminated as far as possible except for the locations, which more clearly reflects the influence of different positions on the signal transmission. As can be seen, although it is relatively easy to identify the categories of human activities by translating the CSI patterns at a single location, it may not be possible to ensure good classification accuracy for location-independent sensing. A practicable solution is to minimize the distance of the same activity in different locations, while maximizing the distance between different actions, and apply this learned metric relationship to the target domain. For this reason, a metric learning-based approach is selected for location-independent human activity recognition.

In order to further explore the influence of activities on signal transmission, we illustrate the distinction of the signal between the empty environment and the activity-influenced environment. The three-dimensional maps of the signal are shown in Figure 6, which indicate that the fluctuation of the signal in an empty environment and activity-influenced environment. Each point on the stereogram represents the amplitude of signal corresponding to the frame and subcarrier. From the figure, we can see a higher level of chaos in the three-dimensional waveform of the activity-influenced environment than the empty environment.

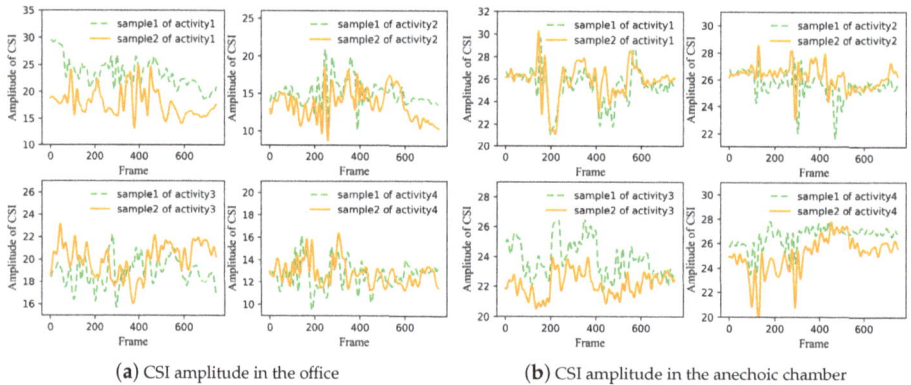

(**a**) CSI amplitude in the office   (**b**) CSI amplitude in the anechoic chamber

Figure 4. CSI amplitude of four different activities at the same location in two experimental scenes. (**a**) CSI amplitude in the office. (**b**) CSI amplitude in the anechoic chamber. Two curves in each subgraph are two samples for the same activity. The horizontal axis of each subgraph represents the frame, the ordinate of each subgraph indicates amplitude of CSI.

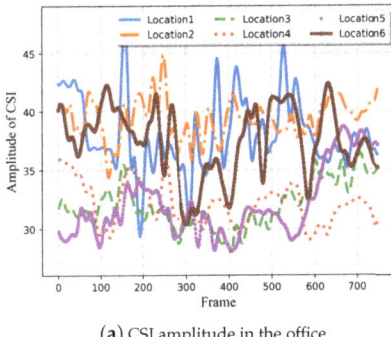
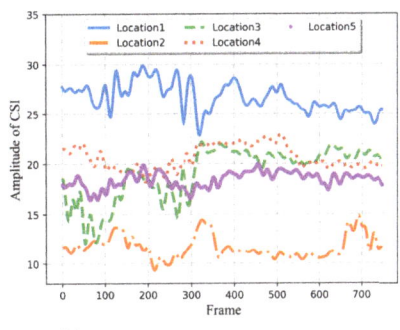

(**a**) CSI amplitude in the office   (**b**) CSI amplitude in the anechoic chamber

Figure 5. CSI amplitude of the same activity at different locations in two experimental scenes. (**a**) CSI amplitude in the office. (**b**) CSI amplitude in the anechoic chamber. Each curve in each subgraph represents an activity sample at one location.

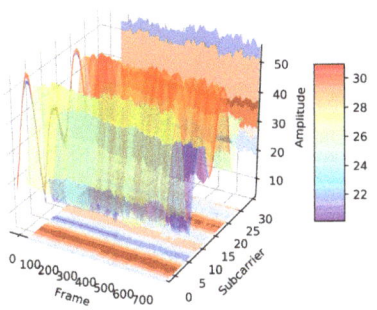
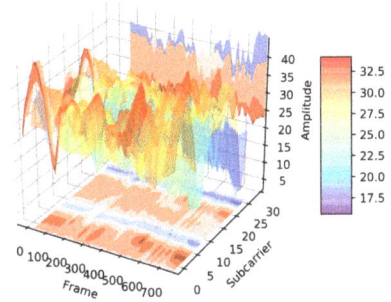

(**a**) Three-dimensional map of signal in empty environment.   (**b**) Three-dimensional map of signal in activity-influenced environment

Figure 6. Three-dimensional map of the signal in empty environment and activity-influenced environment. (**a**) Three-dimensional map of signal in empty environment. (**b**) Three-dimensional map of signal in activity-influenced environment. The three coordinate axes are frame-axis, subcarrier-axis, and amplitude-axis, respectively. The three-dimensional waveform can be mapped to three planes, including the planes parallel to the subcarrier-axis and frame-axis, and perpendicular to the amplitude-axis.

To demonstrate the difference more clearly, Figure 7 shows the two-dimensional maps corresponding to the two vertical planes in Figure 6. As can be seen in Figure 7a, compared with the activity-influenced environment, the amplitude of each subcarrier is almost constant in the empty environment. In other words, the signal waveform changes smoothly with time when there is no human activity interference, while it changes obviously when the signal transmission is affected by human activity. In addition, the activity has a great influence on some subcarriers and a relatively small influence on others.

In Figure 7b, we name the curves channel waveforms, which could reflect the channel state to some extent, revealing the states of each subcarrier. The curve will change with the influence of the activity and the surrounding environment, such as other signal sources, interior layout, and furnishings, especially obstacles on the line-of-sight path. In the left figure, the amplitude of each subcarrier is almost unchanged within 3.5 s, while, in the right figure, the amplitude of each subcarrier varies to different degrees. In each environment, there is a basic channel waveform describing the channel situation (shown as the subgraph on the left of Figure 7b). After being affected by human activity, the curve generates an additional perturbation based on the basic waveform (shown as the subgraph on the right side of Figure 7b). The thickness of the whole curve represents the fluctuation degree of CSI subcarriers, which shows the extent to which human activity and the surrounding environment affect the transmission of signals. Therefore, we should pay more attention to the added activity-related changes. Deep learning methods can be used to extract action-specified characteristics.

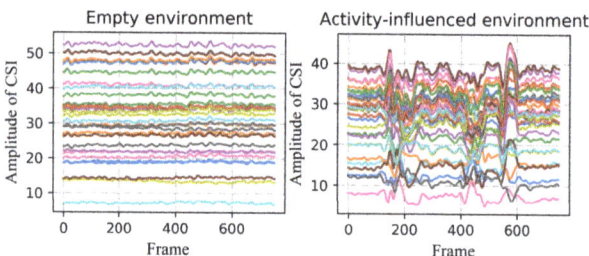

(**a**) Signal waveforms in empty environment and activity-influenced environment.

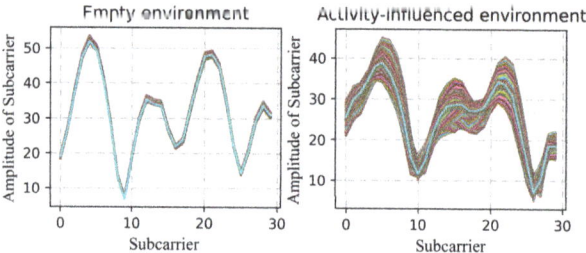

(**b**) Channel waveforms in empty environment and activity-influenced environment.

Figure 7. Two-dimensional map of signal in empty environment and activity-influenced environment. (**a**) The horizontal axis represents the frame/packet, the ordinate indicates the amplitude of CSI. Each curve in the figure represents one of the 30 subcarriers; (**b**) the horizontal axis represents the subcarrier index, the ordinate indicates the amplitude of the subcarriers. Each curve in the figure represents one of the 750 curves, which illustrate the amplitude change of each subcarrier within 3.5 s (The sampling rate is 200 frames/s).

We also investigate the CSI measurements in different TX-RX antenna pairs. As shown in Figure 8, we can see it intuitively, the three subgraphs of each row vary largely, and the three subgraphs of each column are similar in amplitude changes, with a horizontal shift, which can be explained by the phase shift caused by the delay of different transmitting antennas arriving at the receiving antenna. Therefore, the information carried by $1 \times 3 \times 30$ subcarriers from one transmit antenna and three receive antennas is enough for a sample description. Although more subcarriers cover richer information, it is more desirable to extract sufficient activity characteristics from only one transceiver antenna pair, which can effectively reduce computing costs and obviate the need for the number of antennas. In this paper, we hope that the proposed method can be applied to data samples with a small number of antennas and subcarriers.

In this part, we study the signal affected by human activity with different sampling rates. As shown in Figure 9, as the sampling rate decreases, the signal becomes smoother. It may remove some of the noise, but, more importantly, it will lose some of the details referring to the activity. In this paper, while realizing the location-independent human activity recognition, we try our best to ensure the sensing performance of the data samples with a small sampling rate.

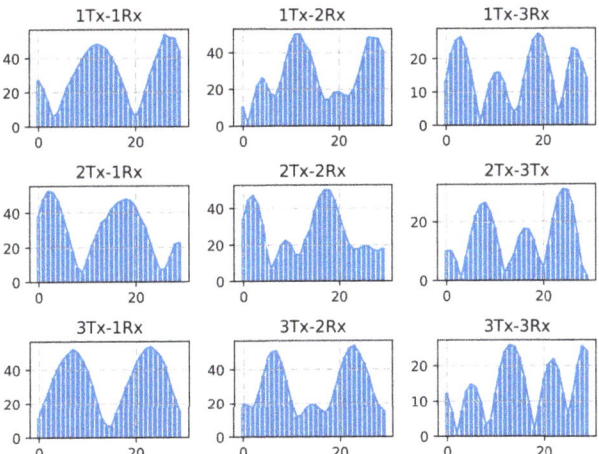

Figure 8. Amplitude of subcarrier of nine TX-RX antenna pairs.

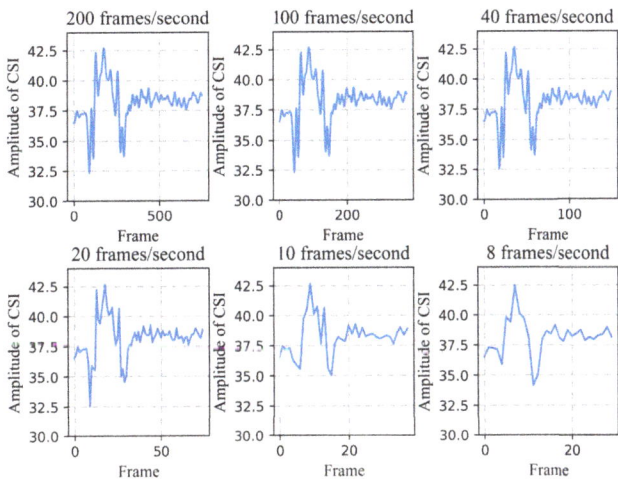

Figure 9. CSI Amplitude of the human activity with different sampling rates.

3. WiLiMetaSensing

In this section, we provide a detailed introduction to the proposed WiLiMetaSensing system. We first present the system overview. Then, a CNN-LSTM-based feature representation method is described. Finally, an attention mechanism enhanced metric learning-based human activity recognition method is presented.

3.1. System Overview

The workflow of the location-independent human activity recognition system WiLiMetaSensing is shown in Figure 10, which mainly consists of four parts, including data collection, data preprocessing, feature representation, and model training/testing. In the data collection phase, we collect the raw CSI measurements, which describe the changes in the environment. In the data preprocessing step, the amplitude is calculated by the raw complex CSI. Due to the noisy raw data, a 5-order lowpass Butterworth filter is utilized for denoising. Beyond that, the collected data are divided into samples with the size of time × subcarrier, which indicates the number of frames corresponding to an activity multiplied by the number of subcarriers. Then, we map the data samples to high dimensional embedding space to fulfill the feature representation through CNN and LSTM. Finally, in order to achieve location-independent perception with as few samples as possible, regarding a few-shot learning problem, the human activity perceptive method based on metric learning is proposed. Subsequently, we will introduce the system in detail.

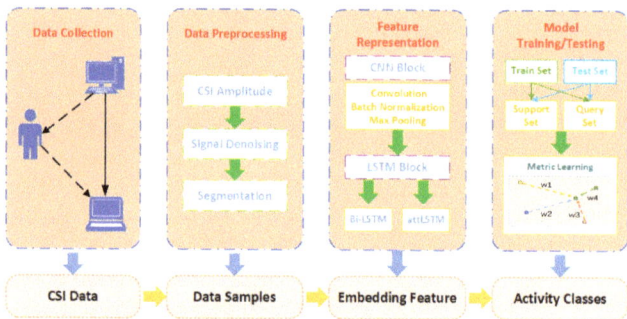

Figure 10. The workflow of WiLiMetaSensing.

3.2. CNN-LSTM-Based Feature Representation

In this section, in order to extract activity-specified and location-independent features from input samples for few-shot learning, deep learning methods, including CNN and LSTM, are introduced for feature representation shown as Figure 11. Following the learning strategy of meta learning, the data samples are divided into two parts, including the support set and the query set with the same data selection strategy, which will be presented in detail in the next section.

We use x_i and $\hat{x}$ to denote the samples from the above two sets. $S = \{x_i\}, i \in 1, \ldots, n \times k$ indicates the support set which is made up of samples from n categories, and k samples for each class. $g(x_i, S)$ and $f(\hat{x}, S)$ are modeled to achieve feature representation of x_i and $\hat{x}$ fully conditioned on the support set, respectively.

The feature embedding function $g(x_i, S)$ for each sample x_i can be expressed as:

$$g'(x_i) = CNN(x_i) \tag{3}$$

$$\overrightarrow{h_i}, \overrightarrow{c_i} = \overrightarrow{LSTM}(g'(x_i), \overrightarrow{h}_{i-1}, \overrightarrow{c}_{i-1}) \tag{4}$$

$$\overleftarrow{h_i}, \overleftarrow{c_i} = \overleftarrow{LSTM}(g'(x_i), \overleftarrow{h}_{i-1}, \overleftarrow{c}_{i-1}) \tag{5}$$

$$g(x_i, S) = \overrightarrow{h_i} \oplus \overleftarrow{h_i} + g'(x_i) \tag{6}$$

The samples are first mapped to high-dimensional embedding space through CNN to capture the feature in subcarrier and time dimensions. Specifically, the embedding model is made up of a cascade of blocks, each including a convolutional layer, a batch normalization layer, and a MaxPooling layer, followed by a fully-connected layer. The activation function is a rectified linear unit (ReLU).

The samples embedded by CNN form a sequence, which serves as the input of bidirectional long short-term memory (Bi-LSTM). It consists of a forward propagation LSTM and a backward propagation LSTM. The basic structure of LSTM is shown in Figure 12, which consists of three control gates, including an input gate i_t, a forget gate f_t, an output gate o_t. In addition, a memory cell c_t and a hidden unit h_t are also significant components. With the current input x_t, the hidden state h_{t-1}, and cell state c_{t-1} at time $t-1$, the LSTM parameters at timestep t can be calculated as follows:

$$f_t = \sigma\left(W_f[h_{t-1}, x_t] + b_f\right) \tag{7}$$

$$i_t = \sigma(W_i[h_{t-1}, x_t] + b_i) \tag{8}$$

$$o_t = \sigma(W_o[h_{t-1}, x_t] + b_o) \tag{9}$$

$$\tilde{C}_t = \tanh(W_c[h_{t-1}, x_t] + b_C) \tag{10}$$

$$C_t = f_t \times C_{t-1} + i_t \times \tilde{C}_t \tag{11}$$

$$h_t = o_t \times \tanh(C_t) \tag{12}$$

where W_f, W_i, W_o are the weight and b_f, b_i, b_o are the bias of the three gates. σ and tanh denote sigmoid and hyperbolic tangent activation functions, respectively. $\times$ stands for the element-wise multiplication.

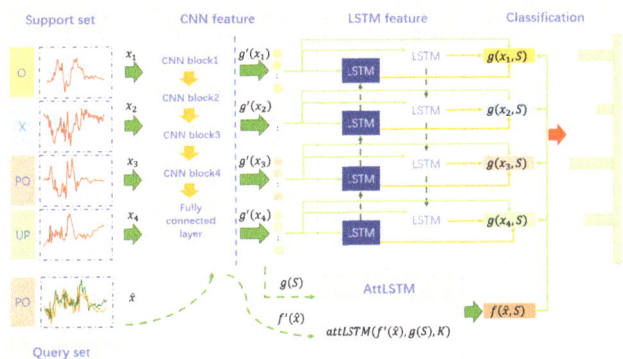

Figure 11. The architectures of human activity recognition method.

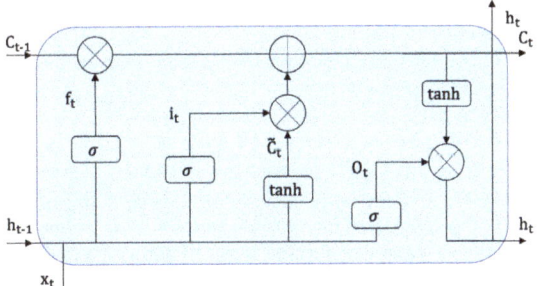

Figure 12. The structure of the LSTM cell.

Through the forget gate, the previous memory cell can be selectively forgotten. The input gate controls the current input, while the output gate determines how the memory unit is converted to a hidden unit. However, the LSTM network processes the sequential data in one direction resulting in only partial categories of features that can be utilized. Therefore, the Bi-LSTM is leveraged to merge the information from two directions of the sequence. The final hidden vector of the Bi-LSTM at the $t - th$ moment can be expressed as:

$$h_t = \overrightarrow{h}_t \oplus \overleftarrow{h}_t \tag{13}$$

where $\oplus$ is the concatenation operation, $\overrightarrow{h}_t$ and $\overleftarrow{h}_t$ are the outputs (hidden vector) of the forward LSTM and the backward LSTM, respectively.

Through the above CNN-LSTM feature representation, we aim to leverage the common characteristics of different activities to calibrate the high-dimensional embedding of each sample. In other words, in the feature representation of each class sample, the information of other class samples can be used. As we all know, the received CSI measurements contain not only dynamic activity information but also static environment information and varying location information. Therefore, there are some common features about the background for different samples in each category. We hope that the model can learn and memorize the common characteristics of different types of activities, as well as the distinct information of different categories. The distinct information can be utilized to increase the distance of inter-class, and reduce the distance of intra-class.

The embedding function $f(\hat{x}, S)$ for a query sample $\hat{x}$ is defined as follows:

$$f(\hat{x}, S) = attLSTM\big(f'(\hat{x}), g(S), K\big) \tag{14}$$

where f' is a neural network, the same as g'. K denotes the number of "processing" steps following work from Vinyals et al. [37]. $g(S)$ represents the embedding function g applied to each element x_i from the set S. Thus, the state after k processing steps is as follows:

$$\hat{h}_k, c_k = LSTM\big(f'(\hat{x}), [h_{k-1}, r_{k-1}], c_{k-1}\big) \tag{15}$$

$$h_k = \hat{h}_k + f'(\hat{x}) \tag{16}$$

$$r_{k-1} = \sum_{i=1}^{|S|} a\big(h_{k-1}, g(x_i)\big) g(x_i) \tag{17}$$

$$a\big(h_{k-1}, g(x_i)\big) = soft\max\Big(h_{k-1}^T g(x_i)\Big) \tag{18}$$

Noting that the $LSTM(x, h, c)$ in both g and f follows the same LSTM implementation defined by Sutskever et al. [38].

3.3. Metric Learning-Based Human Activity Recognition

Our location-independent activity recognition task can be described as a few-shot learning problem and a meta learning task. Meta learning trains the model from a large number of tasks and learns faster on new tasks with a small amount of data. Unlike the traditional meta learning and few-shot learning methods, which apply the model learned from some classes (source domain) to the other new classes (target domain) with very few samples from the new classes, our work is intended to utilize the model to the data with the same label, but with different data distribution.

Meta learning includes training process and testing process, which is called meta-training and meta-testing. In our task, samples in part of locations are selected as the source domain data, while samples from other locations are the target domain data. Both the source domain data and the target domain data are classified into the support set and query set with the same data set selection strategy.

Assuming that there is a source domain sample set S with n classes, and a target domain set T with the same n classes. We randomly select support sets $S' = \{(x_i, y_i)\}_{i=1}^{n \times m}$ and $T' = \{(x_i, y_i)\}_{i=1}^{n \times k}$, query sets $S'' = \{(\hat{x}, \hat{y})\}_{i=1}^{n \times l}$ and $T'' = \{(\hat{x}, \hat{y})\}_{i=1}^{n \times t}$ from S and T datasets. m and l, k, and t are the number of samples picked from each class of source domain and target domain, respectively. This is the so-called k-shot learning. More precisely, leveraging the support set S' from the source domain, we learn a function which can map test samples $\hat{x}$ from S'' to a probability distribution $P(\hat{y}|\hat{x}, S')$ over outputs $\hat{y}$. P is a probability distribution parameterized by a CNN-LSTM feature representation neural network and a classifier. In the target domain, when a new support set T' is given, we can simply use the function P to make a prediction $P(\hat{y}|\hat{x}, T')$ for each test sample $\hat{x}$ from T''. In short, we predict the label $\hat{y}$ for the unseen sample $\hat{x}$ and a support set S' can be expressed as:

$$\hat{y} = \arg\max_y P\big(y|\hat{x}, S'\big) \tag{19}$$

A simple method to predict $\hat{y}$ is calculating a linear combination of the labels in the support set as follows:

$$\hat{y} = \sum_{i=1}^{N} a(\hat{x}, x_i) y_i \tag{20}$$

where a is an attention mechanism which is shown as:

$$a(\hat{x}, x_i) = \frac{e^{c(f(\hat{x}), g(x_i))}}{\sum_{j=1}^{N} e^{c(f(\hat{x}), g(x_j))}} \tag{21}$$

It is softmax over the cosine similarity c of the embedding functions f and g, which are the feature representation neural network. In addition, the cosine similarity is calculated as:

$$c(f(\cdot), g(\cdot)) = \cos(f(\cdot), g(\cdot)) = \frac{f(\cdot) \cdot g(\cdot)}{\|f(\cdot)\|\|g(\cdot)\|} \tag{22}$$

The training procedure is an episode-based training, which is a form of meta-learning, learning to learn from a given support set to minimize a loss over a batch. More specifically, we define a task T as a distribution over possible label sets L (four activities in our experiment). To form an "episode" to compute gradients and update our model, we first sample L from T (e.g., L could be the label set X, O, PO, UP). We then use L to sample the support set S and a batch B (i.e., both S and B are labelled examples of X, O, PO, UP). The network is then trained to minimize the error predicting the labels in the batch B conditioned on the support set S. More precisely, the training objective is as follows:

$$\theta = \arg\max_{\theta} E_{L \sim T} \left[E_{S \sim L, B \sim L} \left[\sum_{(x,y) \in B} \log P_{\theta}(y|x, S) \right] \right] \tag{23}$$

where θ represents the parameters of the embedding function f and g.

4. Evaluation

In this section, we evaluate the performance of the proposed WiLiMetaSensing system through extensive experiments. The evaluation contains the following three parts. Firstly, we explore the feasibility and effectiveness of our system. Then, we investigate the system Modules. Finally, the robustness of the system is discussed by demonstrating the influence of different data samples.

4.1. Experiment Setup

We first evaluate the performance of our sensing method in a traditional way, including the single location sensing and the mixed locations sensing. In addition, we validate the effectiveness of location-independent sensing. There are 50 samples for each activity at each location for each person, 60% of which are randomly selected as the training set, 20% as the validation set, and the rest as the testing set. For single location sensing, we train and test at the same location. For mixed locations sensing, we apply the activities of all the locations for training and testing. For location-independent sensing, we show the overall average accuracy with four locations for training and 24 locations for testing. In this section, we show the overall accuracy for one-shot learning using the samples with 200 frames/s sampling rate, which lasts for 3.5 s, and 90 subcarriers. According to the training strategy of meta learning method, when we test for k-shot learning, we set the number of samples in each category of the support set as k for the testing sets. We set the support set of training and validation sets the same as the testing sets.

Specifically, the CNN embedding module consists of four CNN blocks, each including a convolutional layer, a batch normalization layer, and a 2×2 max-pooling layer, followed by a fully-connected layer with 64 neurons. In addition, 64 filters with the kernel size 3×3 are used. In the Bi-LSTM embedding module, the number of hidden units is $n * k$, which is the number of activities multiplied by the *k*-shot. The input size of Bi-LSTM is decided by the dimension of a fully-connected layer which is 64. The number of hidden layers is 1. Hidden size (the dimension of the hidden layer) is 32, while, in attLSTM, it is 64. We minimize the cross-entropy loss function with Adam to optimize the model parameters. The exponential decay rate $\rho1$ and $\rho2$ are empirically set as 0.9 and 0.999. The learning rate is set as 0.0001. The total number of training iterations is 300. The batch size is set as 16. Unless otherwise specified, the following evaluations follow the above settings.

4.2. Overall Performance

Table 2 illustrates the recognition average accuracy of our method compared with the traditional deep learning method CNN and WiHand [25]. WiHand is based on the low rank and sparse decomposition (LRSD) algorithm and extracts the histogram of the gesture CSI profile as the features, which outperforms the other location-independent approach. It can be seen that our system outperforms these two methods in both location-dependent sensing and location-independent sensing. All the methods can recognize with high accuracy for single location sensing and mixed locations sensing. For the location-independent sensing, WiLiMetaSensing can also obtain an average 91.11% recognition accuracy, which is about 7% higher than CNN, and about 9% higher than WiHand. Specifically, the confusion matrix of a test for our location-independent human activity recognition method is shown in Figure 13 with a 91.41% accuracy. We can see that all of the activities can be recognized with high accuracy. Note that Table 2 shows the optimal recognition accuracy of WiHand with 30 subcarriers and 20 features. We analyze the reason why WiHand did not perform as well as the original dataset, including (1) The nine data collection locations of WiHand are relatively close to the TX and RX, while our 24 locations have a wider coverage. (2) The sampling rate of WiHand is 2500 packets/s, which is much larger than our 200 packets/s. (3) WiHand could extract CSI streams of all 56 subcarriers from the customized drivers, while ours is 30 subcarriers. A higher sampling rate and more subcarriers may provide richer fine-grained information. After the matrix decomposition, more activity-related information will be preserved.

Table 2. The recognition accuracy for single location sensing, mixed locations sensing, and location-independent sensing.

Accuracy (%)	WiLiMetaSensing	CNN	WiHand [26]
Single location	99.13	99.00	96.15
Mixed locations	98.36	95.53	91.50
Location-independent	91.11	84.02	82.20

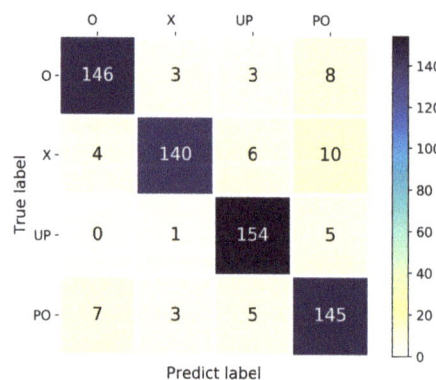

Figure 13. The confusion matrix of location-independent human activity recognition.

4.3. Module Study

Comparison with different feature representation modules. In this section, we explore the effect of the embedding module g (Bi-LSTM) and f (attLSTM) for the samples from the support set and the query set. We test for one-shot learning using the samples with 90 subcarriers. From Table 3, we can see that both modules enhance the performance of the method. Leveraging all the activity samples from the support set, common features can be obtained to adjust the feature representation, so as to pay more attention to the location-independent features. The embedding module for the query set enables the sample in the source domain to effectively calibrate the feature representation of the sample in the target domain.

Table 3. The recognition accuracy with different embedding modules.

Embedding Modules	Accuracy (%)
WiLiMetaSensing with Bi-LSTM with attLSTM	91.11
WiLiMetaSensing with Bi-LSTM without attLSTM	90.25
WiLiMetaSensing without Bi-LSTM without attLSTM	88.73

4.4. Robustness Evaluation

Performance of location-independent sensing in terms of different number of training locations. The activity samples of each position have different data distributions. The further the distance of the locations, the higher the probability of a broader distribution distance will be. Therefore, when it comes to the samples collected for training the models, we hope the positions of the training samples become more decentralized. We adopt a fixed training position selection strategy, in which the positions should be distributed as far as possible in the entire space, instead of clustering together in a line parallel to the transceiver. We choose 4/6/8/12/24 locations for training and 24 locations for testing. The selections of fixed 4/6/8/12 training positions are depicted in Figure 14. Specifically, for 4/8/12 training locations, the positions where the same colored straight line goes through, or the inflection points and the enthesis of the same colored broken lines, constitute the training samples. For six training locations, the straight lines or broken lines together with the same colored marked locations form the training pairs.

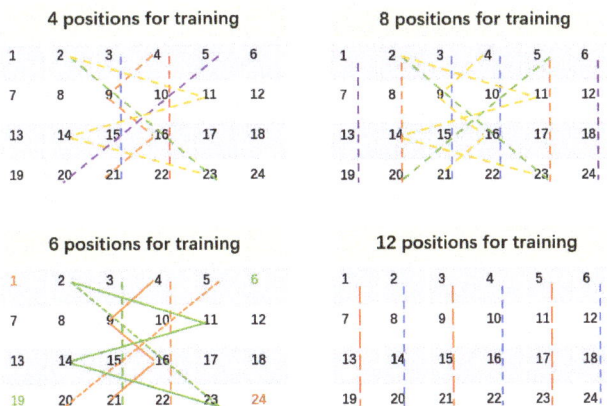

Figure 14. The layout of the training locations.

As demonstrated in Table 4, when we pick four training locations and 1-shot, the accuracy is 91.11%. When eight training locations and 1-shot are selected, the accuracy is 92.66%. The results indicate that the more training positions there are, the higher accuracy the recognition obtains.

Table 4. The average recognition accuracy for different numbers of training locations.

Number of Training Locations	4	6	8	12	24
Accuracy (%)	91.11	92.23	94.98	96.00	98.36

Performance of location-independent sensing for samples with different numbers of subcarriers. We explore one-shot human activity recognition with different numbers of subcarriers. As illustrated in Table 5, the recognition accuracy reduces with the decrease of the number of subcarriers. However, it still maintains an acceptable recognition rate when there are only 30 subcarriers from one pair of antenna.

Table 5. The accuracy for different number of subcarriers with four training locations.

Training Locations	90 Subcarriers	60 Subcarriers	30 Subcarriers
3,8,15,20	92.63	91.75	86.75
1,10,13,22	91.25	88.50	87.50
2,8,14,20	91.75	90.75	87.75
3,9,15,21	89.13	89.00	85.13
1,8,15,22	91.25	89.50	85.75
4,9,14,19	90.63	90.13	85.00
Average accuracy (%)	91.11	89.94	86.31

Performance of location-independent sensing for different TX-RX antenna pairs. We investigate the recognition accuracy with 30 subcarriers from different TX-RX antennas. As shown in Table 6, different antenna pairs have similar recognition effects. The difference reflects that different antenna pairs contain more or less diverse information. Therefore, 90 subcarriers which integrate these features can obtain superior results. Note that, in Table 6, iTX-jRX represents CSI data from i-th TX and j-th RX.

Table 6. The accuracy for different TX-RX antenna pairs.

TX-RX	1TX-1RX	1TX-2RX	1TX-3RX
Accuracy (%)	86.31	87.00	85.60

Performance of location-independent sensing for different number of shots. We explore the number of samples in support set for testing. As examples, we also select four locations for training and 24 locations for testing. The samples with 90 subcarriers are used. The identification results are listed in Table 7. It is noted that all the average accuracy is above 90%, and the accuracy will increase with the growth of the sample size.

Table 7. The accuracy for different number of shots with four training locations.

Number of Shots	1-Shot	2-Shot	3-Shot
Accuracy (%)	91.11	92.25	93.21

Performance of location-independent sensing for samples with different sampling rates. We collect CSI measurements at the initial transmission rate of 200 packets/s, and down-sample the 750 CSI series to 375, 250, 150, 75. The one-shot results with different sampling rates are shown in Figure 15. As can be seen, when he sampling rate decrease to 20 frames/s, the method can still obtain satisfying accuracy.

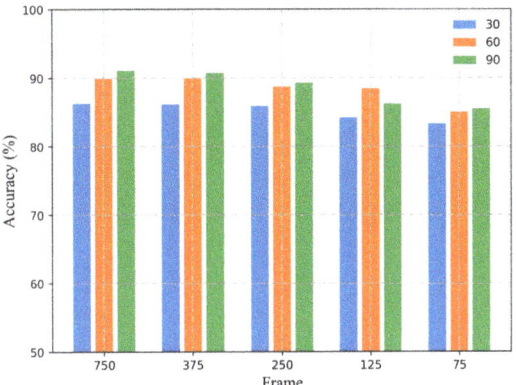

Figure 15. The recognition accuracy with different number of subcarriers and sampling rates.

5. Limitations and Future Work

Although the proposed WiLiMetaSensing system realizes location-independent sensing with very few samples, there remain many challenges to be overcome. First of all, there are some strict restrictions in the data collection process. For example, volunteers are required to perform the same activity facing nearly the same direction in the same room. Consequently, except for the types of activity and location variations, other factors that would affect the transmission of the signals are not seriously taken into account, such as the status of a person (e.g., pose and direction) and the environmental variations (i.e., altering the room or the locations of surrounding objects). In addition, as signals can be easily blocked, reflected, or scattered by different targets, the existence of other people would also result in different signal patterns. However, the impact of interference from the other person on the classification accuracy was either not considered. As a result, in future work, we will further explore the generalized and robust human activity recognition method with an adequate account of these aforementioned factors. Only in this way can human activity recognition technology develop from academic research to industrial application.

6. Conclusions

In this paper, we present a novel human activity recognition system, named WiLiMetaSensing. It realizes location-independent sensing with very few samples in the Wi-Fi environment. Inspired by the idea of meta learning, we endow the system with the ability that can utilize the knowledge acquired from one location for others. Technically, we propose a CNN-LSTM feature representation and metric learning-based human activity recognition system. The model focuses on the common characteristics of different locations and extracts discriminative features for different activities. The performance evaluation is conducted on the comprehensive dataset we build. It demonstrates that the WiLiMetaSensing system can achieve an average accuracy of 91.11%, with four locations for training, given only one sample for other testing locations. More importantly, it can well adapt to the data samples with a small number of subcarriers and a low sampling rate. Therefore, we can firmly conclude that the presented approach is feasible and robust for location-independent sensing.

Author Contributions: Conceptualization, X.D. and T.J.; methodology, X.D. and Y.Z.; software, X.D. and Z.L.; validation, X.D and Z.L.; formal analysis, X.D. and Y.H.; investigation, X.D.and Y.H.; resources, T.J.and Y.Z.; data curation, X.D. and Z.L.; writing—original draft preparation, X.D.; writing—review and editing, X.D., T.J.,Y.Z., Y.H., and Z.L.; visualization, X.D.,Y.H.; supervision,T.J.,Y.Z. ; project administration, T.J.; funding acquisition, T.J. All authors have read and agreed to the published version of the manuscript.

Funding: This work is supported by the National Natural Sciences Foundation of China (No.62071061, 61671075, 61631003), and the BUPT Excellent Ph.D. Students Foundation (No. CX2019110), and Beijing Institute of Technology Research Fund Program for Young Scholars.

Institutional Review Board Statement: Not applicable.

Informed Consent Statement: Informed consent was obtained from all subjects involved in the study.

Data Availability Statement: Not applicable.

Conflicts of Interest: The authors declare no conflict of interest.

References

1. Ma, Y.; Zhou, G.; Wang, S. WiFi sensing with channel state information: A survey. *ACM Comput. Surv.* **2019**, *52*, 1–36. [CrossRef]
2. Kim, E.; Helal, S.; Cook, D. Human activity recognition and pattern discovery. *IEEE Pervasive Comput.* **2009**, *9*, 48–53. [CrossRef]
3. Lara, O.D.; Labrador, M.A. A survey on human activity recognition using wearable sensors. *IEEE Commun. Surv. Tutor.* **2012**, *15*, 1192–1209. [CrossRef]
4. Wang, J.; Chen, Y.; Hao, S.; Peng, X.; Hu, L. Deep learning for sensor-based activity recognition: A survey. *Pattern Recognit. Lett.* **2019**, *119*, 3–11. [CrossRef]
5. D'Sa, A.G.; Prasad, B. A survey on vision based activity recognition, its applications and challenges. In Proceedings of the 2019 Second International Conference on Advanced Computational and Communication Paradigms (ICACCP), Majitar, Sikkim, 25–28 February 2019; pp. 1–8.
6. Zhang, H.B.; Zhang, Y.X.; Zhong, B.; Lei, Q.; Yang, L.; Du, J.X.; Chen, D.S. A comprehensive survey of vision-based human action recognition methods. *Sensors* **2019**, *19*, 1005. [CrossRef]
7. Zhang, R.; Jing, X.; Wu, S.; Jiang, C.; Yu, F.R. Device-Free Wireless Sensing for Human Detection: The Deep Learning Perspective. *IEEE Internet Things J.* **2020**. [CrossRef]
8. Liu, J.; Teng, G.; Hong, F. Human Activity Sensing with Wireless Signals: A Survey. *Sensors* **2020**, *20*, 1210. [CrossRef]
9. Ding, C.; Hong, H.; Zou, Y.; Chu, H.; Zhu, X.; Fioranelli, F.; Le Kernec, J.; Li, C. Continuous human motion recognition with a dynamic range-Doppler trajectory method based on FMCW radar. *IEEE Trans. Geosci. Remote Sens.* **2019**, *57*, 6821–6831. [CrossRef]
10. Adib, F.; Kabelac, Z.; Katabi, D.; Miller, R.C. 3D tracking via body radio reflections. In Proceedings of the 11th USENIX Symposium on Networked Systems Design and Implementation (NSDI 14), Seattle, WA, USA, 2–4 April 2014; pp. 317–329.
11. Yang, Z.; Pathak, P.H.; Zeng, Y.; Liran, X.; Mohapatra, P. Monitoring vital signs using millimeter wave. In Proceedings of the 17th ACM International Symposium on Mobile Ad Hoc Networking and Computing, Paderborn, Germany, 4–8 July 2016; pp. 211–220.
12. Lien, J.; Gillian, N.; Karagozler, M.E.; Amihood, P.; Schwesig, C.; Olson, E.; Raja, H.; Poupyrev, I. Soli: Ubiquitous gesture sensing with millimeter wave radar. *ACM Trans. Graph.* **2016**, *35*, 1–19. [CrossRef]
13. Zhong, Y.; Dutkiewicz, E.; Yang, Y.; Zhu, X.; Zhou, Z.; Jiang, T. Internet of mission-critical things: Human and animal classification—A device-free sensing approach. *IEEE Internet Things J.* **2017**, *5*, 3369–3377. [CrossRef]
14. Zhong, Y.; Yang, Y.; Zhu, X.; Dutkiewicz, E.; Zhou, Z.; Jiang, T. Device-free sensing for personnel detection in a foliage environment. *IEEE Geosci. Remote Sens. Lett.* **2017**, *14*, 921–925. [CrossRef]
15. Huang, Y.; Zhong, Y.; Wu, Q.; Dutkiewicz, E.; Jiang, T. Cost-effective foliage penetration human detection under severe weather conditions based on auto-encoder/decoder neural network. *IEEE Internet Things J.* **2018**, *6*, 6190–6200. [CrossRef]
16. Zhong, Y.; Yang, Y.; Zhu, X.; Huang, Y.; Dutkiewicz, E.; Zhou, Z.; Jiang, T. Impact of seasonal variations on foliage penetration experiment: A WSN-based device-free sensing approach. *IEEE Trans. Geosci. Remote Sens.* **2018**, *56*, 5035–5045. [CrossRef]
17. Zhong, Y.; Bi, T.; Wang, J.; Wu, S.; Jiang, T.; Huang, Y. Low data regimes in extreme climates: Foliage penetration personnel detection using a wireless network-based device-free sensing approach. *Ad Hoc Networks* **2021**, *114*, 102438. [CrossRef]
18. Yousefi, S.; Narui, H.; Dayal, S.; Ermon, S.; Valaee, S. A survey on behavior recognition using wifi channel state information. *IEEE Commun. Mag.* **2017**, *55*, 98–104. [CrossRef]
19. Shi, Z.; Zhang, J.A.; Xu, Y.D.R.; Cheng, Q. Environment-Robust Device-free Human Activity Recognition with Channel-State-Information Enhancement and One-Shot Learning. *IEEE Trans. Mob. Comput.* **2020**. [CrossRef]
20. Zhong, Y.; Wang, J.; Wu, S.; Jiang, T.; Wu, Q. Multi-Location Human Activity Recognition via MIMO-OFDM Based Wireless Networks: An IoT-Inspired Device-Free Sensing Approach. *IEEE Internet Things J.* **2020**. [CrossRef]
21. Yang, J.; Zou, H.; Zhou, Y.; Xie, L. Learning gestures from wifi: A siamese recurrent convolutional architecture. *IEEE Internet Things J.* **2019**, *6*, 10763–10772. [CrossRef]
22. Wang, Y.; Liu, J.; Chen, Y.; Gruteser, M.; Yang, J.; Liu, H. E-eyes: Device-free location-oriented activity identification using fine-grained wifi signatures. In Proceedings of the 20th Annual International Conference on Mobile Computing and Networking, Seattle, WA, USA, 2–4 April 2014; pp. 617–628.
23. Wang, W.; Liu, A.X.; Shahzad, M.; Ling, K.; Lu, S. Device-free human activity recognition using commercial WiFi devices. *IEEE J. Sel. Areas Commun.* **2017**, *35*, 1118–1131. [CrossRef]

24. Virmani, A.; Shahzad, M. Position and orientation agnostic gesture recognition using wifi. In Proceedings of the 15th Annual International Conference on Mobile Systems, Applications, and Services, Niagara Falls, NY, USA, 19–23 June 2017; pp. 252–264.
25. Yang, J.; Zou, H.; Jiang, H.; Xie, L. Fine-grained adaptive location-independent activity recognition using commodity WiFi. In Proceedings of the 2018 IEEE Wireless Communications and Networking Conference (WCNC), Barcelona, Spain, 15–18 April 2018; pp. 1–6.
26. Lu, Y.; Lv, S.; Wang, X. Towards Location Independent Gesture Recognition with Commodity WiFi Devices. *Electronics* **2019**, *8*, 1069. [CrossRef]
27. Yue, Z.; Yi, Z.; Kun, Q.; Guidong, Z.; Yunhao, L.; Chenshu, W.; Zheng, Y. Zero-Effort Cross-Domain Gesture Recognition with Wi-Fi. In Proceedings of the 17th Annual International Conference on Mobile Systems, Applications and Services (MobiSys '19), Seoul, Korea, 17–21 June 2019.
28. Jie, Z.; Zhanyong, T.; Meng, L.; Dingyi, F.; Petteri, N.; Wang, Z. Crosssense: Towards cross-site and large-scale wifi sensing. In Proceedings of the 24th Annual International Conference on Mobile Computing and Networking (MobiSys '18), New Delhi, India, 29 October–November 2018; pp. 305–320.
29. Wu, X.; Chu, Z.; Yang, P.; Xiang, C.; Zheng, X.; Huang, W. TW-See: Human Activity Recognition Through the Wall with Commodity Wi-Fi Devices. *IEEE Trans. Veh. Technol.* **2018**. [CrossRef]
30. Zhou, Q.; Xing, J.; Yang, Q. Device-free occupant activity recognition in smart offices using intrinsic Wi-Fi components. *Build. Environ.* **2020**, *172*, 106737. [CrossRef]
31. Jiang, W.; Miao, C.; Ma, F.; Yao, S.; Wang, Y.; Yuan, Y.; Xue, H.; Song, C.; Ma, X.; Koutsonikolas, D.; et al. Towards environment independent device free human activity recognition. In Proceedings of the 24th Annual International Conference on Mobile Computing and Networking (MobiSys '18), New Delhi, India, 29 October–2 November 2018; pp. 289–304.
32. Lake, B.; Salakhutdinov, R.; Gross, J.; Tenenbaum, J. One shot learning of simple visual concepts. In Proceedings of the Annual Meeting of the Cognitive Science Society, Boston, MA, USA, 20–23 July 2011; Volume 33.
33. Vilalta, R.; Drissi, Y. A Perspective View and Survey of Meta-Learning. *Artif. Intell. Rev.* **2002**, *18*, 77–95. [CrossRef]
34. Vinyals, O.; Blundell, C.; Lillicrap, T.; Kavukcuoglu, K.; Wierstra, D. Matching Networks for One Shot Learning. *arXiv* **2016**, arXiv:1606.04080.
35. Bellet, A.; Habrard, A.; Sebban, M. A Survey on Metric Learning for Feature Vectors and Structured Data. *arXiv* **2013**, arxiv:1306.6709.
36. Halperin, D.; Hu, W.; Sheth, A.; Wetherall, D. Predictable 802.11 packet delivery from wireless channel measurements. *ACM Sigcomm Comput. Commun. Rev.* **2010**, *40*, 159–170. [CrossRef]
37. Vinyals, O.; Bengio, S.; Kudlur, M. Order Matters: Sequence to Sequence for Sets. *arXiv* **2016**, arXiv:1511.06391.
38. Sutskever, I.; Vinyals, O.; Le, Q.V. Sequence to Sequence Learning with Neural Networks. *Adv. Neural Inf. Process. Syst.* **2014**. [CrossRef]

Article

Impact of Scene Content on High Resolution Video Quality

Miroslav Uhrina *, Anna Holesova, Juraj Bienik and Lukas Sevcik

Department of Multimedia and Information-Communication Technology, University of Zilina, Univerzitna 1, 010 26 Zilina, Slovakia; anna.holesova@uniza.sk (A.H.); juraj.bienik@uniza.sk (J.B.); lukas.sevcik@uniza.sk (L.S.)
* Correspondence: miroslav.uhrina@uniza.sk

Abstract: This paper deals with the impact of content on the perceived video quality evaluated using the subjective Absolute Category Rating (ACR) method. The assessment was conducted on eight types of video sequences with diverse content obtained from the SJTU dataset. The sequences were encoded at 5 different constant bitrates in two widely video compression standards H.264/AVC and H.265/HEVC at Full HD and Ultra HD resolutions, which means 160 annotated video sequences were created. The length of Group of Pictures (GOP) was set to half the framerate value, as is typical for video intended for transmission over a noisy communication channel. The evaluation was performed in two laboratories: one situated at the University of Zilina, and the second at the VSB—Technical University in Ostrava. The results acquired in both laboratories reached/showed a high correlation. Notwithstanding the fact that the sequences with low Spatial Information (SI) and Temporal Information (TI) values reached better Mean Opinion Score (MOS) score than the sequences with higher SI and TI values, these two parameters are not sufficient for scene description, and this domain should be the subject of further research. The evaluation results led us to the conclusion that it is unnecessary to use the H.265/HEVC codec for compression of Full HD sequences and the compression efficiency of the H.265 codec by the Ultra HD resolution reaches the compression efficiency of both codecs by the Full HD resolution. This paper also includes the recommendations for minimum bitrate thresholds at which the video sequences at both resolutions retain good and fair subjectively perceived quality.

Keywords: ACR; H.264/AVC; H.265/HEVC; QoE; subjective assessment

check for updates

Citation: Uhrina, M.; Holesova, A.; Sevcik, L.; Bienik, J. Impact of Scene Content on High Resolution Video Quality. *Sensors* **2021**, *21*, 2872. https://doi.org/10.3390/s21082872

Academic Editor: Carlos Tavares Calafate

Received: 1 March 2021
Accepted: 13 April 2021
Published: 19 April 2021

Publisher's Note: MDPI stays neutral with regard to jurisdictional claims in published maps and institutional affiliations.

1. Introduction

In recent years, the number of various types of surveillance and data collection cameras located both indoors and outdoors have been constantly increasing. Popularity of home security cameras is also growing as even high-quality models become more affordable. Typical surveillance cameras applications include public safety, protection of facilities against theft or vandalism, remote video monitoring, traffic surveillance, weather monitoring, or more special cases, such as animal monitoring or data collection, for statistical or marketing purposes. Today, due to the pandemic situation, face recognition with and without a protective mask is also becoming a point of interest for researchers in cooperation with technology companies [1–3]. It is important to realize that each such employed sensor produces a tremendous amount of data to be subsequently transmitted over the network or further processed, which calls for effective video compression. Furthermore, whether the image or video is presented to a live person or a machine learning algorithm (most often for its classification or segmentation), the best results can be achieved when the image is of the highest achievable quality. This implies one common goal for the distributors, communication service providers, or even broadcasting companies, to optimally set the compression parameters so that perceived video quality is maximal, while the bandwidth requirements are minimal. This challenge leads to increased interest in the analysis of video content followed by the individual setting of the compression parameters of video sequences with different types of scene content. Even though many

243

studies deal with the video quality assessment using subjective methods, the demand exceeds the supply; there is still a lack of video quality datasets, as well as recorded subjective tests, conducted on these datasets. Very popular and extensively used datasets, such as References [4–27], come from the University of Texas and were developed by the Laboratory for Image and Video Engineering. Another very popular option is the VQEG-HDTV database [28], which is a result of international project of VQEG (Video Quality Experts Group) consortium. Other well-known datasets are BVI-HD [29], BVI textures [30] and BVI-HFR [31] developed at the University of Bristol, AVT-VQDB-UHD-1 database [32] made by the Ilmenau University of Technology, Ultra Video Group (UVG) dataset [33] composed at the Tampere University, SJTU 4K video quality database [34] from the Shanghai Jiao Tong University, Image and Video Processing Subjective Quality Video Database [35] developed at the Chinese University of Hong Kong, collection of IRC-CyN/IVP databases from the Institut de Recherche en Communications et Cybernétique de Nantes [36], Konstanz Natural Video Database (KoNViD-1k) made by the Universitaet Konstanz [37,38], MCL-V [39], and [40] databases from the MSC University of Southern California, Scalable Video Database [41,42] composed at the EPFL, ReTRiEVED Video Quality Database [43] made by the Universita Degli Studi or TUM databases [44,45] developed by the Technical University of Munich. Taking into account the demand and importance of measuring the performance of video quality assessment techniques, a number of studies on perceptual evaluation was presented. Most of them merely compare the quality of video sequences with various characteristics evaluated by different subjective methods and do not examine the content aspect. Rerabek et al. [46] examined a rate-distortion performance analysis and mutual comparison of one of the latest video coding standards H.265/HEVC with VP9 codec. Ramzan et al. [47] presented a performance evaluation of three coding standards—Advanced Video Coding (H.264/MPEG-AVC), High-Efficiency Video Coding (H.265/MPEG-HEVC), and VP9, based on subjective and objective quality evaluations. Two different sequences at both resolutions (Full HD and Ultra HD) were tested using the DSIS method. Bienik et al. [48] measured the impact of the compression formats, namely H.264, H.265, and VP9 on perceived video quality. The evaluation was performed on four Full HD sequences using the Absolute Category Rating (ACR) and DSCQS methods. Xu et al. [49] presented a subjective video quality assessment on 4K Ultra-High Definition (UHD) videos using the DSCQS method. Six different test sequences were used for the evaluation. Herrou et al. [50] focused on a performance comparison between HEVC and VP9 in the HDR context through both objective and subjective evaluations. Dumic et al. [51] offered findings on subjective assessment of H.265 versus H.264 Video Coding for High-Definition Video Systems. For the evaluation, a database consisting of 120 degraded HD video sequences with 4 contents encoded at various compression rates to H.265/HEVC and H.264/AVC formats was compiled. Milovanovic et al. [52] subjectively compared the coding efficiency of three video coding standards (MPEG-H HEVC, H.264/MPEG-4 AVC, and H.262/MPEG-2). Sotelo et al. [53] presented a subjective quality assessment of HEVC/H.265 compressed 4K Ultra-High-Definition (UHD) videos in a laboratory viewing environment. Kufa et al. [54] explored coding efficiency performance of High Efficiency Video Coding (HEVC) and VP9 compression formats on video content in Full HD and UHD resolutions. Deep et al. [55] focused on the comparison of HEVC and VP9 based on both subjective and objective evaluation on various (720p, 1080p, and 2160p) test videos. Akyazi et al. [56] examined the compression efficiency of HEVC/H.265, VP9, and AV1 codecs based on subjective quality assessment. Our survey of research papers shows that there is still a lack of databases of video sequences annotated according to subjective evaluation. Therefore, this paper brings new subjective results and also explores the impact of the video content on the subjective assessment. We decided to compare today's most used compression standards—H.264/AVC and H.265/HEVC—on video sequences at Full HD and Ultra HD resolutions. Our publication follows Reference [57], where a new 4K video dataset was compiled with full subjective scores (Mean Opinion Score (MOS)) of videos at different bitrates compressed by HEVC/H.265 codec evaluated by the Double

Stimulus Impairment Scale (DSIS) method, variant II. For our measurements, we decided to use the Absolute Category Rating (ACR) method.

2. Dataset Description and Preparation

2.1. Dataset Description

For our measurements, we used the dataset from the Media Lab of the Shanghai Jiao Tang University [34]. We selected eight sequences with various scene content, illustrated in Figure 1, classified according to the Temporal Information (TI) and Spatial Information (SI) from this database. SI defines the amount of spatial detail in an image and is higher for more spatially complex scenes, while TI represents the number of temporal changes in a video sequence and is higher for high motion sequences [58]. The spatial perceptual information is based on the Sobel filter and is represented by the formula:

$$SI = max_{time}[std_{space}[Sobel(F_n)]],\qquad(1)$$

where F_n stands for video frame, and std_{space} for the standard deviation over the pixels in each Sobel-filtered frame. The temporal information is computed as:

$$TI = max_{time}[std_{space}[M_n(i,j)]],\qquad(2)$$

where $M_n(i,j)$ is the difference between pixels at the same position in the frame belonging to two consecutive frames, i.e.,

$$M_n(i,j) = F_n(i,j) - F_{n-1}(i,j),\qquad(3)$$

where $F_n(i,j)$ is the pixel at the i-th row, and j-th column of n-th frame in time [58]. Both of these parameters were calculated for each sequence using the Mitsu tool [59] and plotted in Figure 2. The general specification of the dataset is given in Table 1, and the content of individual sequences is briefly described in Table 2.

| (a) Bund Nightscape | (b) Campfire Party | (c) Construction Field | (d) Fountains |
| (e) Marathon | (f) Runners | (g) Tall Buildings | (h) Wood |

Figure 1. Printscreens of used test sequences. Reprinted with permission from [60], Copyright 2021, Uhrina.

Table 1. Parameters of test sequences.

Resolution	Chroma Subsampling	Bit Depth	Aspect Ratio	Framerate [fps]	Length [Seconds]
3840 × 2160 (UHD)	4:4:4	10 bits per channel	16:9	30	10

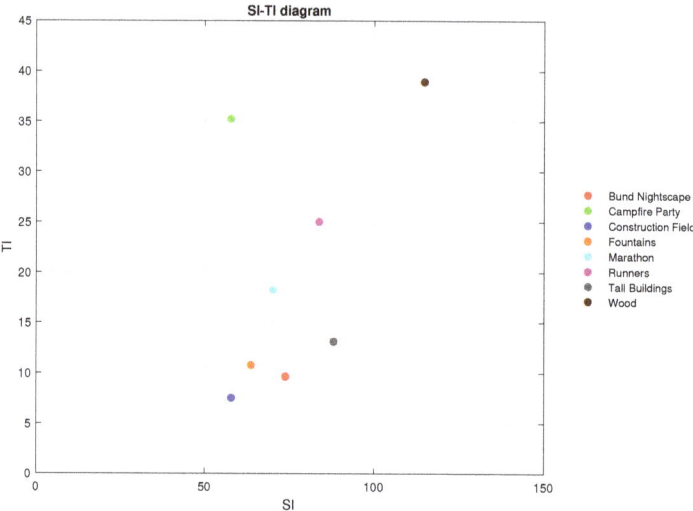

Figure 2. Spatial Information (SI) and Temporal Information (TI) diagram of used test sequences. Reprinted with permission from [60], Copyright 2021, Uhrina.

Table 2. Characteristics of the test sequences.

Test Sequence	Description	Test Sequence	Description
Bund Nightscape	is a video sequence portraying the above view of a night city crossed by a busy road next the river. The time-lapse video is captured from a high angle with a steady camera as one extreme long shot. The scene is relatively static, except for the accelerated movement of cars driving on the road, people passing by, flags waving in the wind and flashing lights.	Marathon	is a video sequence picturing a large group of people in colorful apparel running a race on an asphalt road on a rainy day. The sequence was filmed from bird's eye perspective with almost no camera movement as a very long shot. The scene is rather dynamic, given almost the entire frame is filled by running marathon participants and raindrops falling on the wet road.
Campfire Party	is a night time video sequence depicting a group of people posing for a photograph behind a large campfire. The long shot is captured by a stationary camera, which zooms in slightly at the end of the video. The motion in the scene is caused mainly by a flashing fire in the foreground and a woman who briefly runs out of and back into the shot.	Runners	is a video sequence that captures athletes running on a tree lined road in a cloudy weather. The racers in the very long shot are approaching the stationary camera, which is positioned approximately at their eye level. The scene contains a considerable amount of motion caused by rushing contestants and by the wind in the treetops.
Construction Field	is a very still video sequence capturing construction equipment in the middle of a building site during excavation work. A hand-held camera was used to film the very long shot from a high angle. The only moving objects in the scene are an excavator digging a foundation pit and people slowly walking in the background.	Tall Buildings	is a video sequence portraying the tallest skyscrapers and busy intersections in Shanghai, with a grand river in the background. The video was captured from a bird's eye view using a camera that slowly pans to take a panoramic extreme long shot. The movement in the scene is primarily a result of the panning motion of the camera and partially of the cars driving fast at a deep distance.

Table 2. *Cont.*

Test Sequence	Description	Test Sequence	Description
Fountains	is a video sequence focused on several fountains in the center of a housing estate with multiple trees and apartment buildings in the background. The video is captured by a static camera as a long shot. All the motion in the scene can be attributed to water gushing from the fountain jets and droplets evaporating into the air.	Wood	is a video sequence picturing a tall forest during a sunny autumn day. The video was filmed from a low angle as a long shot with a camera performing a moderately fast panning motion. All the movement in the scene can be attributed to the camera pan and the resulting change in the angle of the sunlight rays incident on the lens.

2.2. Dataset Preparation

In our research, we decided to explore the quality of 8-bit video sequences at two commonly used resolutions, i.e., Full HD (FHD) and Ultra HD (UHD) with a typical chroma subsampled YUV 4:2:0 format. Because original sequences were uncompressed and YUV 4:4:4 color format at Ultra HD resolution with 10-bit depth was used, we had to convert them to the appropriate formats. Therefore, all test sequences were first chroma subsampled from YUV 4:4:4 to YUV 4:2:0 format and also the bit depth was changed from 10 to 8 bits per channel. Subsequently, all these conversion steps were repeated for Full HD resolution utilizing the FFmpeg tool [61]. As we wanted to assess also Full HD in addition to Ultra HD, the resolution also had to be altered. For all these conversion steps we used once again the FFmpeg tool [61]. Correspondingly, two uncompressed test sequences were generated (Figure 3) for each type of content, which adds up to 16 videos. We call them the source video sequences (SRCs) for the rest of this paper.

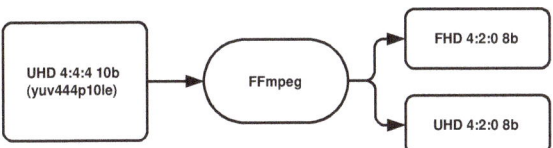

Figure 3. Process of preparing the test sequences: chroma subsampling, bit depth, and resolution changing.

2.3. Coding Process

All these test video sequences (SRCs) were afterwards encoded to both compression standards to be evaluated, i.e., H.264/AVC and H.265/HEVC. As a quality restriction parameter, we decided to use the constant bitrate. We selected 5 various target bitrates: 1, 3, 5, 10 and 15 Mbps based on our previous research [62] which have shown the efficiency of codecs growing nonlinearly with increasing bitrate. We have limited the number of bitrates to 5 as a compromise between the complexity and time requirements of subjective testing and precision of the measurements. For the purposes of our research, we decided to use the Group of Pictures (GOP) length typical for video intended for transfer over a noisy communication channel. The GOP length is based on the framerate of used video sequences and is commonly set to half of the framerate value. Accordingly, given that test video sequences had a framerate of 30 fps (frames per second), we chose the GOP length of 15 frames, i.e., M = 3, N = 15. The first number, labeled with M letter, expresses the distance between two anchor frames (I or P) and the second number, denoted with N letter, stands for the distance between two key frames (I). For this coding process, we used once again the FFmpeg tool, which contains libraries x264 and x265 for H.264/AVC and H.265/HEVC codec, respectively [61], creating the total of 160 video sequences for the subjective quality assessment. We refer to them as PVSs (Processed Video Sequences) for the rest of this paper. The FFmpeg command example for encoding the Wood test sequence to the H.264 format at 1 Mbps bitrate is:

ffmpeg -i Wood_1920x1080_30fps_420_8bit_YUV.yuv -vcodec libx264 -command example-params keyint=15:min-keyint=15:bframes=3:b-adapt=1:bitrate=1000:vbv-maxrate=1000:vbv-bufsize=1000 Wood_1920x1080_30fps_420_8bit_H264_01M.mp4.

3. Subjective Quality Assessment

During the subjective testing, all created PVSs were shown to people of different ages and genders to evaluate their quality. We decided to use the Absolute Category Rating (ACR) method [58,63] which belongs to the category of Single Stimulus (SS) subjective video quality assessment techniques. The principle of this method is that the degraded sequences are presented to the observers one at a time, and they are asked to rate its quality on a five-level grading scale, where 1 indicates the bad quality, and 5 stands for the excellent quality. The measurement was conducted in two laboratories separately: one situated at the University of Zilina (UNIZA), and the second at the VŠB – Technical University in Ostrava. The video sequences were presented on three types of displays (Table 3) depending on the resolution of the test sequences in the laboratories under normal indoor illumination conditions.

Table 3. Types of used displays.

Type of Assessment	Type of Display
UNIZA – FHD	Samsung LE40C750R2W FHD
UNIZA – UHD	Samsung U24E590D UHD
VSB – FHD + UHD	24" Dell P2415Q UHD

Thirty participants, mostly students, were involved in the testing in each laboratory. All of them were naive observers which means they had no expertise in the image arte-facts that may be introduced by the system under test. Naturally, they were thoroughly acquainted with the method of assessment, types of impairment, grading scale, sequence, and timing as required by Reference [58]. The statistical distribution of the number of men and women who took part in the tests, as well as the average age of all observers, is shown in Table 4. The course of the entire subjective assessment process is represented by Figure 4.

Table 4. Statistical characteristic of the observers.

University	Resolution	Number of Men	Number of Women	Average Age
UNIZA	FHD	25	5	24
UNIZA	UHD	21	9	22
VSB	FHD + UHD	15	15	25
UNIZA + VSB	FHD + UHD	61	29	24

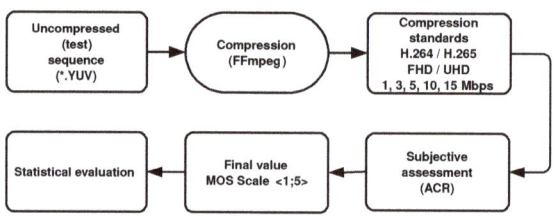

Figure 4. Complete process of coding and assessing the video quality.

4. Statistical Analysis and Presentation of the Results

After performing the subjective tests, we processed all collected results statistically; for each test sequence, codec, and resolution, the Mean Opinion Score (MOS) and 95 percent Confidence Interval (CI) in accordance with Reference [64] were calculated and plotted in graphs, a shown below. The presentation of the results could be divided into five parts. In the first part, the cross-comparison of the results obtained from different laboratories, i.e., from UNIZA and VŠB, is performed using the Pearson correlation coefficient (PCC) and the Root Mean Square Error (RMSE). In the second part, the bitrate impact on the perceived video quality depending on the scene content is plotted. The third part deals with the Analysis of Variance (ANOVA) which was applied on the acquired data. In the fourth part, the impact of the bitrate on the perceived video quality in terms of the used codec and resolution is presented. Finally, in the fifth part, the minimum bitrate thresholds at which the video sequence should be encoded to reach certain quality are determined.

4.1. Correlation between the Results from Individual Laboratories

To compare the MOS values obtained from both laboratories, i.e., from UNIZA and VŠB, and, to find out the correlation, the Pearson correlation coefficient (PCC), as well the Root Mean Square Error (RMSE) were calculated. All computations were done for both codecs and resolutions, as well as for all test sequences. The results are plotted in Figures 5 and 6 and are shown in Table 5.

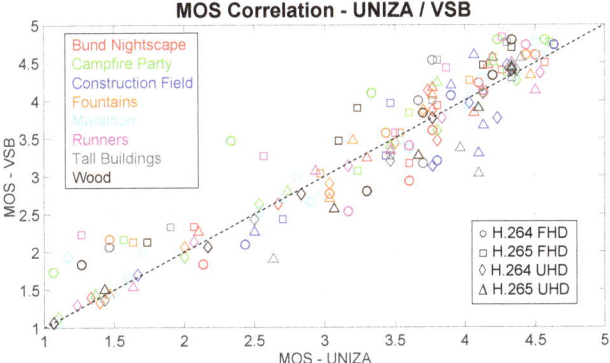

Figure 5. Comparison of Mean Opinion Score (MOS) values obtained from different laboratories. Each spot represents MOS values for corresponding codec, resolution, and test sequence.

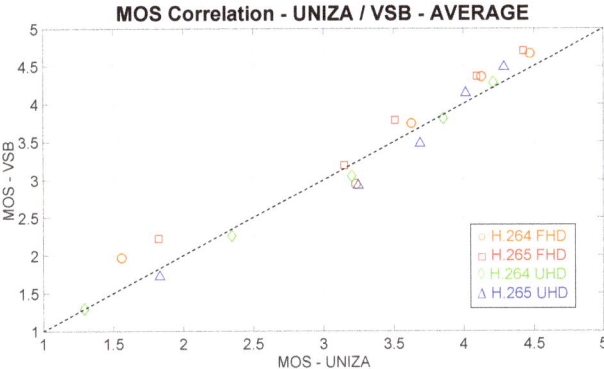

Figure 6. Comparison of MOS values obtained from different laboratories. Each spot represents averaged MOS values from particular test sequences for corresponding codec and resolution.

Table 5. Correlation of MOS score between the laboratories.

	Pearson CC	RMSE
FHD-H.264	0.97	0.30
FHD-H.265	0.99	0.31
UHD-H.264	1.00	0.10
UHD-H.265	0.98	0.23

As we can see from Figures 5 and 6, as well as from Table 5, there is a high correlation between the results from both laboratories. The lowest correlation was reached by the combination of Full HD resolution and H.264 codec. This is most likely due to the different displays used in the assessments; at the UNIZA laboratory, the Full HD display was used, while, at the VŠB laboratory, the Ultra HD display was used. Vice versa, the highest correlation rate was achieved by video sequences encoded to H.264 at UHD resolution.

4.2. Impact of Bitrate on Video Quality Depending on Scene Content

Figure 7 shows the impact of the bitrate on the perceived video quality (defined by the MOS with associated CI). In this figure, eight graphs are inserted considering used codec, resolution, and laboratory where the evaluation was conducted. Sequences with different scene contents are color-coded in the graphs; each curve represents MOS values for a given test sequence. Figure 8 shows the average MOS values obtained from UNIZA and VSB laboratories.

It is apparent from the graphs that the sequences with the lowest SI and TI values, such as the "Bund Nightscape" and the "Construction Field", reached the best MOS value. Vice versa, the observers rated the sequences situated in the middle of the SI-TI diagram, such as the "Marathon" or "Runners", as of worst quality. Interesting cases are the "Campfire Party" and the "Fountains" sequences. The "Campfire Party" contains a lot of movement (high TI values) but not many details (low SI values) and reached low MOS value, while the "Fountains" sequence lies near to the "Bund Nightscape" and the "Construction Field" sequences, meaning it has low both TI and SI values and also scored low on the MOS scale. A special case is the "Wood" sequence which is situated at the upper right corner of the SI-TI diagram. Nevertheless, its quality was perceived as similar to the sequences "Fountains" and "Runners". All these differences are more pronounced:

- at low bitrates—with increasing bitrate, the perceived quality rises, too, and approaches the perceived quality of sequences with low SI-TI values,
- at Ultra HD resolution rather than at Full HD resolution, and
- at H.265 codec rather than at H.264 codec.

Based on these results, we can state that the compression efficiency and related video quality depends on the content of the sequences. However, the sequence representation and description only by the spatial and temporal information is not sufficient and should be the subject of further research. We suggest other parameters should be used to describe the scene, such as, for instance, the luminance and contrast or the colors occurring in the scene. In addition, the psychological factors should be considered. Based on the results, we can also state that the temporal information has greater impact on the perceived quality than the number of the objects defined by the spatial information.

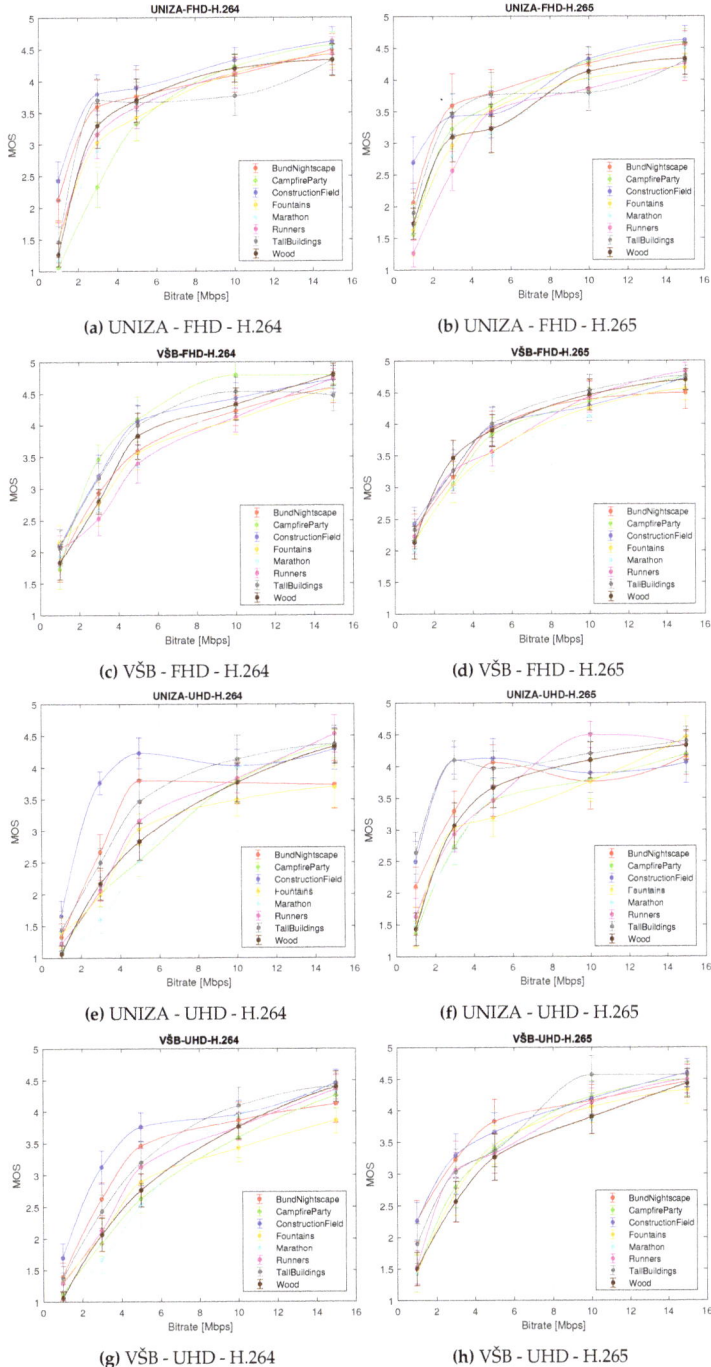

Figure 7. Bitrate impact on the perceived video quality (defined by the MOS score with associated Confidence Interval (CI)) depending on codec and resolution for both laboratories independently. Each curve represents MOS values for each type of used test sequence.

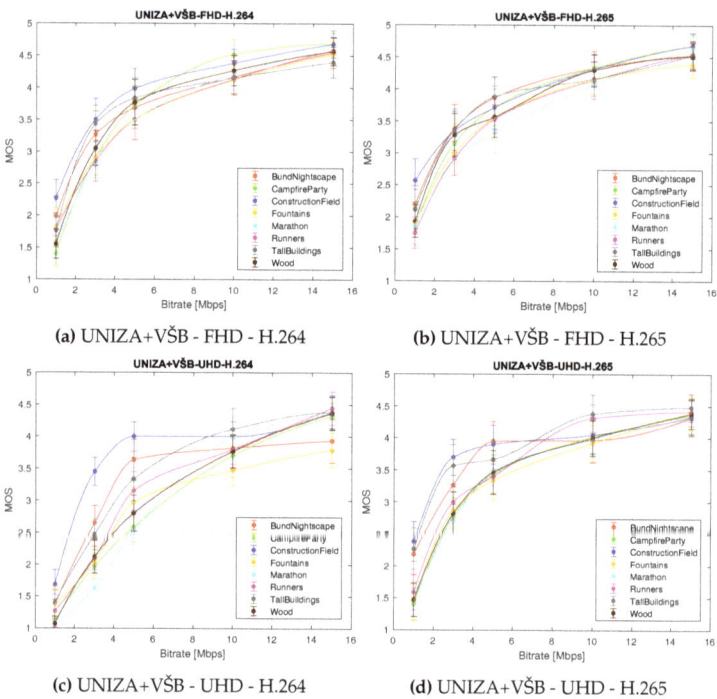

Figure 8. Bitrate impact on the perceived video quality (defined by the MOS score with associated CI) depending on codec and resolution for both laboratories jointly. Each curve represents averaged MOS values from both laboratories for each type of used test sequence.

4.3. Analysis of Variance

To verify what stemmed from the graphical representation of the subjective evaluation results, the ANOVA was applied on the data [65]. The three-way ANOVA was used to compare the significance and influence of individual sequence parameters on the resulting perceived video quality. The interaction between three independent variables, bitrate (X1), content (scene type) (X2), and resolution (X3) in Table 6 or compression standard (X3) in Table 7 was examined, with video quality being considered a dependent variable. Tables 6 and 7 depict the three-way ANOVA matrices. The *F*-value, also called the F-ratio is calculated as the variance of the group means divided by the mean of the within group variances (Mean Squared Error). Greater *F*-value indicates more significant variation. In ANOVA, the *p*-value, i.e., the probability of getting the observed result at random, is also determined. For the source of variation to be regarded as insignificant, the *p*-value must be higher than a given alpha level, commonly set to 0.05. When performing ANOVA, the *p*-value is also determined to investigate the probability of rejecting the hypothesis.

Based on the analysis of the tables, the following conclusions can be drawn. Table 6 indicates that for H.265 encoded sequences, the effect of resolution can be ignored, since this variable was deemed statistically insignificant. In contrast, in the case of the H.264 codec, this negative phenomenon does not occur and resolution is the second most important parameter that determines the subjectively perceived quality. For both codecs, an alteration in bitrate results in a maximum change in the subjective MOS. According to Table 7, the impact of compression format on the perceived quality is considered statistically insignificant for Full HD video sequences. However, that is not the case for Ultra HD resolution, where deployed codec is the second most influential variable. Equivalently to Table 6, the bitrate has the greatest effect on the subjective video quality assessment results.

All remaining ANOVA test results in both tables can be regarded statistically significant based on their *p*-values.

Table 6. Three-way Analysis of Variance (ANOVA) using video codec as a criterion.

H.264					
Source of Variation	**Sum of Squares**	**Degrees of Freedom**	**Mean Square**	***F*-Value**	***p*-Value**
Bitrate (X1)	2541.95	4	635.488	982.84	0
Scene Type (X2)	134.03	7	19.148	29.61	0
Resolution (X3)	106.68	1	106.682	164.99	0
X1*X2	106.58	28	3.802	5.89	0
X1*X3	34.24	4	8.561	13.24	0
X2*X3	12.16	7	1.737	2.69	0.009
Error	1518.18	2348	0.647		
Total	4453.83	2399			
H.265					
Bitrate (X1)	1875.05	4	468.764	669.56	0
Scene Type (X2)	90.96	7	12.994	18.56	0
Resolution (X3)	0.12	1	0.12	0.17	0.6784
X1*X2	88.31	28	3.154	4.51	0
X1*X3	7.96	4	1.99	2.84	0.0229
X2*X3	30.65	7	4.379	6.25	0
Error	1643.85	2348			
Total	3736.91	2399			

Table 7. Three-way ANOVA using video resolution as a criterion.

Full HD					
Source of Variation	**Sum of Squares**	**Degrees of Freedom**	**Mean Square**	***F*-Value**	***p*-Value**
Bitrate (X1)	2210.04	4	552.509	806.21	0
Scene Type (X2)	82.43	7	11.776	17.18	0
Compression Standard (X3)	0.01	1	0.007	0.01	0.9214
X1*X2	79.43	28	2.837	4.14	0
X1*X3	11.11	4	2.779	4.05	0.0028
X2*X3	16.25	7	2.322	3.39	0.0013
Error	1609.13	2348	0.685		
Total	4008.4	2399			
Ultra HD					
Bitrate (X1)	2186.06	4	546.515	842.85	0
Scene Type (X2)	156.8	7	22.4	34.55	0
Compression Standard (X3)	112.23	1	112.234	173.09	0
X1*X2	145.9	28	5.211	8.04	0
X1*X3	52	4	12.999	20.05	0
X2*X3	12.31	7	1.759	2.71	0.0084
Error	1522.48	2348	0.648		
Total	4187.78	2399			

4.4. Impact of Bitrate on Video Quality Depending on Codec and Resolution

Figure 9 shows the impact of the bitrate on the perceived video quality (defined by the MOS with associated CI) plotted separately for each type of video sequence. In this figure, eight graphs are inset, considering examined test sequence, which show the impact of used codec and resolution on the perceived quality of a given sequence; curve represents averaged MOS values from both laboratories for a given codec and resolution.

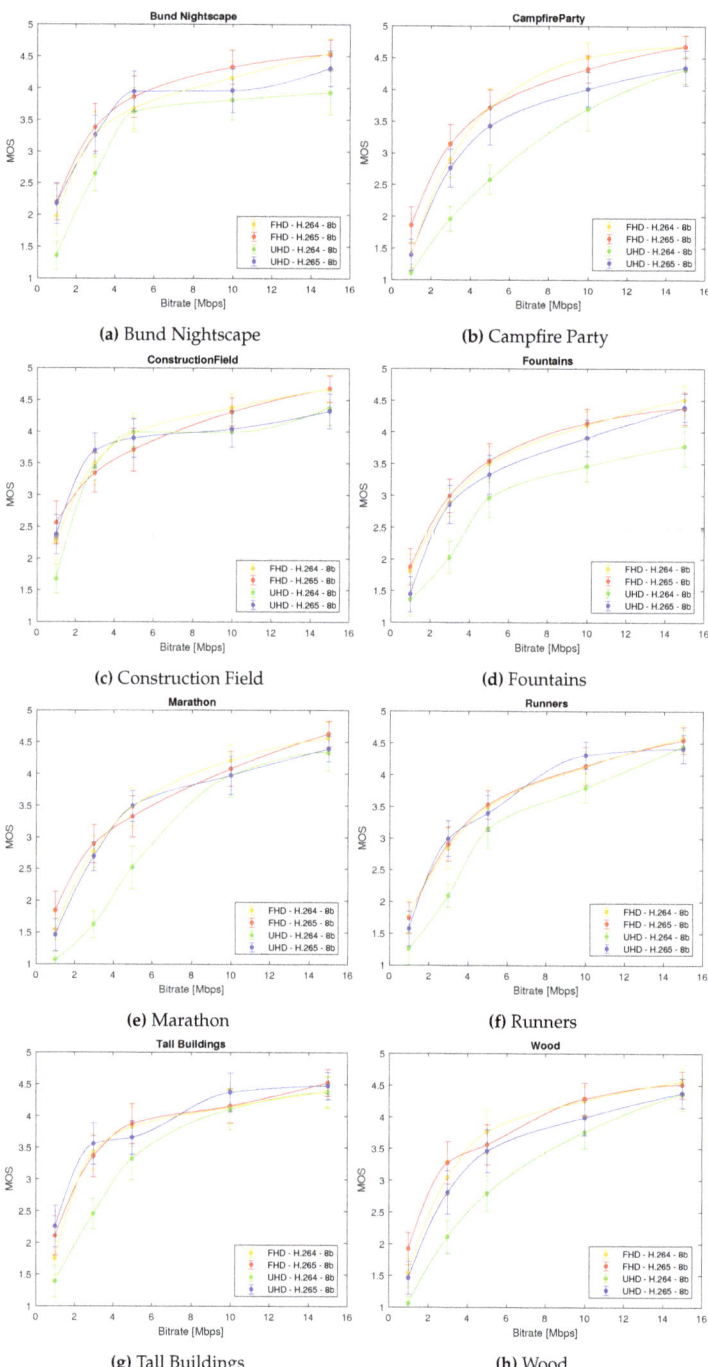

Figure 9. Bitrate impact on the perceived video quality (defined by the MOS score with associated CI) depending on used test sequence. Each curve represents averaged MOS values from both laboratories for corresponding codec and resolution.

In Figure 10, the averaged MOS value from both laboratories from all used test sequences for each codec and resolution is plotted.

We can draw several conclusions from Figures 9 and 10. Firstly, it is apparent that the H.265 compression standard yields better quality than the H.264 codec. This is a generally known fact and we expected it. But what is interesting and important is that the efficiency difference between these two codecs is negligible for the Full HD video sequences. Therefore, it is inessential to use H.265 compression standard at this resolution, as the observers will not see any notable differences. The use of H.265 codec is relevant only for the videos at the Ultra HD resolution, particularly at low bitrates. This is due to the fact that the quality of H.264 encoded video sequences increases with the rising bitrate up to the point where it reaches or even surpasses the perceived quality of H.265 sequences. Secondly, the compression efficiency of the H.265 compression standard at the Ultra HD resolution reaches the compression efficiency of both codecs at the Full HD resolution.

Indisputably, the conclusions drawn from the Analysis of Variance (ANOVA) and the graphical representation of the subjective quality evaluation results coincide. These findings could be beneficial for visual media content providers and broadcasting companies, as they indicate how to adjust video compression parameters to improve its quality. The fastest growth of perceived video quality is apparently due to an increase in bitrate. Specifically, the quality increases most rapidly until the bitrate reaches a value of approximately 5 Mbps. The analyses also revealed which combination of resolution and compression format is best used so that the resulting quality of visual content is perceived by viewers as good as possible.

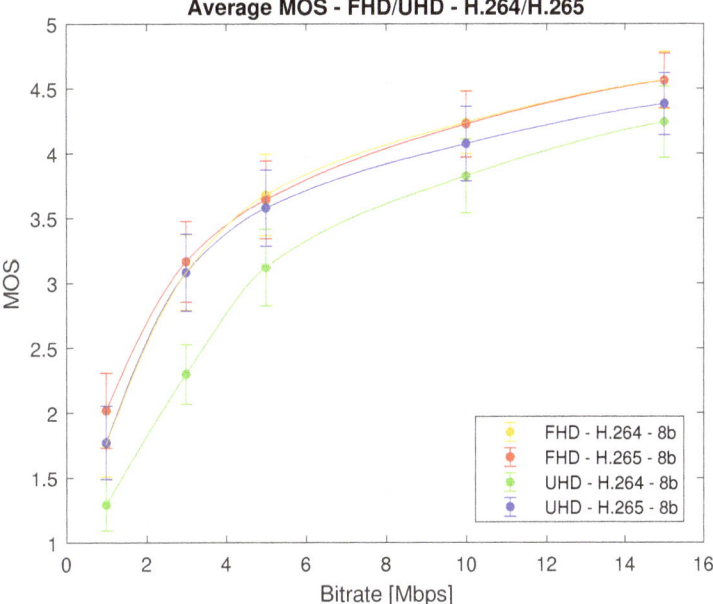

Figure 10. Bitrate impact on the perceived video quality (defined by the MOS score with associated CI). Each curve represents averaged MOS values from both laboratories for corresponding codec and resolution—average MOS score.

4.5. Minimum Bitrate Thresholds Suggestions

Finally, Figure 10 shows the minimum bitrate thresholds at which the video sequences should be encoded to achieve good (4) or fair (3) quality. These quality thresholds are based on MOS values of used ACR method and are important for the bitrate setting of each codec to maintain a certain quality. Table 8 shows the mentioned minimum bitrates.

Table 8. Minimum bitrate thresholds to achieve good (4) and fair (3) video quality.

MOS Scale	FHD-8b		UHD-8b	
	H.264	H.265	H.264	H.265
Good (4)	7.50 Mbps	7.50 Mbps	11.55 Mbps	9.00 Mbps
Fair (3)	2.80 Mbps	2.60 Mbps	4.50 Mbps	2.80 Mbps

From Table 8, it follows that to achieve a good quality (value 4 on MOS scale), the video sequence must be coded to minimum 7.50 Mbps by both codecs for Full HD resolution and to 11.55 Mbps by H.264 codec and 9.00 Mbps by H.265 codec for Ultra HD resolution. To reach fair quality (value 3 on MOS scale), the minimum thresholds for the bitrates are 2.80 Mbps by H.264 codec and 2.60 Mbps by H.265 codec for Full HD resolution and 4.50 Mbps by H.264 codec and 2.80 by H.265 codec for Ultra HD resolution.

5. Conclusions

This paper dealt with the content impact on the perceived video quality evaluated using the subjective Absolute Category Rating (ACR) method. Eight types of video sequences with various scene content were evaluated. Two widely used video compression standards H.264/AVC and H.265/HEVC in combination with Full HD and Ultra HD resolutions, were tested. In the coding process, we selected 5 various bitrates based on our previous research, which showed that the efficiency of codecs grows nonlinearly with increasing bitrate. The number of bitrates was a compromise between the complexity and time requirements of subjective testing. In total, we created an annotated database which contains 160 different video sequences coded at constant bitrates with GOP set to half of the framerate value which is typical for video intended for transfer over a noisy communication channel. The perceived quality of the sequences was evaluated employing the subjective ACR method. The assessment was conducted in two laboratories: one situated at the University of Zilina, and the second at the VSB—Technical University in Ostrava. First, we calculated the correlation of the MOS values between both laboratories using the Pearson correlation coefficient (PCC) and the Root Mean Square Error (RMSE). The correlation proved to be considerably high. After that, we described the impact of the bitrate on video quality depending on scene content defined by Spatial (SI) and Temporal information (TI). The results showed that even if the sequences with low SI and TI values reach better MOS than the sequences with higher SI and TI values, these two parameters are not sufficient for scene description, and this domain should be the subject of further research. Subsequently, we described the impact of bitrate on video quality depending on codec and resolution. Based on the results, we concluded that the employment of the H.265 codec for compression of Full HD sequences is inessential, as the people did not observe any significant differences. Furthermore, we stated that the compression efficiency of the H.265 codec by the Ultra HD resolution reaches the compression efficiency of both codecs by the Full HD resolution. We also applied the ANOVA to verify what stemmed from the graphical representation of the subjective evaluation results. Finally, we determined the minimum bitrate thresholds at which the video sequences at both resolutions retain good and fair subjectively perceived quality.

Author Contributions: Conceptualization, A.H. and M.U.; methodology, J.B. and L.S.; validation, J.B., L.S. and M.U.; formal analysis, A.H. and J.B.; investigation, J.B. and L.S.; resources, M.U.; data curation, J.B. and L.S.; writing—original draft preparation, A.H. and M.U.; writing—review and editing, A.H., L.S. and M.U.; visualization, L.S. and M.U; project administration, M.U. All authors have read and agreed to the published version of the manuscript.

Funding: This work was supported by the Slovak Research and Development Agency under the project PP-COVID-20-0100: DOLORES.AI: The pandemic guard system.

Institutional Review Board Statement: Not applicable.

Informed Consent Statement: Not applicable.

Data Availability Statement: The data presented in this study are available on request from the corresponding author.

Conflicts of Interest: The authors declare no conflict of interest. The funders had no role in the design of the study; in the collection, analyses or interpretation of data; in the writing of the manuscript, or in the decision to publish the result.

References

1. Damer, N.; Grebe, J.H.; Chen, C.; Boutros, F.; Kirchbuchner, F.; Kuijper, A. The Effect of Wearing a Mask on Face Recognition Performance: An Exploratory Study. In Proceedings of the 2020 International Conference of the Biometrics Special Interest Group (BIOSIG), Darmstadt, Germany, 16–18 September 2020; pp. 1–6.
2. Joshi, A.S.; Joshi, S.S.; Kanahasabai, G.; Kapil, R.; Gupta, S. Deep Learning Framework to Detect Face Masks from Video Footage. In Proceedings of the 2020 12th International Conference on Computational Intelligence and Communication Networks (CICN), Bhimtal, India, 25–26 September 2020.
3. Tan, W.; Liu, J. Application of Face Recognition in Tracing COVID-19 Fever Patients and Close Contacts. In Proceedings of the 2020 19th IEEE International Conference on Machine Learning and Applications (ICMLA), Miami, FL, USA, 14–17 December 2020.
4. Seshadrinathan, K.; Soundararajan, R.; Bovik, A.C.; Cormack, L.K. Study of Subjective and Objective Quality Assessment of Video. *IEEE Trans. Image Process.* **2010**, *19*, 1427–1441. [CrossRef] [PubMed]
5. Seshadrinathan, K.; Soundararajan, R.; Bovik, A.C.; Cormack, L.K. A subjective study to evaluate video quality assessment algorithms. In *Human Vision and Electronic Imaging XV*; Rogowitz, B.E., Pappas, T.N., Eds.; SPIE: Bellingham, WA, USA, 2010.
6. Moorthy, A.K.; Choi, L.K.; Bovik, A.C.; de Veciana, G. Video Quality Assessment on Mobile Devices: Subjective, Behavioral and Objective Studies. *IEEE J. Sel. Top. Signal Process.* **2012**, *6*, 652–671. [CrossRef]
7. Moorthy, A.K.; Choi, L.K.; Veciana, G.; Bovik, A. Subjective Analysis of Video Quality on Mobile Devices. In Proceedings of the 6th International Workshop on Video Processing and Quality Metrics for Consumer Electronics (VPQM), Scottsdale, AZ, USA 19–20 January 2012; Volume 720, pp. 1–6.
8. Chen, C.; Choi, L.K.; de Veciana, G.; Caramanis, C.; Heath, R.W.; Bovik, A.C. A dynamic system model of time-varying subjective quality of video streams over HTTP. In Proceedings of the 2013 IEEE International Conference on Acoustics, Speech and Signal Processing, Vancouver, BC, Canada, 26–31 May 2013.
9. Chen, C.; Zhu, X.; de Veciana, G.; Bovik, A.C.; Heath, R.W. Adaptive video transmission with subjective quality constraints. In Proceedings of the 2014 IEEE International Conference on Image Processing (ICIP), Paris, France, 27–30 October 2014.
10. Chen, C.; Choi, L.K.; de Veciana, G.; Caramanis, C.; Heath, R.W.; Bovik, A.C. Modeling the Time—Varying Subjective Quality of HTTP Video Streams With Rate Adaptations. *IEEE Trans. Image Process.* **2014**, *23*, 2206–2221. [CrossRef] [PubMed]
11. Chen, C.; Zhu, X.; de Veciana, G.; Bovik, A.C.; Heath, R.W. Rate Adaptation and Admission Control for Video Transmission With Subjective Quality Constraints. *IEEE J. Sel. Top. Signal Process.* **2015**, *9*, 22–36. [CrossRef]
12. Choi, L.K.; Cormack, L.K.; Bovik, A.C. On the visibility of flicker distortions in naturalistic videos. In Proceedings of the 2013 Fifth International Workshop on Quality of Multimedia Experience (QoMEX), Klagenfurt am Wörthersee, Austria, 3–5 July 2013.
13. Choi, L.K.; Cormack, L.K.; Bovik, A.C. Motion silencing of flicker distortions on naturalistic videos. *Signal Process. Image Commun.* **2015**, *39*, 328–341. [CrossRef]
14. Choi, L.K.; Cormack, L.K.; Bovik, A.C. Eccentricity effect of motion silencing on naturalistic videos. In Proceedings of the 2015 IEEE Global Conference on Signal and Information Processing (GlobalSIP), Orlando, FL, USA, 14–16 December 2015.
15. Choi, L.K.; Cormack, L.K.; Bovik, A.C. LIVE Flicker Video Database. 2015. Available online: http://live.ece.utexas.edu/research/quality/live_flicker_video.html (accessed on 18 April 2021).
16. Ghadiyaram, D.; Bovik, A.C.; Yeganeh, H.; Kordasiewicz, R.; Gallant, M. Study of the effects of stalling events on the quality of experience of mobile streaming videos. In Proceedings of the 2014 IEEE Global Conference on Signal and Information Processing (GlobalSIP), Atlanta, GA, USA, 3–5 December 2014.
17. Ghadiyaram, D.; Bovik, A.; Yeganeh, H.; Kordasiewicz, R.; Gallant, M. LIVE Mobile Stall Video Database, 2016. Available online: http://live.ece.utexas.edu/research/LIVEStallStudy/index.html (accessed on 18 April 2021).
18. Ghadiyaram, D.; Pan, J.; Bovik, A.C.; Moorthy, A.K.; Panda, P.; Yang, K.C. In-Capture Mobile Video Distortions: A Study of Subjective Behavior and Objective Algorithms. *IEEE Trans. Circuits Syst. Video Technol.* **2018**, *28*, 2061–2077. [CrossRef]
19. Ghadiyaram, D.; Pan, J.; Bovik, A.C.; Moorthy, A.K.; Panda, P.; Yang, K.C. LIVE-Qualcomm Mobile In-Capture Video Quality Database, 2017. Available online: http://live.ece.utexas.edu/research/incaptureDatabase/index.html (accessed on 18 April 2021).
20. Bampis, C.G.; Li, Z.; Moorthy, A.K.; Katsavounidis, I.; Aaron, A.; Bovik, A.C. Study of Temporal Effects on Subjective Video Quality of Experience. *IEEE Trans. Image Process.* **2017**, *26*, 5217–5231. [CrossRef] [PubMed]
21. Bampis, C.G.; Li, Z.; Moorthy, A.K.; Katsavounidis, I.; Aaron, A.; Bovik, A.C. LIVE Netflix Video Quality of Experience Database, 2016. Available online: http://live.ece.utexas.edu/research/LIVE_NFLXStudy/nflx_index.html (accessed on 18 April 2021).

22. Ghadiyaram, D.; Pan, J.; Bovik, A.C. A Subjective and Objective Study of Stalling Events in Mobile Streaming Videos. *IEEE Trans. Circuits Syst. Video Technol.* **2019**, *29*, 183–197. [CrossRef]
23. Ghadiyaram, D.; Pan, J.; Bovik, A. LIVE Mobile Stall Video Database-II, 2017. Available online: http://live.ece.utexas.edu/research/LIVEStallStudy/index.html (accessed on 18 April 2021).
24. Bampis, C.G.; Li, Z.; Katsavounidis, I.; Huang, T.Y.; Ekanadham, C.; Bovik, A. Towards Perceptually Optimized End-to-end Adaptive Video Streaming. *arXiv* **2018**, arXiv:1808.03898.
25. Sinno, Z.; Bovik, A.C. Large Scale Subjective Video Quality Study. In Proceedings of the 2018 25th IEEE International Conference on Image Processing (ICIP), Athens, Greece, 7–10 October 2018.
26. Sinno, Z.; Bovik, A.C. Large-Scale Study of Perceptual Video Quality. *IEEE Trans. Image Process.* **2019**, *28*, 612–627. [CrossRef] [PubMed]
27. Sinno, Z.; Bovik, A. LIVE Video Quality Challenge Database, 2018. Available online: http://live.ece.utexas.edu/research/LIVEVQC/index.html (accessed on 18 April 2021).
28. VQEG Database, 2010. Available online: https://www.its.bldrdoc.gov/vqeg/projects/frtv-phase-i/frtv-phase-i.aspx (accessed on 18 April 2021).
29. Zhang, F.; Moss, F.M.; Baddeley, R.; Bull, D.R. BVI-HD: A Video Quality Database for HEVC Compressed and Texture Synthesized Content. *IEEE Trans. Multimed.* **2018**, *20*, 2620–2630. [CrossRef]
30. Papadopoulos, M.A.; Zhang, F.; Agrafiotis, D.; Bull, D. A video texture database for perceptual compression and quality assessment. In Proceedings of the 2015 IEEE International Conference on Image Processing (ICIP), Quebec City, QC, Canada, 27–30 September 2015.
31. Mackin, A.; Zhang, F.; Bull, D.R. A study of subjective video quality at various frame rates. In Proceedings of the 2015 IEEE International Conference on Image Processing (ICIP), Quebec City, QC, Canada, 27–30 September 2015.
32. Rao, R.R.R.; Goring, S.; Robitza, W.; Feiten, B.; Raake, A. AVT VQDB UHD 1. A Large Scale Video Quality Database for UHD 1. In Proceedings of the 2019 IEEE International Symposium on Multimedia (ISM), San Diego, CA, USA, 9–11 December 2019.
33. Mercat, A.; Viitanen, M.; Vanne, J. UVG dataset. In Proceedings of the 11th ACM Multimedia Systems Conference, Istanbul, Turkey, 28 September–1 October 2020.
34. Song, L.; Tang, X.; Zhang, W.; Yang, X.; Xia, P. The SJTU 4K video sequence dataset. In Proceedings of the 2013 Fifth International Workshop on Quality of Multimedia Experience (QoMEX), Klagenfurt am Wörthersee, Austria, 3–5 July 2013.
35. IVP Database, 2011. Available online: http://ivp.ee.cuhk.edu.hk/index.shtml (accessed on 18 April 2021).
36. Péchard, S.; Pépion, R.; Le Callet, P. Suitable Methodology in Subjective Video Quality Assessment: A Resolution Dependent Paradigm. In Proceedings of the International Workshop on Image Media Quality and Its Applications, IMQA2008, Kyoto, Japan, 5–6 September 2008; Volume 6.
37. The Konstanz Natural Video Database. Available online: http://database.mmsp-kn.de/konvid-1k-database.html (accessed on 18 April 2021).
38. Hosu, V.; Hahn, F.; Jenadeleh, M.; Lin, H.; Men, H.; Sziranyi, T.; Li, S.; Saupe, D. The Konstanz Natural Video Database (KoNViD-1k). In Proceedings of the 2017 Ninth International Conference on Quality of Multimedia Experience (QoMEX), Erfurt, Germany, 31 May– 2 June 2017; pp. 1–6.
39. Lin, J.Y.; Song, R.; Wu, C.H.; Liu, T.; Wang, H.; Kuo, C.C.J. MCL-V: A streaming video quality assessment database. *J. Vis. Commun. Image Represent.* **2015**, *30*, 1–9. [CrossRef]
40. Wang, H.; Gan, W.; Hu, S.; Lin, J.Y.; Jin, L.; Song, L.; Wang, P.; Katsavounidis, I.; Aaron, A.; Kuo, C.C.J. MCL-JCV: A JND-based H.264/AVC video quality assessment dataset. In Proceedings of the 2016 IEEE International Conference on Image Processing (ICIP), Phoenix, AZ, USA, 25–28 September 2016.
41. Lee, J.S.; Simone, F.D.; Ramzan, N.; Zhao, Z.; Kurutepe, E.; Sikora, T.; Ostermann, J.; Izquierdo, E.; Ebrahimi, T. Subjective evaluation of scalable video coding for content distribution. In Proceedings of the International Conference on Multimedia—MM '10, Firenze, Italy, 25–29 October 2010; pp. 65–72.
42. Lee, J.S.; Simone, F.D.; Ebrahimi, T. Subjective Quality Evaluation via Paired Comparison: Application to Scalable Video Coding. *IEEE Trans. Multimed.* **2011**, *13*, 882–893. [CrossRef]
43. Paudyal, P.; Battisti, F.; Carli, M. A Study On The Effects of Quality of Service Parameters on Perceived Video Quality. In Proceedings of the 5th European Workshop on Visual Information Processing, EUVIP 2014, Paris, France, 10–12 December 2014.
44. Keimel, C.; Habigt, J.; Habigt, T.; Rothbucher, M.; Diepold, K. Visual quality of current coding technologies at high definition IPTV bitrates. In Proceedings of the 2010 IEEE International Workshop on Multimedia Signal Processing, Saint-Malo, France, 4–6 October 2010.
45. Keimel, C.; Redl, A.; Diepold, K. The TUM high definition video datasets. In Proceedings of the 2012 Fourth International Workshop on Quality of Multimedia Experience, Melbourne, VIC, Australia, 5–7 July 2012.
46. Řeřábek, M.; Ebrahimi, T. Comparison of compression efficiency between HEVC/H.265 and VP9 based on subjective assessments. In *Applications of Digital Image Processing XXXVII*; Tescher, A.G., Ed.; SPIE: Bellingham, WA, USA, 2014.
47. Ramzan, N.; Pervez, Z.; Amira, A. Quality of experience evaluation of H.265/MPEG-HEVC and VP9 comparison efficiency. In Proceedings of the 2014 26th International Conference on Microelectronics (ICM), Doha, Qatar, 14–17 December 2014.
48. Bienik, J.; Uhrina, M.; Vaculik, M.; Mizdos, T. Perceived Quality of Full HD Video—Subjective Quality Assessment. *Adv. Electr. Electron. Eng.* **2016**, *14*. [CrossRef]

49. Xu, J.; Jiang, X. Assessment of subjective video quality on 4K Ultra High Definition videos. In Proceedings of the 2015 8th International Congress on Image and Signal Processing (CISP), Shenyang, China, 14–16 October 2015.
50. Herrou, G.; Hamidouche, W.; Ducloux, X. HDR video quality evaluation of HEVC and VP9 codecs. In Proceedings of the 2016 Picture Coding Symposium (PCS), Nuremberg, Germany, 4–7 December 2016.
51. Dumic, E.; Grgic, S.; Sakic, K.; Frank, D. Subjective quality assessment of H.265 versus H.264 Video Coding for High-Definition Video Systems. In Proceedings of the 2015 13th International Conference on Telecommunications (ConTEL), Graz, Austria, 13–15 July 2015.
52. Milovanovic, D.; Milicevic, Z.; Bojkovic, Z. MPEG video deployment in digital television: HEVC vs. AVC codec performance study. In Proceedings of the 2013 11th International Conference on Telecommunications in Modern Satellite, Cable and Broadcasting Services (TELSIKS), Nis, Serbia, 16–19 October 2013.
53. Sotelo, R.; Joskowicz, J.; Anedda, M.; Murroni, M.; Giusto, D.D. Subjective video quality assessments for 4K UHDTV. In Proceedings of the 2017 IEEE International Symposium on Broadband Multimedia Systems and Broadcasting (BMSB), Cagliari, Italy, 7–9 June 2017.
54. Kufa, J.; Polak, L.; Kratochvil, T. HEVC/H.265 vs. VP9 for Full HD and UHD video: Is there any difference in QoE? In Proceedings of the 2016 International Symposium ELMAR, Zadar, Croatia, 12–14 September 2016.
55. Deep, V.; Elarabi, T. HEVC/H.265 vs. VP9 state-of-the-art video coding comparison for HD and UHD applications. In Proceedings of the 2017 IEEE 30th Canadian Conference on Electrical and Computer Engineering (CCECE), Windsor, ON, Canada, 30 April–3 May 2017.
56. Akyazi, P.; Ebrahimi, T. Comparison of Compression Efficiency between HEVC/H.265, VP9 and AV1 based on Subjective Quality Assessments. In Proceedings of the 2018 Tenth International Conference on Quality of Multimedia Experience (QoMEX), Cagliari, Italy, 29 May–1 June 2018.
57. Zhu, Y.; Song, L.; Xie, R.; Zhang, W. SJTU 4K video subjective quality dataset for content adaptive bit rate estimation without encoding. In Proceedings of the 2016 IEEE International Symposium on Broadband Multimedia Systems and Broadcasting (BMSB), Nara, Japan, 1–3 June 2016.
58. ITU-R. Recommendation ITU-R BT.500-14—Subjective Video Quality Assessment Methods for Multimedia Applications. 2019. Available online: https://www.itu.int/rec/R-REC-BT.500 (accessed on 18 April 2021).
59. Mitsu. Mitsu Tool. Available online: http://vq.kt.agh.edu.pl/metrics.html (accessed on 18 April 2021).
60. Uhrina, M.; Bienik, J.; Mizdos, T. QoE on H.264 and H.265: Crowdsourcing versus Laboratory Testing. In Proceedings of the 2020 30th International Conference Radioelektronika (RADIOELEKTRONIKA), Bratislava, Slovakia, 15–16 April 2020; Volume 30, pp. 1–6.
61. FFmpeg. A Complete, Cross-Platform Solution to Record, Convert and Stream Audio and Video. ffmpeg.org. Available online: https://www.ffmpeg.org (accessed on 18 April 2021).
62. Uhrina, M.; Bienik, J.; Vaculik, M. Coding efficiency of HEVC/H.265 and VP9 compression standards for high resolutions. In Proceedings of the 2016 26th International Conference Radioelektronika (RADIOELEKTRONIKA), Kosice, Slovakia, 19–20 April 2016.
63. ITU-T. Recommendation ITU-T P.910—Subjective Video Quality Assessment Methods for Multimedia Applications. 2008. Available online: https://www.itu.int/rec/T-REC-P.910-200804-I/en (accessed on 18 April 2021).
64. ITU-T. Recommendation ITU-T P.1401—Methods, Metrics and Procedures for Statistical Evaluation, Qualification and Comparison of Objective Quality Prediction Models. 2020. Available online: https://www.itu.int/rec/T-REC-P.1401-202001-I/en (accessed on 18 April 2021).
65. Judd, C.M.; McClelland, G.H.; Ryan, C.S. *Data Analysis: A Model Comparison Approach to Regression, ANOVA, and Beyond*; Routledge: Oxfordshire, UK, 2017.

MDPI

St. Alban-Anlage 66

4052 Basel

Switzerland

Tel. +41 61 683 77 34

Fax +41 61 302 89 18

www.mdpi.com

Sensors Editorial Office

E-mail: sensors@mdpi.com

www.mdpi.com/journal/sensors